Nels L. Nelson

Preaching and Public Speaking

a manual for the use of preachers of the Gospel and public speakers in general

Nels L. Nelson

Preaching and Public Speaking

a manual for the use of preachers of the Gospel and public speakers in general

ISBN/EAN: 9783337284824

Printed in Europe, USA, Canada, Australia, Japan

Cover: Foto ©Lupo / pixelio.de

More available books at **www.hansebooks.com**

PREACHING

AND

PUBLIC SPEAKING

A Manual for the Use of Preachers of the
Gospel and Public Speakers
in General.

BY

N. L. NELSON,

Professor of Rhetoric and Elocution in the Brigham
Young Academy, Provo City, Utah.

Salt Lake City, Utah:
Deseret News Publishing Company.
1898.

PREFACE.

This book is the outgrowth of ten years observation and reflection. The conviction that such a work is needed came to the author while on a mission to the Southern States, where he had frequent occasion to deplore the fearful waste of time, money, energy, and opportunity to save souls,—to say nothing of the mental anguish,—which is involved before the raw missionary, with no other guide than blundering experiment, is changed into the fairly capable preacher. The conviction was intensified by his acting as clerk of Sabbath meetings for three years, and having to record the substance of the sermons there delivered. If any one would know how strong is the sense of duty among Latterday Saints, even in the face of peculiar discouragements, let him note how, in spite of our preaching, they still continue to attend meeting on the Sabbath day.

But much as he saw the need of such a work, he naturally hesitated before putting his thoughts on paper; as who would not, in view of the general sentiment respecting criticism of preaching? The matter came to a head, however, in the following manner:

A much respected but wordy brother had occupied the time of the congregation for one hour. Try as he would, the clerk could get nothing coherent from the sermon. Turning to the Elder sitting nearest him,—Hon. W. H. King, if that gentleman will pardon the liberty of mentioning his name—he asked: "What in the name of consistency can I put into the record today?" "Oh, say that our brother made some desultory remarks on the Gospel," was the kindly, good-humored reply. And so it was recorded.

That day on leaving the Tabernacle the author confided to Elder King his intention of preparing a number of lectures on preaching, and was warmly encouraged to go ahead. For a time he was undecided how best to get his ideas before the people, but finally concluded to write a series of articles for the Contributor.

But he has never felt satisfied with the results; first, because these articles, though they ran through eighteen numbers and were favorably received wherever read, left the subject only half finished; secondly, because the views there set forth, having been written on the time demand of a publisher, were often but crudely elaborated, and were in some instances rash and inconsiderate; thirdly, because the Contributor, being on its last legs, so to speak, had but few readers at that time, and so it seemed like putting ideas into a coffin.

"Preaching and Public Speaking" is a recast of the whole subject. Time and matured reflection have enabled the author to produce a work which, it is believed, will be helpful to speakers desirous of improving their power of expression. Fourteen years contact with young men of Zion in the classes of the Brigham Young Academy has given him exceptional opportunities of knowing just what is wanted. The book has been written mainly for these young men; for it would hardly be reasonable to expect much of a change in the mental habits of the older generation. In view of this fact the latter will, it is hoped, kindly bear in mind that in passages where certain abuses are unmercifully scored, the intention is not to hurt the feelings of Elders guilty of such faults, but merely to prevent younger brethren from falling into the same errors.

The author desires it distinctly understood that the views here published are subject to the acceptation, rejection, or modification of every reader as the Holy Spirit shall enlighten his mind. Throughout this treatise he has constantly kept before him the fact that no human art or learning can take the place of the Holy Ghost in converting souls; nor can a knowledge of rhetoric and elocution offset that humility which is so necessary to the enjoyment of the Spirit as a daily, hourly guide. He fully realizes that an Elder must be as clay in the potter's hands, and believes that the principles here set forth will have a tendency to break the dry clods of inexperience and help make the clay fit for the Potter's use. In short, he believes that thinking about how to preach can have no other effect than to make our minds pliable to the slightest whisperings of that Voice which is to give us in the hour thereof what is meat in due season.

N. L. N.

CONTENTS

CHAPTER I.
Consideration of Objections.

	PAGE
I.—Problem: Is there a Need for this Book?	1
II.—Misconception of the Words "Take no Thought."	3
III.—Doing Presupposes having Learned How	8
IV.—Non-preparation Tested by Scripture	13
V.—Non-preparation Tested in our Missionary Fields	19
VI.—Non-preparation Tested by Results at Home	24

CHAPTER II.
Qualifications of the Preacher.

I.—Sermons Should be Made up of Logical and Progressive Thought	29
II.—A Well-stored Mind and Meekness the True Qualifications of the Preacher	34
III.—The Need of Humility Illustrated by an Experience	39
IV.—As a People we are Evidently in Love with Glittering Generalities	44
V.—Another Chapter about Glittering Generalities	48
VI.—How Glittering Generalities are Helping to Shape our Destiny as a People	52

CHAPTER III.
Subject-Matter for Sermons.

I.—Importance of the Point of View	57
II.—Effect in Religion of Difference in Point of View	63
III.—The True Point of View Both for Science and Religion	66
IV.—Point of View of Latterday Saints in Actual Practice	70
V.—Scope or Range of Subject-matter	74
VI.—Relationship of the Gospel, the Church, and the Saints	80

CONTENTS.

CHAPTER IV.

The Art of Thinking.

PAGE
I.—The Importance of Latterday Saint Elders' becoming Thinkers 86
II.—The Value of Thinking as Compared with Thought-gathering 91
III.—How to Set the Wheels of Thought Moving 97
IV.—Thinking may or may not be Acquired in School 101
V.—How Objects in Nature may Develop the Thinking Powers . . 105
VI.—How One may Learn to Think in the Library 110
VII.—The Meaning of Apperception. How to Apperceive 115
VIII.—Thinking as Related to Expression—a Concrete Theme . . 118
IX.—The Self-questioning Process as Applied to an Abstract Theme 123
X.—An Elder should not only Learn to Think, but Learn to Think Justly 128

CHAPTER V.

Characteristics of the Sermon.

I.—Importance of Choosing a Subject when Beginning to Speak . 136
II.—How to Choose an Appropriate Subject 140
III.—General Examples Showing the Effect of Unity 144
IV.—Effect of Unity and want of Unity in the Sermon 149
V.—Unity Violated by Making the Subject too Broad—An Illustration from the School Room 155
VI.—Effect in the Missionary Field of Sweeping Generalizations . 159
VII.—General Effects of Triteness and Indefiniteness 165
VIII.—Want of Clearness and What it Leads to 171

CHAPTER VI.

Kinds of Sermons.

I.—Devoted to Those who Ridicule Rhetoric, Elocution, and Kindred Studies 177
II.—The Relative Value of Oral and Written Sermons 180
III.—Sermons based on the Nature of the Congregation—Doctrinal Sermons 183

CONTENTS. ix
                                                                PAGE
IV.—The Weakness of the Doctrinal Sermon 188
V.—Missionary Sermons—What they Should be Like 192
VI —The need of Adopting more Popular Methods in Preaching . 196
VII.—The Real Value of the Doctrinal Sermon—The Topical Sermon 200
VIII.—The Exhortation and its Cumulative Miseries—The Missionary Report 205

CHAPTER VII.
Methods of Communicating Thought.

I.—Essential Characteristics of a Narrative 210
II.—Essential Characteristics of a Plot 213
III.—Essential Characteristics of the Description 217
IV.—The Process of Describing 224
V.—Essential Characteristics of the Exposition 232
VI. Methods of Exposition 237
VII.—Methods of Exegesis 242
VIII.—Principles and Methods of Argumentation 247
IX.—Principles and Methods of Argumentation Continued 253
X.—The Conduct of a Discussion 259
XI.—Principles Underlying Persuasion 266
XII.—Essential Conditions of Persuasion 273
XIII —Qualifications of an Orator 279

CHAPTER VIII.
Analysis of the Sermon.

I.—The Introduction; Effect of Personality 286
II.—Rendering an Audience Keenly Alert Intellectually 281
III —Placing an Audience in Sympathy with the Views About to be Expressed 296
IV.—As to the Length of an Introduction 301
V.—The Introduction Should be Simple, Direct, and Suggestive . . 306
VI.—Moderation and Modesty in the Introduction 311
VII.—The Discussion; a Definite Proposition Necessary 314
VIII.—Should the Proposition be Stated to the Audience? 322
IX.—The Need and Value of Divisions in the Discussion . . . 328
X.—Factors that go to Determine What Divisions Must be Made . 333
XI.—Illustrations of Various Methods of Division 338
XII.—Essential Characteristics of the Conclusion 343

CONTENTS.

CHAPTER IX.
Rhetorical and Elocutionary Embellishments.

PAGE

I.—The Acquisition and Use of Words 349
II.—The Sentence and Sentence-making 357
III.—Imagery and Illustration—Examples 366
IV.—Imagery and Illustration Continued 370
V.—Imagery and Illustration—Faults 375
VI.—Personal Bearing—How to Cultivate a Fine Personality . . . 382
VII.—Breathing and Voice Development 390
VIII.—Articulation, Pronunciation, and Accentuation—Common Faults and How Remedied 395
IX.—Styles of Delivery and Forms of Voice 402
X.—Quality of Voice, Force, Stress, Pitch, Movement, and Grouping 409
XI —Action: Movements of Head and Torse—Position of Feet—Improper Attitudes 416
XII.—Action: General Meaning and Scope of Gesture 421
XIII.—Stages of growth: First, Crude Natural; Second, Conscious Artificial; Third, Artistic Natural 430

APPENDIX.

A Sermon by President Wilford Woodruff 435

Preaching and Public Speaking.

CHAPTER I.
CONSIDERATION OF OBJECTIONS.

I.

PROBLEM: IS THERE A NEED FOR THIS BOOK?

A Parable.—A certain rich man desired to make for himself a spacious garden. Straightway he sent to every land for laborers whom he could trust. He enquired neither as to their skill nor their experience, but only if they were honest men. When he had thus gathered a goodly number he led them to a wide field and said: "Behold, here I have planted trees and vines and flowers of every variety that delight the eye and furnish food for man. In the richest spot thereof I have planted a tree choice above all other trees; for whereas these do but satisfy a mortal appetite, the fruit of this tree ministers to the soul of man. Again it is choice because it is the only tree of its kind in the world, albeit there are in every garden many wild varieties of it. This garden I now leave to your care till my return: see that ye betray not this trust."

Now the soil was virgin and the laborers industrious and willing to learn: so the garden throve exceedingly. Especially did the sacred tree (for so they called it) grow and thrive—almost, it seemed without the thought or care of the laborers; so that long ere the other trees began to bear, this tree put forth its fruit; and great was the harvest and luscious the flavor thereof: and such joy did they experience who ate of it, that the fame thereof spread to many lands, insomuch that multitudes came to the garden to partake of the goodly fruit.

Now after many years, when the other trees began to bear abundantly, each laborer betook himself to a special part of the garden, and soon became burdened with the much fruit thereof. And the sacred tree became no one's care. The weeds grew rank about its trunk, and many of its limbs began to show dry ends; for the life-giving stream was used elsewhere. On stated days the laborers assembled about the tree, and many were sorrowful when they looked upon it, and the people murmured among themselves when they saw how it was neglected. Nevertheless the laborers went back again, each to his burdensome labors, and forgot all about it.

At length there arose a man with a cunningly devised speech: "Behold," said he, "is not this tree sacred? And doth not its fruit fit men for heaven? What then are we that we should presume to dig about it and prune it? Hath the divine any need of the human? Are not the wild trees of this kind in other gardens thus cultivated by human hands? May not this become wild like unto them if cultivated according to our poor finite skill?"

Now the saying pleased some of the laborers and satisfied others; for they all were loaded with the cares of other parts of the master's vineyard. But many of the people came no more to eat of the fruit, for they said it was become dry and tasteless; and they that came, often ate in bitterness of soul, being roundly upbraided the while because of them that staid away. Some of the laborers stoutly declared that the fault was not in the fruit; for, said they, the fruit is the same as it always was, or at least it is as the master would have it. How could it be otherwise, growing upon the sacred tree? These moreover, declared that the fault was in the taste of them that ate; and they pointed to many things which showed that the taste of the people was become worldly.

But some among them saw that the fault was both in the fruit and in the taste. They saw also that the first was largely the cause of the second; for, they said to themselves, if the fruit of the sacred tree had remained luscious and well-flavored as at first, would the people have been so readily tempted to wander in other parts of the garden for their food and pleasure? But these discreetly held their peace, lest they should be accounted malcontents, and so it is even unto this day.

What now would the master say should he suddenly return? Would he not say: "This is the most precious tree in the garden and behold how ye have neglected it! The trees on all sides of it ye have labored with, even the trees whose fruit is worldly—so that their tops do overshadow this choice tree, and almost shut out the sunlight of heaven from it. Go to, now, cut down those trees and spare not. Then dig about and water and prune this sacred tree, till it stretch forth its glad arms toward heaven, and again bear fruit that is luscious, so that multitudes shall flock hither as to a feast."

II.

MISCONCEPTION OF THE WORDS "TAKE NO THOUGHT."

Introductory.—In opening this discussion, dear reader, I do not feel sufficient self-confidence to proceed without first halting to make your personal acquaintance, to feel the warmth of your sympathy, and to hear you wish God's blessing on this humble endeavor. How would the young Elder—your own son or brother—feel; with what heart and courage would he enter upon the duties of a foreign mission, so new and strange to him, if sent from home with no loving farewell; if, instead of the encouraging words ringing in his ears, and the group of warm, sympathetic faces locked in the album of his heart—he must look back for two or three years upon a leave-taking of the coolest business formality? And yet a foreign mission is now so common that it need excite neither novelty nor dread; but here I stand before a mental mission unopened hitherto, so far as I am aware, among the Latterday Saints; how much greater my need of your sympathy and prayer!

Preaching is what we all do and have done almost from the beginning. Both sexes, and all ages, participate in public speaking in some one or more of the numerous meetings of the Church organization. Elders, venerable with age and good works, whose lives are half within the veil; babes in the Primary Associations, whom the angels still hold by the hand—alike stand up and give vent to the Spirit.

"Who then are you, that presume to discuss this subject?" Who am I, indeed, if God does not bless my thoughts! But, surely, what concerns Latterday Saints so generally, it must be profitable to reflect upon. If preaching, or public speaking, be so prominent a part of our mental and spiritual food, can this food be improved —in seasonableness, in flavor, and in nutritiveness—by thinking about how to prepare it and how to serve it? I shall proceed in this work, guided at every step by the conviction that it can be; that preaching, like praying, like teaching, like farming, in short, like any activity of mind or heart or muscle, is clearly capable of improvement—even as these occupations are capable of improvement —by studying carefully the 'why' and the 'how.'

Stereotyped Objections.—But many Elders do not agree with me in this. The good will of these I desire also to carry with me from the start in this discussion. It is only just therefore that I stop briefly to consider their objections.

Whenever it is urged that due attention be given to the manner of preaching, these at once cry: "Prepared sermons! sectarianism! that's what we left the world to get away from. No, 'Take no thought about what ye shall say'—that is the only kind of preaching God is pleased with."

One gray-haired father in Israel whom I approached for ideas, intimating the purpose I had in view, answered quickly and with warmth: "There is nothing to discuss: the word of God says that he who would preach, must do so by the Holy Ghost, and if he have not the Holy Ghost, he should not preach. Now that is the beginning and the end of the whole matter; for if a man have the Spirit to dictate him, all the rules and discussions in the world won't help him, and if he doesn't he will not need them for he is not permitted to preach."

Now these answers are certainly discouraging enough, especially to the young and inexperienced Elder who may be feebly thinking about self-improvement in this important matter. The objection carries enough truth and authority so that, to minds unaccustomed to keen discrimination, it appears to be a leveling argument. But it is, in fact, only a great Shibboleth, that gets away with the reasoning by killing the reasoner, so to speak.

It is related of a certain dogmatic Elder, who generally carried his weapons loaded to the muzzle with single, conclusive shots, that he once held up a well-dressed citizen on the public highway and demanded, eying him sternly:

"Do you believe Joseph Smith to be a prophet of the Lord?"

"No, sir, I do not," replied the man indignantly.

"Well, I wouldn't give much for your skin, then. Good-day, sir."

In like manner all the work of the Elders might be concluded with a single passage of Scripture: "He that believeth and is baptized shall be saved, and he that believeth not shall be damned." But would this conclusion conclude? And if men were brought into the Church by such preaching, would it be faith or fear that moved them? Now of such a kind is the objection urged by that aged father in Israel against studying preaching as an art. But let us examine his objection more closely.

Observe first how admirably this argument is adapted to

justify our indolence and flatter our holiness. The gray-haired Elder in our Sabbath meeting, the young man before the Improvement association, the Seventy before his quorum theological class —all stand up and claim a merit for not being prepared. Their minds, they start in by saying, are utterly vacant. Now, if they would sit down after making this confession, they might count on the pity and perhaps the sympathy of the audience. But alas! it is not so: they go on exhibiting the vacancy.

Sleep, Phantasy, or Mental Torture.—When we strike a barrel and it gives us a hollow sound, the first stroke is a pleasure because it gives some information to us, viz: that the barrel is empty. The second stroke does not even arouse curiosity; and the third, if we are compelled to bend our attention upon it, becomes painful. Try to sense the cumulative pain then of having to listen attentively and expectantly to one hour of such aimless drumming!

Of course, if we pay only the dreamy attention that we give to a waterfall, allowing the mind to busy itself elsewhere, we can sit it through without getting nervous. The agony begins when one bends his mind for ideas, and gets only sounds. In the case of the empty barrel, one never thinks of bending the mind. But it is not so with the empty preacher. In his case we feel called upon to listen; and the pain we feel is evidently caused by the conflict of our sense of duty and our knowledge: the duty we feel of paying strict attention to one who speaks in the name of the Lord, and our conviction by the first stroke of his tongue that his head is empty. When such a speaker announces that he has nothing on his mind to say, we contemplate the fact in connection with the man and the occasion. But when he proceeds to take a whole hour of our time in saying it, one of three things happens: we sleep—blessed escape! —we wander, or we are mentally tortured.

Would that for three consecutive Sundays there were but one channel—the last—for the mind of every Latterday Saint. Would that sleep were impossible, and mind-wandering furnished no escape valve; that every Latterday Saint were compelled to bend his attention for ideas—connected, logical ideas—and feel the excruciation of getting empty sound, or, in lieu thereof, mere scraps and platitudes! How eagerly we should then turn to the Scriptures to see if God has really promised to put thoughts and ideas into vacant heads; to discover if infinite wisdom may really be expected to rest upon the man who virtually says: "Here I am, Lord; I have a mouth and a good pair of lungs, which I will lend you for a brief season; fill me with wisdom that I may edifiy the people."

Self-Stultification. — But the truth is, we can and do too easily become listless and heedless; and having yawned the hour away without any attempt at bending our attention, we are doubtful whether the fault is with the preacher or with ourselves, that we go home empty and leaden-hearted. The stream of sound, we say to ourselves, went fluently on: what grand ideas may not have escaped us! "Fine sermon we had today," says some one who feels conscience-smitten for having fallen asleep. "Beautiful!" we reply for a similar reason.

Each thus convinces the other that the fault lies, not with the speaker, but with himself; and while I do not take the ground that there is not some truth in this view, since, as is well known, the attention or want of attention of an audience never fails in aiding or retarding the speaker, the point I insist upon is, that aimless preachers inflict their talks upon us again and again, simply because there are three ways of sitting through them—sleeping, mind-wandering, and mind torture—instead of one way—the last. For if there was only this last way, we should protest to a man against allowing the abuse to continue.

III.

DOING PRESUPPOSES HAVING LEARNED HOW.

A Personal Digression.—Right here, kind reader, I ask your indulgence while we understand each other on another point. As I re-read the last chapter I observe that my habit of putting things strongly, a habit I can scarce control at times, is manifesting itself in no uncertain way. Do not be offended thereby. My only apology for touching this subject at all, is the laudable hope of improveing—reforming. Surely there is need of it. If, therefore, you bid me go on, you will give me some latitude in the choice and use of my weapons. He who would build better must often tear down and cart away in order to get place for a foundation. The reformer rarely escapes becoming an iconoclast, though the iconoclast does not always become a reformer.

Relative Merits of Ridicule and Praise.—Now my experience as a teacher convinces me that when a truth has reached a point in expression where we may say it is plain, there is still something needed—some force or energy—to carry it home. Truth, it seems to me, is effective only when in motion; at rest, or feebly moving, it needs apologizing for. To use just enough powder to bring out the charge is idle firing; it serves only to befog the air.

If my illustrations are harsh or extreme, the seeming so to you indicates that they were intended for sensibilities less keen than your own. If I resort occasionally to satire when you think I should excite emulation by praise, it is because I believe human nature to be so constructed that every man accepts greedily the praise for himself—and recommends the emulation to his neighbor.

Then, too, praise, while it is the natural stimulus of healthy growth, is a poor reformer. For instance, let a certain complexion be praised by every tongue, and while one girl will go to the gymnasium ten will go to the drug store. Praises, like balms and healing ointments, serve frequently only to "film the ulcerous place." But ridicule probes. Satire cauterizes—burns away the proud flesh; and I hope I shall apply my literary caustics to nothing else than proud flesh. Let us not, then, despise these merciless instruments. He who refuses heroic treatment must often live and die a cripple.

If the reader, now, will pardon this personal digression, and let it be my standing apology throughout this discussion, I will proceed from where I left off.

A Jonah's Gourd Under which to Shirk.—We were considering the objection of certain Elders against the study of preaching for preaching's sake. Such Elders read the passage, 'Take no thought about what ye shall say' and count it the end of argument, because, forsooth, it chimes with their inclinations. It was made clear, however, that this summary manner of firing at your opponent a single quotation of Scripture assumed to be conclusive, and then refusing to listen further, is a disposition of the question that does not dispose of it. As well cut out your adversary's tongue, and then boast that you have silenced him effectually. Elders, by the way, who have been refused a night's lodgings on the authority of a certain text in John about heretics, will appreciate the force of this truth.

This argument against the study of how to preach is generally carried to the absurd length of doing nothing and expecting the Lord to do it all. How such an interpretation can be placed upon the words, 'take no thought,' is inexplicable on any other ground than that it furnishes a convenient Jonah's gourd under which to shirk. If for no other purpose than to take away this shield of idleness, this self-flattery of saintliness, it is to be hoped that the worm is at work to tumble the argument on the heads of those that confide in it.

Common-Sense Aspect.—The scriptural aspect of the objection I shall consider in the next chapter. Here let us consider the question, Is it common sense to hold it sacrilege to prepare for preaching? Take any other activity that engages the human mind, and what is the measure of success? Not energy, nor much energy, but much wisely-directed energy. What is it that enables us wisely to direct any energy? Hercules' mighty labors illustrate the prowess of brute force; but a babe can do mightier today by merely touching a button. Wisely-directed means scientifically directed, and this again means directed according to law. But directed according to law presupposes a knowledge of law, and hence we say knowledge is power.

What do you think of the man that builds a mill exactly as his father and grandfather did? He thereby gets only five per cent of the power of the stream, while the latest turbine would give him ninety-five. He obstinately refuses to open his eyes to "new-fangled notions." What is he? You are ready to call him bad names.

Let us not be too hasty. We might strike too near home. He is simply a gentleman who chooses to follow his "innate good sense and God-given intelligence," rather than adopt the results of the thoughts and labors of mankind. If he could thus "go it blind" for a thousand years, the rude shocks of experience might bring him eventually to the turbine. Thus also, in all other vocations: we may shut our eyes and with all the glorious independence (?) of following the bent of our natural intelligence, we shall not fail to be harnessed, like blind Sampson, to the prison mills of a bygone age; or we may open them, and become the heirs of six thousand years' thought and experience.

Not understood, the forces of nature make slaves of men. Understood, the reverse is true. It is not a question of greater energy in modern times, but of greater wisely-directed energy, that makes one man's effort count against the efforts of a thousand in ancient times. The difference is traceable to a careful study of the 'why' and the 'how.'

These thoughts are so elementary and familiar to all that they can scarcely be put tersely enough to relieve their triteness. The marvel is that there should be men unwilling to concede them to be applicable to preaching. What is preaching but one of many methods of teaching—one of many avenues to reach and influence the human mind? Now the human mind and the means of influencing it, have been studied by the wisest men of every age since the days of Aristotle. No field of investigation shows greater activity today than does this one; all which indicates that much still is unknown. But shall we on this account refuse to avail ourselves of the many truths that are known? Shall the farmer refuse to give up his crude methods because all is not yet known in the science of agriculture?

Preaching not the only Divine Occupation.—"But it is different with preaching," urges the objector. "Preaching is from God."

So is farming, yea, digging canals, hauling wood, and building bridges. Who shall rise up and say of the very least agency which contributes to make man like his Father, that it is not of God? This distinction between things human and things divine is a sectarian notion, unworthy the enlightenment of a Latterday Saint. All truths are divine. We live upon a divine earth, breathe a divine atmosphere, refresh ourselves at divine fountains, admire the beauties of a divine landscape, draw our very life's blood from divine elements. What different men and women we shall become when we learn to reverence all God's gifts as we do the single gift of his Word! Brigham Young never preached a more eloquent sermon than when he said to Brother Maeser: "Do not attempt to teach even the multiplication table without the Spirit of God."

God Helps Those who Help Themselves.—"But," it is

urged, "inspiration levels all. The humblest mind inspired, becomes the mightiest power for good."

True; but inspiration is modified in effect by the medium through which it works, nevertheless. For instance, without humility the most cultured mind is a non-conductor, if I may use so material an expression. Of two equally humble and God-fearing men that set out to till the soil, he is blest with the better harvest that has the greater skill. It is no whit different with preaching, else why should one preacher be more effective than another?

He has a greater talent, you urge. That merely shifts the question, but enables me to exhibit another phase. The notion prevails that a talent is something arbitrarily bestowed—given as God lists, not as man deserves. Nothing could be more inconsistent with all we know of God's dealings with man. Watch how God gives a talent in this life, if you would know how he gave it before this life. If a man be born with the talent for preaching developed, it argues a careful cultivation of it during pre-existence. If not well-developed it argues indifferent cultivation. Now, if preaching be a talent, may it lie buried in the ground, save only as it is dug up weekly, or occasionally, simply because it is the preaching talent?

Learning by Imitation. — There is another argument — that drawn from necessity. Strictly speaking, the doing a thing pre-supposes the having learned how. He that plays by ear cannot claim that he has not studied. Attention he must have paid to his art but not wisely-directed attention, since he refuses to avail himself of laws which are the heritage of the race. In like manner all, or nearly all studies may be undertaken either logically or empirically. Those who pursue a study logically stand in a comparatively short time upon the shoulders of their predecessors; or to vary the figure, reach the frontier of investigation, and may themselves become discoverers and inventors. Those who follow the other method seldom pass the dead level of mediocrity. The Elder that preaches, be that preaching good, bad, or indifferent, must have given attention to it, even if it be only the attention of imitation. But imitation is only an echo, which rarely succeeds in reproducing the force and clearness of the thing imitated. Besides, when applied to preaching, imitation becomes a peculiarly unfortunate process: what is a merit in the original often changes to a defect in the copyist.

But why pursue this argument further? The objection against a careful study of preaching as an art can come, it seems to me, only from thoughtlessness, or at least from immature reflection. Pages ago I felt, as no doubt has also the reader, that I was beating the air, there being no opposition. If, then, the general principle is conceded, which I now assume, that preaching, like any other activity, can be improved, both as to matter and manner, by a careful study of its underlying laws, the question next arises, Do we as Latterday Saint Elders sufficiently prepare ourselves for the ministry?

IV.

NON-PREPARATION TESTED BY SCRIPTURE.

The Non-Progressive Elder and His Sermon.—The Elders that preach before the Latterday Saints may be divided into four classes: (1) those that read much and think much; (2) those that read little, yet think much; (3) those that read much, yet think little; (4) those that read little and think less. The last class, in this year of grace, is a big one.

I should be tempted here to devote a paragraph of kindly advice to this class, were I not hopeless of its ever reaching them. Solomon wrote many striking proverbs about wisdom, and them that refuse to seek it. But it is very unlikely that they were ever read by the people whose attention he tried to catch. At any rate the wise man felt like "braying them in a mortar," but confessed it very doubtful whether even this would improve them. Let me not seem satirical. These are generally good men—goody-good. The only mistake they make in preaching is in setting their tongues wagging and then going off and leaving them.

Seriously, I profess no charity for the Latterday Saint who has ceased to grow, especially if he be an Elder. Progressiveness —this grand device is not alone emblazoned on our banner; it is the very genius that carries the banner. It is not a time to bury our talents. Thought today must breed fast, talents must duplicate themselves daily, hourly. For us that have the whole world to move, it is a crime to stand still, or merely beat time.

Mormon theology embraces such a variety of truths that nothing which affects the temporal or the spiritual welfare of man, can come amiss on Sundays if selected by the Spirit of inspiration. Indeed, anything that arouses attention and stimulates thought—be it Gospel principle or advice about husbanding crops—will be not only listened to but relished by Latterday Saints, such is our boundless respect for all God's truths.

But it requires thought to arouse thought. What then can be expected from men that never think themselves? What can the Spirit find there to edify the people? Often there is but a very scant store to draw from, even of the ideas of others. Such minds resemble second-hand junk-shops. The sermons drawn therefrom are a wearisome patchwork, made up of thoughts and ideas disconnected; aged but not venerable; worn out by having been said a thousand times before; dressed in a garb of insufferable phrases, old and hackneyed; platitudes with the green mould clinging to them.

And yet such sermons are generally prefaced by a commiseration of sectarian preaching and by thanks to heaven that Elders in this Church are required to take no thought about what they shall say. Is it not the case of the Pharisee and publican over again?

Is it not like saying in effect: "O Lord, I thank thee that I who take no thought am a fit vessel for thy inspiration, and that I am not like yonder publican (or sectarian) who doth meanly grub among books and men for thoughts and ideas"?

What the Scripture Says.—What justification have such Elders from Scripture? Let us examine what the Lord has said on the subject. In a revelation given to Joseph the Prophet, September 22nd and 23rd, 1832, occurs the following passage:

"Neither take ye thought beforehand what ye shall say, 'but treasure up in your minds continually the words of life,' and it shall be given in the very hour that portion that shall be needed unto every man." Doctrine and Covenants, Sec. 84: verse 85.

I have taken the liberty to put part of this passage in single quotations. The first and the last part have been repeated so often, that I thought it well by way of a change, to direct special attention to the middle part—the kernel, without which the passage becomes an empty shell. Looking at this middle part, one feels a certain relief in the thought that he need not credit—or charge—the Spirit of inspiration with all that he listens to under the name of preaching. In this, as in all other matters, the Lord does not depart from the natural. He has never promised to quench the thirsty from a dried-up well, nor feed the hungry from an empty store-house. He has, indeed, promised that there shall be given in the very hour that portion which is mete for every man; but only on the condition that he who is called to mete out what is thus needed shall have stored his mind continually with the word of God.

This thought is re-enforced by considering the office of the Spirit of inspiration: "But the comforter, which is the Holy Ghost whom the Father will send in my name, he shall teach you all things, and bring all things (i. e. stored-up truths) to your remembrance, whatsoever I have said unto you."—John xiv: 26. But what if there be nothing stored up to bring to remembrance?

"He shall teach you all things." Again: "He will guide you into all truth."—John xvi: 13. But what if the Elder is too indolent or careless to be taught or guided? What if he has ceased to be an ardent student under this divine Teacher? What if, like a tree that has been neither pruned nor watered, he has practically died in all his branches save memory, and even this returns year by year a scrubbier fruit? Do we not too often have to listen to reiterated sermons which are but the remnants—the scraps and dried bones—of former feasts?

Direct Command to Prepare for Preaching.—In the following passage, which I quote from the eightieth section of the Doctrine and Covenants, the obligation of preparing for the ministry is not left to inference. As will be seen from verse eighty, the command is addressed to Elders called on missions. I commend it to my brethren who have put an easy interpretation on the words, "Take no thought:"

77. And I give unto you a commandment, that ye shall teach one another the doctrine of the kingdom;

78. Teach ye diligently and my grace shall attend you, that you may be instructed more perfectly in theory, in principle, in doctrine, in the law of the Gospel, in all things that pertain unto the kingdom of God, that are expedient for you to understand:

79. Of things both in heaven and in earth, and under the earth; things which have been, things which are, things which must shortly come to pass; things which are at home, things which are abroad; the wars and the perplexities of the nations, and the judgments which are on the land, and a knowledge also of countries and of kingdoms.

80. That ye may be prepared in all things when I shall send you again to magnify the calling whereunto I have called you, and the mission with which I have commissioned you.

Perhaps it will be profitable to offer a few comments on the passage. The first two verses enjoin the diligent study of the principles of the Gospel as ordinarily comprised in the plan of salvation. Verse seventy-nine goes further, and commands the acquirement of knowledge concerning all things that interest mankind, whether in heaven, on earth, or under the earth, whether past, present, or future; all to the end that the preacher may be prepared for the mission and calling whereunto God has commissioned him. This may be regarded as the Lord's own commentary on the words, "Take no thought," and should settle the question forever. As will be pointed out in subsequent chapters, the wide range of information here required of the Elder is necessary in order that the Spirit may have material from which to draw in making plain and enforcing the truths of the Gospel.

Preachers by Miracle.—This brings into consideration the last refuge of those who still believe that it is God's part of preaching to bring to our Sabbath meetings the bread of life already baked, sliced, and buttered; man's only to distribute it. By way of bolstering their position, these Elders frequently relate how the Lord called them: from the loom, from the work bench, from the mine, or from the plow; placed them before eager audiences to preach the Gospel restored to earth. How they were utterly unprepared by previous training—in many cases not knowing how to read; how the Spirit descended upon them, and they became eloquent; thoughts unknown before grew into discourses; the Bible became a Urim and Thummin, from which they quoted at will to support the new doctrines; finally how the occasion passed, the inspiration ceased, and they became their unlettered selves again, yet overwhelmed with astonishment.

Now, this circumstance, often marveled at, is not marvelous save in the same sense that every sunrise is marvelous. God has always worked so. The real marvel would be if he made this dispensation an exception. But this is by the side. My point is the shallowness of the conclusion, first so, always so, which some Elders draw from this object-lesson. It seems to me that only childish reasoning could lead to the conviction that because the Lord at first gave everything but voice, that thereafter the Elder is required to furnish only voice. What man will argue, because his father once carried him in his arms, and his mother fed him with a spoon, that they should always feed and carry him? And yet occasionally we find a man who insists that the Lord must do this very thing for him, intellectually speaking, as if he were still an infant in the Gospel.

Reasons for this Miraculous Aid.—It must be remembered that the men of whom such miracles in preaching are recorded, could hardly have been held responsible for not being familiar with the Gospel—for not having "treasured up in their minds continually the words of life." The truth had not been on the earth to treasure up. When the message first came, it found few men whose natural powers had been cultivated ready to receive it; for where men were thus prepared, their education had generally so biased their judgments as to make them unable or unwilling to understand the truth. The Spirit had, therefore, to educate preachers; and it began in many instances, where minds were humble and pliable enough, by giving whole sermons, apparently without the aid of other natural powers than the speaker's voice alone.

But it hastened to educate these natural powers. Look over the names of great men in the history of the Church, and name one if you can, that did not end his career by being in the truest sense an educated man. And where men had a good foundation to begin with, as in the case of the Pratts, John Taylor, Wilford Woodruff, Oliver Cowdery, Sidney Rigdon, Orson Spencer and others that might be named, they were, by so much, the more useful in the ministry, right from the start.

Humility not Ignorance, the Essential.—What I contend for is that it is not ignorance that fits men to become powerful instruments in the hands of the Lord; it is humility and freedom from bias; or at least a strength of native honesty which will cause them to give up their bias in the presence of truth. Does any one doubt that had Peter and his fellow Apostles been possessed of

Paul's learning, and yet had none the less of their own humility and willingness to be guided, they would not have been more effective in preaching the Gospel?

Suppose that an Elder, who has been thus miraculously aided in preaching, should cease to exert himself and lean like a dead weight wholly on the Lord. How often, think you, would he thereafter be assisted? Most of this class have apostatized, but we still have a few in the Church. They are pretty dry sticks. When they arise to speak today, they can do little else than brag of what the Spirit once did through them.

I use the word brag, for while I believe that miraculous experiences generally are faith-promoting, the influence drawn from this particular kind of experience is so pernicious in its bearing that I feel justified in using this word. Who can calculate to what extent the poor preparation of our missionaries is due to their inference that God will in like manner put sermons ready-made into their mouths?

V.

NON-PREPARATION TESTED IN OUR MISSIONARY FIELDS.

The Raw Missionary.—Consider in this connection the effect of another circumstance: Here is the scion of a prominent family, a young man who has literally run wild; who knows all about lassoing and riding a broncho, about stock raising and maverick-hunting, yet is utterly ignorant of the Gospel; hopelessly so, unless—strange alternative—unless called on a mission. And so he is called. Two or three years pass swiftly. Ere his friends have ceased to miss him, he returns and is invited to address his brethren and sisters.

Can it be possible! Is this the same young man that broke down in a half minute farewell talk? What fluency in speech, what aptness in quoting scripture! What force of character, what warmth of spirit! "Is it not marvelous what the Lord can do in so short a time! Verily, as the scriptures say: 'Take no thought of what ye shall say'—this is the only school for the true preacher."

Such is the impression—at least among the unthinking, and that means a great number of similar young men, who go on in serene thoughtlessness, blindly trusting that when they shall be called, some miracle will transform them also from cowboys to preachers of righteousness.

The Transforming Process.—They are right. A miracle will be worked; but the Lord will take care that they are the workers of it. You, young man, who have just returned—let me put you upon the stand. Did you find a mind utterly untrammeled with ideas a good preparation for preaching? Did you excite astonishment, or did you excite pity in your first congregation? in your tenth? in your fiftieth? How did the miracle that transformed you begin? Are you anxious to pass through the beginning again? Nay, be not impatient; dwell upon it for the benefit of these lazy young hopefuls.

Ah, how the Lord made you suffer, as only a condemned soul can suffer, for your past indifference and indolence! How you were laughed at and hooted! Ignoramus that you were! You that knew scarcely the first syllable of the Gospel—you to set up for teacher of mankind!

Such were the taunts that directly or indirectly reached your ears. Try as you might, the Lord would not suffer you to feel the consolation of a martyr; in the keenest manner possible, he burned it into your soul: "This is your true self."

On the way to your field of labor you already felt qualms of incompetence. But these you set aside by the fond trust: "I am God's servant; he will not suffer me to be defeated." But in this, how cruelly you were undeceived! He not only suffered you to be ignominiously defeated time after time, but did not interfere when you were utterly routed.

How fearfully discouraged you were after such encounters! You dreaded your meetings, for you had nothing to say. Your mind seemed utterly empty—and was quite so, no doubt. How could you ever become a preacher? The torture you were passing through prevented you from remembering anything you read. You prayed, but the heavens were brass above you. Your soul was dark and dull as chaos, and your heart was burdened with the leaden weight of despair. Amidst it all one wild impulse possessed you—to give up and go home. In this only did the Spirit come to your assistance. You resolved to stay, no matter what might happen. "If it be God's will for me to remain, useless though I am, I'll do it even though it kills me."

The Light Breaks.—This was a splendid resolution. It brought you nearer to your God than all the efforts of your previous life together. Somehow it made a great difference in your way of looking at things. What cared you now for the mocks and jeers of your enemies? You felt you could gladly suffer these things, and love them all the more. Even the ties of friends, relatives, and loved ones, which hitherto had seemed your only support, paled into insignificance by the side of this new friendship which was springing up in your bosom.

You now formed the habit of stealing into the woods alone that you might converse, as it were, face to face with this New Friend. You told him of your unworthiness to fill this mission; confided to him how the despair of your wasted life was almost killing you; clung to him as your only hope, and promised him with a fervor and earnestness which stirred the inmost recesses of your soul, that now you would begin to study and work as you had never studied and worked before.

On these occasions you shed tears—blessed tears; tears that came from the deep; tears that unburdened a black cloud. You were reminded of childhood days when you were wont to weep your sorrows away in the arms of a loving mother. But what was that love compared with the infinite pity and mercy and love of this new found Father! Under the caresses of your parents you had a sense of perfect rest and security. But then you were a child and within the protecting walls of your childhood home. Now you felt a thousand-fold that same sense of rest and security, and your home was the protecting roof of the universe! From these meetings with your Heavenly Father you came away with a light step and with eyes beaming like a May morning after a shower.

Work the Law of the Universe.—Such is a brief history of how you were humbled—crushed to the earth. Such also is the meaning in our day of sack-cloth and ashes,—of a broken heart and a contrite spirit. You scarcely expected that the miracle of your transformation would have a beginning of this kind. You rarely refer to this episode in your career. It would be profitable for the young men, the future preachers of Zion, if you would do so often —picturing it in its native colors, as I have tried to do But you shrink from even recalling it. It is so much more pleasant to tell of the success after, than of the failures before this time. And then there is your egotistic self, persuading you even now that perhaps after all you were really a martyr and did not deserve the probation in purgatory which your first few months in the mission field gave you.

But the fact remains. In your heart of hearts, you expected great things of the Lord; you expected that, when he looked upon your helplessness, rather than see you put to open shame, he would somehow fill your mind with eloquent sermons ready made, as he did some of your brethren in the early history of the Church.

You forgot to take into account that they were all called on a moment's warning and could not be held accountable for ignorance of the Gospel; while you had spent your whole life in Zion and had shunned the very schools, associations and meetings designed to prepare you for this work. You forgot that the Lord never gives; he rewards. You forgot the law of equivalents, as true in religion as in farming or trading: you cannot get something for nothing; and that other law, as true in preaching as in teaching: you cannot give what you have not got. These are profound yet very elementary truths. But you had to be brought low before you could be made to feel the force of them—before you could realize that the great law of the universe is WORK.

Learns the Lesson at Last.—But once you did realize it, how eagerly you began to repair the waste of your past life! The Bible became your dearest friend. Day and night you read and thought and prayed. And the light began to dawn. The sun rose brighter, and the world looked lovelier, and mankind became dear—inexpressibly dear, to you. As each truth flashed upon your mind, you longed for the tongue of an angel to proclaim it to the whole world. When that world turned but a dull ear, you were saddened but not discouraged. "Thank heaven," you exclaimed, "I shall profit by it, if you do reject it."

Your growth was now so rapid, truths now multiplied so fast, as to seem like revelation. Worlds past, present, and future, opened to your mind like a vision, and you saw exactly your place in the economy of the universe. And no wonder; for you were now a student with the surest of all guides, the Spirit of truth, for your teacher.

Thus was the miracle accomplished; thus was the cowboy transformed to a preacher of righteousness.

VI.

NON-PREPARATION TESTED BY RESULTS AT HOME.

The Goodish Preacher.—Now, kind reader, look carefully at the case recorded in the last chapter. Can you find anything in it to justify the hope that God will reward indolence? What a question you say. Well, suppose it to be a fond, trusting—yea, prayerful indolence? If a man neglect by observation, by reading, and by thinking, to get ideas, may he reasonably expect, when called upon to preach, that the Lord will come to his rescue, and put oil into his lamp?

That, you say, is an easy question. Well, I want to make this thought hit the mark squarely. Suppose he be a good man (goodish is a better term), one who prays earnestly the prayer of habit, who pays his tithes, etc., but nevertheless one who, in spite of all these good qualities, is mentally lazy. What will be the quality of his sermon? Whom shall we praise or blame for it?

I answer this question only for myself. I cannot think of a more profitless hour than that spent in listening to an aimless speaker; whose "remarks" are spread out from Dan to Beersheba, and actually touch nothing but the peaks of thought; whose worn-out generalities one sees with dread afar off, as one by one they come, each caused by the speaker's stumbling upon some familiar word, which like a stone in the road, bobs up in the distance and throws the discourse into a rut.

The weary length of these ruts must be painfully familiar to Latterday Saints. Occasionally one is beguiled into an idle curiosity as to whether there will be a variation this time. But generally one is doomed to be disappointed; for the man that can inflict platitude after platitude upon a congregation, is not the man of sufficient mind-activity to draw new applications from old truths.

What is my duty, then? May I stay away from meeting? No; I will go, even though I know such a rambling talk is coming. The real blessing of a Sabbath meeting—the strengthening of one's determination and the renewal of one's covenants, which come from thoughtfully and prayerfully partaking of the sacrament—no preacher can take away. This blessing received, I can sit back to an hour's punishment, if need be, and count it among the blessings of adversity.

A Side Talk.—And now one word to those of my brethren who will rise up and say this criticism comes from a disaffected mind and a fault-finding spirit. I am fully aware of the danger I run of being misjudged by thus speaking right out. I know, too, how a man's usefulness is crippled once it is believed he is "on the road to apostacy." Indeed, it is from fear of this misjudgment that ten men think what they will not say, where one man says what he thinks. Let those who doubt this, visit and talk confidentially with the multitude of Latterday Saints who now seldom go to meeting. For myself, let me say, it has given me no pleasure to handle without gloves what I regard as a serious abuse. But the chapters I still have in view on preaching necessitate the establishing of clear-cut views on the points I have discussed. I might have used language so polished in phrase and distant in meaning as to arouse no objection; but this would have left the matter untouched, and burdened the pages of this book with empty words. For the present, then, let my candor and bluntness count for evidence of honesty and sincerity.

Effect of Aimless, Rambling Sermon.—But after all what matters any one's opinion? The question still remains. An aimless, rambling sermon is or is not profitless; it is or is not inspired by God. Perhaps it will help us to decide by watching its effect upon any congregation. Among the portion that sleep, some of whom are on the stand, may be counted here and there leading members of the ward. Of the portion awake, the majority show the leaden eye and lackadaisical expression, which, were it in the school-room, would be the agony of a teacher accustomed to sparkling attention. There remains then the third class, the punished few, who have been vainly trying to gather and combine something from this aimless scattering. These you can generally tell by the squirming way they have of trying to fit their seats. After meeting, go and have a confidential chat with one of them. You will be edified; or, if you are of the goody-good kind—shocked.

Are all Sermons Inspired?—Be patient, kind reader. I am almost through fault-finding—at least on this particular subject. To what purpose, it may be asked, is the objection against studying how to preach, discussed from so many points of view, and illustrated by such a variety of phases? Chiefly that we as a people may choose intelligently between these two alternatives:

First. 'That every Elder is inspired who first asks for the faith of the Saints and then launches out on a sermon.' Those members of the Church who still persist in clinging to this fiction will sometime have these very curious consequences to reconcile:—

    a. No matter how scattering or irrelevant the sermon, being inspired, it is as God would have it; consequently,

    b. Those who felt punished in listening, and those who staid away to avoid hearing it, must be accounted on the highway to apostacy, since they find fault with what is inspired.

    c. The only ones, then, who are really benefited by the sermon are those who slept and those whose minds wandered; that is to say, those who did not hear it (which is doubtless true).

Now, Mormons who are capable of swallowing the above proposition, will, I have little doubt, also be able to stomach the consequences I have named. They may moreover defend themselves by these most excellent reasons: (1) Such a belief is likely to leave one free from those disquieting aspirations for something nobler and better, which disturb the serenity of those respectable people who are satisfied with good enough. (2) It will tend to keep up the prestige and reputation of antedated preachers and so enable these good men to live and die with exalted opinions of themselves. (3) It is an admirable device for thinning out congregations and thus cutting down the burden of building new houses (during these hard times).

All Sermons Not Inspired.—In spite of these reasons however, I very much fear that most Latterday Saints will be likely to believe,—

Second. 'That the Lord is ever ready to inspire a speaker provided he has complied with the conditions of such inspiration; and consequently, that if he has not thus complied, he speaks from the fulness or emptiness of his own head.' This proposition also leads to some important consequences:—

a. Latterday Saints will occasionally feel at liberty to characterize a sermon with the same force and brevity that they speak of a mismanaged, weed-grown farm, and not fear that their standing may be misjudged on account of doing so. It seems to me a healthy rule to count that charity misplaced which fosters the evil it feeds, be it beggary or bad preaching. There was a time, not long ago, when most of our school rooms were filled by just such inattentive, sleepy gatherings as I have been trying to portray. Would they not have remained so till now, had the teachers been covered by the charity so unwisely thrown round our Elders? Let us not fear a healthy public awakening on this point. Marvels will grow out of it, for—

b. Stereotyped preachers will break through their shells and begin to grow again. Young men will feel that the first qualification of a preacher is to know something, to feel something, and to think something. Elders who refuse to learn the lesson will at least, out of very shame, forbear to inflict upon the congregation the hackneyed phraseology of musty memories. Thus,

c. Preaching will be made a study both as to subject matter and method of delivery, just as teaching has already been; and equally good results may be expected to follow. If the teacher has found the secret of interesting little children, let not the preacher despair of finding the way to interest grown-up children.

CHAPTER II.

QUALIFICATIONS OF THE PREACHER.

I.

SERMONS SHOULD BE MADE UP OF LOGICAL AND PROGRESSIVE THOUGHT.

No farmer expects to irrigate with an unopened spring, nor is there anything in nature that can so counterfeit water as to cause him to wait, shovel in hand, the approach of a dried-up stream. It is quite different in speech; here we frequently have a stream without having water—a stream of empty words. And the man who could not be imposed upon in the first instance, sits in the second through a whole hour mentally trying to direct an empty channel upon the gardens of his mind and heart. But he goes home still thirsty. He cannot understand it. There was fluency enough. A great many good things—trite good things— were said upon as many good subjects, but somehow they didn't reach the spot. What was lacking?—Thought.

Thought we must have, first of all; logical, consistent, progressive thought; thought that builds part by part, roofs in what has been built, then garnishes the whole structure so that we may actually feel the warmth and comfort of a finished thing. But thoughts scattering and fragmentary or piled up haphazard—what are they at best but brick? Perfect, perhaps, as brick, and always suggestive of a house. But are we warmed and cheered by the sight of heaped-up building material? On the contrary, is it not the very suggestion of what logical structures might be made of these word-brick, while we stand shivering by, that is so exasperating?

Bigotry and Narrow-Mindedness.—What then? Is it enough that a man think clearly and constructively on a subject? The sectarian generally does this. So do the atheist lecturer, and the Bohemian preacher, whose conscience responds not to principle, but to the highest cash bid. Surely says the young Elder of more zeal than judgment—surely, these facts ought to condemn the principle you contend for. Not so fast, my friend. Clear and constructive thinking is not what makes men atheist in belief or Bohemian in tendency. Such thinking makes them powerful even in the propagation of error. How much more powerful then would it make them in the defense of truth? Let us realize, once for all, that even the devil uses mainly truth to accomplish his purposes. Shall we therefore, despise truth? Shall the keen blade no more be used because the assassin occasionally paints it red?

Let me devote one paragraph to this tendency among Latter-day Saints, to cast away not only the false, but also the true and good, which happens to be in bad company. In spite of the thirteenth Article of Faith, many of us are woefully bigoted and narrow-minded. Let us confess this freely, and keep it daily in mind until we shall feel our cramped souls stretch out to the full stature of the image of our Father. We are narrow, not because of, but in spite of, our religion. It is the smell of sectism still lingering in our clothes. The distant heathen we can easily account our brother; but the carpet-bag preacher who comes here to lure away our children—and gets the very money with which to do it, by telling monstrous falsehoods about us to his eastern dupes—in this well meaning but misguided son of our Father, we cannot distinguish the good from the bad—it is all bad, and differs only in degrees of badness.

Not all Bad in Sectarianism.—This is not the only instance of our own narrowness. For instance I have no doubt that the barn-like structures that do duty in so many of our towns, for places of worship, maintain their architectural barbarity so long and so brazenly, largely because of the pretty, neatly-painted sectarian chapels that stare them in the face. True, within these chapels are taught fables and man-made doctrines, as we believe—a mere form of godliness without the power thereof. But is that any good reason why we should despise the beauty of the architecture?

The naked walls, the bare floors, and shackly benches in our houses of worship are apologized for on the plea of poverty. But how shallow is this pretense! The cost of furnishing almost any parlor in the ward, which represents what each member might do, would so adorn the meeting house as to make the very walls breathe a spirit of worship. The real cause is lack of disposition to make beautiful the house of the Lord; and this disposition has been induced, I fear, by fatal glimpses into sectarian churches. *

And so also of sectarian preaching. In our disgust for the upward rolling eye, the canting tone, the tearful voice, and the wearisome "firstly," "secondly," "thirdly," of an attenuated text, we throw away, likewise, the logical development of the theme, which is often so admirable a feature of these sermons. But permit me here to remind the reader, I am not contending that we should come to sectarian ministers for this merit, no more than I would urge that we beautify our houses of worship because they do. Let us rather come to our own leading speakers for models in logical arrangement. What I maintain is that it is folly for us to hold a thing bad merely because sectarians count it good; and it is worse than folly to act on the blind assumption that we are only safely right when directly opposed to them.

For the rest, it is with preaching as with teaching, as with any principle of the Gospel, we have the decided advantage; our source of information may be divine, if we are humble and full of faith

---

*This paragraph was written and published five years ago. It is hardly true today. The wards throughout Zion seem now to vie with one another in building and beautifying their places of worship, which fact may be taken as an example of the swiftness with which reforms move among us.

enough to be guided by the Spirit of truth; their source is confessedly human, for they repudiate the very idea of revelation in our day. Revelation is truth to them only if it has filtered for ages through channels of human interpretation. To us the newer the revelation the truer; as being the less likely to be mixed with human ingredients. To put it figuratively, what they are willing to drink only from the ditch, we prefer to get from the fountain.

Mind Wandering Not a Merit.—Let us not, then, make a merit of wandering as some of our Elders actually do who foolishly believe that to be exact, clear, and constructive in their sermons, is to imitate sectarian preachers. Nor need we fear that the Spirit will be grieved; for it is not the Spirit as these Elders fondly believe, that leads so idly and uncertainly along; it is the flickering of a feeble memory amid the darkness of a poorly organized mind; which, like the blue lights of a bog, faintly illumine now this spot now that.

In any other business than that of preaching, the logic of circumstances settles this question without need of words. What, for instance, becomes of the teacher that does not form the habit of thinking clearly and consecutively upon subjects he is expected to teach? Started perhaps at Highville, by the influence of friends, he ends by being refused a position at Scrubtown. Between these two points who shall mark his devious course! It was his mind that first began to wander, but his legs perforce soon caught the infection. This experience is no doubt duplicated also in the case of preachers, especially in those churches that follow the salary plan. It is probably too often true, also, of our own Elders who travel month after month without opening a field of labor.

The Lecturer and the Preacher.—This brings forward again the question as to whether the qualifications that make a lecturer suffice to make a preacher. Certainly as compared with the piece-meal speaker, the preacher who lectures is to be preferred every time; he actually moves his listeners forward in some direction while the other merely keeps them beating time. But after all is said the lecture-sermon is a very cold-fire; we see the flames truly, but must stop to reason about it, before we become conscious of any warmth. Let such a speaker be ever so gifted in rhetoric and elocution, we still feel that something is lacking—something of the heart, rather than of the head.

The true sermon transcends the lecture as the day does the dawn. The pleasure of the lecture, like that of the dawn, consists in the sensation that what is dark about us begins to yield definite shapes and outlines. We become sensible that our vistas lengthen and our expanses widen even while we look. Our imaginations are full of what the light of day may possibly reveal! And somehow we feel that all this has grown out of ourselves—that we are the centers of light. The true sermon is all this, save the last; we feel that the light comes from above. But we feel in addition a warmth as of mid-day that penetrates the soul we know not how; and a gladness that may be compared to nothing so well as the smile of a flower garden in a bath of sunshine.

The Melody of a Sermon.—Spiritually we are a very finely-strung people. In the simplest exhortation as well as in the most persuasive eloquence, we detect instantly the presence or absence of the still, small voice. I am told—what a pity that some of us need to be told!—that in the most severely classic of musical pieces, which the dull-eared hear only as marvelous acrobatic feats in sound, there is to the musician a sweet, simple melody running like the notes of a nightingale amid the rumblings of thunder. It is this same melody in the sermon, to which I am trying to call attention. However unskillful to discover it in music, all that live their religion detect it readily in speech; and when it is found wanting in the pretentious sermon, the disappointment is much keener than when it is wanting in the rambling talk, where it is scarcely looked for; just when we almost reach the altitude of some delight, we suffer keenly the disappointment of a pleasure that would scarcely have entered our minds had we remained in the prosaic valley below.

Thus it happens occasionally that a sermon, which might be considered meritorious as a lecture, fails to satisfy the spiritual hunger of the Saints on the Sabbath day. And it takes but one or two such disappointments to arouse prejudice. No doubt in the case of many readers, my severe criticisms against aimless sermons have been met by the remark: "Well, I'd rather have such a talk than listen to the highfalutin' preaching of so and so."

They are about right. The sermon that is cut and dried, is tasteless spiritual food for Latterday Saints, who are accustomed to have their fruit directly from the orchard, full of the juice and flavor of freshness. Nor should we lose sight of this important fact: the true source of a sermon is a perpetual Garden of Eden whence fruit in its season is always ready to pick. But are our minds such gardens? If so there is no need to cut and dry; if not, the remedy is still not to cut and dry but to dig about and prune and cultivate.

Granting all this, however, does it offer any justification for the rambling, disconnected sermon? On the contrary, it proves that while a sermon should have all the merits of a lecture, it must have something more. What is that something?

II.

A WELL-STORED MIND AND MEEKNESS THE TRUE QUALIFICATIONS OF THE PREACHER.

An Oft Repeated Incident.—"Well, my boy, what can I do for you this morning?"

"Oh, Brother Maeser, I'm utterly discouraged. I think I'd better go home. I don't know anything, and I'll never be able to learn anything. I did think I knew a little something when I left home, but when I get into the classes here, they're so far advanced, and everything I did know leaves me, and I sit there looking on stupid, and can't say a word, or understand a question that's put to me. I can't stand it any longer. I'll have to go home."

"My dear boy,"—with a caressing touch of the hand—"you have learned the first great lesson, and I'm glad you have learned it so well. This is the Lord's way of starting a student in aright. Be thankful that you have learned so soon that you know nothing. No student can remain here long who does not learn the lesson of humility. Even if he could, he never would be a real student. Go now, my dear boy; make the Lord your friend. The light will soon begin to shine, and you will find yourself in a new world."

How many times this little scene was enacted in Brother Maeser's private office in the Brigham Young Academy! Hundreds of young people in this State will recall such an interview as the turning point in their lives.

Vanity and Self-sufficiency.—But this experience is by no means peculiar to any one school in Zion. Elders in the missionary field must begin in the same way, if the Lord is to make any use of their talents. Is there, in fact, any place in the Church that a man can fill without this lesson of humility? Nor is it enough generally to be humbled once. Latterday Saints need to visit themselves every little while in the private office of the Spirit of truth, and learn the lesson over again. I am convinced that nine-tenths of the Elders that preach before the Latterday Saints, should at this very writing be humbled to the dust. We are too well satisfied with ourselves as preachers. I have said many uncomplimentary things in this line of thought. Let me be candid. I am preaching to myself. The tendency to feel satisfied and pleased with one's self is so insidious that I aim directly at it. I want to kill your vanity and my own. I am severe because I feel nothing short of severity will reach me.

Vanity, self-sufficiency, or want of humility is supposed to be the peculiar weakness of Elders that "take thought" as to what they will say. But this is surely a mistake. Frequently those who are emptiest and least logical are most vain.

Years ago, returning from a mission, I was invited to preach in the Tabernacle. I said some beautiful things. More than one of my hearers confirmed me in this view. But there was one who told me the truth in two short sentences, viz: that I had trampled over every thing generally, and reached nowhere in particular. He was my true friend. I have often pondered his rebuke since, and find I am in a numerous company; but unlike him, I have not had the moral courage to be "cruel in order to be kind." Perhaps these chapters on preaching will atone for my want of candor to individual speakers whom I might have aided by being plain.

How It Grows.—Too often this personal vanity begins in the missionary field—and here, let it be remembered, is where nine-tenths of our preachers become preachers.

"How long," says the young missionary, "did I hold out this time?"

"Twenty-four minutes."

"Well, that's encouraging. That's ten minutes better than I did last time. I'm growing."

Before the Elder returns he has learned to "hold them" an hour, and alas for the poor Saints in the valleys thereafter! I say alas! for it is the Elder who thus measures his growth that needs most of all to learn again the great lesson of humility. But will he learn the lesson? Not as long as we are imposed upon by the belief that he speaks by inspiration. Not until some friend does for him what my friend did for me; that is, rebuke his volubility, and make him realize what a puffed-up creature he is.

The Four Classes.—In the last chapter I maintained that though a sermon should have all the merits of a lecture —that is, clearness and logical arrangement—it should have in addition the warmth of the Spirit of God. But this latter element is impossible without humility in the speaker. We have then four cases to consider. (1) The rambling talker who is not humble. He is of all preachers the most insufferable. (2) The rambling speaker who is humble. He does not edify much, but we say of him, He has a fine spirit. (3) The logical speaker who is not humble. He interests, that is, conveys information, but does not warm us spiritually. (4) The logical speaker who is humble. This is the ideal preacher, a man whose mind is richly stored and who is pliable enough to let the Spirit choose what is meat in due season.

The first two of these cases we may now dismiss. Let us consider the third.

Prepared Sermons.—The disposition to prepare a sermon, as we prepare a lecture, which, indeed, makes a lecture of it, results from want of humility and a fearfulness that the Lord will perhaps fail to "give in the hour thereof," what is needful for the congregation. It is perhaps nearer the truth to say that this want of trust in God results from want of humility. For, if the preacher be not humble, and have not this childlike trust, the sermon must proceed unaided by the Spirit of inspiration, no matter how many good things may be stored in the mind. This conclusion may, I think, be fairly drawn from the following passage: "Therefore, verily, I say unto you, lift up your voices unto this people, speak the thoughts that I shall put into your hearts, and you shall not be confounded before men; for it shall be given you in the very hour, yea, in the very moment, what ye shall say. But a commandment I give unto you, that ye shall declare whatsoever ye declare in my name, in solemnity of heart, in the spirit of meekness, in all things."—Doctrine and Covenants, Section c: 5-7.

A Well Stored Mind and Meekness.—Here then are the two conditions on which the Lord promises to put into the heart of a speaker the thoughts he shall give utterance to: First, he must "treasure up in his mind continually the word of life." Second, he must stand before the congregation "in solemnity of heart and in the spirit of meekness." Without the first condition, the Spirit finds nothing to draw thoughts from, and without the second, the Spirit cannot enter, no matter how well filled the mind may be.

A well-stored mind and meekness! What an admirable criterion by which to judge the preacher; or rather by which the preacher may judge himself. Let the mind review the names of eminent speakers of this dispensation, many of whom are among us today. These two conditions will be found present in every case. As set forth in a previous chapter, God has wrought miracles through Elders without the first qualification, i. e. a well-stored mind, where the want of it could not be counted to them a moral fault. But I do not call to mind an instance where a preacher has been instrumental for good without the latter qualification; save only on the general principle that the Lord makes every movement help forward his plans. Sidney Rigdon and Oliver Cowdery are striking cases in point. As long as these men were filled with a spirit of meekness they spoke as with the tongues of angels. When they fell there was still the material for sermons in their minds; but the divine Spirit was no longer there to draw thoughts from it.

I remarked above that I could not call to mind any instance where men were able to preach Mormonism successfully without the meekness and humility so necessary to the enjoyment of the Spirit of God. I did not mean that the principles we teach could not, even aside from inspiration, be made powerful towards influencing the human mind. When we see what marvelous results in religion-making are attained by the skillful use of fragments of the Gospel among the sects, who can doubt that much more marvelous results would be reached, if the human thought and eloquence in sectarian pulpits were but given themes so familiar to us? And I believe that when Satan is driven to the wall on every other subterfuge, he will at last masquerade under all our doctrines, including that of divine authority. Then it will be seen how powerful a preacher of these tenets may become, even without meekness,

PREACHING AND PUBLIC SPEAKING. 39

and how these principles alone will "convert" thousands and millions of human beings. This sect will then swallow all the sects.

True Conversions the Work of God.—In the meanwhile, let us remember that no man was ever really and truly converted without the Holy Ghost; and this comes only through meekness. Nor will there ever be such a conversion save in the true Church. · A true conversion is the work of God, and not of human eloquence. Man can never become so wise and learned that he needs not the Spirit of truth to search out the wants of a congregation. Skillful he may become in looking into the human heart, and noting its motives and impulses; but psychology can never supplant the need of inspiration. Because man has contrived the electric light, shall he presume to get along without the sun?

Let us then continue to believe that we are to take no thought about what we shall say, that we are to rely implicitly upon the Lord's giving in the hour thereof what is mete for every man. But let this trust never be an apology or a justification for minds in which nothing has bloomed and ripened since the days we were on missions. Let it mean what God designed it to mean, that we are not to prepare sermons by rote. The manna of distrust will always be full of worms. Nor are we even to choose the sermon beforehand. To do either of these would bespeak so little faith in God's promises as not to call down his blessings upon the effort. By way of illustrating this principle, let me close this general discussion with an experience of my own.

III.

THE NEED OF HUMILITY ILLUSTRATED BY AN EXPERIENCE.

Introduction to a Dunker Community.—Some years ago my traveling companion and I were called to open a new field of labor in the northern part of West Virginia. Having a letter of introduction to a family in Williamsport, we were kindly received, and made arrangement to hold meeting the following Sabbath. In the meanwhile, we made house to house visits, distributing tracts and getting acquainted. The people belonged generally to the Dunker persuasion, a Quaker-like sect, which professes to follow literally and exclusively the teachings of Christ.

In the first four principles of the Gospel, there is so little difference between us, that I began to be concerned as to what I should preach about. These people, I reasoned, teach faith and repentance as we do, and though they differ a trifle as to the mode of immersion, they agree in all the rest, so that a sermon on any of these subjects will hardly command their attention. Plainly, I must begin on divine authority, the point on which we differ.

My First Missionary Sermon.—This was to be my first sermon in the missionary field. My companion begged me not to expect more than a three minutes' talk from him. The great responsibility of opening the field devolved upon me, and I felt it grow heavier day after day. I spent hours memorizing passages and getting off the admirable arguments of Orson Pratt on divine authority. I went often into the woods to pray that I might succeed, then straightway reviewed my points. It seems, as I look back upon it now, that I was determined the Lord should not leave me in the lurch. I was "taking thought" with a vengeance. I had mentally sized up my listeners and prepared to convert them all at one fell swoop.

Pen-picture of My Audience.—Sunday came, and punctually at the hour our audience dressed in Dunker worshipping attire were seated, the women on one side, the men on the other. This sect counts it a mark of worldliness to wear buttons. For a similar reason, they aim to use only the natural colors of the wool. Their clothes, which they fasten with hooks and eyes, are purposely antiquated and ill-fitting, that pride may be crushed. To cut the hair or shave the beard like other mortals, would be a dangerous imitation of Babylon. They have therefore a tonsorial fashion of their own, in which, as in their costume, they take great pride.

Picture then, several rows of clean-shaven faces, each with a fringe-like (or goat-like) beard under the chin from ear to ear. And on the other side of the aisle, corresponding rows of—night caps I shall have to say for want of a word to describe them: white head coverings adorned by a severely plain hem, and strings tied under the chin. A cool curiosity pervaded the room, not unlike an early autumn frost. Our hymns seemed neither to thaw nor freeze the air. Elder C——— arose and read our articles of faith and bore his testimony. Not a single kindly look was yet to be seen.

Effect of Announcing My Theme.—Then I arose and announced that I should prove from the Bible—their own Bibl —that Joseph Smith was a Prophet of God. Presto, what a change! The temperature fell fathoms below zero in an instant. So fell also my heart, and for the remainder of that miserable hour it thumped dull as if its walls had been of lead. The points in my argument were still clear, and my memory did not fail on passages. I had announced that I would prove Joseph Smith to be a prophet and I proceeded to do so—with about as much effect on my congregation and pleasure to myself as if I had been beating with naked fists against a granite wall.

No sooner did I pronounce the name Joseph Smith than one-third of my audience wheeled about and turned their backs on me. I distinctly remember, as part of my annoyance, the haggling way in which one old man's hair had been cropped. I realize now, however, that I should have been more punished still had not every stony eye been turned away from me.

Direct Results of the Meeting.—This meeting and its results had evidently been determined by the Lord for my instruction rather than for my hearers. Our friends became alarmed and would not take us home with them any more. After meeting, a ribald crowd surrounded us and we were led into a running debate that even now gives me a twinge of shame. At last to my stupid mind came Christ's warning about pearls and swine, but not until some of the most sacred truths of the Gospel had been trampled into the mire. Then we broke away with the laughter and jeers of these devils ringing in our ears, till we hid ourselves in the depths of a grove.

Here I tried to pray, but I could utter nothing but words. The heavens were brass. Surely the man who invented that expression can sympathize with me. This was the first time I had really sensed it. We had fasted that morning for the success of our meeting. Strange inconsistency! to fast and pray that the Lord may be with us and then proceed to take precautions lest He should fail! We were now ravenously hungry, and and must seek lodgings. I shall never forget that tramp. Instinctively we felt that we must get outside of the circumference of my late sermon. But we were innocently ignorant of the distances people in the woods will assemble to hear a new preacher. It seemed that we would never get beyond the influence of my talk on divine authority. As we approached successively each new house, my companion would remark: "Look, there comes out another one of them. It's no use trying here."

Sure enough ere we had reached the stile of his rail fence he would be there—fringe beard, sanctimonious face, stony eye and all. (What a harsh, cold, inhuman countenance a Christian Pharisee can put on!)

"You uns can't stay here. 'Behold, in the last days false prophets shall arise and deceive many.'"

Indirect Results.—It was about ten o'clock that night when we paused beside the turnpike, attracted by a deep gully filled with leaves. The March air was chill, and the sun had not yet loosened the rills which a month later would combine to make a brook in every hollow.

"Let us lie down in those leaves. Thank heaven, we need ask only God's permission to do that," said Elder C.——.

It was a simple remark, but it opened the door of a new world, full of food and warmth and light. God's permission! Did not this whole world belong to Him? And were we not His servants? Now I felt full of prayer, and withdrew to give vent to my feelings:

"Father, thou hast opened my eyes. Thou hast said: 'Take no thought about what ye shall eat nor what ye shall drink,' and yet it has been my care and anxiety by night and day. Thou hast said: 'Take no thought about what ye shall say, for in the hour thereof shall be given what is mete,' and I have not trusted thee. Forgive me, Father. Henceforward let me be as clay in thy hands. Help me to make my spirit bend to thine, even as the leaf stirs to the evening breeze. Now I feel that thou hast forgiven my headstrong course this day. Do with me, then, as thou wilt, for I am here to do thy will, not my own. Is not all this world thine? And we are thine. Open thou the way for us. But if it be thy will that we shall stay here tonight, I am content and happy, for I have found a Friend. What need have I of other friends when thou art near? Where'er I go, I am still in thy house; and what roof can compare with the glorious star-decked firmament above me, what food with that which has now refreshed my soul? Father, I am content, and thank thee for this humble spot, and when thy sun shall rise glorious on the morrow, it will warm and cheer and gladden me as it ne'er hath done before."

Blessed tears! ineffable joy! Heavens, what a load I had been carrying! Never did child rescued from awful danger nestle so securely in its mother's bosom, as did I that night, with unquestioning confidence, throw myself into the arms of a loving Father.*

---

* For those of my readers who may be interested in this story, aside from my use of it as an illustration, I give herewith the sequel: After presenting our case to the Lord, we both felt like going on, though finding lodgings at this time of night was certainly not ordinarily to be expected. We had not proceeded more than half a mile when one of those large

Now, kind reader, do you get my meaning? I do not abate one jot my urgency that we must study to preach, both as to matter and manner; but with all the training of mind and voice, of thought and delivery, let us not forget the lesson so often taught to Elders in Israel—the lesson I have just set forth in my own humble experience.

IV.

AS A PEOPLE WE ARE EVIDENTLY IN LOVE WITH GLITTERING GENERALITIES.

If some writer should present for publication an essay of a few thousand words gravely arguing that, before a miller begins making flour he should see to it that he has some wheat to grind, would he get into print? Perhaps. At any rate, it seems that I am in print to the extent of a few thousand words on a similar proposition. In the light of this comparison, the work of holding up the thought that the preacher should know something, should be a man of some ideas, is humorous enough. But my justification is the wide-spread notion that preaching, like luck, is a gift to be waited for, which notion, if true at all, is true only of the "gift of gab."

There is an admirable motto which is fast becoming popular with Latterday Saints. It is this: "Let us be not only good but good for something." Now as applied to preaching, the "gift of gab," must certainly be counted good; and it becomes "good for

---

plantation houses, looking hospitably light and warm, presented itself to view. What astonished us most was the warm supper apparently awaiting our arrival, explained by the delay of the master in reaching home that night. We had no inkling of the real feeling of our host toward us till the next morning, when the door of our bedroom was unlocked and we were invited down to breakfast. We learned subsequently that he was the ring-leader of Mormon haters in that neighborhood. When chaffed by his friends for having lodged and fed the objects of his hate, he excused himself by saying he feared we were bent on stealing his horses so he took us in that he might lock us up.

something," when the instrument in question (the tongue), having ceased to vibrate to mere muscular irritation, responds promptly to the dictates of a well-stored mind and a chastened heart.

Interchange of Terms is Not Explanation.—Now comes the question: What should the mind be stored with? How should the heart be chastened? In other words, what may the Elder use as subject matter for sermons? What spirit should animate, i. e. make alive, this subject matter? To the first of these questions every Sunday school child can truly answer: the word of God; and to the second: the Spirit of God. The revelations quoted in former chapters declare that an Elder must continually treasure up in his mind "the words of life;" and that he must speak "in solemnity of heart in the spirit of meekness."

But what is meant by the 'words of life' and by the 'Spirit of God?' Certainly no Latterday Saint would hesitate long in answering these questions. But would they be answers, or merely changes of expression? Let the reader try a number of replies. He will find it difficult to get beyond mere synonyms. Suppose we say the words of life signify "all that God has revealed, and all that He will reveal." What does the expression mean?—the Bible, the Book of Mormon, and other such revelations? Surely it must mean more than this. What of the truths and beauties of history, of literature, and of science? What of that most precious of all records, known as common sense, written by the rough pen of experience on every man's "book of life"? Shall these be included or excluded? In short, where shall we limit the meaning of "words of life"?

Infinite Extent of Subject-matter.—The fact is, these familiar expressions mean little or much according to the mind that uses them. They are general names only, which to one soul brings a sound and to another a universe. To the simpleton such an expression as the "words of life" causes less mind-activity than does the latest slang phrase. But to the sage, all that is known and a million things besides which he despairs of knowing in this life, are comprehended in the words. In chemistry, in botany, in astronomy, in each of a thousand sciences and arts, stand men staring in dismay at the ever-expanding field before them Divisions and subdivisions have been made in each, and men have chosen narrower and still narrower branches of research, and life is then too short. Yet all this is included in the possible subject matter of an Elder in Israel. If all that men have observed, or thought, or discovered, or invented, or come in contact with in any way, were combined and preserved so as to be within reach, it might take a million years for one man to master it all; yet what part of the meaning of "words of life" would he even then have gained? For answer, drop a bucket into eternity and when it is filled, see what intelligence is still left to draw from. Try to locate the place where the vessel was filled. Only in some such way as this can we bring home the conception of the stupendous truth.

No doubt every Elder whose mind has been lighted up by the Spirit of truth, has had a glimpse into the vistas of eternity and gained some perception of what the Gospel embraces. Scarcely a Sunday passes that we do not hear some general expression of this as: "The Gospel comprehends all that is good and true in all the world and in all the eternities." The thought is turned over and over, and illustrated by calling in the heathen, the sectarian, the infidel, and even the devil himself to contribute what truths they may have, to our system. And thus we glory, not to say gloat, over the thought that God has been so kind to us; that all the beautiful, the good, and the true, in the universe is ours—ours to have and to enjoy.

Bragging is not Enjoying.—But we do not enjoy. Too often we merely brag about the greatness and extent of our riches. No sooner do we get through with the catalogue of our good and great things than we begin over again.

"All the truths of history," says the Elder enthusiastically, "are ours, and God gives us his Spirit to understand them."

"Is that so? Stop, preacher, I am overwhelmed with the multitude of these truths that are ours! They are far from me and I see them only as I do the stars, with dim light and no warmth. My soul is sick and faint with all this immensity. Give me one, just one, of these truths, with its human bearings and relations. Clothe it in mortal garb and story form as Christ did.

"'Nature,' you say, 'proclaims the handiwork of God. Our Father may be seen in all His works.' Give me, then, some of these sublime lessons. Show me the loving Father in one of His works. Open my eyes to the beauties of nature. Only one lesson about a flower, one truth about the sunrise and the rainbow in the dewdrop, and I shall be content. But no; you pass on still telling of the wealth that is ours. Not one specific idea! Words, words, words. Alas, alas!

> "'Water, water everywhere,
> But not a drop to drink.'"

Such is the cry of the hearts which here and there in our meetings can articulate . But others are dumb and cannot tell what it is that pains them; others still are entirely oblivious to the want, and are perhaps even gratified by a childish vanity that "we own so much."

Silent Conclusions in the Audience.—Is it not pitiable to be told that this glorious Gospel of ours embraces all the truths known to man, and immediately thereafter have to sit and listen for an indefinite period to the same old ideas dressed in the same old clothes? Might not a cynic be pardoned if he sat through such a meeting drawing silent conclusions like these: "Is that so? Well, I don't think all the truths in the world have been canvassed in this ward; suppose we have a fresh one or two today. * * * 'The Lord's table.' That gives me an idea. Now, if all the good mental eatables in the universe belong to this Gospel, why must we sit down today to husks?

"'Shakespeare and Milton inspired?' Heard it before. Now, I wonder if you're going to give us a single inspired passage to prove it? No. Did you ever read a page of Milton or Shakespeare? I'm afraid you're one of the nine out of every ten, that praise but never read Shakespeare or Milton. They'd give you ideas.

"'Heard all these truths when you were a boy?' So did I. 'Good to have 'em said often, over and over again?' I suppose so—if whatever is, is good. But—good—that must mean good for somebody. Whom, I wonder. Not for Brother Puffy who's been snoring for half an hour. The lounge at home would have been decidedly better. Not for that row of boys. They'll be, next Sunday, where their minds have been today. To me, perhaps? I've listened, so I must have developed the power of voluntary attention. There's a little grim satisfaction in that. But I feel for all the world as I used to when as a boy they kept me in the same grade three years after I knew all the lessons off by heart. How I used to lam that old third reader down when I got home, and swear I'd never go again. Good? Yes, I suppose we'll have to call it good, but I can't help wishing that the sermon had been, not only good in general, but good for something or somebody!"

Latterday Saint sermons are so largely made up of glittering generalities on every subject that will glitter, that one must conclude that we as a people are pleased with that sort of tinsel.

V.

ANOTHER CHAPTER ABOUT GLITTERING GENERALITIES.

The Cow in a Bovine Paradise.—Have you ever observed the action of a cow just taken from the remnants of a winter's hay stack and placed in a fresh new pasture where the tender grass

PREACHING AND PUBLIC SPEAKING.   49

and meadow flowers wave in the spring breeze? She gets excited. Her eyes grow wickedly large, and each becomes a mirror for a square rod or two of daisies and dandelions. Her tongue, long whetted on cornstalks, mows away at all this beauty and innocence like the scythe of fate. Like fate, too, it mows here and there. Stopped for a moment in her mad fury by the necessity of swallowing, she gazes over the beautiful expanse of this bovine paradise, and away she goes! No more rest for her this day. Oh, for a pair of infinite jaws to gather and masticate all this greenness in one greedy bite! Not succeeding in this wish, she snips here, then runs, and snips there, and tramples into the ground a hundred times what she eats.

I deliberately introduce this bit of descripton for the sake of an illustration. Perhaps I ought to apologize for dragging a cow into this book on preaching. However, one must often choose between elegance and force. Without stopping to call attention to the analogy that might be drawn between the preacher and the cow on the change from cut and dried fodder to the living, growing food, I simply desire to point out that Elders too often imitate this unromantic animal in their manner of getting food for sermons. There is, however, this difference: that while the cow's rambling is a mere intoxication seldom repeated more than once or twice, with the Elder it frequently becomes a habit.

The Specific vs. the General.—The notions thus picked here and there from the field of truth have been well named "glittering generalities." God has wisely endowed us with the power to take general views. Without it we should never be able to see the grand whole; never be able to relate part to part in co-ordination or subordination, as the case might require. We should, in fact, be irretrievably lost in the labyrinths of particulars. Let us then duly sense the greatness of the endowment. But shall we for this reason neglect the specific, the particular? What would you think of the farmer, for instance, who dipped into the work on his plantation as some Elders dip here and there into the field of truth? Depend upon it, the world has scarcely any place of influence left for the man of merely general notions. And the reason is plain. He who cannot get down to specific ideas demonstrates the fact that so far as thinking is concerned, his mind is still inert; and ability to think is certainly required of one whose duty is to arouse thoughts and produce convictions in others.

Besides, this dwelling upon generalities and constantly cataloguing and enumerating the points in which we surpass the 'isms' of the sectarian world, not infrequently begets a pride as superficial and empty as that of the bibliomaniac, who is always buying books and committing to memory their names, but who never reads one. This self-complacency is the most fatal malady a mind can get, so far as progress is concerned; and when it strikes in upon an Elder about the time he has the first glimmering outlines of the Gospel, it stultifies his mental powers by puffing out his vanity, and leaves him a mere automaton capable thereafter of canvassing the entire scheme of salvation from beginning to end in one sermon!

Recklessness in Statement.—But on the other hand, many who are not thus self-satisfied, who are in fact vaguely dissatisfied, seem to have lost the power to think themselves out of the rut of generalities into which habit has thrown them. For instance: it is so easy a thing to keep in memory, so indicative of profundity, to say: "The cure for all the ills that curse society is to be found in the Gospel, and only in the Gospel. The vain philosophies of men only lead mankind farther away from the light." This may be true. It is no purpose of mine to dispute it if it were not. Here we have a sweeping generalization very gratifying to minds constituted like the one that gave utterance to it. Analyze that gratification for a moment. Does it come from perception of truth? No. It comes from praising our side and hitting the other side. What good comes from such a remark? How are those who hear it made better able to realize in acts the truths which the generalization sets forth?

Absolutely no better, unless it be counted a gain to have a better opinion of ourselves and a worse one of our opponents.

But the awakening mind is not satisfied with such generalities. Here is an Elder that makes reckless and sweeping assertions on three points: (1) ills that curse society; (2) cures in the Gospel for such ills; (3) the vain philosophies of men. Surely the preacher who dares thus generalize must have concrete ideas on these points.

An Instance Tested.—"Tell us, Mr. Preacher, which are the ills that curse society? Well, name one ill. Why is it an ill? Do all men believe it such? What is the extent of it? To what sex and age and class of people does it do harm? What causes it? What are its effects, as already observed upon man—physically, mentally, morally, socially, religiously? Its ultimate effect upon society if not eradicated?

"The Gospel, you say, has a cure. I believe you, because of my faith in God. Please point out this cure. I want to find it, for I see this same evil right in our own midst. Don't tell me it is in the Gospel, tell me where it is, what it is. That is your business as a preacher. I am anxious to apply this cure. No, it will not do to tell men to live according to the Gospel. That merely shifts the question. You must draw from the teachings of the Gospel a cure just as far reaching and specific as is the evil. It may be done, perhaps, but evidently you cannot do it.

"Then I notice you make a sweeping denunciation of the philosophies that attempt to deal with these evils. I was not prepared to go so far, as I have read only a few of them. Of course you have weighed them all in the balance and found them wanting. What, for instance, is wrong with 'Progress and Poverty?' With 'Looking Backward?' With—'haven't read any of them?' " (—!—!!—!!!)

General Statements Should be Analyzed.—Now every general statement such as the one I have used for illustration admits of analysis. And this is the only way we can get down to things. A dozen sermons, for instance, might be preached from the reckless generalization just cited, and each one would then go to the spot, if my readers will pardon the phrase. Moreover, what is true in it would be strongly exemplified; and instead of merely having our vanity tickled, we should be stirred up to action; and what is unjust or false in it would likewise be shown, and we should have charity rather than contempt for the efforts of our fellow-men.

I am thoroughly convinced that the Lord has revealed truths unto us, the light of which, if turned upon the subjects that engage men's thoughts today, will result in revolutionizing the knowledge of the world. But I am convinced that, from a variety of circumstances, not least of which is a sanctimonious self-sufficiency, we are scarcely beyond the word-period in the elaboration of these truths. I believe also that we shall conquer the world in the exact ratio that we realize in clear, specific thought and action, the revelations which the Lord has given us in this dispensation.

VI.

HOW GLITTERING GENERALITIES ARE HELPING TO SHAPE OUR DESTINY AS A PEOPLE.

Consider for a moment the channel into which our missionary efforts in the world have been driven. What class of people, as regards their mental qualifications, have our Elders been able to reach? Humility is their supreme virtue, nor could any man have a higher. But what of the mental and material acquirements—or rather want of acquirements—that make them thus more humble than their fellow-men? That mental and material wants are not to be counted among the virtues—although they seem to make the virtue of meekness possible—is best evidenced by the fact that as soon as these people accept the Gospel, we make strenuous efforts to educate them and make them well-to-do. The problem with us is to preserve the humility and yet take away its apparent conditions. It is a mighty problem, not often solved successfully.

But this is not my point. I merely wish to call attention to the correspondence between the preaching of our Elders and the minds of their converts. Sermons full of generalities will go begging for an interested audience until they reach minds untutored and unaccustomed to thinking. Here they will find lodgment, and this, too, when more specific ideas would be unheeded and misunderstood.

Now, if we compare the sermons preached in the early history of this Church, as we have them in the "Journal of Discourses," with the ordinary sermons of today, we shall be forced to the conclusion that we have gained nothing. On the contrary, we have lost much of the freshness and vigor of those early efforts, and become more and more contented with glittering generalities.

Where General Preaching Leads Our Elders.—It is a striking occurrence that, with this decadence in preaching consequent upon going from the specific to the general, our Elders have been forced gradually from populous and cultured centers to the backwoods and country hamlets. I am aware that other explanations of this circumstance might be suggested, such as the greater facility for slander and misrepresentation in cities where all have access to the daily papers. To which I may reply that no Elder expects to find a field of labor where the Mormons have not been painted black. Country people know just about as much of us that is bad as do city people, and with them it makes a much deeper impression and lingers longer in memory, not being covered up so quickly by the rubbish of succeeding sensations. I believe, therefore, that after these things are duly balanced, it will be found that we make converts mostly among the uncultured because these find our general talks interesting enough to set them to investigating; and that the cultured, whose minds have been accustomed to severe exertions, find so little in them to arouse thought, as not to be set investigating. Indeed, if further confirmation be needed of this view it may be found right at home in the fact that the brainy men of our communities, commonly known as worldly-minded, go with reluctance to our Sabbath meetings.

Our Preaching Must be Made Specific.—Here then is the conclusion I have been aiming at. If a process of generalizing, or rather becoming vague and indefinite, has led our proselyting from the centers of intelligence, a process of specializing will as surely lead it toward the centers again. All the institutions of mankind are just now in very unstable equilibrium. Society is everywhere in a turmoil. Even where things appear quiescent, forebodings hang like black clouds. Ministers in the sects are alive to these evils and have this advantage over us: they have made a careful diagnosis of the ills into which mankind are plunged. But here their advantage ceases. So far as the remedies they propose are concerned, they are the by-word of thinkers. That only seems popular which is atheistic in conception with perhaps a few pious incidentals.

Why should not we enter into this field, and grapple hand to hand with these evils? We actually have the remedy. The science and philosophy of the world—the knowledge which is alike the spring of the hopes and the fears of mankind—remains to be rewritten from the Latterday Saint point of view. Think what a revolution the single element of pre-existence will make in the learning of mankind, when its bearings are worked out! What then, also, of a personal God, the perfected man; of a Savior who is our elder brother, in the truest, holiest sense; of family ties for eternity; of a heaven not floating around in etherial nothingness, but connected with soil and trees and flowers and birds and sparkling rivulets? What of all these principles so specialized as to combat point for point the silly superstitions that are now disgusting mankind under the name of Christianity?

How it is to be Done.—But these principles must be specialized, must be made concrete, must be humanized, must be dressed in the garb of the nineteenth century. It will not do to stand aloof from intelligent men and poke faith, repentance, and baptism at them with a long stick. Pardon the remark, if it seems irreverent. But is not this what we do when we refuse to enter into their councils, and treat with scorn what they hold dear; when we say, in effect: Throw all those things down! They are worthless. About face! Have faith— the faith that Paul defines; repent—with the kind of repentance that Peter commands; be baptized—or you shall be damned! The man chooses the latter alternative and walks away.

The principles of the Gospel can never become antiquated while the universe is organized as it is. But does it occur to the ordinary missionary that perhaps the garb of these principles, the statement, the explanation, and illustration of them, may? Does it occur to every Elder that faith in God may be taught in as many ways as there are blades of grass on the hillside? That every impulse and emotion of the heart is a possible door to repentance, if we but hold the key? But not so; we are sticklers for the Jewish garb of these principles. Men must see through Paul's eyes ere they can see our faith. But there are thousands of honest men who have lost all faith in the Bible; who have become so disgusted with Biblical disputation, that the very naming of these things is a signal for impatience. Sectarians are wily enough to take advantage of this. Their doctrines, stripped of verbiage, are frequently the most absurd of superstitions; but they so manage to dress them in modern garb and life-like illustration that they win the converts while we stand by and call it trickery.

Perhaps it is. "Use a little guile," said Paul. It seems to me that it is not our business as missionaries to make men bend to the stiffness which we mistake for dignity. We should so love mankind as to make our ministration of the word fit their wants and necessities. Get them by hook or crook to begin investigation— only get them. Truth will take care of the rest.

In conclusion let me say to my fellow-laborers: I scarcely expect your plaudits for the merciless way I have spoken of certain kind of preaching that abounds today. Perhaps I am unjust. It is quite certain that I shall be misunderstood. But let me say, it is not so much to gain you to my way of thinking as to stir up mind-activity upon this important subject, that I write thus pointedly. Above all I have a savage desire to 'wake up' certain of us that are steeped head and ears in a vain self-sufficiency that bars all hope of progress and growth. Even as a people we are great admirers of ourselves. Far be it from me to disturb the balmy sweetness of this repose, but—

CHAPTER III.

SUBJECT MATTER FOR SERMONS.

I.

IMPORTANCE OF THE POINT OF VIEW.

Father Smith, in a vision, was told by an angel to walk through the mountain. "Impossible," cried the venerable patriarch. "Can a human being pass through a granite wall?" "Look," replied the angel, "do you not see one step before you? Take it then." And when he did so, there were two steps before him, and so on until he was soon in the midst of the mountain, which proved to be only a cloud.

The Eye of the Mind.—The mountain before me is the subject matter for sermons. I penetrate but dimly as yet. One step is, however, clear—the point of view from which all subject matter is to be treated. Let us take this step, resolutely trusting that the way will be opened further.

Before doing so, however, we must try to sense how important is the point of view to a proper comprehension of any subject that can claim human attention. So essential is it that we clearly sense this importance that I shall devote this chapter to examples showing how the point of view causes most of the differences, strifes, and contentions in the ideas of mankind.

For instance, let a photographer expose his sensitive plate for but a moment in one place, then move his camera to complete the exposure in another, and what kind of picture will he produce? Blurred and confused almost beyond recognition. Can you expect anything better for the human mind with a constantly changing point of view? But in the case of the photographer, you urge, the impression depends upon an inert piece of glass. The human eye, the camera of the mind, instantly adjusts itself to every change.

This may be true to a limited extent—the extent to which the mind, through former experience, has trained the eye to anticipate the change. But outside the range of this experience, the eye must learn to adjust itself exactly as it did within this range, by being alternately confused by the impression, then clarified by the mind.

Effect of Change in Point of View.—No two persons ever saw the same rainbow, nor indeed did any one person for two consecutive minutes, unless he stood stock still; for if he moved but an inch, the combined refraction from an entirely different set of rain-drops brought a new rainbow to his eye. For a similar reason no two persons ever see the same identical landscape, even though the powers behind the eye be equal, which is never the case. One step disarranges the whole. We may not, indeed, become sensible of the fact until we have walked a long distance; but that the view is changed by every step will readily be admitted by anyone who has climbed a mountain and stopped occasionally to look behind him. At every pause for breath new effects are sprung upon his surprised vision and old ones have faded from sight.

Now, what is true of the outer eye, is equally true of the inner or mental eye. Why is it that in reading or listening we so often lose the drift of the thought, and feel a sense of confusion? We seldom have the patience to seek the cause. If that which confuses us be a book, we throw it down, or hastily pass on to some clearer passage; if it be a person, we are usually fearful to interrupt and ask that the thought be cleared, lest the keenness of our powers of interpretation be questioned. But if we should stop to analyze the cause of confusion, we should, in nine cases out of ten, discover it to be a reckless, or perhaps unconscious, change of base on the part of the writer or speaker. Let him begin a narrative, a description, or an exposition from one point of view, and then, without warning to the reader or listener, finish it from another, and utter bewilderment will be the result, unless the latter shall guess at the cause of the obscurity.

Violation of Unity is the technical name for this fault, and it may occur in any product requiring the co-ordination or subordination of parts. Thus, if in any work of art or literature there be found want of clearness, expressiveness, or power to move the feelings, and this, too, while we confess that talent and perhaps even genius has produced the work, the fault may usually be attributed to the fact that our minds are distracted by conflicting purposes. But what causes the distraction? Confusion in the artist's point of view. Where this point is correctly taken and persistently maintained, while we may not be pleased with the composition, it is quite safe to say that failure to appreciate will not result from failure to understand.

The Correct Point of View.—But, it may be asked, what is the correct point of view in any given case, and how shall it be determined? If no two persons viewing the same object can see it exactly alike, even though they themselves be alike—which is impossible—whose point of view shall we say is the correct one? And if we should select one, would not our point of view in making the decision be disputed at once? The fact is, the differences and disputations rife among mankind could be harmonized, if such a thing were desirable, only by casting every human being in the same mold, and then making all human beings thus cast, stand in the same pair of shoes.

Now, what is so obvious in the material world concerning the point of view and its relation to the product, is equally true, though perhaps less obvious, in the thought-world—the realm of ideas. In the former the criterion is the natural eye and the physical organs; in the latter it is the eye of the mind and the powers of association.

And as there is in the panorama spread before the natural eye much more uniformity of interpretation than in the domain over which the mind's eye gazes—since men generally agree as to color, form, and extention,—we should expect to find the differences among mankind chiefly in the world of thought and belief, and this is the case. Ten thousand winds of varying force and direction playing upon the ocean, do not produce more choppy waves and ripples upon its glossy bosom than do the agitations of thought and emotion upon the minds of mankind. And as on the ocean, forces occasionally arise which drive all opposition before them, so in the realm of mind philosophies spring forth that lead mankind irresistibly in a single direction. But not for long; both in due time are stopped, and this too by finite shores: the waves by barriers they cannot surmount, the philosophies by phenomena they cannot explain.

Why Views Prevail.—Here it will be profitable to inquire why one man's views prevail over those of his fellow-men. The reason will be found in two circumstances. First, his point of view is more nearly correct than theirs. They concede this because it explains phenomena which theirs cannot. Secondly, he has the persistence not to leave his point of view. This is his center and he strives to make all knowledge bearing upon the subject revolve about it. Orbit after orbit is created as this philosopher reaches out and draws floating, cometary truths within the attraction of the assumed center. For the first few orbits outward, things move harmoniously enough, and apparently according to fixed law; but strange to say, many of the truths thus fixed, revolve equally well around a rival system. The fact is, truth, contrary to many wise old saws, accommodates itself much better to a theory, than does error. For truth, like a faceted diamond, or like a star, shines from every face and angle, thus throwing light upon hypothesis perhaps diametrically opposed; while error, which may be counted the diamond's charcoal counterpart, shines not at all, and is serviceable only as a foil against the rays of truth not wanted.

But the philosopher, poor dupe, engrossed as he is with his own conceptions, and prejudiced against others, forgets this fact and comes to believe that truth shines only in his direction. At first he finds little to stagger his belief: but, if he would die an honest man, it were well that he die early, ere his theories have reached remoter connections; otherwise his venerable age will be given to the disreputable trickery of bolstering an artificial system; of straining facts, suppressing daylight truths, and inventing unheard-of devices and explanations to keep men's faith in a philosophy which so far as eternity is concerned is as ephemeral as a sky-rocket.

Human Points of View Finite.—But what, it may be asked, has all this to do with the importance of the point of view? Much. I desire thereby to show that the learning and wisdom which sway the world now this way now that, are and can be in fact, only the judgment of fallible men from finite points of view; that what passes for truth in philosophy, is nothing more than the aspect things present to the eye of the philosopher; that, consequently, there may be as many philosophies passing for true as there are philosophers with different points of view; that truth shines in all directions, thereby frequently giving equal plausibility to very diverse theories; that, in consequence, the opinions of mankind revolve in orbits which cross and recross and interlock in such a multitude of intricacies, that did each leave a luminous track behind it, there would be presented a tangle past the power of angels to unravel; and that when these opinions for any given period revolve mostly in a similar direction, it is owing to one (or both) of two causes; either (1) a new and correcter point of view has been found, (i. e., one which harmonizes a greater number of things); or (2) a more determined effort is made by the arts of sophistry to make things fit an old point of view.

From all which we may justly conclude, first, that the thing of most importance in entering upon a subject is the correctness of the point of view; and second, that he who would influence his fellow-men, must not desert his point of view, which is only another way of saying that he must not be desultory or scatter-brained. But enough of abstractions. Let us consider a few concrete examples and see whether they illustrate the foregoing deductions.

Abandoned Points of View.—Take, for instance, the history of the development of science. One of the earliest Greek philosophers held that water, or rather the ocean, is the source of all life, vegetable and animal, including even man. Also that the earth has been built by the ocean and is constantly being changed by it.

Surely, says the reader, such a point of view must have been taken by a sheer guess. By no means. It was, on the contrary, a glorious conception for that day So far from being a guess, it took keen observation and close reasoning to discover that all things visible on the earth were a unit with the ocean as a center. It is marvelous, indeed, what things may be explained from such a point of view. There can be no vegetation without water. Deserts are but the neglected children of the great mother of all—the ocean. The earth—is it not being eaten away by the waves, and moved hither and thither by the rains? Even man—does he not quickly perish when water is withheld from him? And seven-eighths of his body is water. Is it any wonder that such a theory found believers?

But another philosopher arose who pointed out that the ocean is but the servant of a greater power—the sun. All the facts which lent themselves so readily to the old system, now accommodated themselves equally well to the new. And since that day, how the center of things has shifted and changed! The last generation has gone mad over the Darwinian point of view—Evolution.

Modern-Science Point of View.—Curiously enough this latest rerum omnium mater is closely allied to the first, differing only in keener penetration. Somewhere in the boundless deep, say the science of today, a protoplasmic speck found itself and began forthwith to evolute! Thus again men believe all things come from the ocean, including the lords of creation themselves. How like children with wise old heads must these sage philosophers appear to the angels—disposing and arranging the works of creation, as if they were the furniture of a doll-house, to suit now this whim, now that!

But evolution has struck the rock. It utterly fails to explain the spiritual life. Like all other systems it has stranded on a finite shore, unable to encompass even one little globule of space, the planet on which we live. A system that cannot harmonize the few scattered facts which man in his short years of mortal life can gather—how can it be depended upon to explain the universe?

II.

EFFECT IN RELIGION OF DIFFERENCE IN POINT OF VIEW.

The question will perhaps be asked, what has all this to do with the subject matter for preaching? The answer is, everything; for the material—the truths thus far discovered or yet to be discovered—which the puny philosophies of men seek to marshal into systems, is the same stock of facts with which the preacher must deal. Nor can we afford to despise any of these truths. Our question must be, not, Is the fact convenient? but Is it true? If true it belongs to the Gospel and becomes material for sermons.

Difference between Fact and Inference.—But there is a wide difference between accepting a fact for itself and accepting a fact coupled with some theorist's inference from it. We cannot escape the truths which the researches of men are piling up daily from ten thousand fields of mind-activity. But we can and must refuse to view them in the light of man-made theories.

A new point of view is needed—one as far from this earth as the Pleiades. In astronomy the world long ago gave up the notion that we are the center of the universe; but the same absurdity remains yet to be abandond in theories respecting the origin and destiny of human beings. Spiritual life as exhibited on this plane of being is no more accidental than the earth is accidental; and if men recognize that the earth has a relationship to the universe, why should they shut their eyes to the fact that life on earth has equally a relationship to something beyond? But how shall we get a true conception of these relationships? Certainly not from this earth.

Finite Points of View in Religion. — In the last chapter I discussed the babel of unrealized theories that has scattered mankind intellectually. But what of the scattering of mankind spiritually? A thousand-fold more numerous and fantastic have been the points of view in this domain. From the same sun and moon and stars and earth and sea and light and darkness and life and death, what diverse religions have sprung! Surely I need draw no illustration from what are called Pagan beliefs; enough if I devote a paragraph to the sects professing to believe in the one God of Abraham, Isaac, and Jacob, and to follow in the footsteps of the one Savior of the world.

Let us consider then the one broad stream of divine truth, the Bible, enlarged and enforced at intervals down the valley of time, by new messages and revelations from the Divine Teacher. Along its banks are a thousand contentious sects, drawing more diversities than unities from the same stream. What is the explanation of it? Not to carry the figure further, how can divine truth be made to support such varying and opposite opinions? Only for the same reason that similar truths in nature have supported in turn all the theories of science. Truth, as before remarked, shines from all sides. Half its rays intercepted or unheeded, it becomes a dangerous lie—dangerous because it still passes for truth. Men draw

PREACHING AND PUBLIC SPEAKING. 65

opposite systems of religion from the same passages in the Bible, just as philosophers from the same facts in nature support antagonistic theories of the origin of things.

How Sects Originate. -- It is simply the question of the point of view again. Every distinct sect in Christendom means merely the aspect of things divine as presented to the spiritual eye of the founder. Having selected his point of view, he proceeds to marshal the sacred writings into line with it as best he can. He soon finds it impossible to unify the Scriptures. First class passages bend readily; second class yield after much twisting; third class require acrobatic feats in exegesis; all other passages will not bend at all, so he dubs them mysteries.

He is now ready to go forth and convert the world! What his share of souls will be depends upon his enthusiasm, his combativeness, and his persistence. Soon he will have a lot of preachers about him, who, "though vanquished, yet can argue still." And now listen, for there is noise in the land. The air is full of writhing and contorted scripture. The people take sides, and shout and sing and pray and sprinkle and pour and baptize! The air vibrates to hallelujah songs and damnation sermons enough to arouse spirits of every stripe and color. But many people go away disgusted with this jangle and wrangle of interpretations. Shall these be lost? No; anon comes a Wesley with a new creed, also from the Bible, specially adapted to capture the emotional class. There remains then the "submerged tenth," about whom General Booth has written so well.* These are hunted in slums and gutters by drums and tambourines. How it makes one's ears buzz to picture all this sanctifying strife!

And There Can Be No End.—Learned men only add learned, but still human, points of view to complicate the difficulty.

---

*Darkest England and the Way Out, by General Booth of the Salvation Army.

What Tom Paine said is literally true: "If thou dost not believe as thy neighbor doth, what is it but a proof that thy neighbor doth not believe as thou dost? And there is no power on earth that can decide between you."

Nor is there. For, unlike the differences in science, whose subject matter is here on earth for re-examination, religious disputations turn on what will transpire in another world; and every disputant is quite ready to await the trump of Gabriel.

And yet what is all this strife but multiplied proof of man-made religions! Systems whose ability to fulfill the promises made to mortals is no greater than their power to influence the stars! Shall the Scriptures be counted contradictory then, that they occasion all this confusion? To hold such a view is to discredit their divinity. No; there must be some key to the whole, some point of view from which every revelation harmonizes with every other revelation Like the key to the mysteries of nature this point of view can be known to man only by the Divine Author's revealing it. This he has done in our dispensation as in every dispensation of the Gospel. To us is given the key to the mysteries of heaven and earth. We have been made to see the point of view whence the works of eternity correlate.

III.

THE TRUE POINT OF VIEW, BOTH FOR SCIENCE AND RELIGION.

The last chapter closed by asserting that to Latterday Saints it has been given to see the true point of view of the universe. I should rather say it is our privilege to see if we live for it. But the novelty of possession has satisfied us. We have put off the day of exploring. Outside the knowledge necessary to confound the wise among the sects, we have not sought these hidden treasures.

But when they shall be sought and applied to the problems of the world, there will be such a revolution as will make all things new.

The True Point of View.—Only from the summit of eternity can the works of creation be viewed in their true relations. Try to sense with me the meaning of this expression—'the summit of eternity.' When we wish to get an untrammeled view on this earth we climb to the summit of the highest mountain in our neighborhood. But no earthly mountain is high enough to view the true order and significance of creation. Conceive the highest point—the summit—of the universe: the point where God stands and views all things in relation—here we must stand also. Is such a thing possible? How shall mortals attain this summit? Only by the revelations of the Master Builder. God himself sees things in their true relation only by the Spirit of truth; whoever has this Spirit in its fulness has the key to the universe; and every man will see the true point of view in exact proportion as he has the Spirit. It is only in this way that man can see it; if God does not thus reveal it to his children, mankind must yet wait for the true understanding of world-building.

This is the point the Elder must ever keep in view. Whatever be his topic, he must seek to see it as God sees it—from the summit of eternity; and not as man sees it, amid the fog and smoke of mortality. So viewed, the Fall becomes a blessing and the Atonement a natural sequence; the trials of adversity and the pangs of death are mercies in disguise, and wealth and pampered ease oft-times curses.

One of our visitors viewing the Temple made the observation that there seems to be ages of anticipation in every representative act of the Latterday Saints. The remark falls short of the truth. There should be 'eternities' of anticipation in every representative act.

It was this lofty point of view that made Christ incomprehensible to the Jews. When he closed his sermon on the Mount, it was not some earthly ideal he held up for emulation, but said he: "Be ye perfect as your Father in heaven is perfect." Probably the true point of view has never been more tersely stated than by Joseph Smith: "As man is, God once was; as God is, man may be." Expanded and worked out in all its relations, this is the key to the knowable universe.

Consequences of This Point of View.—It will be found that the point of view whence all Scripture becomes consistent and intelligible, is likewise the point whence all true science harmonizes. Herbert Spencer, after fifty years of attempting to construct a universe without a God, comes to this sublime conclusion: "Amid all mysteries, there remains one absolute certainty: we are ever in the presence of the Infinite and Eternal Energy, from whom all things proceed."

It has been counted the most glorious achievement of this age of science that the forces of nature known as sound, heat, light, electricity, etc., are demonstrated to be only varying manifestations of the one great force which Spencer calls the "infinite and eternal energy" of the universe. But all this is revealed in the eighty-eighth section of the Doctrine and Covenants. It is, moreover, pointed out that the power of intelligence, known to psychologists as consciousness, is only another manifestation of this infinite and eternal energy; that this force, variously known in the Bible as the Spirit of God, the Spirit of truth, the Holy Ghost, is in fact the eternal energy that gives life to all things that are in a state of development, and is the motor-power of the universe.

So also concerning the law of the conservation of energy, pronounced by Tyndall the greatest discovery of the age. Years before, Joseph Smith proclaimed the doctrine that nothing can be created, nothing destroyed. I might go on citing other instances, such as the Word of Wisdom, where science has but recently caught up with revelation, but 1 will content myself by remarking that in spite of mighty truths thus made plain, some of these same revelations are a sealed book to most Latterday Saints, perhaps to all. They await a time when the minds of Zion's youth, enlightened by the Spirit of truth, shall be able to grasp their sublimities and be prepared to apply them for the redemption of the world.

Counter Points of View.—In conclusion let us glance briefly at the points of view Latterday Saints must meet in the thought-world. In science the central idea is confessedly unstationary. Every scientist holds himself ready to adapt his point of view to new truth whenever it shall come. Not so in the religious world. Here bigotry reigns. The Roman Catholic point of view examined in the light of science or reason, becomes pitiful; which is probably the explanation of why that church absolutely denies the right of reason or science to question it. Note now wherein its strength lies. While in a few flexible details this church flatters every popular movement by concessions, it maintains its central heresies with undeviating consistency and dogged pertinacity. Let us learn from this church the lesson not to leave our moorings for speculative excursions.

The Protestant sects have never had well-defined points of view. The Calvanistic wing has, it is true, pretty strongly entrenched itself behind the cast-iron doctrines of the great expounder of predestination. But those doctrines are crumbling now under the battering-ram of every heretic who, like Briggs, dares to strike for reason and common sense. The Wesley wing "rely solely on the merits of Jesus." Other point of view than this one I have been unable to discover among emotionalists. But as long as men are found who will risk an easy route to heaven this creed will be popular.

"Religion must keep pace with science; creeds are antedated. Science must be the interpreter of religion as it is of life." Such is the way the sects are now tearing loose. And "Mother Church" smiles grimly, knowing full well that a routed army finds no time to intrench itself. Again we should learn the lesson, this time from the weakness of fugitive sects, not to desert our point of view even in an exhortation.

The controversy of the future, the great religious Gog and Magog, will be between the Latterday Saints and the Roman Catholics. No need of the light to ask the darkness what the end will be. But in the meanwhile it may be well to bear in mind that only in one particular do we now excel them, viz: the point of veiw. In power and resource and persistence in holding to our great central truths, and in making them bear down upon and modify the institutions of the world, we have scarcely made a beginning as compared with them.

IV.

POINT OF VIEW OF LATTERDAY SAINTS IN ACTUAL PRACTICE.

An Incident from Agassiz's School of Science.—It is said that a student bearing pretentious degrees from a number of prominent colleges, once presented himself for a course in science under Louis Agassiz. The great teacher after asking him a few test questions, handed him the skeleton of a fish, which the young man took to his study room.

Next morning he presented himself for a new specimen, but his teacher after a few searching questions, sent him back again. This procedure was repeated for ten days, at the end of which time, the student began to see some new things in the common-place skeleton—that is to say, his eyes began to open. He had been blind all these years, with the very worst kind of blindness—that which is convinced it sees all there is to see.

As a teacher and an observer of human nature, I am convinced that the majority of mankind "have eyes and see not" in the same way. And in nothing else are we so blind as in that with which we are most familiar. It is because the theme of the last three chap-

PREACHING AND PUBLIC SPEAKING.   71

ters is so very self-evident and the truth of it is so well-known, that I am going to make my readers take it over again.

A Review.—These chapters called attention to the importance of the point of view; to the fact that it is this chiefly which determines the final shape and coloring of all observation and thought; that the religions and philosophies of the world, though able to arrange about them more or less extensive areas of truth, fail nevertheless ultimately, because their center is finite; that it is as unreasonable to hope for the explanation of things natural or spiritual from a merely human point of view, as to assume that the center of universal gravitation is this little old earth of ours; that the true point must in fact be external; that when found, it will harmonize and correlate all truths, no matter what specific names they may bear here below; that the Creator has revealed to us mighty truths with reference to this eternal point of view, and has yet "hidden treasures" of knowledge to make known when we shall comprehend what we already have; that the philosophies of mankind need to be rewritten from the Latterday Saints' point of view; and that instead of going resolutely to work modifying the world with our ideas, most of us stand struck with admiration for ourselves as receptacles singled out by Deity for these mighty truths.

It was also pointed out that not alone in the correctness of its point of view does a system depend for growth and perpetuity, but also upon aggressiveness and an undeviating consistency in maintaining this point of veiw. Indeed the latter condition alone, as in the case of the Roman Catholic church, often prolongs the life and vigor of the baldest superstitions. Whence the conclusion was drawn that in all our efforts of instruction we should not forget for a moment the lofty central truths that enable us to see this world with all its manifold relations swing into line with the universe; and also that by observing both the cause of strength in the Catholic church and the cause of weakness in the Protestant churches, we should arouse all our power and resources, and present an unbroken phalanx to the world on all the frontiers of human controversy, as we have successfully done on one.

Now all this discussion about the point of view seems, as I read it over, very common-place talk indeed; scarcely rising above the dead-level of the platitude against which I am waging such war. What everybody talks about it is very difficult to make emphatic. No spot in the ear is so hard to make vibrate as that made callous by having been often drummed upon. It is only the fearfulness that my readers have not bent their minds to the magnitude of the difference caused by the point of view, that leads me to discuss the subject from other aspects.

Applications.—Consider the point of view with special reference to any principle, doctrine, or ordinance of the Gospel. What means it, for instance, to be an Elder? From man's point of view, an honor scarcely worth crossing the street for. The lowest office in a lodge is sought for more eagerly, or even the captaincy of a base ball nine.

But from God's point of veiw! Place the humblest Elder along side the mightiest potentate of earth. Compare the dignity and perpetuity of their respective offices. Even while we wait, breathless, and ere the pulse of the universe throbs once, the mighty change has come which lays the king low and exalts the Elder to dominion and power worlds without end. Do you, my young missionary friend, so value your office and calling? Do you realize that when you enter any man's dwelling, you honor him as no prince of earth can honor him? Or do you feel like a beggar or a tramp asking for a night's lodging? Does your Priesthood re-enforce your manliness, or do you drag it in the mire? Tell me how you act and I will tell you what is your point of view.

What is baptism? Something to attract an ide crowd; or—think of the miracle caused by change of view—the gate to the City Celestial! Marriage? A mere convenience to escape idle gossip; or the fulfilment of that supreme law whereby worlds and lives are perpetuated throughout eternity! And so of every principle, or hope, or fear, whether great or small.

Still Grubbing Among Things Earthly.—When I behold throughout Zion the indifference, the want of reverence, almost the contempt, manifested toward sacred things—our houses of worship, the ordinances of the Gospel, the holy Priesthood, sometimes even Deity himself—I am led to exclaim, "Alas! how cheap we hold the sublime gifts of eternity!" How many on the Sabbath day really sit down at the table of the Lord, and behold resplendent a risen Redeemer as they put forth their hands to partake of the Sacrament!

Now, brethren, let us ask ourselves, why is there so much gross-mindedness among us? As a people, I grieve to say it, we are almost strangers to the rapture of devotion which dictated the Psalms. For real reverence, the sects in our midst often put us to shame. Is it not largely owing to the fact that often we carry into our places of worship the same off-hand, matter-of-fact spirit with which we plow, and sow, and swap horses? Whatever be the cause the remedy is plain; if we could but preach alike the simplest and the sublimest truths from the point of view which angels would take, were they in our midst; if we could but approach every sermon, whether drawn from revelation, from personal experience, from the discoveries of science, or the achievements of art, as if we were viewing it from the summit of eternity, how quickly then would the blatant brute within us be silenced by the ascendancy of the angel! And, heaven be praised, this will yet be, and we shall live to see it!

Hold All Things Divine.—I spoke just now of plowing, sowing, and trading as if these pursuits were to be followed from human points of view, but I spoke of what is, rather than what should be. Let all your out-goings, and all your in-comings be unto the Lord. When President Young counseled the Saints to stay upon their farms and not rush to the gold fields of California, he spoke from God's point of view, not man's. Nothing is more touching in President Woodruff's "Leaves from My Journal" than the simplicity of faith with which he dedicates the commonest things unto the care of the Lord. I can think of no act or word or even thought that a Latterday Saint can hope to escape—or should desire to escape—the dread Omniscient Eye. If before we undertook anything, whether of little or of mighty moment, we paused long enough to place ourselves, in mind, at the point where loving angels view our deeds, how different would be the issue of our lives!

I hope that the point I have been striving for is now clear and forcible; the preacher before all other men engaged in shaping the human mind, needs to rise in imagination to the lofty point of view of eternity, ere he seeks to utter a word; for he more than any other is the voice of God unto man.

V.

SCOPE OR RANGE OF SUBJECT-MATTER.

Having disposed of the first question, viz.: from what point of view all subject-matter should be treated; or to use Father Smith's vision once more, having taken the only step visible to me a short time ago, like him I now find two steps before me opening into this important subject, viz.: 1.—'What is the scope or range of subject-matter available for sermons?' 2.—'Having determined the scope or range, how shall we determine the order of importance of subjects for sermons?' The first question will be treated in this chapter, the second in the next. A moment's reflection will show how important it is that the preacher have clear ideas on these questions.

Predetermined and Chance Sermons.—As to the first, it certainly must go without argument that subject-matter drawn indiscriminately from God's work-shop, the universe, will be fitting for Sabbath service only by chance. And yet all that God has said or done in his manifold creations is good. Now, too often we hear chance-sermons,—sermons not even consistent with themselves. The speaker, running out matter, grasps frantically at floating straws of truth, and is led hither and thither, by no law but phantasy; and where he will end, not even a prophet can guess.

But, says the Elder, it is clear that we are not deliberately to select our subject, nor by any power of will predetermine what we shall say. This is the work of the Spirit of truth. How then can these efforts be called chance sermons?

This remark brings forward two questions: (1) What it means to predetermine what we shall say, and (2) why aimless sermons may be called chance sermons. In considering the scope or range from which subject-matter for sermons may be chosen, it would of course be a good general answer to say: just that scope and range which the Spirit of God dictates, no more, no less. No one will dispute this for a moment. But is it to be understood that we must never expect aid from the Spirit save when we are on our feet before an audience? If so, I must stop with this paragraph. But as I believe the Spirit will guide me as well here at my desk as when on the stand, I proceed trustfully.

If now my objector in saying we shall not by power of will predetermine what we shall say—means to cut off communion with the Spirit before the meeting as to what will be best to say, then decidedly I think him in error. But if by predetermining, he means learning by rote, in a way that shall give the Spirit no play in the delivery, then I agree with him most heartily.

As to the second point, it is safe to affirm that sermons inspired by the Spirit of truth will never be wandering, inappropriate, or haphazard. It is equally safe to affirm that sermons which do exhibit these evidences of chance, are not inspired, however fondly the preacher may be deluded that they are. All that I contend for here is, that the Spirit of truth is a spirit of order and system. And if we accustom our minds to order and system, they will bend readily to the direction of the Spirit, even as clay in the potter's hands; but if we do not, we shall find our thoughts flying the shining track of inspiration and following instead, the vagaries of our own fancy.

Order in the Sequence of Gospel Instructions.—Then as to the order of importance of sermons, will not the Spirit lead us to think about those things concerning which it would be timely and seasonable to speak? For there is surely as much need of order in the sequence of Gospel instruction as in any other work of man.

For instance, all materials entering into the construction or embellishment of a temple may be good—in their time and place. But what utter waste, confusion, and demoralization would ensue if these materials were brought and laid down indiscriminately—glass, wood, stone, mortar, paintings, upholstery, etc., without regard to need or fitness! No one is so crude as not to see in such a work the absolute necessity of order in the selection and use of materials. But the analogy I would draw from it is far from being distinctly perceived. In building the temple of our faith the preacher very often piles up materials in just that haphazard sort of way. And the same confusion and demoralization follow. We may not be aware of it, but we should be aware of it, did we but have the clearness of vision respecting causes and effects in the spiritual world that we have in the natural world. As it is, we merely feel a sensation of weariness, flatness, incompleteness, or dissatisfaction. Hash, as we are familiar with the term, is not an adequate name for much material used in faith-building; hash, from a recipe that I could write out, might perhaps describe it.

Suppose we should build temples by the same rule of mind that some prescribe for preaching, viz,: 'Take no thought, etc.,' should we not have all the confusion pictured in the above paragraph? But is this confusion any the more Godly that human souls rather than building material are the objects of it?

Inspiration at Home as well as at Meeting.—Need I say anything further on the importance of order and gradation and logical sequence in our preaching? On the need of some definite, general scheme or classification of subject-matter for sermons, based on the wants of the people? Not an artificial plan such as might be gotten up by reference to logic, rhetoric, and ethics, but one that takes note of the varied requirements of Latterday Saints, physical, mental, social, spiritual; and adapts itself as any one of these sides of man's nature is observed to advance or retrograde? The central purpose always being so to co-ordinate and subordinate these various interests, as to make the Church advance like a unit toward perfection? Is there need of discussing such a plan?

All will agree that we need such a plan; but, I seem to hear some one say, can any one other than the Spirit of truth be trusted to decide what are the wants, physical, mental, social and spiritual, of the people? Certainly not. But will not the Spirit aid us to understand what these wants are out of meeting as well as in meeting? Will it not aid us to think about them, write them down, if need be, and otherwise so accustom our minds to consider them that when in meeting the Spirit would lead us to speak of them, we shall not be stubborn or unpliable to its dictation?

This view is, I am sure, vaguely recognized by almost every Elder, as witness the spasmodic efforts against besetting crazes, such as Sabbath breaking, and the follies of the world that inundate our shores. Do we wait till meeting opens before thinking of these things? At present, however, our preaching on these subjects is mostly of the nature of scolding; useless scolding, too, since generally it waits till the evil is done.

Now it seems to me that we must be made thoroughly to realize what it means to be "on the watch-tower." In some way the ten thousand preachers of the Latterday Saints must be made to work as parts of one grand unit. Instead of the desultory and fragmentary preaching of today, when each comes laden with some material, be it glass, wood, mortar, or stone, remotely fit or unfit for the grand temple, every Elder must realize that he is a laborer with some definite part to do in a glorious, consistent, and progressive plan of salvation.

Scope of the Subject-matter for Sermons.—Let it not be supposed that I am going to propose such a scheme. No wisdom short of Deity could do that. The scheme is already with us, and working in part. I only ask that the Lord will help me to make it plainer than it seems to be to some of my brethren as well as myself.

First then, let me say that all our preaching must be within the scope of theology. How wide a scope this is, let any one that does not know, turn to Parley P. Pratt's definition in the Key to Theology. Here is another definition quite as broad with the advantage of being more briefly put: 'Theology is the science of God; of his being, his attributes, and his works.'

There is nothing in the universe that this definition does not cover. To say then that our preaching must be within this scope, seems but to leave us in the midst of an eternal abyss; but in fact it determines our point of view, God, and locates our field of investigation—his attributes, and his works; for, satisfied of his being, what is there for man to study, (i. e., develop in himself) in order to become like him, if it be not his attributes and his works?

But where shall we begin? The subject is so vast, so infinite, that for man's puny mind to begin unaided at any point, let alone to take the risk of finding the only correct point, is as if he would stretch his baby arms from space to embrace the great globe, his future home, as it revolves with terrific momentum, swathed in mists and clouds.

Yet a beginning must be made, and, as a matter of fact, a beginning has been made, by every rational being that ever lived upon the face of the earth. Indeed, were the spirits of heaven, endowed as they are with the undeveloped attributes of Deity, merely permitted to wander aimlessly through their Father's workshop, the universe, they must make a beginning of this endless study, by the very creations they would come in contact with.

The Divine Order of Studying Truth.—But unaided by the Almighty Father, what kind of beginning would it be? Let me rather ask, what kind of beginning is it—even in the case of the great intellects of the nineteenth century, the pride of whose learning hath made them mad? Who alone can start these students of eternity aright? Who alone can grade the system of instruction, so as to develop the child to the full stature of the Parent?

Consider this illustration: Here are the material and intellectual resources for a splendid university; libraries, laboratories, apparatus, equipments, teachers, and students. Now, is it enough merely to bring these factors together? How long, think you, would it take by such desultory, unsystematic association, to make educated men and women of these students? The very first requisite of such an institution is a carefully worked-out plan of study—a plan whose beginning is based upon the capacity of the weakest of the weak among those permitted to enter upon the course; a plan whose development is as nearly parallel with the natural unfolding of the human mind as psychology is able to make it. Indeed, other things being equal, one school excels another as its plan parallels more nearly the natural evolution of the divine attributes.

Now, the university of all universities is the universe itself. Unnumbered worlds, filled with intelligencies, are its laboratories. Gods in embryo, the children of the Supreme Father, are its students. Angels and just men made perfect are its teachers;

while presiding over all is the Infinite Teacher, who by means of the Spirit of truth, impresses upon all things his will, his individuality, making a unit of what is without beginning or end. If the college president can do nothing without graded courses of instruction, is it possible that God proceeds in the education of his children without a plan of study? I was about to say: Just as the president of a university calls about him his council of professors, so the Supreme Teacher—but what sacrilege! As well might the rain-drop say to the globe toward which it is swiftly descending: "How remarkably you resemble me in form." The fact is, if in all the departments of human endeavor there is ever an increased tendency to system and classification, let us be assured that it is because our minds come to this earth freighted with just such impressions of pre-existence. In displays of order, as in all achievements that approach the precision of nature, our ideas are but the echoes, as it were, of a higher, more perfect life. Would it not be surprising, then, if we should fail to find in God's revelations a definite plan of study pre-arranged for the mighty school of which we are members?

VI.

RELATIONSHIP OF THE GOSPEL, THE CHURCH AND THE SAINTS.

God's Graded Plan of Education.—What, then, is the name of this graded scheme of divine education? In revelation it is called the plan of salvation. But salvation is synonymous with true education; that is to say, there can be no true education which does not lead, step by step, to salvation. The English translators, finding no exact equivalent of the idea, coined a new word from two Anglo-Saxon words (God spel, God's story), and the name of the divine plan of education is therefore the Gospel.

"Is that all you have been driving at?" I hear some hasty

reader remarking. "The Gospel—faith, repentance, baptism, etc., —why, I've heard about that ever since I can remember. I thought we were really on the eve of receiving something new."

Alas, that the marvel of this plan should ever cease, and that its name should become cheap by shallow reiteration! Is it then to be counted so trite a thing that the council of the Gods, out of the boundless resources known to us as the universe, should, with the infinite wisdom gained through experience, lay out a graded plan of development for the spirits of heaven? A plan whose operation began with our pre-existence, and will never end "till we come to the fulness of the knowledge of God, unto a perfect man?" A plan that does not proceed, like man-made plans, by vacillating experiments in education, such as those that have caused nations to flourish and fail in the world's history; but one which by the directest route leads the child back to the mansions of the Father? Surely nothing but a shallow comprehension of this eternal plan could lead anyone to count it commonplace, no matter how often it is lightly named.

Theology and the Gospel.—We may now consider some pertinent relationship growing out of this discussion. As will be seen, the Gospel, while it draws all its material from theology, is not coextensive with theology—at least not in this life. Ages of progress will have passed ere this plan will have need of those higher principles of theology which now excite wild and foolish speculation. The Gospel is a graded plan and program in theology —a system of progressively related divine principles for the education of divine children. Theology is all knowledge known to man or to God—a universal encyclopedia; the Gospel is a series of textbooks carefully adapted to the gradual unfolding of the mind. Eternities will have passed ere these text-books absorb the encyclopedia.

If now this relationship is clearly perceived, we are ready to define more distinctly the scope of preaching. Elders in Israel must preach the Gospel, not theology; that is to say, they must preach from that portion of theology which constitutes the next lesson in the Gospel. It is not enough that the subject matter of a discourse be true; is it a truth that can be assimilated? Is it the truth that is needed now? Will it help or hinder the growth of the people at this very time? Thus it will be seen that the subject must be neither too elementary nor too advanced. If it be too elementary, it will be counted trite and fail to awaken mind activity; if too advanced it will not be understood or will perhaps be misunderstood. Primary lessons before academic students, and academic lessons before primary students, are equally ridiculous and futile.

The Divine School.—Taking the Ground that the Gospel is a a divine plan necessitates another relationship—the school. The Church of Jesus Christ is the school. Dwell for a moment on this exalted and exalting thought. What school ever had such an organization as this? The Presidency, the Twelve, the High Priests, the Seventies, the Elders, the Priests, Teachers, Deacons, helps, governments—what are they all but teachers—each with a definite work if he will but find it. And then the plan and program of studies!—what school ever had these drawn and perfected in a council of heaven? And like a halo over all—over students and teachers alike—permeating their minds, quickening their intelligences, and enlightening their souls, is the Spirit of truth, which leads into all truth—what human school howe'er famous, can lay claim to this?

Ah, my dear brethren, when we shall awaken to the real meaning of the Gospel and get rid of the idea that we have learned it all in a few dogmatic tenets supported by as many hackneyed texts; when we shall break through our shells of self-sufficiency, and begin to grow again; when we shall learn to adapt our preaching and all our ministrations of word and works to some clearly perceived want of this school, instead of talking to fill up time as we do largely now—then Zion will arise and shine and be truly a light unto the nations!

The Students.—There remains then the last relationship, the people to be educated—the students in this divine school. To the preacher the understanding of this relationship is most important of all. First, it may be remarked, the Gospel as a plan of education was made for man, not man for the Gospel. The history of God's dealings with mankind, since the days of Adam, sufficiently illustrates this fact. In our day we have helps and governments, such as the Improvement Associations, Primaries, Relief Societies, etc.; not expressly contemplated in the revelations—organizations made to meet special conditions which the Church will outgrow. Only in the Sacrament and the ordinances is there anything approaching inflexibility, and here inflexibility is necessary to preserve the unity. But it must be remembered that the ordinances have no power of salvation in themselves, save only as the candidate is worthy of receiving them. Administered to an unfit person, they avail nothing toward salvation, but are solemn, fearful mockeries that cannot fail to call down the wrath of heaven. Ordinances are to the divine plan of education what admissions and promotions are to the ordinary school. Let us understand the thought of this paragraph clearly; it is not the eternal requirements which bend or change; these are invariable. It is the methods of bringing the people to these requirements that are flexible; not alone as to new devices and expedients, but also as to the stimulating now of this now of that side of man's nature, as it shall be observed to be weak.

The Need of Profound Study.—But before we can adapt methods to the needs of a people, we must see distinctly and with certainty what we are adapting them for; no blind strokes—goody-good talks or scolds—will strengthen the weakness. Consequently, before we set up for preachers, that is, teachers, we ought to make a profound study (1) of our plan of instruction, the Gospel; (2) of our school, the Church, and (3) of our pupils, the members of the Church. I say profound, for nine-tenths of us have made but a very shallow study thus far, and the worst of it is, we are satisfied.

But what means a profound study? Leaving the question unanswered as to the first two items, the Gospel and the Church, what does it mean to study profoundly a people—say the Latter-day Saints? There is not space in this treatise to answer the question. It would require a book.* I must content myself by observing that such a study would take many directions. Not least of these would be a careful study of the material interests of the people; for ignore and disclaim it as much as you like in rhetorical flourishes, the prosaic fact remains: the almighty dollar plays a wonderful part in salvation. Then there are the social interests, the intellectual, the moral, the spiritual—each with its manifold relations bearing mightily for weal or woe upon the destinies of these children of the universe. Studied in their proper order and from the true point of view, these transcendent lessons are easily mastered, as logical sequences of one another; even as one who views the valley from an eminence, takes in at a glance all its bearings and relations; but if studied spasmodically, and in haphazard fashion, the results will be the same as if the observer should attempt to master the bearings and relations of things in the valley, by going from detail to detail, without order and without perspective. He will never cease groping—save out of sheer discouragement.

Conclusion.—By way of summary let me add in reply to the questions as to the scope or range of subject matter, that sermons may touch upon any subject that affects the weal or woe of man in any capacity, whether physical, social, intellectual, or spiritual;

---

* Let me observe in passing that I know of no book that needs so much to be written as one making a profound study of the Gospel, the Church, and the People, in their relationship of Plan of Studies, School, and Students. Such a book would give our Church schools a renewed, vigorous, and permanent growth.

the only conditions being that the matter treated shall be of immediate application to the needs of the people; being neither so elementary on the one hand as to seem trite and uninteresting, nor so advanced on the other as to lead to idle speculation or deep-water mysteries; in a word, the scope or range of sermons is the Gospel, not theology.

Respecting the order of importance among the multitude of themes thus included within the proper scope or range of subject matter, it may be said that the question can be determined only by a constant examination of the spiritual barometer of the Church, as the Holy Spirit shall make it manifest. What themes should take precedence, will perhaps differ in every branch and ward of the Church. "Meat in due season," is the safe rule.

CHAPTER IV.
THE ART OF THINKING.

THE IMPORTANCE OF LATTERDAY SAINT ELDERS BECOMING THINKERS.

In the chapters devoted to the scope and the order of importance of subject-matter, I urged that Elders acquaint themselves, (1) with the Gospel, which is the divine plan and program of our eternal education; (2) with the Church organization, which may be counted the school including the teaching; and (3) with the people, who may be called the pupils of this school. Nor should we be satisfied with the shallow, superficial study generally made of these factors. Nothing but a logical, a profound acquaintance with these things can make us powerful as preachers; for, as was pointed out, it is as irrational to hold that a man, unacquainted with the art of teaching, unskilled in school management, and ignorant of the natural growth of child mind—is capable of conducting successfully an institution of learning, as to believe that the preacher, alike ignorant or superficially informed, is prepared to lead men's souls to salvation. The principle that before you do a thing, you must know how, holds as well in the one instance as in the other.

A Common Objection Answered.—I wish to meet at its fullest force an objection I anticipate here, viz.: "I was always under the impression," says the habitually unprepared preacher, "that it is no part of the Elder's business to cast about him as to the needs of the people when he arises to preach: that this is exclusively the function of the Spirit of truth. Is it not almost blasphemy for the preacher to try to figure out the wants of a congregation? How many chances of going astray against one of choosing aright! No, no; the Holy Ghost alone can search the hearts of men, and give meat in due season. Let not the duty be put upon man's observation and judgment."

Now, it is difficult to reply to this objection unless the truths it contains be first drawn away from the lurking error. First, it certainly is no time for the Elder to begin to study the wants of the people, after he has been called upon to speak; such study should have been the constant bent of his previous life. Further, it is certain such study should never be undertaken save under the guidance of the Spirit of truth. Surely the objector will not urge that the only time the Spirit will lay bare these wants is before an assembled audience! Is it blasphemy, then for man under such an influence to form his judgment concerning the needs of the Latterday Saints? Who will dare to be so presumptuous as to say this? Indeed, so far from dissuading him, will not the Spirit if interrogated, expressly lay upon the preacher the duty of forming just and accurate ideas on the Gospel, the Church, and the people? For if the speaker have not such just and accurate ideas when called upon to speak, how can the Spirit bring them to his mind? Even though the Spirit search out the needs of the congregation, what is there in the store-house of such a speaker to supply these needs? Suppose that the Spirit would, for the good of the congregation, supply the spiritual food needed by sheer word-for-word revelation—would the mind of the Elder be pliable enough to permit such a thing to be done? In ninety-nine cases no; in one case yes, perhaps; but in this case the man would be unconscious of using his own powers, oblivious to what he had said.

"Out of the fulness of the heart the mouth speaketh." There is ordinarily no other way. If a man knows only how to raise potatoes, potatoes will be his sermon, let the Spirit strive as it will.

For the demonstration of this truth, I only ask that you go to meeting and listen. In nine cases out of ten the Spirit will fail to lead us into paths which we have not previously broken, faintly at least, by observation and reflection. But this is not the fault of the Holy Ghost; it is because we, in the unpliability of our spirits, will not trust inspiration to lead us out of the beaten track. Depend upon it, if we would be as clay in the potter's hands, we must see to it that the clay is well mixed before we come to meeting.

I trust the reader will pardon this digression by way of review, the more so, as in a way it serves to introduce the subject of this chapter, which is how to mix the clay; in other words, how to think and get into the habit of thinking.

Surprising how Few People Think.—The common expression "thoughtless multitude," is no merely rhetorical phrase. Nothing is truer, even of well-informed people. It was believed that universal education would make all men thinkers, but this hope has not been realized. It has merely furnished, universally, thoughts ready-made. The ratio of real thinkers remains about the same. Indeed, it would not be reckless to hazard the opinion that they are probably fewer in this age of newspapers and electricity; for many educated people whose heads are now filled with thoughts from books, might have been thinkers had they been thrown more upon their own powers.

It seems to me that our Elders, be their information meagre or extensive, must become thinkers if they would have their preaching virile enough to breed thoughts and acts in their hearers. Let me develop further the figure contained in this word virile, for in it is set forth, I believe, the vital distinction between first-hand and second-hand thoughts.

Look over the circle of your acquaintances and pick out a man whom everybody praises for his brilliancy. Gifted primarily with a splendid memory, he has added to the charms of a vivacious mind the graces of rhetoric and elocution. In fete or social circle he is the admired of all admirers. Now, by the first impulse of one's reasoning it would be natural to conclude that such a man must have many disciples. Nothing could be further from the truth. If he has followers at all, depend upon it, they are the most superficial of imitators. Why is this?

Now look over the circle again, and pick out the man who actually has disciples—and by this I mean men who go to him to form their judgments and who quote him in evidence on any scheme. In point of dazzlingness, if I may coin a word, he does not begin to rival the first; yet in real power to shape the destiny of the people among whom they live, these two men are not to be compared at all. As a preacher the first will generally charm us, but the second seldom fails to warm us. In most movements, we applaud the first, but we heed the second. To the first we come for entertainment, to the second for counsel. The one may indeed be an electric fountain, but its waters at best will taste of the pipes; the other is nature's spring, sparkling forth amid the beaded moss of rocky cleft and cavern. The first, conscious of borrowed ideas, guards jealously the machinery that enables him to produce such splendid effects, and hence we can only guess at his inner life; the second, glowing with the warmth of original discovery, makes us feel rather what he is than what he does.

POWER TO THINK VS. POWER TO ABSORB THOUGHT.

What then is the specific difference between these minds? It is a question of native thinking; the one is a mere lodging house for thoughts; thoughts polished, brilliant, cosmopolitan, perhaps, as lodgers are apt to be, but always disguising their real origin; the other is a home, a birthplace of thoughts—crude, unpolished, even homely perhaps, but withal loving and lovable, as children are likely to be. That we should reverence and be influenced by the latter more than by the former is not strange; for it is incontestable that we trust whom we love, not whom we admire merely.

Thinking may thus be called the virile power of the mind; and minds will be fertile in reproducing themselves—that is, in attracting disciples—just in the ratio that they are vigorous and exact in their power to think correctly.

In minds that do not breed or reproduce we may note two varieties, the impotent and the emasculated. The impotent may again be divided into two classes, viz.: (1) those that develop neither the power to think nor the power to gather thought. Such minds after acquiring the trick of the lowest order of routine work, speedily petrify and are thereafter machines, helpless save as they are set to work by superior minds. (2) Those that, failing to develop native thought-power, are yet so unfortunate as to become lodging places for the most vicious thoughts of others—such thoughts as come from street lore, trashy literature, and sensational plays. It is from this class that saloons, gambling dens, houses of ill-fame, prisons and insane asylums are recruited.

Emasculated minds, if the reader will forgive the harshness of the epithet, are minds which, though still full of energy, have had the virility of their thinking powers altered or diverted to channels of uncreative activity. For the working purposes of the world such minds are still most useful. They are mirrors reflecting, prisms refracting the discoveries, inventions, and thoughts of mankind; they are cisterns filled by rills of knowledge from every point of the compass; reservoirs whence are drawn by mere compilation most of our text-books, literary hash-books, reviews, essays, lectures, sermons.

But all such minds desire to seem profoundly original. As editors they mix in vituperation in the hope that muddiness may be mistaken for depth. As teachers they sometimes change text-books that the source of their supplementary talks may not be known to students. As preachers (in the world) they swap sermons, suppress quotation-marks, look learned, and still say in sepulchral tones: "Thou shalt not steal." Yet all these people are the very woof, if not the warp, of society.

There may in fact be, as already pointed out, much brilliance with very little native thinking power. Indeed, it might seriously be contended that, for mere purposes of conveying facts and increasing the circumference of enlightenment, minds trained to voice the thoughts of others are superior to native thinkers as having a wider range and being, as it were, a sort of books with tongues. But where character is to be formed, where evil habits are to be uprooted, and good ones planted in their stead, there is need of a warmth and positiveness of conviction never found dissociated from genuine thinking.

It is for this reason, I maintain, that whatever else they may or may not be, Latterday Saint preachers must be thinkers. And so, it may be said, they are, in every case where their discourses tell for good among their fellow-men.

II.

THE VALUE OF THINKING AS COMPARED WITH THOUGHT-GATHERING.

In a former chapter I had occasion to divide our Elders into four classes, viz: (1) those who read much and think much, (2) those who read much and think little, (3) those who read little yet think much, and (4) those who read little and scarcely think at all. The last might better be classed under minds impotent, since they have neither thoughts of their own nor of any one else's. But I have paid my respects to this class in a way sufficiently pointed in former chapters.

Thinkers vs Readers.—It will be seen that the parallel I have attempted to draw in the last chapter is between the second and third class—those that read much yet think little and those that read little and think much. Now, it is quite safe to affirm that most of the marvels accomplished by preaching in this dispensation have been by men of the latter class. Nothing is more common than to read in the biographies of the natural leaders among us that they enjoyed no advantages of scholastic training. So also must we pronounce those men thinkers that from a religious, a social, or an economical point of view, dominate society among us today.

When these men arise to speak, they say something, because they have been thinking something. The people listen, heed, and act upon the counsel given—such is the power of real thought. Their sermons are often crude in composition, illogical in argument, and lacking in consecutiveness; seldom do they possess the external graces of oratory. What matter? Latterday Saints ceased to look for acrobatic feats in word-building when they left sectarianism. Sufficient for them if their minds be stirred to activity; they are not scrupulous as to the way it is done. Had there been no worse sermons than these, I should not have been induced to write these criticisms on preaching. However, let it not be thought that there is no room for improvement in this class. But more of this later.

Necessity as a Teacher.—What made these men thinkers? Dire necessity. Thrown face to face with mankind and with nature, and not having the thoughts of others in their heads, they were compelled to think what to do and how to do it. This emergency set the wheels of thought in motion, and that is all that was required. Once started, they go on forever. No one but the angel of death can stop them; nay, even he cannot; he but oils the bearings that thereafter they move noiselessly.

These men have sons that might become all that is implied in the first division—men that read much and think much; but too often they fall early victims to a system of fact cramming. Thoughts ready made are so easily accessible, so tastily dressed, and so immediately effective for display, that these youths never awaken to the need of the thinking faculty. Indeed, if their teachers, by a combination of circumstances, force the birth of a homeling, it is so misshapen by comparison with book-thoughts as immediately to be disowned.

Son and sire are now pitted against each other as preachers; book-learned brilliancy against rough-hewn thought. As before pointed out, the people are entertained by the first, but counseled by the second. But note this tendency: the rising generation, incapable of thought-discrimination, are insensibly caught by externals. The more the artistic culture of the world finds its way into our schools, the more difficult does it become for these scions to appreciate the homely thoughts of their fathers. The fathers, with clearer perception, accustomed to weigh things rather than words, are grieved at the high-falutin shallowness that they see becoming popular with the young. The breach is likely to widen. On the one hand the fathers, having the choosing of the preachers, will continue the good old sermons; on the other, the children, unwilling to look upon truth in a homely garb, will find—do find —a thousand pretexts for staying away from meeting.

The Transition.—Let us give this problem a little thought. In this wide-spread captivation for outward form may be seen, by any one who will give it a moment's reflection, one element of a mighty intellectual evolution just now beginning to sweep over Zion. Thinkers we must call those Elders who, in the past, have deserved the name of preachers at all; but God never intended that they should stop short of becoming cultured thinkers, as are most of our leading speakers now. There will be no resting place below the summit. A similar evolution has already swept over us in methods of agriculture, in style of architecture, and in the amenities of dress and social usage. Nor have we failed to appreciate the blessings of these changes. It seems to me, therefore, worse than idle to stand in opposition to this greater evolution of mind.

In the past, preachers who read little and thought much have sufficed for our growth. Preachers that read much and think little may mark the transition. Their time will be short; perhaps I should be more exact to say, are marking the transition. The preachers of the future will be they who read much and think much; by which I mean men of wide general culture and profound thought; men that will study the art of preaching both as to matter and manner, with no other motive than that they may be able to save souls.

Why Our Elders Must become Thinkers.—There are many reasons why this must be so. No greater compliment can be paid a man's intelligence than to say he is a thinker. But a carpenter is not always an architect, though both be thinkers. The difference is one of culture. Thinking is like fire: it needs fuel. The more fuel the greater warmth, the brighter the light. Thinking is conditioned by the amount and the variety of material gathered into the mind's work-shop. That many work-shops are turned into mere store-houses does not count against the need of material for thinking.

The material gathered from the area of but a single life's experience may be sufficient to produce a thinker; the thinking may even be clear and intense, but it will be too narrow to be wise or trustworthy. Thinking that shall benefit a city must be based on a clear perception of the needs of the whole city, not alone on those of the individual thinking; thinking that shall benefit a state must be from knowledge at least commensurate with the state lines; thinking that would benefit a nation must spread out the map of the whole country; thinking that would benefit the world cannot afford to despise any knowledge.

Now, this last is what we set out to do. It is for this reason that we need the broadest culture that education can give, coupled with the profoundest thought that the mind is capable of. That our thinking at present is shallow is best evidenced by the fact that we fail, sometimes ignominiously, to control matters and things in a very narrow precinct.

The Thinker and the Thought-Gatherer.—My next question is: What is thinking? Before I attempt an answer, let me show you the thinker at work as compared with the mere gatherer of thought.

The first goes to nature and trusts rather his own eyes and ears than books; the second will climb to the top shelf of the library, fight his way through cobwebs quivering with busy spinners, seize hold of a dust-begrimed book on zoology—all for no other purpose than to find out how many legs a spider has! That he might have caught one of these little creatures and examined for himself does not occur to him.

If the thinker be appointed to lecture, or to write an essay, he prepares the skeleton of it and takes stock of his mental material. Thus he discovers at once wherein he will need to read further or observe more accurately. But the collector of thought, if given a task, asks immediately: "Where can I find something on it?" And this will be true of him, even though it be a matter in which he is supposed to be better informed than anyone else. He distrusts his own powers of observation and thought, and well he may, as one who has leaned on others all his life. Other eyes have looked for him, other ears heard, other imaginations conceived, other minds composed and written; his work has been chiefly to transfer bodily to his own mind the finished product of another as he finds it on the printed page. Books are the end of argument to him. "It is written" is his guide, and he applies it as well to books in general as to Holy Writ.

The thinker also uses books, but only to get the material for thought. He so far distrusts the material thus found that he will read many authors, so as to be positive of the data from which he reasons. Books are generally a lengthened tissue of inferences. For every conclusion whose premises are given, ten are baldly stated without reasons. These ten he might accept, as does his unthinking colleague, without question. Surely it would save time and mental effort. But his mind is too vigorous. Having developed a sharp set of mental teeth he cannot bring himself to feed on hash; that is on thoughts masticated and made ready for swallowing, by other mouths.

"What brought the author to this conclusion?" he asks. "I will call up the fact again and try them over." Often he proves these conclusions wrong, and learns thereby to distrust the generalizations of other men. And even when conclusions are found to be just, this retracing the history of a thought proves most excellent for mind discipline, and yields him pleasure second only to the original finding of thought. So, too, his mind grows in another direction; for the habit of seeking out the springs of human thought leads naturally to the searching after reasons for divine thought, as expressed in nature and in revelation. And this is the very essence of true philosophy—thinking the thoughts of God after him.

Another distinction is to be noted between the thinker and gatherer of thought in the habits they form. The thinker, pausing as he does to verify the important conclusions of his author, finds that he can read but few books during a year, hence he is exceedingly jealous of the company he keeps in the library. Books trashy, frivolous, illogical, re-hashed, his mind instantly detects and rejects as unwholesome. His colleague, not having this mental gauge, reads everything indiscriminately, having no other rule of selection than keeping up with the latest craze. He probably reads ten books to the other's one, but the ratio of real power gained thereby is as ten to one in favor of the thinker.

III.

HOW TO SET THE WHEELS OF THOUGHT MOVING.

I am now ready to discuss the question how to learn to think. It may be remarked, as a preliminary, that the difficulty in setting the thinking faculty in motion increases with years. Especially is this true where it has atrophied through non-use while adjacent faculties are highly developed. The mental energy has in such a case cut its channel, and it is exceedingly difficult to stop it long enough to make it rise above its banks and overflow the arid regions of thought. But where the stream can hardly be said to have begun flowing in any direction, as in childhood, or where it has spread out and dried up or stagnated, as in the great mass of stolid adults that never read nor think—it can be induced by skillful management to flow as readily through the channel of thought-making as of thought-gathering. But the volume and force of the current will depend upon how easily and how assiduously this management takes place.

Mental Laziness.—Thinking is a difficult process to set going under any circumstances. Talk about laziness! For every physical drone in our communities there are one hundred mental sluggards. And the reason is not far to seek. The man that feels like shirking physical labor is driven by sheer force of shame and ridicule to work the lazy microbes out of his muscles. But what of the mental shirks? There are no such weapons wielded over them. But who would wield them? A smutty face need fear no ridicule if it goes only into a coal mine. Those who might wield the weapon are so few comparatively, as to be neither heard nor heeded; besides, their time is too profitably taken with themselves. And so it happens that the slothful in mind are received with open arms by the society that frowns upon the slothful in body. Received by society, did I say? Bless their darling insipidities! They are society, if my drawing-room recollections serve me truly.

The Other Fellow.—But why continue the parallel further between those that think and those that let others think for them? Surely it is not necessary to prove it a desirable thing to become a thinker. It will be difficult to find people of any intelligence who, according to their own estimation, do not believe themselves already so. Perhaps not half a dozen readers of this book will say, "These parallels have been drawn especially for my benefit"—so good an opinoin does the average man have of himself. And yet, my self-complacent brother, you are the very man I have in my eye. Now, ask yourself candidly: Is my course continually upward intellectually? The thinker, you will bear in mind, is never truly delighted save when going up-hill—that is, bending his mind a little harder today than he did yesterday. It is the bending that gives him pleasure; and as the faculty grows more vigorous by the exercise, it requires a little harder task each day to bring the accustomed delight. Hence if you would have a man's course continually upward, make him truly a thinker. Are you such a one?

It is much more likely that you are a thought-gatherer. If so your gait will be upward and downward as the publishers lead. Perhaps in the majority of cases, if you are a man, you will end by walking the dead-level grade of the newspaper, and, if a woman, by going the down-hill grade of the sensational novel.

Everlasting Curiosity.—Then how shall an Elder in Israel set to work to get his mind into the habit of thinking? The answer will be found in any good work on logic or psychology. The technicalities and abstractnesses of these sciences do not, however, suit the purpose I have in view, which is to assist the multitude of our preachers whom, without training leading up thereto, these explanations would only confuse.

Have you a little four-year-old son? Bless his bright eyes, he is the book I want. His tiny mental clock was last wound up by the angels; watch its movements if you would know how they do things in heaven. Can you find an egg more full of meat than he of the finding-out spirit? It would seem that everything he eats and drinks turn into wriggling question-marks. And they are all alive, too. Like imps they lurk in his ears, peek from his eyes, insinuate themselves among his fingers and cling to whatever his hand touches. On every breath they float outward like motes on a sunbeam. He was a wise man that invented the interrogation point and made it a hook! Is there anything great or small to which a child will not attach one of these little harpoons?

Now, why does the Creator thus organize the child? First of all for the child's own sake, that it may rise above its environments. But is there not sometimes a sly suggestion—as if the angels had said: "Now, if this bright soul is sent there, will he not help to make a stupid father think?" Be this as it may, any father that will answer all the questions of a wide-awake son will not fail to become a thinker.

Thinking a Process of Questions and Answers.—Here then is the key-note of learning to think. Be as endlessly inquisitive as a child. But, unlike the child, answer your own questions, otherwise this spirit of inquiry may lead you to be merely a book worm.

"But suppose we can't answer them?" Alas for the can't! One of the first messages the thinking faculty sends back on being given a difficult question is: "Too much for me." Now, what will you do? I ask, what did you do when your arms and back said the same thing to the question involving a shovel and a muddy ditch? Did you heed the flinching of your arms? No; had you done so your children would have cried for bread. Neither heed the cry of your brain, lest thereby you loose the bread of life. I cannot emphasize this point too strongly; hang to the question, even though apparently it be like looking into black chaos. The light will break in time. The mist is behind not in front of the eye.

Neither allow your mind to slip cogs. I remember a student coming to me for the solution of a difficult problem. "No, my dear friend," said I, "I will not give you the solution, but will ask you such questions as shall enable you to discover it." Half a dozen replies were satisfactorily given; three more and the light would break. But at the next she exclaimed pettishly: "Oh, why don't you tell me, do you multiply or divide?"

Want of attention causes the mind to slip cogs. Cultivate such concentration that a cannon fired over your head will not make you lose grip of your thought. A mosquito will do it now, no doubt.

The Half-Thinker.—You may have observed potatoes, in one case growing all to vines, and in another going all to seed, leaving scarcely enough top to locate the precious crop below. Now, men are often thinkers by halves in the same way. One man is full of questions that he cannot answer; another is full of answers that he cannot call to mind. Neither one is a thinker. But put them together and much thought will be evolved.

How many men are like the last—able to acquit themselves clearly, voluminously, and refreshingly, if some one will but work the pump-handle! How grateful they are to the man that enables them to spout thus gushingly! But these are not thinkers. The living wells only, whose waters overflow by internal force, are worthy such a name. A cow that loses the power to raise her cud fails to thrive and grows sick; something similar to this takes place with the man who, unaccustomed to commune with himself, has lost the companionship that was wont to stir his mind to activity. The "cud" must be restored in one case and the "crony" in the other, or disaster will follow.

The thinker must not only be able to ask himself questions far remote from his immediate thought, but must, as the thought progresses, see at every turn of word or phrase the associations and objections that a merciless critic would see. He must in fact be his own adversary, and an unrelenting adversary; and though his critical self utters no word, yet will he heed all his silent objections and reply to them as if they were formally made.

IV.

THINKING MAY OR MAY NOT BE ACQUIRED IN SCHOOL.

Taking Thought Canned.—In my last chapter I pointed out how difficult it is to get people into the habit of thinking—especially where the channel of mental energy is cut deeply in the direction of thought-gathering; that is to say, in the case of the multitudes that feed upon books and lean upon men. In the language of psychology, these do not apperceive. They remind one of the city cousin, who, being invited to help himself to peaches as they hung ripe and luscious on the tree, replied with conscious pride in his better bringing up: "No, thanks, I take my fruit canned." And so of the multitudes; but few people are willing to come in contact with thought until it is canned. Loaves, not seed wheat, is what they demand. The healthful mental toil of sowing, reaping, threshing, milling, baking, and we might add masticating, their minds have contracted a dis-relish for.

During a number of years I have made careful observations in the case of hundreds of students whose mental habits come befor me every day. It is amazing to find what a small percentage of them are real students; that is to say, young people that think independently of books and teachers; young people of whom you can say, stopping school will not stop their mental growth. And yet their teachers are, so far as I am aware, all alert to the evil, and are making special efforts so to shape their methods so as to compel thought.

Mistakes in Thought-Training.—The fact is, our whole system of education, both secular and religious, is grievously one-sided. Constant and unremitting effort is directed to putting in, putting in, and very little attention paid to drawing out. History, science, language, literature, even logic and philosophy, are taught in such a way as to contribute great ease and facility in thought-gathering, but little skill in real thinking. Is it not proverbial that college graduates have poor judgments?

Mathematics, though also largely directed toward memory, is, it would seem, the only study that cannot be utterly spoiled for developing thinking power. But mathematical thinking does very little to arouse general thinking. Every community is full of mathematical thinkers whose minds for the varied and complex reasoning of life are quite as impotent as minds that feed only on books. Perhaps even more so, from the very reluctance they have to getting out of their cherished mathematical grottos. Mathematical thinkers are like locomotives, able to draw heavy loads and reach conclusions with undeviating exactness, provided an unobstructed track lies before them; but for hauling wood out of our canyons, or scraping out our canals, they are not an unqualified success—the locomotives, I mean.

To get our young men resolved to become thinkers, in spite of the teacher and the preacher, must then be my excuse for prolonging this aspect of the question. The purpose of the last paragraph is to protest against the wide-spread fallacy that mathematics will accomplish this needed reformation. It is not even among the best studies for this purpose. Its value lies chiefly in the exactness it contributes; but this benefit is largely offset in the narrowness and exclusiveness of its reach.* It is the opposite of this last that makes the thinker great, viz.: the ability to hold in mind and correlate a thousand factors, apparently unrelated.

Manner Rather than Matter of Study.—The remedy is not to be sought in the matter but in the manner of study; and no better manner can be found than that already pointed out: Be endlessly inquisitive concerning everything that engages your attention, and answer your own questions. Conceive every object bristling with question-marks as thick as berries on the juniper. Try to discover the most natural and rational order to tackle these questions—which proceeding, by the by, would itself illustrate the very process of thinking I am trying to explain—in this case the answering of questions about how to tackle questions. This is very important. The proper order discovered, the subject yields readily to a logical development.

Generally speaking this order will be as follows: 1. What is it? 2. How is it? 3. Why is it?

What, How and Why Questions.—It will be seen that the first is pre-eminently the question of the child. Everything he touches, sees, hears, smells, tastes—brings up the question, what is it? He must know what to call his "finds," else how can he talk about them? Like Adam, he is called upon by nature to name things anew as they pass by. Ideas without names may lurk in the darkness of a mind, but they cannot be induced "to go a-visiting," for they are naked. The child by instinct, as it were, seeks to clothe his ideas, in which respect he is often wiser than his parent. Witness the amusing attempt of the latter to express

---

* A friend to whom I read this MS. found for me the note which I herewith append. I am delighted to know that my own experience and judgment correspond with the views of so great a thinker. (*The italics are mine:*) "If we consult reason, experience and the common testimony of modern and ancient times, none of our intellectual studies tend to cultivate a *smaller number of the faculties, in a more partial or feeble manner, than mathematics.* This is acknowledged by every writer on education of the least pretension to judgment and experience; nor is it to be denied by those who are the most decidedly opposed to their total banishment from the sphere of a liberal education."—*Sir William Hamilton.*

himself at times: "And then the man took the-the-the thing-umbob and gave the-the-the duphunny a turn or two, and off it come."

The second question, how is it, is almost as characteristic of children. It is this wormy thing in his mind that makes Johnny smash his toy locomotive and pull out the tail of his hobby-horse ere he has had them a day. But after all, the spirit behind this activity is only curiosity. The adult should never be less eager to find out the how of things, but he should be impelled by genuine interest, a force compared with which the child's motive is but a straw in the wind.

These two questions are valuable as furnishing material for thought; but a man may have in the highest degree the aptitude to ask them and yet fail to become a thinker. It is the third question, why is it, that stimulates and develops thinking power. Children rarely ask this question, and when they do, parents, instead of encouraging the disposition, answer: "Oh, 'cause"—precisely as the children would reply were the case reversed. Unfortunately the vast majority of adults are but grown-up children in respect of not seeking cause-relations. Indeed, nothing short of a drawn sword across the heavens would rouse a why in some men's minds. And yet the whys are more numerous than all the other questions combined. For every what, how, where, when, there is an endless troop of whys lurking in ambush. The why may be called a key, opening as it always does, into new mysteries. When you have exhausted the how of a problem, just ask a why concerning the how, and an entirely new set of relations are sprung upon the astonished vision. Young men, if you would learn to think, make much of the why question.

Rounding up Ideas.—If a man unaccustomed to thinking should be given a familiar object, say a pocket-knife, and be told to talk about it consecutively and without repeating ideas for half an hour, would he, even under pain of death, be able to accomplish the feat? And yet it is certain that a bright boy of ten has enough ideas about it to do that very thing. The question is, can he collect them? Ideas, like cattle upon a broken range, seem meagre and scattering, indeed, as one looks inward upon his mind; but a round-up soon makes a respectable showing. Now the power of making an instant round-up of one's ideas, and of moving them hither and thither and making new combinations of them—should be sought for and cultivated as the supreme habit of mind. Where the preacher fails, not from poverty of ideas, but, as he puts it, from "want of words to express his thoughts," the fault in reality lies in his inability to recollect or make a mental round-up of his ideas. Surely, it is worth determined and prolonged effort to gain this power. I know no better way than to begin to form the habit of logical self-questioning. This is slow work, but very fruitful. Do not imagine that the burden of it can be thrown upon a school. Men go through colleges and universities without learning to think. First or last, thinking must come, when it does come, by down-right, native self-effort. The storing process will not count. The right kind of school will facilitate the growth of thought-power, the wrong kind will stultify it.

V.

HOW OBJECTS IN NATURE MAY DEVELOP THINKING POWER.

Self-Questioning Out of School.—Darwin, the profoundest thinker on natural science of this or any other age, was, it is said, a most stupid school-boy. Carlyle, the great English philosopher, tells us in his memoirs how he stood in awe of the superior attainments of Sandy McPherson, a smart student who took a savage delight in making him the butt of the school. Agassiz found his early school-life intolerable, and played truant to ramble in the woods and fields whenever he could. Yet these men rose to towering eminence, while the Sandy McPhersons and other "smart-alecks" of the school, became shop-keepers, petty politicians, perhaps tramps. What is the explanation?

It is this. These boys were so organized that they could not proceed, save by the self-questioning process. They were slow in storing their minds, simply because they must untie and examine everything—and this takes much time, especially with a child. The gross material which they took into their mental work-shops they must stop to work up into products, ere they could find rest. Is it any wonder that they seemed dull in comparison with students that merely piled up lumber? And so, too, is it any wonder that they became thinkers, while their glib class-mates remained thought-gatherers to the end of life? Let it not be inferred that the school was detrimental to them. Far from it. They probably owed their greatness to their school-life, though thinkers in limited spheres they would have been even had they never seen a school.

The beauty of the self-qustioning process is that it may begin as well on the farm as in the school-room. For the sake of illustrating this theme let us take one day out as a common field hand, and see what interrogations may strike us:

While Doing Chores.—"The sun rises red this morning.—Why, I wonder.—Cause cannot be in the sun itself; must be between the sun and the earth.—In the air?—Must be, but still not the air itself.—What then?—Vapor—dust—smoke—which? Where could dust come from?—Desert winds and volcanoes.—Where smoke?—Forest fires perhaps; and that reminds me, I read yesterday about great forest fires in Michigan.

"How near must that smoke be to come between me and the sun?—That's quite a problem. Let's see. The ray of light is the hypothenuse of a right angled triangle, of which the perpendicular is the height of the atmosphere above the earth—say fifty miles. Question is, to find length of base and thereby length of hypothenuse.—Can it be done?—A question in geometry. I'll try it at noon.—But would smoke rise fifty miles?—Hardly, by the way it ordinarily hangs on the mountain side.—Approximately, how far is that stratum of smoke?—Not over 100 miles as I begin to perceive now—perhaps not over ten.—But how did it get west?—Winds.—Must examine my map to see what direction and also to calculate how fast it must have come.—But why do we not feel winds here? Are there strata in the atmosphere as in the earth? Meteorology must be a very interesting science.

"But—so boss!—but why does smoke turn a flame red?—It always does; I noticed that fact when Jones's barn was burning. Let's see, now. The sun's light is pure white, and white light I remember is a combination of violet, indigo, blue, green, yellow, orange, red.—Does the smoke absorb all the colors save red or does it refract them upward into the sky?—I must examine the tints in other parts of the sky.

"There's surely a difference. Moisture at sunrise or sunset makes all the tints of the rainbow more or less visible across the sky, but this leaves the sun a red disk surrounded by a yellow umbra. That's the orange next to the red, so there must be slight refraction.—How can I settle it?—Smoked glass?—But is that the same?—Let me see. In the one case the particles of soot float and in the other—what did you say?—Breakfast? Good. After feeding and currying four horses, and milking six cows, I'm ready for it, I assure you. * * * * * *

While at Breakfast.—"Thank you, but I'll not take coffee; I've been studying its effects for the last month. I find it makes me borrow too much on future capital. I would rather spread my strength out equally over the whole day, than feel so unusually ambitious for a few hours in the morning, and then be utterly exhausted for the rest of the day.

"What did you say about over-coats?—No, you are mistaken I think; it won't rain today. That sign may hold in England or in the Eastern states but not in Utah. I don't know the reason yet.

I only know it's so, and I'll find out the reason. Besides it's not because of moisture that the sun was red this morning,—it's because of smoke.—'How do I know?'—I'll tell you as we drive to the field. I thought it out as I was milking this morning. * *

During the Forenoon.—"The sun is about an hour high —Why has its color changed to a reddish yellow?—Sixty miles to the west it is now just rising.—Is it red there? If so what does it prove concerning the position of the smoke and the movements of the air currents? Can I predict that the sun will get brighter as it rises?—Yes.—Why?—Why does it get hotter as it gets brighter?—Yes, that must be the reason.

"But clouds are beginning to form.—What if it should rain after all?—I'd never hear the last about my 'thinking;' still I'm certain that red sun was no sign. But, now I remember, we may expect showers any time,—just as the lucern is all down.—Why? —Surely not because the devil is permitted to plague mortals by reason of their sins, as Daddy Slocum said. There must be some natural cause.—Let's see. If the rain comes down it is an evidence that the air had more moisture than it could hold.—I have it. One hundred thousand acres of lucern perhaps was cut last week. Now, for every ton of hay, four or five tons of water must have gone somewhere—into the air. Five hundred thousand tons of water swallowed, besides the millions sucked up from lakes and streams, irrigated lands, and the exhalation of growing plants! No wonder the atmosphere is getting leaky. * * * * *

During the Dinner Hour.—"How those horses enjoy their dinner! The rythmic crunching of their teeth, with their periodical snorts, is music to me. Somehow it makes me happy, and I feel the impulse to get up and pet them.—Why, I wonder.—The farmer's life is a joyous one. What prince approaches his plates of silver and goblets of gold with half the zest with which I open my dinner pail!

"As I sit eating, my eye catches a curious sight. A bunch of dandelion stems, in gray hoods, stand there full four inches above the tall lucern. I must secure one of these stems.—Eighteen inches! and yet but a few feet away on the bare road they are scarcely four.—Why such a difference in identically the same soil? —As I blow upon the winged seed I perceive the reason. Marvelous! what taught you the need of out-growing the lucern, in order that the wind might scatter your offspring? Do you have intelligence like myself? Let me see that performance—puff! Away go your babies.—What! they settle with a spiral motion, seed downward? And that wind mill attached?—ah, I see, it is so constructed that the wind will keep it boring till the seed is imbedded in the soil. Wonderful! You and all your tribe have truly learned to take care of yourselves. Would that I could do as well in my sphere!

"What is this I see—a spider in a panic? Surely it is!—What can be the cause? Can it be that insignif—no, spiders are not afraid of flies.—Move out from your covert, Arachne, I desire to see the combat.—Swoop! that was a stinger! Another such a stab and you bid good bye to earth.—Out again, I am willing to sacrifice you to science.—Whew! How savage that attack!—There, you are dead—poisoned to death; and there, I have your assassin. I must examine him.—A fly, long-winged, slender, about one third the size of a house fly! —What put such mettle and power into your trim body? When did you become the champion of the fly tribe, against the terrible spider? What necessity called you into being?—What marvelous wisdom in you to know exactly when and where and how to strike! Like lordly man, you first frighten your enemy and then the victory is yours, even against a thousand odds. And that lubberly dead spider—how different the emotion you inspired in him from that inspired by the music of your clumsy cousin, the house-fly! * * * * *

Only Self-Effort Educates.—"It is time to go to work again, and still my fellow laborer sleeps. I must wake him—but hold!

Here is a chance to study the nature of a snore. I've always heard that snoring occurs because the mouth is left open.—Now, if I place my hand so—oh, you awake, do you? I hope you have had edifying dreams—for life is too short to sleep away, unless you thereby learn something. But perhaps you have been studying Theosophy?—'What have I learned by keeping awake?' Man, man, I have neither time nor ability to put oil into your lamp; you, and you alone can do it."

VI.

HOW ONE MAY LEARN TO THINK IN THE LIBRARY.

I have just finished a chapter which attempts to illustrate the kind of mind-employment that the common laborer may have every day, if he will but set the wheels of thought going. This was the very school in which Robert Burns gained some of his sublimest thoughts. For instance, what was there marvelous in plowing up a mountain daisy or unnesting a mouse from the stubble? To ten thousand plowboys such an occurrence would be of less significance than overturning an unusually large clod. But the rustic poet of Scotland saw in it perfect revelations of thought and feeling. Read his poems entitled respectively, "To a Mountain Daisy," and "To a Mouse," if you would know how much little things and little events may do towards forming and vitalizing our mind-powers. The thinker can never be alone if he but have a spear of grass or a pebble for company.

Reading to Assimilate.—But let us learn this same lesson also from another point of view. When your evening chores are done, take your chair in the library. Select some book,—let it be a thoughtful, that is, a full-of-thought book,—and begin the thinking habit by inserting how and why question marks after every important word and phrase. Curb that American propensity to get over ground. Suppose you finish but one page by bedtime. Nay, do not cast an impatient eye upon the volumes yet unread in your library. One page an hour is splendid progress, especially if the thought has been made your own; if it has become so truly a part of your soul-fibre as to lose all trace of its origin. The pleasure of conscious growth and possession will more than compensate for the loss of the accustomed exhilaration obtained from race-horse skimming. I am constrained to attempt an illustration of how thought-activity may be stirred by the manner of the reading. Suppose the selection be the following from Holmes:

"I would have a woman as true as death. At the first real lie which works from the heart outward, she should be tenderly chloroformed into a better world, where she can have an angel for a governess, and feed on strange fruits which will make her all over again, even to her bones and marrow. Proud she may be, in the sense of respecting herself; but pride, in the sense of condemning others less gifted than herself, deserves the two lowest circles of a vulgar woman's Inferno, where the punishments are smallpox and bankruptcy. She who nips off the end of a brittle courtesy, as one breaks the tip of an icicle, to bestow upon those whom she ought cordially and kindly to recognize, proclaims the fact that she comes not merely of low blood, but of bad blood. Consciousness of unquestioned position makes people gracious in a proper measure to all; but, if a woman puts on airs with her equals, she has something about herself or her family she is ashamed of, or ought to be. Better too few words from the woman we love, than too many; while she is silent, nature is working for her; while she talks she is working for herself. Love is sparingly soluble in the words of men; therefore they speak much of it; but one syllable of woman's speech can dissolve more of it than a man's heart can hold."

How to Chew and Digest What is Read.—"Some books," says Bacon, "are to be tasted, some to be swallowed, and some to be chewed and digested." It is the last kind which our Elders should read for the most part, for these only teach how to think. I have chosen the above extract to illustrate my idea of what is meant by reading matter that is to be chewed and digested. If one would really enjoy the full flavor of such books, he must linger over them, analyze every conceit, develop every hint, image every figure, follow every suggestion to its lair, and disagree with conclusions generally till every doubt is vanquished. Let me try to convey some faint idea of the process.

"Woman as true as death,"—why not man also? Surely there is greater need in his case. Or does the author wish to insinuate that it is more unnatural for women to be untrue,—that the gentler sex have the reputation of angels to maintain,—unspotted angels? That reminds me that the Bible speaks frequently of sons of perdition, but never of daughters of perdition. Of the angels that fell, none were women. They stood the supreme test in heaven,—they ought not to fall here.

"True as death,"—did you ever hear of such a comparison before? Woman and death! Death is pretty true to his professions. I am inclined to agree that it would be good for woman to be equally true to hers. This would still give her a great deal of play to indulge those delightful uncertainties, which make a crabbed old bachelor here and there classify her with March weather and the moon; for death, though inexorably true, plays us many a prank before he finally stops our breath.

"At the first real lie,"—then lies may be classified?—as for instance, untruths and falsehoods; fibs, fables, and "whoppers;" bluffs and personal reminiscences; white lies and black. But what is a real lie in the case of a woman? Not the petty deceptions of toilet, not her gossiping proclivities, not the wiles and snares she lays for man, not even the kiss she gives to woman.

What then? It is the lie "which works,"—smallpox-like—"from the heart."—not the head,—"outward." Here is the key to his thought. The lie is real when it involves the heart,—when this spring of purity and holiness, heaven's fountain to thirsty mankind, has been polluted for gold or fashion or power. When this has happened "she should be tenderly chloroformed,"— woman should always be treated gently,—"into a better world,"— always a better world. She improves by sunshine, never by storms. —"where she can have an angel for a governess."—one of her primeval sisters, one of the shining hosts,—"and feed on strange fruits,"—from the tree of life which the Cherubim guarded with flaming swords,—"shall make her all over again even to her bones and marrow." That would take seven years according to physiology. Yes, I am convinced the world could spare some of its women for that length of time, especially in view of such a purpose.

"Proud she may be in the sense of respecting herself"—what a blessed pride is that! Self-respect—whoever loses this is lost indeed, even though wealth and station and fame take its place; but whoever maintains it inviolate may look angels in the face, and sleep the sleep of a child, though friends desert him and fortune frowns—"but pride in the sense of contemning others less gifted than herself"—less holy, less rich, less fashionable, or less beautiful, or whom she imagines to be so—for pride of this sort is apt to be associated with little judgment and much personal vanity— "deserves the two lowest circles of a vulgar woman's Inferno."

What does he mean—vulgar woman's Inferno? Oh, yes, I remember, the allusion is to Dante's Inferno, a kind of ghastly circular chasm with galleries from top to bottom, the punishment of the damned increasing in horror as you go down. At the end of this "bottomless pit" near the center of the earth is Dis or Satan, huge as a mountain, frozen to the armpits in everlasting ice, holding the traitor Judas between his teeth and crunching his bones, whenever the pains of hell rack his own huge frame. So, the vulgar woman's Inferno is a private establishment of this kind, in the two lowest circles of which, "the punishments are small-pox and bankruptcy!" Ideal punishments, these. Small-pox! yes, that would fix her vanity, and bankruptcy would as effectually take the wind out of her false pride.

"She who nips off the end of a brittle courtesy as one breaks the tip of an icicle"—he alludes to the cold, stiff movement that passes for a bow—"comes not only of low blood but bad blood." What is the distinction? Let me see. Low blood produces coarseness—dough-like features, towzy hair, low aspirations, animal propensities, and a laugh that cracks glassware. Nevertheless such people may be roughly honest; their moral nature, if it is not the most refined, is at least not honeycombed by deceit nor rottened by gilded vices. But bad blood is all the last and more. Yet bad blood may produce the highest and most refined types in outward seeming. When this is the case the villainies it hatches pass for strokes of genius. It is when bad blood and low blood are joined that we have monsters among men—and "brittle courtesies" among women.

"Better too few words from the woman we love than too many. (How true!) While she is silent nature is working for her; while she talks, she is working for herself." And what a spectacle it is, to see woman thus "working for herself"—working, one is almost tempted to say, with tongue, tooth, and claw! A volley of words from a woman's mouth are like a charge of bird shot from an old-fashioned blunder-buss; there is tremendous noise, and everything is bespattered within fifty yards of the mark. When woman thus begins "working for herself," the angel in her retires behind the scenes, as by a dissolving view, and only the devilish, harsh-faced vixen remains. No wonder she must then work for herself!

"Love is sparingly soluble in the words of men." After one is wearied to death by the hackneyed images of ordinary writers, it is refreshing to light upon such a metaphor as this. Love has been figured as anything and everything, and now it is tested in the laboratory: to determine, forsooth, whether it is soluble—capable of being dissolved like sugar or salt! But the words of men, so our author asserts, will absorb scarcely enough of the precious chemical, to give them a coloring,—"hence they speak much of it" —that is, make up in quantity what their love-making lacks in quality. "But one syllable of woman's speech can dissolve more of it than man's heart can hold." Woman should therefore take care to dilute it well and to give in broken doses, lest man's digestive powers be overtaxed and there be a serious overflow of bile. This is no satire; sentimental nausea is extremely common in the sterner sex.

VII.

THE MEANING OF APPERCEPTION. HOW TO APPERCEIVE.

Throughout this book I have very frequently used the terms apperceive and apperception. The words are so significant in psychological processes, that I doubt very much whether the reader has been able to get from the dictionary anything like adequate definitions. I have waited for some corner to turn up in this discussion where I might, without violating unity, devote a few paragraphs to their meaning and importance, and now the opportunity has come.

Etymology of the Word.—The reader will doubtless be quite familiar with perceive and perception. I only wish to caution him against narrowing their meaning to the work of the eye alone. To perceive is to receive a definite impression through any of the senses. It may perhaps signify more than this to a psychologist, but for my purpose this definition is sufficient.

Now, dropping one of the terms,—since they mean the same thing save that one is a verb, the other a noun—what is apperception? Simply ad-perception, the d having been softened to p for the sake of euphony. Ad-perception signifies a perception to which something has been added.

This something is really in the nature of a second perception. You have heard the expression "going in at one ear and out at the other." This exactly describes a perception that has failed to become an apperception. Our senses,—seeing, hearing, tasting, smelling, feeling—are so many distinct avenues from the outer world to the inner, or the soul. Now conceive each of these entrances to have an ante-room or lobby. It is here that perceptions come. When they pass the inner door we call them apperceptions. The inner room is the holy of holies—the sanctuary of the God within us. Thoughts entertained here become part of our existence and are never forgotten; but those received in the lobby pass quickly on or melt away into the darkness of non-being as lightly almost as they came.

Illustrations.—Test yourself. You have just returned from a walk in the city. What lingers on your mind? Your eyes saw a thousand things, from the pebbles beneath your feet through all the range of being to church steeples and cloud-mountains in the blue of heaven. Get a pencil and set down in order what remains of these impressions. Or call to mind one sound, if you can, out of the thousand that your ears must have gathered last Wednesday. You cannot. Then all these were mere lobby visitors.

It is in the impression-world as in the social world; for every acquaintance whom we take to our homes and our hearts, we allow ten thousand to pass us by with scarcely a recognition. And I might add, that just as our social standing depends upon the number and the quality of the people whom we grapple to our bosom, so precisely does our mental life depend upon apperception.

It will be seen now that I have already thoroughly illustrated the process of apperception by the two chapters which precede this one. In the first, two men beheld, or might have beheld, identically the same objects in nature; but one was made wise, and the other sleepy. To which class do you belong?

In the second an attempt was made to illustrate creative reading; in other words, that play of the mind without which it is impossible to apperceive the thoughts of others. It is a slow process of getting through books, but it is a most delightful and profitable one. For the encouragement of the reader, let me add that it does not always remain slow. The mind soon braces itself for the vigorous exercise thus required of all its faculties, and ere long is able to move at a comparatively rapid rate.

Results of Failure to Apperceive.—One of two things speedily happens to minds that do not apperceive: (1) Both the inner and the outer senses become dulled and indifferent, and the mind wraps itself in a stolidity which nothing but animal appetites can excite,—a condition that enslaves its millions yearly; or (2) the inner senses come out to the lobby, so to speak, for entertainment. By the latter, I mean that class, also numbering its millions, whose mental life centers almost wholly in their physical senses, —in seeing sights, hearing sounds, and gratifying the palate. Do you belong to either of these classes?

The latter class soon develop morbid tastes and vagrant habits. Sensual excitement burns in them; and as they cannot afford to see, hear, smell, and feel all things for themselves, their minds seek the best substitute,—sensational literature. Accounts of murders, rapes, and divorces; fires, floods, and cyclones; scenes of lurid squalor, private debauch, and public prostitution,—these spectacular images, for the supply of which every "wide-awake" newspaper of today is a veritable Police Gazette—are greedily taken into the imagination and gloated over, until the mind becomes as unclean as a bagnio.

Only a trifle wiser and healthier are the minds that gormandize on books. "I read seventeen hours a day," boasted a fiend of this vice, in a voice that made a bid for praise. "When in h—l do you find time to think?" was the more forcible than elegant rejoinder of his teacher. When a man or woman boasts of reading two or three volumes each week, depend upon it the mind is out in the lobby. Thoughts by the thousands are disposed of like visitors at a White House reception. How vitiated is the taste that finds pleasure in mere glimpses of ideas in a row; and what a "common road," as Shakespeare says of a certain female character, is that mind which gives them entrance and exit.

Mental Digestion.—Apperception is to the mind what digestion is to the body. Let us develop this parallel for the sake of exactness in the meaning of the word. First, there is chewing, which corresponds to perceiving; both should be vigorous and complete to insure physical and mental health. Then there is digestion, which corresponds to self-questioning. This in both cases is an analyzing process, a tearing apart of the elements. Assimilation depends on the thoroughness with which this is done. Next comes the distributing process, in which, by chemical changes in the one case, and psychological changes in the other,—the marvel of which is unequalled and unparalleled elsewhere in nature,—the same blood supplies the various wants of the body, and the same ideas incorporate themselves into the complex associations and operations of mind. Lastly, behold the results: A body capable of more intricate adjustments than all the machines of the world combined; and a mind capable of inventing combinations and adjustments still beyond the powers of the body. Do you digest well? Learn also to apperceive well. Let not the animal be more true to its life-mission than the soul.

VIII.

THINKING AS RELATED TO EXPRESSION—A CONCRETE THEME.

Impression and Expression.—Hitherto we have discussed thinking in its relation to the assimilation of ideas; the apperception of sensations that reach us directly from the outer world, and of thoughts that reach us through the medium of men and books—all which may be called impression. It now becomes necessary to take the next step, viz.: to discuss methods of giving out to others what we have apperceived—which method summed up may be called expression. But before attempting so abstract a thing as a sermon, let us try to illustrate the art of self-questioning by some concrete object with which we are very familiar. For instance, let our subject be a half-hour's talk on the apple.

A Concrete Theme.—Our first is manifestly a question of procedure—how shall we think upon this subject? Plainly, to take ideas as they happen to come, is to abandon the mind to the workings of chance; and surely the mental faculties should be as well under control as the muscles. We determine that there must be a rational order of treating this subject, the question is only how to find it. First we curb with iron will the impulse to ask some one else how to proceed, and also the impulse to ransack the library in the hope of "finding something on it." There is the question plainly enough before us, and we force our thinking minds to face it.

It would be tedious, and indeed would carry me far beyond the limits of this chapter, to write down the varied questions that arise in settling this first proposition. Suffice it to say that after a little vigorous thinking, some definite order more or less imperfect is fixed upon to guide the mind. Suppose it to be the following: I. Introduction—Why this subject is brought forward. II. Description of this apple. III. Classification. IV. Kinds. V. Cultivation. VI. Use.

These general heads can be easily kept in mind; and it is quite essential that they be kept in mind, otherwise the lecture would fail to move forward, and disjointed ideas and repetitions would be inevitable. These heads form a sort of guide to the thought: ideas intruding themselves out of relation, can be set aside till the proper sub-heading is reached.

The Introduction.—Every discourse should have an introduction the purpose of which is to awaken interest and center the attention. To do these things well we must have an audience of whom to judge and for whom to shape our introduction. We shall therefore suppose our listeners to be a class of boys eager to enlarge the range of their ideas. For such minds preliminary remarks might arouse interest and attention, if made somewhat in this fashion:

"Boys, it was an apple that suggested to Newton the law of gravitation. He was lying under an apple tree, you will remember, deeply engaged in thinking how this world came about and what would become of it at last, when a ripe apple let go its stem and fell near him.

"'There,' said he, 'is an example of part of this great mystery. Now, why did not that apple fall the other way? Wouldn't it be a strange world if things had to be tied down to keep them from falling up? And yet—why not?'

"You see he asked why, then hung to his question, and kept thinking and thinking till he got the answer.

"I suppose he ate the apple, if it was a good one—just as I see by your eyes you would like to eat this one—but it was not eating it that made him great; it was thinking about it. Boys, anything that will set you thinking will help to make you great; and as Newton didn't do all the thinking there is to be done about the apple, we are going to see what it can teach us today.

"'Pooh,' I imagine I hear some of you saying. 'I know all about apples; give us something new.' Let us not be too hasty. I is often the things we handle every day that we know least about. Would you believe me if I told you that a hundred volumes could be written about the apple family and not exhaust the subject? But to proceed with our object-lesson. Our first business must be to get a clear idea of this apple."

It is not my intention to write this lecture. Were I before a class I should make the students think it all out, from my ques-

PREACHING AND PUBLIC SPEAKING. 121

tioning. In doing so, I should have two objects in view, viz.: (1) the conveying of information and (2) the development of power to think. The reader will bear in mind that it is only the latter of these objects that I can strive for in these pages. Accordingly I give only so much of this lecture as will illustrate the process of thought-evolution. The sub-heads following the introduction would naturally be:

Description of the Apple.—This is most conveniently treated under the following divisions:

(a) Size—Very large—how many inches—weight—why so large—young tree—budded fruit—old tree same kind near by with scrubby fruit—why should age of tree make difference?

(b) Shape—Like a pear—why—what other shapes—does shape indicate quality—my experience.

(c) Color—First tinge of red on one side—why not on both —did sun strike it—was it light or heat that turned it red—result of chemical action—what—what does red signify as to quality—apples of other colors—what quality goes with green—russet—yellow?

(d) Parts—Skin—glossy—why—to keep air out—effect of air on pulp—effect after picking—why not same before—power of nature to mend—effect of bruises in picking—why such an effect—how avoided. Stem—how long—thickness—deep indentation—why—attached to core—why not to pulp—purpose of stem—feeds apple—how does apple grow—from core outwards. Pulp—tart—crisp—juicy—discolors knife-blade—why—what else will do it—doesn't grow mellow by time—how long—what chemical action causes change—(unlike some people I know). Core—sections—perfect—seeds—size—color—number—grow if planted —what kind of fruit—curious law—why?

(e) Blemishes—Pit marked—why—how prevented—worm hole—when—what kind of worm—under what conditions does it attack the apple—what becomes of it—how is it best destroyed, etc., etc.

The description is by no means exhausted. The questions here given are such as would suggest themselves to the most ordinary intelligence and most of them can be answered by a wide-awake boy or girl that loves an apple. Yet this same boy or girl could push the how and why questions on this subject quite past the researches of science to the very boundary line of the unknown and the unknowable. It does not take long to reach the frontier of investigation, even with so commonplace a thing as an apple. And whoever thinks clearly on this frontier will command the attention of the cultured and thoughtful of the world.

Vastly too Broad.—The man who would have staggered if placed before a class and given point blank the apple for a lecture, discovers by a little thinking that the subject is vastly too broad. The half hour is gone ere he has finished the description, and yet this is really the least extensive heading in the list. Think what might be said under Kinds, the causes of variety, and the characteristics of each variety. So under Cultivation, the relations of climate and soil and stock would come in for consideration; also the arts of budding, pruning, and pest-killing. Under Use, the material is no less varied and extensive, involving preserving, cooking and others arts. In short, it would be found that, as in the case of Bunyan's "Pilgrim's Progress," thought would be added to thought, until, instead of a meagre half-hour's talk, he would have a respectable volume or two on pomology.

Such is the fertility of a mind that thinks. I have emphasized the fact that this mind-action should be made a habit, so much so that it shall not need the will to spur the faculties into activity. The mind shall instantly seize upon every object it touches, for no other reason than that it is more natural for it to do so, than not to do so. Let this habit be formed from the contemplation of all things that come before the senses.

The Need of Imagery and Illustration.—I chose my illustration, the apple, from among concrete rather than from among abstract things, for another reason. Whatever may be the exculsiveness of the qualifications for sectarian ministers, Latterday Saint preachers must be accustomed to think upon all subjects. Whatever bears upon the material, the intellectual, the social, or the spiritual interest of the people is germane to a Mormon sermon. Besides, even if we grant that the sermon deals chiefly with the moral and spiritual side of our nature, how shall these truths be brought home to the congregation unless the preacher be a sharer of their experiences? It is from what occurs during the week that imagery and illustration can best be drawn to make plain and enforce the moral lessons on Sunday. It is from the secular that we get the dress for the religious thought. We can reach men only though those channels to their minds which have been opened and enlarged by contact with every-day things and events. So, let us not wait to put on our thinking cap until we take down the Bible and the Book of Mormon. On the contrary, let us count only that too trivial for thought which is too trivial for attention.

IX.

THE SELF QUESTIONING PROCESS AS APPLIED TO AN ABSTRACT THEME.

Will it be profitable to illustrate by another chapter the art of thinking on a given subject? I do not wish to overdo any part of this treatise; but when I remember what desperate straits some of my young missionary companions were in for want of knowing how to set their minds going, I am led to believe that this particular part cannot be easily overdone. Indeed, if the present chapter shall seem useless to any of my readers, they may set it down that I am not specially writing for their welfare.

Concrete and Abstract Themes.—Of course, a concrete

subject like that in the last chapter, is much easier to think about than an abstract one. The reason is that we have been familiar with concrete objects from childhood. It will be well to remember in this connection, that what is easier for us to invent thoughts concerning, is for the same reason easier for an audience to understand; so that, though Gospel themes will always be abstract, we should seek to bring the discussion of them within the range of the concrete as often as possible.

How to get a Theme.—Suppose that we now choose an abstract subject, say, Forgiveness. Our first question will be: What do we wish to maintain in respect of it? In other words, what shall be our theme? The aspects in which Forgiveness might be treated are so various as to make this question perplexing. Nor can it be justly settled without taking into account the weaknesses of the congregation.

Suppose then that the sermon is to be delivered before a people that act usually on the principle, 'An eye for an eye and a tooth for a tooth,' and to be given at a time, moreover, when irrigation difficulties, troubles arising out of the cattle and sheep interests, political squabbles, or other general disturbances have roused neighbor against neighbor to a high pitch of resentment. These men are assembled on the Sabbath day, around the table of the Lord and have partaken of the sacred emblems. Now, if ever in their lives a lesson in forgiveness will be opportune. What shall it be? Something that shall not alone touch their feelings; something that shall appeal to their calm judgment, and give them a new criterion of right and wrong. Suppose then, from the well known passage: "I, the Lord, will forgive whom I will forgive, but of you it is required to forgive all men"—we draw this theme:—

Why we should forgive all men, friend and foe alike.

Finding Appropriate Divisions.—There will of course have been an introduction leading the minds of the congregation up to this theme, converging the attention, and arousing interest in the discussion.* The next consideration will be to divide it into such aspects as will best accomplish our purpose. Generally it is safe to place a bulwark of scripture before our thoughts. The word of God is with many men the end of argument. Even with the skeptical it appeals to reverence, and thereby gives the speaker every advantage. Hence our first division will be: What the Lord says on the subject.

To know that the Lord requires a thing should be conculsive reason for doing the thing; and no doubt it would were we of the trusting disposition of Nathaniel. But we are not. Too many are like Thomas. We desire to know why the Lord makes the requirement; hence our second division will perhaps be: To forgive is reasonable as well as scriptural.

But this division may lead us into subtle abstractions, and profound questions of right and wrong. Therefore, before we have drawn too heavily on the mental energies of our hearers, we shall do well to bring the discussion back to the concrete. Our third division might then be: How it affects a man mentally, morally, socially, and otherwise, to hold a grudge.

This division will bring the negative aspect of our theme into view. But it is not well to pause here. Men are moved as strongly by emulation of the good as by fear of the consequences of the bad; hence we may add as a fourth division: How a forgiving disposition contributes to the welfare and success of a man, at home, in society, in business, etc.

We began with an abstract proposition which we amplified (1) by scriptural citations, and (2) by an appeal to common sense. Next we illustrated the theme (1) by a negative and (2) by a positive example. If the discussion has been well conducted thus far, we are ready to narrow its application to indivdiuals, hence our last division—the conclusion—will probably be: How it will help this ward if the feelings caused by such and such things be healed.

---
*See chapter VIII, which treats of the nature and purpose of the introduction.

The first of these divisions requires but little real thinking power, so far as the finding of passages is concerned. Thinking begins (1) when we are led to consider in what order it is best to present them, and (2) when we ask ourselves, after each word or phrase, What—exactly—does it mean? But as in a former chapter I have illustrated how to "read between the lines,"—that is, how to think in connection with reading matter,—I shall take up the second division, viz.: To forgive is reasonable as well as scriptural.

The Second Division Discussed by Way of Illustration.— "Who are the parties concerned in an act of forgiveness? They are first, the Lord who requires it, second, the person who is forgiven, and, third, the one who forgives.—Which one is chiefly benefited by the act?—It cannot be the Lord. True, to save a soul adds to his glory and dominion, and no doubt he feels also the joy of a father when his children are reconciled; but aside from these considerations, how can his status in eternity be affected, either by the love or hate of man toward his fellow man? It must therefore be one of the others that is benefited.

How does the act affect the man forgiven?—If he is unrepentant, not at all; if repentant, much for the man's good.—The former proposition is self-evident, prove the latter.—Well, take the repentant man; he is oppressed by the consciousness of his guilt. He casts his eye down, and dare not look upon the man whom he has wronged. Whenever they meet he can think of nothing else than the wrong, and he imagines the other is thinking of nothing else. He cannot unload his awful consciousness until he has confessed and been forgiven. The two, who were estranged, finally meet on common ground, and the aggressor lays down his load. Unless this were done it would be impossible for him to advance. But look at this case more narrowly: it is really not the forgiveness so much as the asking forgiveness, that enabled him to unload his transgression. Forgiven or unforgiven, he is free when he has asked forgiveness. It cannot therefore be the person forgiven who receives the real benefit of the act.

There is then only the person who forgives. In some way the real benefit is to him. But how?—Well, not to forgive is to hate.— What is hate?—It must be a poison to the soul that harbors it.— Whom does it hurt? Not the Lord—He is beyond the reach of it. Not the being hated; he even gloats to see how deeply the hater is wounded, and his own prosperity is nothing diminished by the mad spleen of another.—Who then is hurt by hating?—The hater himself—like the snake whose fangs have struck his own body.

But how can I make it plain?—I have it. The unforgiving man in going through a hedge, runs a thorn into his flesh. To be quite consistent, he should say, with clenched teeth: "I'll get even with you. Pull out the thorn? Not I! I'll let it stay there till the flesh rots and blood poisoning sets in. I'll teach this wicked hedge what it is to run thorns into me."

But he does not say this. Why? Because the wound is in his body. Is he not thrice a fool, then who does say it and act upon it, when the wound is in his soul? With this conception comes a perfect flood of light on many passages of scripture. Now I understand why our Savior commands us to forgive and love our enemies. It was not the enemies he was concerned about; it was ourselves. He saw that we should be likely to forgive our friends,—those who humble themselves and ask forgiveness. But our enemies—those who glory in the wrongs they inflict upon us—here was the danger. He saw that we should be likely to leave the thorn in our hearts, till it fester and corrupt the very source of our spiritual life—and this, too, under the guise of courage and manliness. Such, indeed, is the manliness of the Caesars and Napoleons of history. Revenge not forgiveness is their watch-cry; and so they breed and multiply the wrongs which they punish. On the other hand, how truly a God was he, who when tortured by wrongs and shames, such as no man before or since has borne, was still able to pray: "Father, forgive them, they know not what they do."

What becomes then of the man who will not free his heart from the poison of hate? What is the record of his downfall—in the family, in the social circle, in the Church—for downfall there must be, in love, and truth, and virtue, and purity of soul?"

The reader will perceive that this question leads me to the third division of our theme, viz.: how it affects a man mentally, morally, socially, and otherwise to hold a grudge—but my space is gone. I trust what I have said will illustrate thinking on an abstract theme, and that if the reader has become interested in this sermon on its own acount, he will think it out to the end.

X.

AN ELDER SHOULD NOT ONLY LEARN TO THINK, BUT LEARN TO THINK JUSTLY.

I have thus far written on how to think; it may be well to devote a chapter in conclusion on how to think justly.

One Sided Thinking.—The preacher is especially exposed to the temptations of one-sided thinking. Taken as a fraternity the world over, no class is more biased and dogmatic in their views. In the first place, the matter of thought relates largely to another world and much of it cannot be disproved or successfully disputed till that other world come. Faulty thinking need fear little, then, from the score of demonstration; for men do not come back and say: "This religion has led me to hell."

In the second place, as to faulty thinking being overthrown by better thinking, it is a very slow and discouraging process; for all thinking is intrenched more or less behind unreasoning walls of emotion—that is behind prejudice. Especially is this true of faulty thinking, and more than ever true when such thinking is on a religious subject. Both speculation and undue feeling should, therefore, be constantly guarded against.

Now, the shortest cut to the end of this matter would be to say: Be always under the guidance of the Spirit of truth when you think, and you cannot fail to think justly. But I apprehend that our Elders do not live lives pure enough to be guided always by this unerring Teacher. We need therefore to set the will on guard like a sleepless sentinel, lest our feelings and infirmities unduly color our thought.

The Mind must be a Complete Court.—We need to have by us at all hours a faithful mentor who shall have no other work to do than to prick our vanities and let out the air; repress our emotions when they tend to bias the thought; and in general, to argue us down into shame-faced humility, save when our reasoning be just. But this is impossible, you say. Not so. The mind is quite capable of creating just such a mentor within itself—a sort of personified justice with eyes cold and clear as a frosty morning and with no trace of sympathy or flattery.

In a former chapter I referred to the need of our having within us an adversary silently to sneer at and find fault with what the mind is concocting—in short to find the same objection before the thought is expressed that a real adversary would make after it is expressed. The better conception is probably to look upon the mind as a complete court, and upon thinking as the process of finding a verdict. The feelings are prosecution and defense, the judgment is jury, and the will, judge. Some minds, however, finding the case so very clear, pronounce judgment when the prosecution is done. Other minds, ignoring the prosecution, come into court only when the defense is ready to begin. This is merely a figure of speech, but it is well to keep it in mind whenever we are thinking upon any subject.

Parental Partiality.—It may be well to note here some of the special conditions under which one is tempted to unjust thinking. One instance is where the matter in question has already been decided upon theoretically. It requires some creative power to construct a plausible theory; hence when a man has succeeded in doing so, he naturally feels a very fatherly interest that it shall live and grow strong. Under such circumstances, it is difficult indeed to be impartial. Like a lawyer with his theory of the case to be tried, such a thinker is keenly alert to facts that support his view and conveniently obtuse to facts that go against it. He is no doubt honest, and means to be just, but how is this possible? There are few Roman fathers, even in the thought world.

Religion has been brought very much into disrepute because of such biased thinking. "The scientist," says Fisk, "is very apt to smile at those people who taking hold of the qusetion at the wrong end, begin by arguing about all manner of fancied consequences. For his knowledge of the history of human thinking assures him that such methods have through all time proved barren of aught save strife, while his own bold yet humble method, is the only one through which truth has ever been elicited. To pursue unflinchingly the method of science requires dauntless courage and a faith that nothing can shake."

These are fine words, and the thought they embody is as true as anything in the Gospel. The preacher can afford, even less than the man of science, to refuse truth a fair hearing for fear "of all manner of fancied consequences." For the latter may make or mar only one life—his own, while the former has hundreds, or perhaps thousands in his keeping.

"Do what is right, let the consequence follow," says the hymn, and Latterday Saints sing it with unusual fervor. Let our hearts respond equally to the sentiment: "Think what is true, let the consequence follow." For depend upon it, when we fear the consequences of admitting incontrovertible facts, we are not fighting for God's cause, but for our own. It is not a truth but a theory which we champion.

PREACHING AND PUBLIC SPEAKING.   131

Religion not Alone in Biased Thinking.—But are preachers alone in thus constructing theories and then making facts bend to them? Grant that the religionist has held the notion that the earth is flat, that the sun, moon, and stars exist only as lamps for man's night and day service—grant that he has tenaciously held these, and a thousand other equally untenable theories; still, can you find anything in his biased thinking to equal the colossal assumption of the evolutionist as to the origin of man?

How can truth assert itself when in the tyrannical grasp of such a giant? Will not every fact in nature be interrogated, not for its unbiased quota of divine truth, but for evidence in support of this assumption? I said will not—better say has not this been done? Take the greatest advocates of Darwinism, and have they not closed their eyes absolutely to half the evidence—the evidence of the spiritual world—in order that their darling hypothesis might forsooth live and thrive? Dogmatically asserting that all intuitions which do not submit to the methods of the laboratory are mere phantasies and hallucinations?

Preconceptions not to be Fallen in Love with.—The fact is, no human being is free from the tendency to be biased in favor of his own conceptions and mental projections. What then? Shall he refuse to project? By no means. Not to theorize is not to advance. For what is theorizing but throwing the more or less feeble light of the known out upon the darkness of the unknown? Without such light we should never leave the beaten track of routine. The remedy is not to cease preconceiving, but to avoid falling in love with any one preconception; not to go forward without a lamp, but to avoid going forward with only one lamp.

There can be no doubt that, had Darwin and his followers begun their great work with faculties as keenly alert to spiritual phenomena, as they were to physical phenomena, we should not have had the gross materialism which immediately succeeded their researches. So, too, if preachers today were not so wedded to pet theories as dogmatically to ignore the daylight truths uncovered by men of science, religion would not so often be held in contempt by thinking men.

Refusal to Entertain Soiled Truth.—A kind of illogical thinking allied to the last is the refusal to make use of certain facts because they have been brought into disrepute by the inferences usually drawn from them. It does not occur to such a thinker that the premises may be true, even though the conclusion be false. For instance, many an Elder is frightened by the name of Darwin, Spencer, or Huxley, simply because these men are avowed evolutionists. How absurd it is to shut our eyes to the light which these men bear, simply because of one smoky spot in the lantern! Is it probable that men who have spent their whole lives in sifting and collating the facts of nature, cannot teach us many truths concerning the works of God—simply because they err in theories drawn from these facts?

Suppression of Inconvenient Facts.—The last case I shall consider is the downright suppression of recognized facts, simply because they run counter to what we have conceived to be true. I cannot find language to characterize the baseness of such self-surrender. It is not merely dishonesty, nor is it merely dishonesty cloaked by cowardice; it is both these and more—it is treason to God and the universe.

Victories gained by such methods are defeats—miserable defeats—even though they be accompanied by all the pomp and circumstances of triumph. For what is gained? Simply the adherence of a few minds too ignorant to detect the imposition. Such acquisitions remain a weight to any cause that would advance. If they remain because they are uninstructed, then their ignorance is the weight; if they remain after they are enlightened, then it is dishonesty. Real victories emancipate man—advance the race toward the likeness of God; but sham victories enslave and debase; for they are the triumphs of error.

PREACHING AND PUBLIC SPEAKING. 133

Other Effects of Suppressing Truth.--When such advances (?) do take place in the spread of a religion—and who that has observed the methods of preachers can doubt that movements of this kind are frequent?—how does it affect men who are intelligent enough to see that unmanageable truths are thus deliberately suppressed? They are too disgusted to ask whether the system demands such a suppression, or whether the advocate of the system is too ignorant to know the real bearing of such facts,—that is, they utterly refuse to investigate the system.

Is not the refusal to entertain facts from groundless fears as to their bearing, a fruitful cause of the distrust of Mormonism? There can be no doubt of it; for if an Elder were but well educated enough, he would be able to marshal all truths into line; but as it is, his unskillful generalship too often causes newly recruited facts to fire into one another's faces. Here is a dilemma: what shall the Elder do? He must either acknowledge his incompetency to command these facts, or deny their competency to serve. Alas, that he should ever choose the latter alternative!

We may make a Choice of Truths.—There is but one other aspect of this question that I desire to discuss. It is this: if we are never to suppress what we recognize as truths, must we on the other hand make no discrimination in the entertainment of truths? That is, must we offer no opposition to the forcing of truths upon our attention?

Well, let us ask what rule we follow in selecting eatables for our tables? Is food for the mind of less consequence than food for the stomach? Again, do we ask every honorable, respectable member of society into our private circle? Then, why should we not be equally choice as to the visitors we admit into our sanctum of thought?

Today I may feel myself quite capable of reading Darwin, Paine, and Ingersoll with profit, but I thank my teachers that these books were not put into my hands ten years ago. And what I say here of books applies quite as well to companions; of two equally pure sources of mind-activity, I may consistently urge my child to become acquainted with the one, and to shun the other—at least for a time.

What answer shall I make then to the man who says I lack independence and calls me coward for not reading a work on atheism? If I do not treat him with the silent contempt which such raw judgment deserves, I might reply: "You say the book is full of good thought. Are there not a hundred volumes in my library with better? And as to your insinuation, I shall deign to reply to it when I find you eating frogs because the French esteem them a delicacy, or crickets and grasshoppers, because the Digger Indians find them nutritious."

Here then is the safest rule to guide one in the discrimination of thought material: Wait to begin the investigation of any controverted system of thought till you can bring to its interpretation a mind that is strong in those characteristics which were weak in the mind that produced the system.

CHAPTER V.

CHARACTERISTICS OF THE SERMON.

I.

IMPORTANCE OF CHOOSING A SUBJECT WHEN BEGINNING TO SPEAK.

We are now to consider the product of preaching—the sermon. By this term I mean, not the elaborate effort generally called by this name in contradistinction to the address, or the informal talk, but rather any oral communication of original composition directed to a religious assembly. These communications take so many forms in Latterday Saints assemblies, apparently obeying no rules whatever, that it will hardly be profitable, at least before we have considered other things, to make distinctions here as to kinds of sermons. Let us rather direct attention to what must be common to all such communications.

Ideal Conditions for Preaching.—First of all, then, we have a oongregation which, if the conditions be as they should be, is made up of minds poised in an expectant attitude; minds that have left business cares and all other mundane affairs at home. The choir by its sweet strains has sought to attune the diverse vibrations of many souls to one solemn harmony. These hearts are also drawn to beat in unison as every voice says "amen" to the opening prayer. As if this were not enough, the way for the sermon is further prepared by the Sacrament, wherein all sit down, as it were, to the table of the Lord; showing forth by this object lesson that all men, high and low, rich and poor, are equal in the eyes of their Heavenly Father. How, indeed, could the fatherhood of man be more solemnly impressed upon a congregation?

After the Sacrament, what next? Such is the attitude of every mind. Here we have not only expectancy as manifested ordinarily by secular audiences, but an ideal expectancy, reinforced as it is by humility, by a spirit of charity and forgiveness, and by a deep, reverential attention. What more could a speaker ask? Shame to the Elder, then, that seeks to satisfy such listening by the echoes of an empty mind, or to feed such hunger on the mouldy crusts of a lazy memory!

But, dropping figures of speech, how shall the Elder avoid doing these every things—avoid hiding his emptiness under cover of many "words without knowledge," or what is little better, how shall he avoid repeating platitudes and scraps of sermons that are as commonplace as remarks about the weather? To make the most of the expectancy of an audience, these trite things should not be said, even for the excuse of gaining time to collect his wits. How, then, let me ask, shall a speaker begin to avoid these things from the time he begins to speak?

The farmer ere he begins to plow takes care to secure a piece of land; the shoemaker does not begin to stitch till he has leather; the weaver does not start his shuttles till he has yarn; but the preacher, alas! often sets his loom going without warp or woof, and regales his hearers with the mere click of machinery.

First Requisite of the Sermon the Choice of a Subject.— Is it not astounding that this proposition needs seriously to be argued? What! do you pretend that there can be preaching without a subject? Preaching—no; but what passes for it—yes. I am not afraid to let every reader draw from his own memory in support of this assertion. How often it happens that a speaker fritters away a whole hour and then sits down without having found a subject! Quite as often we hear him say finally: "Now, what I want to get at is this"—and looking at our watches we discover he has been twenty, thirty, forty minutes in getting at it.

I should have nothing more to say about this fiddling away of time, if people would apply to it the same common-sense reasoning by which they condemn a sheer waste in any other business. But preaching, we seem to feel, is too sacred, too spiritual, to be touched by the rules of common sense, hence abuses grow rank without being molested—nay without even being so little disturbed as to be called by their true names; like a Sunday garden whose soil is too sacred for week-day feet, and whose weeds must be pulled only on the Sabbath, when no man must work!

The temptation to vagrancy as opposed to system and method, is by no means peculiar to preaching. It has struck in on the farming community throughout Utah, as any one who will examine the farms as he rides along, can testify; and it manifests itself more or less in all fields of activity. Every teacher discovers it no matter what the subject or what the school. Where is the child, for instance, that does not naturally perfer slinging ink in meaningless strokes and curves, to following the copy, line for line? Every teacher of penmanship knows, also, how the young sophist when caught at it, justifies the turning loose of his hand as tending to give him flexibility and freedom of movement; when the fact is that scribbling causes him to lose, not to gain control of his muscles.

Aimless talking is mental scribbling and differs from scribbling pure and simple chiefly in that it is harder to cure; for none is so blind as not to see the utter worthlessness of an ink-bespattered sheet of paper, while multitudes, distrusting their own impressions, still cherish a vague notion that there may be some good in a word-bespattered hour of time, from which they have just escaped.

Vagrant Preaching Intrenched.—The difficulty in curing the vagrant habit lies in the fact that it is intrenched behind this delectable piece of reasoning: Whoever speaks by the guidance of the Spirit of God speaks what is good for man. Latterday Saint Elders speak by this Spirit, hence what Latterday Saint Elders speak is good for man. But Latterday Saint Elders are often aimless and wandering in their sermons; hence—well—in some way which we can't exactly see, aimlessness in speech must be good for man. I leave the reader to detect the fallacy.

"I love to count myself only as a fiddle on which the Holy Ghost may play whatever tunes it lists." This remark is credited to one of our eminent leaders, now dead. If this sentiment was intended as an apology for a rambling tongue, then even the uniqueness of its dress ought not to spare its author the just criticism that he is blaming the Holy Ghost for what is a very common human frailty. But so far as I can learn, this Elder always played tunes. He did not realize that his very words would often be used to justify the most discordant noises, or what is little better, the endless tuning up for a sermon, that there is neither time nor patience left to listen to, when it finally begins.

The remedy for all this lies in choosing one subject, sticking to it as long as fresh thoughts spring up concerning it, and sitting down when one is "gravelled for matter," and begins to repeat ideas.

"What! stick to one subject for a whole sermon! Impossible. Some of our most fluent speakers would be floored in five minutes." Well, suppose they are. Would it not be a good thing? What vanity can be more contemptible than that which sacrifices whole audiences that some Elder may have it to say: "I held them an hour!"

Value of Talking to a Single Subject.—But no such results would take place—at least, after the first few trials. These Elders, who now dig a few spadefuls in this garden, then rush madly to that, and so on through the entire field of thought, would find in a single narrow compass, more thoughts, richer thoughts, intenser thoughts, and all this simply because the thoughts would be specific and closely related. The microscope reveals more wonders to us than the telescope, and the truths it reveals are of as much more vital interest to us as they are nearer to us than are the stars.

This confining one's self to a single subject is at once a strong support to self-confidence and a powerful stimulus to thought. The rambling talker, if he will but train his powers for a short time, will be surprised and delighted to discover for himself the truth of this assertion. But it will require a powerful effort of will to realize the new advantage. Perhaps keeping in mind this illustration will aid the will: I once beheld a pesky hen, with worn and bedraggled wing and tail feathers, trying to cover a brood of lordly young turkeys. Picture the ridiculous figure! But ridiculous though it be, it is a valuable comparison for any Elder to keep in mind, who is tempted to do likewise. It has served me on many an occasion when I would otherwise have "spread myself," or attempted to spread myself over all the peaks of thought in a continent of knowledge.

Let us realize, fellow-preachers, that beginning to talk to an audience with nothing before us, on which the mind can rest, is about as senseless as sitting down to a bare table and going through the act of masticating and swallowing food that is not there. Should the preacher, then, predetermine, say on his way to meeting, what topic he will speak upon? Not necessarily so—unless the Spirit so direct him. But let him, when he begins to speak, come to a definite subject as quickly as possible, and then let no vagaries of fancy switch him off the track.

II.

HOW TO CHOOSE AN APPROPRIATE SUBJECT.

The choosing of an appropriate subject is really harder than the speaking upon it after it is chosen. If some one could put to the speaker, as he arises, a specific question, the answer to which would be just the spiritual food needed, not a minute would be lost in aimless and often fruitless foraging for something rational to say. It is not my purpose to teach that any Elder may presume to choose for himself or for another a subject for any given occasion. That must ever be left to the Spirit of truth which searcheth all hearts. What I do maintain is, that Elders should think about subjects—central truths in their relations to the details of life—so that there may be something in their minds to choose from. It is not the Spirit of inspiration we should seek to improve, but our pliability and plasticity to the workings of this spirit. If, then, we think much about what is good and what is bad in preaching, we shall offer less resistance, or perhaps it would be more exact to say, we shall yield more readily, to its suggestions. It is in view of this thought that I invite attention to the discussion that follows as to the nature and choice of a subject.

Three things are to be taken into account: (1) The nature of the occasion; (2) The qualifications of the preacher; (3) The qualities of the subject itself.

1. The Subject should be in Harmony with the Occasion.— Human beings are insensibly influenced by ever-changing environments; springtime and autumn, winter and summer, prosperity and adversity, events political, social, religious, educational; and also by the occupations which for the time being engage their attention. The Elder who is oblivious to the pulse of nature and callous to the touch of mankind is in danger of preaching against the wind.

PREACHING AND PUBLIC SPEAKING. 141

He is not bringing meat in due season. His thoughts are likely to stalk in, dressed in overcoats and fur caps amid the roses of June.

It is not so much in the choice of a subject as in the point of view from which it is treated and the images and illusions by which its truths are brought home to the audience—that the preacher gains by being alive to what for the moment stirs the multitude. Let the preacher ask himself ere he begins: What is in the air today, and in some way or other make this contribute toward impressing upon his hearers the moral lessons of the sermon.

2. **The Subject should be of Present Interest.**—This rule must take into account the people addressed as well as the subject treated. What may be old and stale in one part may be new and fresh in another. We often hear criticisms about "Mormonism forty years old." If applied to truths of the Gospel as advocated forty years ago, the criticism is foolish. Moral principles have no age. They do not change from eternity to eternity. But, certainly, the statement or expression of these principls and the events that cling about their exposition, do constantly vary, and should vary, with the needs of the age and the people. It is the dress then that gets old, and let us not underrate the effect of worn-out or antiquated garments. Fashions in speech hold as well as fashions in dress. Well dressed thought lives, because it finds its way among men and is entertained. Equally good thought, poorly dressed, dies for want of entertainment. But aside from sermons in worn-out dresses, there is a kind of Mormonism forty years old, which is justly censured: sermons which were of present interest one or two generations ago, but which ought never to be heard today out of a museum of relics. So, too, it often happens that Elders on missions acquire so little versatility that on being called to preach at home they launch into a rote sermon, quite oblivious to the fact that they are talking to the Saints, and not to a congregation of unbelievers.

Let every Elder called upon to address the Saints, ask himself the question: Is this of present interest? and it will greatly aid him in avoiding the hackneyed subjects that so often make our meetings dreary. If he discover that he knows nothing about other subjects, let him somehow find the moral courage to sit down, and then prepare himself better for the next opportunity.

3. **The Subject should be Suited to the Intelligence of the Congregation.**—Instinctively the speaker should feel when he is not being understood; should perceive instantly waves of intelligence or of doubt as they pass over the audience, like the alternate lights and shades made by fleecy clouds on a summer day. He will thus be able to adapt his thoughts and diction to the varying needs of his hearers. This rule is oftenest violated in talks before the Sunday schools, which generally go over the heads of all, save the teachers. But it is also the fault of young Elders, dangerously puffed up with a "little learning." They find it so hard to curb their vanity, so delightful to air their scraps of knowledge and enjoy the blank stare of their elder brethren and sisters. Set it down as a rule, that the Elder who thus loves to mystify by grandiloquent words and obscure allusions, is thinking mainly of himself. He speaks, not by the clear, steady light of the Spirit of truth, but by the accumulated gas product of his own vanity.

4. **Only such Subjects should be chosen as are Interesting to the Speaker.**—It need scarcely be argued that what is not interesting to a speaker he will utterly fail to make interesting to the congregation. Moreover, want of interest in a subject is prima facie evidence of want of knowledge—at least of fresh, vigorous knowledge—concerning it. He should, therefore, avoid the subject for the further reason that he would be wasting the time of his hearers in mere general assertions and dreary platitudes. If this rule were invariably followed, three-fourths of our sermons would be on stock-raising, commerce, or farming. What then? Better far to be kept awake by a fresh, vigorous, specific talk on how to irrigate, so as to raise good crops, than to be put to sleep by drowsy emptinesses on a spiritual subject. Of course it is the spiritual subject that

PREACHING AND PUBLIC SPEAKING.   143

we come to meeting to be stirred up concerning. But if the Elder cannot stir us—because he is not stirred himself—let him speak upon a subject in which he can stir us; or, better still, let him give way to the Elder who can interest us in what we came to hear. If we will be guided by the Spirit in the choice of a subject, it will always be chosen from that part of our mind-stores in which we are interested; for the Spirit delights not in scraps and mouldy crusts, and it can find fresh food to draw from only where our ideas are alive and growing. Let us then make it a rule only to speak on those subjects in which we are interested; and if we are not interested in what should be talked about, let us not talk, but sit down and be ashamed of our indolence.

5. The Speaker should Choose only such Subjects as Command his entire Belief.—The tippler and tobacco user will make a poor sermon on the Word of Wisdom. Even if it be faultless rhetorically, it will lack the Gospel ring, for the Spirit does not lend itself to hypocrisy. The first requisite of a preacher is a testimony of the Gospel—an abiding, an ever-burning testimony. It is not enough that an Elder have a passive belief in a subject in order to speak well upon it; his belief must be active—so active as to dominate him, if he would make others believe in it. "I do not want to possess a faith," says a great writer. "I want a faith to possess me."

6. A Subject ought not to be Attempted that is Beyond the Powers of the Speaker.—If this rule be followed it will stop much vain speculation as to the seventh heaven and kindred subjects that may belong to theology but do not belong to the Gospel, at least not in this life. It will also be of aid to the young Elder who, dazzled by the first glimmerings of a mighty subject, rushes into sermons under the delusion that he is the first and only one to whom the glorious truth has been revealed.

We have now treated the choice of a subject as regards the occasion, and as regard the speaker. We have next to speak of this choice as regards the subject itself. The discussion of this part is so important as to require a separate chapter.

III.

GENERAL EXAMPLES SHOWING THE EFFECT OF UNITY.

A Subject should have Unity.—This hits squarely the great fault of most of our preaching. Our sermons are generally a medley of many subjects unrelated or of equal importance. Unity requires that one thought shall be prominent throughout an entire sermon. It must never be lost sight of, even for an instant. A thousand subjects may be grouped about this central thought, if they throw light upon it, but only on this condition. If the subject be faith, then all the principles of the Gospel may be treated in connection therewith, but only as subordinate for the time being to the leading subject. For instance, faith may be treated in its relation to repentance, in its relation to baptism, to confirmation, to tithing, to prayer, to keeping holy the Sabbath day, etc., but the speaker must never lose sight of the fact that it is faith, not repentance, baptism, etc., that is being discussed. If baptism be chosen, then it for the time being is supreme, and all other subjects to which it bears relation are subordinate. To follow any other rule is to draw without perspective, and paint without regard to values.

Unity in the sermon is of such vital importance that I am tempted, even at the risk of seeming prolix, to devote the whole of this chapter and the next to its consideration. And in order that its importance may be the more deeply impressed upon the reader, I shall first consider the effect of unity in respect to other compositions than the sermon.

Unity and Painting.—Examine for instance any of the pictures that hang upon your walls. Instantly you should be able to divine the purpose of the artist. If your judgment lingers between this possible purpose and that, then either the picture lacks unity or you lack the power of interpretation.

Compare three pictures of the same natural objects. Let the first be entitled the Delaware. Here the purpose plainly is to show the river in its majesty and beauty. The season of the year, the cast of the landscape, and the form of animal life, will all be made to contribute to this thought. Let the next subject be Crossing the Delaware. Here it will not be enough to paint upon the other picture a raft or boat loaded with passengers. The want of unity would be detected immediately. Crossing is here the principal thought, and the river itself is made subordinate; made to foam and roar round the up-rooted and plunging giants of the forests, if the crossing is to seem dangerous and heroic; or made to shimmer and dimple under the moonlight if it is to seem romantic.

Let the subject next be: Washington Crossing the Delaware. Neither of the other pictures will answer as a back-ground for this thought. Here everything must be grouped so as to throw light upon Washington. First comes the thought that he is commander-in-chief. His form must loom above all others. There must be an army, visible, however, chiefly by suggestions, else it would detract from the central figure. It is a strategic movement, hence there must be darkness—visible darkness—with the moon for a moment passing a rift in the clouds. Washington is an intrepid commander; hence there will be signs of a heavy snowstorm, with ice-floes and other dangers encompassing his passage.

How Unity may be Sacrificed.—So we might go on naming the characteristics of the picture. No detail is out of place provided it contributes directly or indirectly to the story. Indeed, the more detail the better, if it be of the right kind. But a single touch of the brush conveying thought not in harmony with the general purpose mars the unity, and cannot be justified, no matter how beautiful the thought may be by itself.

While there can be but one adjustment of details whereby perfect unity is secured, there may be a thousand separate adjustments whereby it may be destroyed. Imagine in this picture a choice bit of natural scenery worked into an unused corner, or the waste space of the river utilized by a quaint design in architecture!

But it is not alone by extraneous thought that unity is lost; the same thing occurs if any detail is too pronounced. If in the picture we have been considering, Washington's staff officers, instead of being mere figures, were drawn in as bold attitudes as he, and their features painted as accurately; if other details were so striking that Washington would be lost sight of, and the observer should find himself remarking, "What a splendid river scene!" or "I had no idea such fine boats were possible in the days of the Revolution" —depend upon it, unity has been sacrificed. It is no work of art. The artist has lost sight of his subject. He is not an artist—only a sign painter. He lacks the essential of a true artist—power of harmonious composition. He forgets his purpose in the interest of the execution. He has not the moral courage to paint poorly some parts, when it is so easy to paint them well—to slight details, that the main figure may stand out in bold relief.

The artist, in any line of work, never loses sight of his purpose; always keeps in mind the whole while he is adjusting each part; and resolutely sets his face against beautiful temptations by the wayside. The man of mediocre talent gets lost in the labyrinths of his own creations. He may even excel the master in power of execution, but he knows only indifferently where to emphasize and where to slur. In the first instance the man manages the work; in the second, the work manages the man.

Unity and Music.—Will it be profitable to consider other illustrations of unity? Let the subject be music. Who doubts that in Sousa's band a score of musicians might be found quite as proficient as Sousa himself in the interpretation of music, and perhaps more proficient than the peerless leader in its execution? Wherein, then, lies his pre-eminence as a leader? It is his marvelous sense of unity, his ability to energize or subdue, in short, his ability to manage a hundred instruments of varying sound, volume, and intensity, so that the thought of the composer is expressed in its nicest shades.

Compare with this performance the maddening brass of a country band by which I have lately been tortured. There were a dozen of these merciless instruments agitating the air. Each man played as loud as his neighbor—if his breath held out. It was absolutely a question of lung power. None but a physician could diagnose this music. Oh, it was grand and tall—especially tall! No need to say that the striking feature was want of unity.

Unity in Dress.—Probably in no department are the demands of unity so generally complied with and the want of unity so quickly detected as in dress and personal adornment. Let the young man who is accustomed to wait two agonizing hours in the parlor while his girl in her boudoir is "fixing up," try bravely to possess his soul in patience. He is being sacrificed in a noble cause—the education of his sweetheart in the sense of unity. Could he have but one glimpse within that mystical laboratory of the beautiful, and watch the effect now of this ribbon, then of that lace, as the lovely whole is being harmonized by endless experiment, he would conclude with me that true art, not whimsical fancy was for the time depriving him of her smiles. Happy for him if she has selected the true basis for this unity—her own personality. Too often all things, including the wearer herself, are made to bend to some flashy ornament or costly garment. Steer clear of such a one. She will always seek happiness outside herself. Not so of the girl who honestly "builds her beauty" upon herself —that is, upon her own complexion, face, figure, disposition, and —purse. It is of her that we say: "Everything becomes her, even calico." Depend upon it, she will in the same way, make herself the basis of that greatest of all unities—the unity of the home.

Unity Another Name for Culture.—This question of unity enters into all that we think or say or do. In architecture we as a people are just beginning to realize the meaning of it and to feel pained at the want of it. It is to be hoped that the sense will be fully awakened also in the management of our concerns, our business and other occupation; for without that unity of conception which makes all details bend to one grand purpose, there is no real success in anything. Unity is, in fact, the criterion whence we judge the degree in culture we have attained in any line of thought or work. What is heaven even but a condition in which all things are properly co-ordinated and sub-ordinated according to divine law?

Let me come back again to preaching. I have been copious in my illustrations because I desire young Elders to understand fully the force of unity as applied to composition of any kind, be it painting, or music, or dress, or architecture, or business ventures or preaching. It is the same thing in all: one thing is made the thing, and all its relations are subordinated to it. Success depends upon two things: (1) the choosing of the thing to be made prominent, (2) the making it prominent; that is, the adjustment of all its relations so as to throw the greatest possible light upon it.

Unity in Preaching.—With the more comprehensive view which I trust the reader now has on this point, let us consider specifically the sermon as regards unity. First, then, no sermon can have unity unless it have a purpose. It may have a purpose and still lack unity, for it is not the having, but the constantly keeping in view, the purpose, that insures unity. But lacking a purpose, it may have all the other merits, and it will still be at best a medley.

Nor is it enough that the purpose be a general one as, to do good, to enlighten the congregation on the principles of the Gospel, to get the Saints to renew their diligence, etc. These are not purposes within the meaning of the term as I use it.

To do what good? To get parents to attend diligently to family prayer. Very well, that is a specific purpose. To enlighten on which principle? In what respect? On tithing, and in respect of the spirit in which it is to be paid. To renew their diligence— how? In what respect? In observing fast day, by abstaining so and so, and being actuated by such and such a spirit. Pinning one's self down to a specific purpose prevents wandering, arouses thought, economizes time, and what is best of all, does something.

IV.

EFFECT OF UNITY AND WANT OF UNITY IN THE SERMON.

Vanity, thy Name is Preacher.—Let me ask the young Elder who has just finished the rambling discourse which touched everything in general and nothing in particular: How would you regard yourself if on the road to the field Monday morning, you should discover you really had no definite purpose for going, and then should awaken to the fact that you had no tools with you, and had forgotten to change your Sunday clothes? You cannot conceive of such a lapse of attention. Still, if it did happen, you would be alone with your chagrin, and could go back and prepare yourself for the day's work without letting your neighbors know. But here you have been a whole hour exhibiting just such a condition of mind. And you are not alone this time: hundreds of eyes are upon you, pitying your vacuity. Yet, there you sit upon the stand, apparently pleased that you have "held them an hour!" Vanity, thy name is preacher!

Roust-about Ideas.—Outside of preaching, I call to mind but one occupation where a person may set out to do a thing without a definite purpose in view. That is the occupation of the tramp. Ask the footpad what purpose he has for the day, and he can consistently answer only that he will roust-about.

That may mean going east, west, south, or north; it may be begging, skulking, barn-burning, chicken-stealing, or any other of the possibilities open to this product of the nineteenth century.

No word could be more conveniently general in meaning to suit an empty head, vagrant feet, and sticky fingers than this same word roust-about. For vagueness of purpose, the tramp's negative idea is matched only by the opposite general purpose to do "good," which generally constitutes the end in view of the preacher whose chief qualification is the courage to arise and "let it talk." Instead of the weary legs of Raggles, the rambling instrument in the preacher's case is the tongue. And it is questionable whether the "good" accomplished by the latter is as definite and lasting as is the "bad" accomplished by the former.

My dear young fellow-preachers for whose inexperienced minds I am especially writing: why, you are ready to ask, do I seek to draw my comparisons so scathing? Because I desire to make this reckless talking in the air seem odious; because I am fearful that we shall form the fatal habit of mistaking sound for sense, and thus become too easily satisfied with ourselves; because I desire that we form a high conception of what it means to preach, and then strive to realize that conception in our own preaching. One's usefulness as a preacher will be in the ratio of his ability to preach; hence preaching, both as to forms of expression and power of thought, must be an ever new, an ever fresh study throughout life.

Let us suppose that the first requisite of unity in the sermon, viz., the fixing of a definite purpose in the mind, has been complied with. The question next comes, how shall the Elder avoid losing sight of this purpose? For losing sight of the purpose is little better than having no purpose. It is this point we must discuss now.

The Preacher with Nothing to say.—We will consider first the case commonest of all, the man who has nothing to say. Suppose he has read the passage: "By this shall ye know that ye have passed from death unto life, if ye love the brethren;" his subject might be stated as: The Saints should love one another; and the specific purpose he has in view is to create greater concord and union in this very Ward. So far he has done well. This purpose will be of great aid to him by directing his mind into specific channels.

But now comes the difficulty. What shall he say? He begins probably by saying: "We ought to be more united in this Ward. It is our duty to be more united. To love one another is right in the sight of the Lord, and to hate one another is wrong. It behooves us therefore"—etc. Now this is the end of the whole matter. He can say no more. Twice already he has repeated ideas, and the probability is he will continue in this strain, moving round and round in a circle until the dust of his own tracks flies in his face. His only thought is: "It is good to do it, it is bad not to do it, therefore we ought to do it." As long as he can find new words for the thought, he honestly believes he is giving new thoughts. At length new words fail and he awakens to the fact that he is using the old sentences over again. Perhaps he will justify this by way of clinching the thought; perhaps he will be generous enough to stop.

Want of Power of Suggestion.—What is the matter? The man has not learned to think. His subject, "Love one another," is bristling with suggestion and perhaps his mind is fairly well stored, but he does not know how to question himself. Suppose some good angel could prompt him, each time that he ran short, in some such way as this: "Prove it from the Bible—from the Book of Mormon—from the Doctrine and Covenants. Give examples—from scripture—from history. Relate when it was different with us—our circumstances then—what has caused the change—in what respects we are now disunited. Tell why Latterday Saints especially should love one another—why this Ward should. Show what love does for the family circle—for neighbors—for the community. Make plain how it pays financially—socially—morally—religiously.

Of what interest is it to God that we love one another? Why is heaven impossible unless we learn to do so—etc., etc."

These questions are only a tithe that crowd themselves upon the mind that thinks. The answer to them—keeping the purpose always in view—would make a very interesting discourse—one that would not violate unity.

But no good angel asks the man these questions, and he has not learned to ask them himself, so he has no resource but to sit down, or move on to another subject—then to another—and so on to another, till his time is up. Before such a man shall be able to preach a sermon having unity, he must learn to think.

Uncontrolled Power of Suggestion.—In the case just considered, the real difficulty is a lack of the power of suggestion. In the case which I shall now present, the mind is too full of suggestion; or rather suggestion dominates the mind, leading it in more zigzag and fantastic paths than could any will-o'-the-wisp. Such a mind usually starts headed in the right direction. But three sentences have not been uttered ere some thought needs illustrating. Here begins the difficulty. This mind, lacking the power to keep the whole and its parts in proportionate relations, draws out the comparison to such lengths that it in turn needs illustrating in some intricate part. So the preacher proceeds to illustrate the illustration till his time is up.

But what of the original thought? Gone. Killed by overdressing, and buried in its own finery. Such a mind may set sail for some definite port, laden with choice ideas, but not even the angels of heaven can foretell what island in the sea of thought it will strand upon. The chances too are more than even that some air-spout of fancy will whisp its treasures up and scatter them like spangles upon the heads of the multitude.

An Example of Uncontrolled Suggestion.—While it may be doubted whether a mind can be too richly gifted with suggestion,

PREACHING AND PUBLIC SPEAKING. 153

it is beyond question a weakness not to be able to restrain or direct such a power. I call to mind an Elder whom I met several years ago, a man pre-eminently gifted in this way. It was astonishing the leaps of association he was capable of. From the braying of a donkey to a Chinaman's queue, things utterly dissimilar, was a chain of but two or three links in his mind. I have often pictured his brain as a net-work of mental wires connected and reconnected ten thousand times, so that an impression starting anywhere through eye, or ear, or touch, would almost instantaneously awaken every impression stored within the circumference of his head. Wires or not, such was evidently the state of his mind to judge by the illustrations that poured forth in his preaching, all struggling for life and breath. But he lacked the power of inhibition. Indeed I discovered, that so far from attempting to restrain or direct this faculty, he counted it a particularly fortunate possession,—one that was the secret of his power and popularity. We shall see later how far he was right in this.

After listening to his preaching one day, when his imagination was particularly fertile, I was asked to criticise the sermon. It was early spring, before the leaves had put forth, and we stopped before a poplar tree.

"Here," said I, "do you see this one-year-old sprout, scarcely large enough for a switch. Let that symbolize your opening sentence. When this shall become a tree it may fitly symbolize a perfect sermon. But was yours such a sermon? We shall see. Let each of these buds represent a word in the sentence. Nature, you perceive, is just beginning to build again upon her sermon. To which of these buds will she send her main strength? The top one. Very well. But suppose nature were whimsical, and sent her strength to this bud, it seems a particularly striking one, then to this, then this, and let the top grow but feebly, do you see what a comical little tree (sermon) she would be building? Well, that's you exactly.

"Now, suppose further, that nature chose to let a blue-bell grow from this tiny limb, a larkspur from that, a daisy here, an orange there, and a grotesque thing, say a summer squash, on the top—of course you recognize that all these things may truly be said to be in the imagination of nature—would it not be a remarkable tree? Would it not make people stare? Well, that's you again.

"Your sermon today was nothing like this noble poplar. This tree is a unit—pointing heavenward not only with its trunk but with every branch. The tree you have been building—I scarcely know what it does look like. It is a sprawling vine made up of every green thing that lives, full of flowers of every hue—flowers that bear no fruit.

"Seriously, my friend, dropping the figure, do not be misled by the rapt attention of your audience, into the delusion that you left them wiser or better than you found them. They were simply astonished. An uncultured audience is, in this respect, like the children of the forest that greeted Columbus—pleased with gew-gaws and shining baubles; and that is just exactly how you pleased the people today. True, you said a hundred truths today—each in pretty finery—but they were not connected by other links than the phantasms of your own mind.

"Hereafter, my dear friend, learn a lesson from the poplar. Shoot right upward to the climax of your sermon, having no more branches or foliage than are necessary to support that apex. Have the moral courage to avoid side issues—and I know of no severer test of your moral courage than to refrain from saying pretty things by the side—and you will preach a sermon that has unity, a sermon that will accomplish the purpose you had in view, and actually bear fruit in the lives of your hearers."

V.

UNITY VIOLATED BY MAKING THE SUBJECT TOO BROAD—AN ILLUSTRATION FROM THE SCHOOL ROOM.

In my last chapter I gave the two prevailing instances in which speakers violate unity. The first, wherein the swinging from one thing to another results from poverty of ideas, or inability to round up ideas, is by far the more common. To Elders who feel that this is their special weakness, I respectfully recommend the careful study of those chapters in this book which are devoted to thinking and learning how to think.

The second, wherein want of unity results from inability to control phantasy, is rare, because it goes generally with a highly-cultivated but erratic imagination. Want of unity ought alone to condemn such vagrant posy-gathering. But it comes under even severer criticism as overloading the style with metaphor. But of this I shall speak more at length under the head of imagery and illustration. I have now to name an additional essential of a good subject, the violation of which not only destroys the unity of the discourse, but leaves even the detached fragments vague, hazy, and indistinct as a vanishing cloud. It is this:

A Subject must not be too Broad.—Let me draw an illustration from school-life. Young teachers, like young preachers, are terrified at the thought of running out of material. Especially is this true in the training school, where the lesson is supposed to be a model of preparation and presentation. Thus to be stranded before a class, and have nothing more to say, with a critic teacher in the background taking notes—is a dilemma which embryo teachers instinctively fortify themselves against.

How? you are ready to ask. By refusing to commit themselves

to anything more specific than "arithmetic," "geography," "reading," "U. S. History," etc. I call vividly to mind the consternation of a young teacher at the way I handled a plan which she presented for my inspection. Her exercise was in geography, and she had chosen the subject: North America.

"My dear young lady, what can you possibly say of North America? That is a half-year's work. Choose a more specific subject."

"Well, the United States, then."

"Too broad still."

"Will the New England States do?"

"Hardly; the subject is past all bounds yet. Remember, you have but half an hour. Besides, would it not be well to select something nearer home?"

"Oh, teacher, I dread running out of something to say. How would Utah do?"

"Well, Utah would be a good subject if you had five weeks at your disposal. But you have only half an hour."

This colloquy lasted half an hour, for the critic desired the young aspirant to discover for herself the true principle of human interest. She chose successively, the land surfaces of Utah, then only the mountains, then a part of the mountains, the Wasatch range, and finally was permitted to select from Mount Nebo, Utah valley, the alkali desert, and similarly specific subjects. So, also, descending from the general subject, water surfaces, she was led in the same way to arrange a series of specific subjects such as Utah Lake, Jordan River, the Hot Pots at Midway, etc.—any one of which was alive with interest. So of the vegetation of Utah, the animals of Utah, the political divisions of Utah, the occupations and material improvements of the people, etc. Each great head was sub-divided until the point of sparkling interest was reached.

"Now, Miss R——," said I, "before I took you in hand, you were fearful of running out of something to say; now you seem to be puzzled by the variety of subjects from which to choose. Let the present interest of your pupils decide. Remember, you have a class of boys from eight to twelve years of age, and this is the spring of the year. Think what part of Utah geography these boys are now most interested in, and when you have done so, bring me your plan."

The next morning she brought me this subject well worked out: "Trout-fishing in Provo River." It is needless to say her class bubbled over with enthusiasm. Each boy was eager to contribute what he knew; and from her vantage ground of wider information, the teacher was able to supply many things that the children had not observed. Five minutes did not elapse till there transpired what is the very acme of successful primary teaching. Both teacher and pupils forgot that they were in a school, forgot that a critic teacher was taking notes, forgot that time was passing —till the half-hour ring broke the spell. The teacher looked disappointed; so did her boys. It was a charming vexation all round. Had I been one of those boys, I should have gone fishing that very afternoon, just to verify with my own eyes the new things the teacher had taught me.

Application to Preaching.—Looking over the pages of manuscript that this illustration has taken up I was about to start an apology for my own want of unity; but re-reading it I am convinced that this whole incident in the teacher's experience is germane to the thought under discussion. If any one doubts this, I give him leave to substitute pr for t wherever the word teacher occurs, and I agree to defend the principle involved by the change in each statement. For what is preaching but one of the inferior ways of teaching?—a condition in which the mind is passively engaged (if I may use such apparently contradictory terms) in recording impressions.

The young preacher dreads equally with the young teacher to be "gravelled for want of matter," and, with the same poor judgment, seeks to fortify against the danger by placing a continent of theology between him and his congregation. As in the case of the teacher, he will fail in arousing interest. He is too far away from his hearers. Like the snow on top of the mountains, his theology must flow miles downward ere it can touch thirsty human lips. If he would warm the hearts of his congregation and cause their eyes to sparkle he must imitate the teacher. For as regards the laws of human interest, what are his most sedate hearers but bearded boys and wrinkled girls—a sort of children that have ceased to romp and giggle and chew gum? Somehow, he must keep sub-dividing his theological continent till he gets where the people live, and then make such applications as touch their most vital interests.

Wholesaling the Gospel.—The thought contained in the last paragraph deserves illustration on its own account. Here is an actual case in point:

At a certain conference in the Southern States, I listened an hour and a half to a typical general sermon. The Elder took for his subject the Kingdom of God. A kingdom must have a king. He explained, therefore, our idea of the King. There must be officers. He gave the list. There must be laws. He dwelt upon faith, repentance, baptism, and laying on of hands. There must be privileges and blessings. He illustrated how signs followed the believer. These signs had ceased. He gave a history of the apostasy. An angel was to come again. He gave an account of the restoration, and closed with a sermon on the authenticity of the Book of Mormon!

His fellow Elders gasped at the longevity of his memory. They wondered whether he would leave them a single patch of Orson Pratt's works. He didn't. He put his foot into every subject within the covers of this most excellent treatise. True, he took huge strides, disdaining to touch any but high points. Like some airy giant, his mind stepped quite over the valley, where lived the hearts of the people, and touched again on the opposite mountain top.

All that lay between could of course be discussed by his companions when their turns came; but somehow they felt exasperated that he had thus straddled over it all. For if the truth must be confessed, they were not any more familiar with specific fields of thought than he. These were the very points they would have taken.

Happily he was quite consistent: he took up all the time as well as all the subjects. Night came on and sleep would undo the mischief. In a few hours they might begin again as if nothing had been said. It was quite certain that but very few fragments of this extenuated, loose-jointed sermon would remain upon the memories of the audience next morning. For if five thousand years' study of psychology has made anything clear, it is the utter futility of attempting to plant islands in the human mind. Growth can occur only by accretion. The new can remain in the mind only as it is attached to and absorbed by the old. In the missionary field, so small is the basis of the old, so few the associations to which the new can be attached, that the Elder who takes a hop, skip, and jump through the scheme of salvation need never fear—nor hope either —that the impressions he makes will last over night.

VI.

EFFECT IN THE MISSIONARY FIELD OF SWEEPING GENERAL-IZATIONS.

A Specific Subject.—When conference assembled next morning President Morgan arose to speak. As if to rebuke this cataloguing style of preaching, the spirit led him to choose a very small subdivision of the subject of repentance. This he spoke of in terms with which the people were familiar, drawing his illustrations from their daily lives. Every eye was upon him, every ear was alert, and every heart was stirred as by something divine. His manner was gentle, his words direct and unaffected. I shall not soon forget the effect produced upon me by this unostentatious discourse, nor the impression left upon this simple-minded people. To this day they remember Elder Morgan as a "pow'ful fine preacher."

I was then able only in a vague way to understand why this sermon was so much more effective than the other. It did not convey a hundredth part the number of Gospel truths that the first conveyed; yet as a means of converting minds and hearts, it is no exaggeration to say it did a hundred times the work of the first. So manifest was this difference in general effect, that it set me to thinking and observing; and now I know the reason why one was futile and the other fertile in reclaiming souls.

Effect of Sweeping Generalizations.—Setting aside what was lost through delivery by the first—who spoke to a few hundred cubic feet of air in which people happened to be—and setting aside likewise what was gained in delivery by the second—who spoke directly to human ears while he looked into human eyes—I say, setting the elocutionary aspect of these two sermons aside for discussion in a later chapter, there was enough difference in the matter treated, to account for the almost opposite effects produced.

Think of it! the first speaker went over twenty subjects each one of which, if carefully and logically subdivided, would furnish matter for ten sermons. Sweeping generalizations one after another were hurled upon the audience in breathless haste, and then in the vain hope of fastening them upon the mind—if we may suppose so much thought to have been taken concerning the effect—each general dogma was cunningly "nail't wi' scripture," as Burns would say.

How should the results be otherwise? Such generalizations can be of vital interest only to men familiar with all the intervening ground. The reading of an index often suffices the mind of a scholar as to the contents of the volume; but to the uncultured mind it would be utterly meaningless. What power of apperception has the ordinary audience of the Mormon missionary? As well throw stones at them as sweeping generalizations. They must be spoken to as you would speak to children. Be satisfied if a single principle, which can be stated and proved from scripture in one minute, is understood and felt after one hour devoted to simple illustration.

The Circle of Experience.—Now the second speaker took into account the kind of people he was about to address, the bias of their minds, the easiest point of attack—in a word, he sought the directest route to their hearts. Thus, realizing that he had infant minds to deal with, he took but a single truth and spread it out so widely in illustration that the weakest could not fail to digest it. And it gave immediate pleasure. Nothing gives keener pleasure than mental digestion—just as nothing will more quickly sicken the soul than mental indigestion.

It is the case of teaching over again. Whenever you carry principle into the domain of personal experience men, like children, are interested at once; and this because they become judges, able to verify for themselves the truths presented. But until you do come thus within that magic circle—the circle of experience—which varies in diameter with every human being, your words will remain vague, meaningless, incapable of arousing interest.

Make a Mental Analysis of Your Audience.—Here then we Elders should learn a profound lesson. Instead of loading our minds with passages of scripture and firing them indiscriminately upon an audience, we should make a mental analysis of our hearers. What do they know already? What principles guide them? What prejudices blind them? In a word, how near is their mental horizon, and what are the objects within the magic circle of their experience?

These questions answered, we are ready to proceed. Keeping in view the fact that the unknown can be apperceived or assimilated only as it is directly associated with and absorbed, so to speak, by the known, all our truths will be clothed in the mental experiences of our audience. We need not be mistaken as to the right direction, if we but keep our wits about us. As long as we are giving new, fresh truths and are within the mental horizon of our listeners, their eyes will sparkle with the same interest that aroused the boys to enthusiasm in the lesson on fishing. When we get beyond their mental horizon, or when we are repeating hackneyed truths, their eyes grow lackadaisical, even though their attention remain apparently respectful.

Mistakes in Gathering Material for Sermons.—But do our Elders make such a study? What are the facts in the case? In very many instances they have but vague notions of the Gospel they set out to proclaim. Thrown into the labor with such ill preparations, their first thought is to get thoroughly acquainted with the principles they are to preach. Too often this comes to be the only thought. They load themselves up on the Bible and Orson Pratt's Works, and preach what clings to their memory—which, as we have seen in the case cited, is the high points only. They feel they must hold out a certain time; they have not the mind-power to think in detail; so there is nothing to do but to pass from subject to subject. No attempt is made at unity, unless it be the unity of chronology. Sometimes the order in which the passages have been committed to memory furnishes a kind of link to chain together the fragments.

When all is said, however, the sermon is made up of a succession of subjects, each one of which is too broad to rouse human interest. But what is worse, human interest, that is, the people addressed and the occasion, is not taken into account at all. What is the result? No impression is made. The Elders are not invited home. They trudge on in the middle of the night, believing that there are no honest hearts in this region, no one in whose veins flows the blood of Israel!

The fact is, my dear brethren, we swallow in haste unmasticated mouthfuls of the Gospel, and then literally "take no thought," but with a blind fatuity trust that the Spirit will arrange it all in our heads while we sleep. But it comes out of our heads just as crude and undigested as we stowed it away there; for God is not so poor a teacher as to put a premium on laziness by doing our work for us.

What a mockery it is then to judge as if we were perfect and all the fault lay with our hearers! Just apply this thought to teaching. Let a teacher be as crude in his method of presentation as are many of our preachers, and he would stay no longer in a place than they do.

Let us Learn from Every Source.—One word more in this connection. Let us never become so wise in our own conceit that we cannot learn a lesson from everything. Above all, let us cease ridiculing the success of sectarians in making converts. I do not say we shall imitate them. Far from it. But let us study their methods of reaching the human soul. If men can be won to such doctrines as are often preached by them, then surely the merit must lie in the method of presentation; it cannot be in the thing presented. Let us not be caught by external trumpery, such as anxious seats, mourners' benches, tambourines, drums, and hallelujah excitements. Let us rather watch by what avenues the human heart is approached. I think we shall discover that we disdain any other than the intellectual avenue, which in nine cases out of ten is closed. But are not the emotions as God-given as the intellect? Must all be damned save those who are reached through our dry reasoning on principle?

Think of this a moment. We do not succeed by it even in the few we actually convert. In a majority of cases they are first interested in the Gospel through their emotions. It is because they have learned to love the Elders, not because they are struck with the principles they advocate, nor with our manner of advocating them, that they first begin to investigate. How often the remark has reached me—in a few instances made by men who afterwards were baptized: "Nelson is a fine fellow, but d—— his doctrines!" (It will be seen from this remark that I have been making a righteous judgment, that is, I have been judging my own mistakes.)

Less Extension—More Intension.—But, after all, what is all this but saying in a specific way that it is as much a missionary's duty to study the people as to study the Gospel. For his presentation of the plan of salvation, if it is to do any good, must take into account the conditions in which his listeners are placed. In other words, he can reach the human soul only through the channels that are open. To ignore this fact is to make his sermon thrice a "sounding brass and a tinkling cymbal;" which leads me to remark that the sermons first to be condemned by this rule are those preached from subjects too broad; for they do not even get down to the regions where people live, let alone find their way to men's hearts.

The defect I have been criticising is technically called Extension. The virtue I would have our preachers cultivate is Intension. The latter may also be carried to a ridiculous extreme. It is said of a noted professor of theology in a German university that he preached fourteen sermons on the first verse in Genesis! But we are in no danger from this extreme, nor shall we be for years to come. I know of only one speaker in the Church who is guilty of it. His mind becomes so intense when it reaches some important phase of a subject, that it frequently refuses to move forward for a whole hour together; but in the midst of the general tendency to roam and get over ground, this is a most refreshing fault.

VII.

GENERAL EFFECTS OF TRITENESS AND INDEFINITENESS.

The size and quality of the pattern must largely determine the kind of garment made of it. So well is this fact recognized, that our sisters often exhibit a recent purchase as a new "dress" ere the cloth has been touched by the scissors. In a similar sense, the sermon is largely made when the subject is chosen. If a subject is not chosen, there will be no sermon, any more than there would be a dress without a pattern. There may be a wandering talk, just as there might be an aimless clipping and stitching of scraps; but nothing in the former could possibly compare in utility with what may be the product of the latter—the crazy quilt; for the reason that ideas will not lodge in crazy-patch fashion in the fabric of the mind. I have devoted much space already to the necessity of choosing a subject, and to a discussion of principles that should guide us in such a choice. The importance of a correct selection of the pattern and material for a sermon, must be my apology for taking up the subject again. Besides being a unit, and not being too broad.—

A Subject Should be Fresh.—Stale ideas are taken in by the mind, just as stale food is received by the palate—necessity not interest opens the door to them. In the case of food the necessity happens often; in the case of ideas, rarely; for rather than entertain such humdrum guests, the mind instinctively chooses the alternative of wandering in the fields of phantasy, or of taking a nap.

It goes without saying, therefore, that he who preaches upon a stale subject preaches in vain. No amount of sophistry about its being good for us to hear these things often will alter the facts. Minds do not accommodate themselves to theories contrived as apology or justification for mental laziness. Such an after-talk by a Bishop may soothe the vanity of an Elder who is conscious that his hackneyed sermon has interested nobody; but it will not recall the yawns that have escaped during the dull hour, nor will it bring anything but a pitying retrospect to the minds of the congregation.

This is what it will do: It will make coming to meeting seem a duty in the sense of not being a pleasure. It will stultify all vigorous mind-activity, and throw a flavor of goody-good insipidity over things religious. In the minds of young people, it will make the exclamations, "Oh, he's too religious!" and "He's too soft!" mean about the same thing.

Effects of Stale Sermons.—Young people do not have the charity for platitudes that their parents exhibit—which on the whole is to be counted a promise of better things. Till better things come, however, the blatherskite infidel and the mystic conjurers of occultism, now so numerous among us, will gratify these young people's craving for the new, the fresh, and the vigorous in mental activity. The library of fiction and the pleasure resort will capture that portion who have not a strong intellectual bent. The class that remain then, the class that go to meeting with their fathers and mothers, certainly deserve praise for filial obedience, but are they the flower of Zion? They will be the fruit, certainly; for the bloom of the others will be blasted; but in the sight of heaven, which gave the greater promise? Hitherto we have located the blame for going astray entirely on one side—the side of those that go astray—assuming perfection in those who have the care and feeding of the flock. Will it not be a healthful thing to reverse this judgment for a season?

When I consider that we have the whole world of truth to choose from and have the Spirit of truth moreover to guide us in this choice, I have very little patience or charity for an Elder that inflicts a threadbare sermon upon his congregation. He does not deserve letting down easy by the presiding officer. If he be a young man, nothing should stand between him and the disgust he has called up to the faces of his hearers. Not until speakers are made to feel what a contemptible advantage they take of fellow beings temporarily placed under their voices, shall we have young Elders striving to prepare themselves with something fresh and interesting to say.

Sermons that have Departed this Life.—It may not be unprofitable to consider some of the tendencies that lead to the iteration and reiteration of sermons and parts of sermons that have long ago departed this life. This phase of the subject has already been touched incidentally a number of times; notably in connection with the discussion of the wide-spread tendency among our Elders to gather thought ready-made, rather than think. Where we have speakers of this kind, the inevitable result is a repetition that grows more and more stale and fragmentary with the years.

It is inconsistent perhaps to expect anything fresh and interesting from a preacher that has not acquired the habit of thinking. For he that gets his thoughts from others must at best be second-hand in giving them again. If he be a great reader, however, he may still escape triteness, and may even be interesting. But when as is too often the case, his mind has had a period of growth which ceased years ago and has since become case hardened, it plays thereafter but one wearisome tune; a tune that grows more wearisome as the chords of memory snap one by one, and the mannerisms, feeble at first, become more pronounced and offensive.

An Illustrative Incident.—It is related of a certain Bishop that he had half a dozen Elders of the latter kind who for a period of fifteen years spoke by turns on the Sabbath day.

No sooner was the preacher for the occasion fairly started than the good old man sat back in his easy chair and snored complacently till the sermon was done. Then, aroused as by the sudden ceasing of a familiar lullaby, he would get up and repeat by way of endorsement the leading points set forth.

This ability to sleep and at the same time keep track of the speaker often puzzled visitors. But to regular attendants it was not an astonishing feat. They could all do it. They need not even be present. They might on a Sunday afternoon take their naps on the more comfortable lounges at home, and yet so potent would be the speaker's influence, that his name had but to be mentioned to bring all the points of his sermon to mind.

Was not Sunday a day of rest? What more ideal way of observing it than to sleep and yet lose none of the Gospel truths set forth! So, evidently, thought the good father of the flock, for he rarely permitted a man afflicted with fresh ideas to take the stand. It made him uneasy, and seriously disturbed the Sabbath day for him.

In the chapters of this treatise relating to thinking versus thought gathering, I have sufficiently discussed the chances of improving this class in native thought-power; which power, in its relation to the subject now under consideration, means the chances of getting something fresh from such minds. They are small, indeed, and charity should deter me from alluding to these cases at all, did I not see the fossilizing process going on every day in the case of young men right in the Improvement Associations. We can afford to let the few of the older preachers who are thus hide-bound speak their stereotyped sermons in their stereotyped way, but let us have no servile imitators among the young.

Fresh in Science but Stale in Religion.—But it is not alone those whose minds years ago closed in, like a net, on a single haul of ideas, that give us stale food on the Sabbath day. Men of scholastic attainments who are ever alert to the recent and fresh in science and art, have, on the subject of religion, permitted stationary habits of thoughts to intrench themselves. Their sermons often remind one of the primitive lamp-post with its coal oil wick still aflame under the intense glare of the arc-light overhead, and feebly dancing to the rumble of electric cars! On the material achievements of this marvelous age, their minds flash and scintillate, but when called upon for religious ideas, they merely flicker with the light of bygone days.

It is not the fault of idleness, for these men are never idle. Fourteen hours a day they are delving for the treasures of science and art. Days and even weeks they do not feel are thrown away on the merest detail of their favorite subjects. And special preparations are always made to contribute something fresh and interesting whenever they have an opportunity to appear before their fellows by address or essay. Nor are the relationships which the people bear to these investigations neglected. Mankind is studied from the point of view of politics, sociology, and political economy. Books are read, magazines scanned, original theories made. Every new discovery is tried mentally upon society. Enthusiasm is aroused. Men become interested in men as well as in things.

This I call genuine study. This is investigation which touches fresh things and arouses human interest. But how much of such study is devoted to religion? Do these men read the revelations of God daily, and ponder how the truths of the life eternal can be adapted to the varying needs of humanity? Are the people studied from a religious point of view? Do these men spend days and weeks gathering fresh and interesting material to impart to religious gatherings?

Thinking is Something, though Raw and Crude.—Alas, their rule is also, "Take no thought." From a political, a social, an economic point of view we must take care of ourselves and hence we do our level best to make life fresh and interesting. From the point of view of religion we belong to the Lord, and the Lord will take care of his own. This is the logic of their actual practice, whatever be their conscious theories.

Thus when they arise to speak the chances are ten to one that they will choose a hackneyed subject, and perhaps treat it in a hackneyed way. But generally, being accustomed to thinking, they will get beyond hackneyed lines; which means that they will begin thinking on the subject perhaps for the first time as they stand before the audience.

But even such an effort—disproportioned, loose-jointed, full of repetitions and other crudities of the work-shop as it must inevitably be—is a genuine relief to the congregation that has resigned itself to its fears of a trite sermon.

How humiliated would these same men feel, however, if they acquitted themselves no better before a literary or a scientific society! What apologies they would deem it necessary to make if they were caught so unprepared in a lecture or an address! Yet from the Sabbath meeting they go home quite undisturbed in their feelings. Perhaps this is to be explained by the supposition that the evil one is persuading them that they have done extraordinarily well!

We Must Prepare for Preaching.—These then are some of the general tendencies that lead to triteness in the choice of subjects for sermons. I need not have enumerated them. There is really but one cause. We make no study of preaching. Our only resource is to imitate. The natural instinct in man as in animals is to follow a leader. In most of our preaching one Elder copies from another both as to matter and manner. This being the case, it would be as idle to look for freshness in these reiterated sermons as to expect dew drops to glisten on a dusty trail.

Ere this prime requisite of a sermon can be reached we must prepare ourselves for preaching from two sides: from the side of the subject matter, that we may have something interesting to speak about; and from the side of the people, that we may know how to preach, what to preach, and when to preach. The latter is a most vital consideration. It is not ten days since I heard a splendid sermon wasted because the speaker did not take into account the mental calibre of his hearers.

VIII.

WANT OF CLEARNESS AND WHAT IT LEADS TO.

The last chapter was devoted to the thought that the subject of a sermon must be fresh. Now, while the general means of avoiding triteness must be the accumulation of a large and varied store of information on the one hand; and on the other, the forming of a nice judgment as to what is best to present on a given occasion—it may be remarked that want of freshness like want of unity may often be avoided by avoiding indefiniteness in the subject, and this brings me to the consideration of another essential, viz:

A Subject Should be Clear.—To be quite clear concerning a subject is to know its limitations, that is, to know exactly what it includes and what it excludes. It will thus be seen that unity in one sense depends upon clearness, for manifestly one cannot make a unit of a subject whose limitations are not known. So, too, insisting upon clearness enables a speaker to avoid subjects that are too broad; and since making a subject clear is tracing in outline where the discussion of it will lead to, a speaker thus forewarned is assisted, by having a clear subject, to avoid that which is trite and stale.

Take for illustration the oft-chosen topic, Faith. As here stated, it violates all the essentials of a good subject. First, it violates unity. Life is not long enough for any one being to develop, co-ordinate, and subordinate all the relations of which Faith is the grand unit. The entire scheme of salvation is nothing but a grand unity of which Faith is the center. God only can preach a sermon on Faith, as the word thus stands alone; and he requires for the effort all that grand period which spans the chasm between the two eternities—the chasm which we call time.

The life-time of man, and all that transpires upon the face of the earth in one generation, is but a single paragraph, perhaps but a single sentence, in this eternal theme. If unity may be compared to a tree, then mortality has not soil enough to ground the roots, nor atmosphere to feed the leaves of the tree of which Faith is the trunk.

What would be thought of the man who started to build a house large enough to lodge the inhabitants of the earth? Yet his mind would be no more Quixotic than that of the Elder who expects to preach a sermon having unity on the subject of Faith.

The subject is too broad. This point need not be discussed in view of what has been said in the previous paragraphs. It is because it is too broad that it has no unity. Ten quarto volumes might touch some of the more prominent relations wherein "faith" affects human relations, but no man that knows what he is about will try to bestride the subject in one short hour.

Faith as a Subject is Trite.—Although this topic is so often chosen in just this form, no Elder, as a matter of fact, ever speaks upon it, as it stands thus alone and unqualified. An analysis of any sermon on this subject shows that although the great whole is before the mind of the speaker, he can touch it only by speaking of some infinitesimal part; as, a definition of it, circumstances under which it is manifested, its power in healing the sick, etc.

Now this is the very place where triteness comes in. Each speaker makes the same mistake of trying to cover the grand whole, which, of course, leads to triteness in opening remarks. Then as each finds the task impossible, there is nothing to do but make a running comment on the salient aspects of the subject. But this leads to a sameness in treatment; for leading features strike nearly all preachers alike. The result is a sermon on Faith, which one feels like running away from.

Triteness Illustrated.—If it will make my thought

PREACHING AND PUBLIC SPEAKING. 173

clearer, suppose we substitute "the Earth" for "Faith." I choose this grand globe because one can put his arms around the equator just about as easily as his mind can reach around "Faith."

Conceive then a man—say an Enochite—a few hundred miles out in space viewing the earth as it revolves beneath him. It is his business to describe what he sees to his fellow-citizens of the translated city—if my readers will indulge my use of the pretty fable. If he have one of the mental weaknesses of his untranslated brethren, he will entitle his lecture "the Earth"—taking the whole globe at one swoop. Of course he can say nothing specific on so broad a subject, unless celestial hours are longer than terrestrial. What will he do then? If he be mentally lazy like some of his brethren below, his lecture will be a skipping comment on ocean, island, and continent as they pass by—with perhaps now and then the mention of some such striking phenomena as a snow-capped peak or lurid volcano.

Now, if his listeners have the charity of mortals for such an effort, he will repeat it and eventually make it the tune of his life. Then imitators will spring up all over the land and spread the affliction. Week after week, year after year, the wretched, loose-jointed thing will be reiterated. And when the audience shows signs of impatience, the speaker will appeal to their long-suffering by urging that he has nothing new; what he is about to give they have all witnessed and could themselves give as well as he; but, nevertheless, it is good to hear these things often by way of stirring up remembrance, etc.

The dose is thus swallowed again. But at each successive time that it goes down, the soul gets sicker. At last a general weariness spreads over the land. The sight of the lecturer starts mental nausea, and at length the conclusion is reached that the fault lies chiefly in him, and not in his listeners.

A much Needed Revolution.—The conviction is now forced upon a man here and there that perhaps the old way is not the best way to lecture. The earth is scanned anew. Marvels unheard of burst upon the view. Telescopes are invented. The details of terrestrial life are studied. A new science, Earthography, is invented. Ten thousand books are written about the wonders of the new world. The records of Enoch are searched and it is discovered that this is the identical planet from which their city was taken. Interest is stimulated a thousand-fold by the prediction that the city is to be restored, that this world is to be their future heaven!

What a revolution has taken place in the domain of mind simply because men began original investigation, instead of waiting to catch echoes from one another! No subject can now compare in popular interest with the once wearisome theme.

Perhaps I should beg pardon for my too thinly disguised illustration. I am certain that I should apologize for attributing the plodding qualities of earth to translated beings, however valuable the lesson to be taught thereby. But after all is said, is not my simile true? Is not much of our preaching quite as crude as the lecture I have described? Are its effects not the same? And may we not predict just such universal interest in our religion, if it be but studied aright? Nay, must not such methods prevail, ere Zion's pre-eminence will be recognized in the world? But recurring to the topic, Faith, I remark:

The Subject is not Clear.—It is impossible to say what part of Faith will be treated when the whole is thus taken as a subject. One thing only is certain: the whole will not be treated. The chances preponderate that no one part will be treated. The sermon will be made up of the superficialities of many parts without definite order.

It is this very want of definiteness in the subject that is so perplexing and misleading. As before remarked, want of clearness leads to want of unity, to triteness, and to undertaking subjects that are too broad. Let a preacher realize clearly the extent of

Faith as a subject, and he will not blindly launch out upon it. On the contrary, he will divide it and subdivide it till he gets a subject of which he perceives the limitations. Where a preacher knows beforehand just what to exclude and what to include, there is little danger that he will fail to interest and instruct his hearers, for no man willingly bores a congregation. When this happens it is through ignorance or want of preparation; and nothing more evidently shows ignorance or want of preparation than blindly hacking away at an indefinite subject.

Subjects that are indefinite may generally be known by the fact that, like Faith, they stand alone, as: Virtue, Honesty, Tithing, Baptism, Truth, etc. Such subjects may be made clear by adding words to qualify their meaning, as: "No greatness without virtue," "A virtuous character necessary to the enjoyment of the Spirit of God," "Honesty in the home circle," "It pays to be honest in dealing with the Lord," etc.

It will be seen that making clear any of the usual subjects of the Sabbath day, means nothing more than applying abstract principles to definite relations of life. But, this is the very thing that gives freshness and arouses interest.

It will also be seen that every clear subject is a proposition to be proved, or a relationship that requires definite explanation. Clearness in the subject is thus a powerful aid to the speaker in preventing mind wandering and in rounding up ideas. Like a lantern in a dark night, such a subject keeps his attention in one definite direction. He has but to keep the light in view and follow the bent of his thought in order to say something progressive and coherent from start to finish. That he may speedily learn to do this, is a "consummation devoutly to be wished."

Summary of Essential Qualities.—This finishes the discussion of the essential qualities of a good subject. It may be well to recapitulate:

I.— In order that a subject may be suitable to a congregation: (1) It must be interesting; (2) it must be timely; and (3) it must be in keeping with the intelligence addressed.

II.—In order that the preacher may make the most of a subject: (1) It must be of special interest to him; (2) it must command his implicit faith; and (3) it must not be above his powers.

III.—In order that a subject may be appropriate in itself: (1) It must have unity; (2) it must not be too broad; (3) it must be fresh; and (4) it must be clear.

With these ten points it will be well for every young Elder to become as familiar as with his fingers. Let him think about them till he feels the full force of each, and he will not fail in time to become an interesting speaker. Nor are they of benefit to the preacher alone. They apply as well to the essay, the story, the address, the lecture, the oration, as to the sermon. No man ever succeeded, or ever will succeed, in influencing his fellowmen for good save as he did it or shall do it, by observance of these principles. They are by no means all the essentials that go to make a good preacher, but they constitute a splendid start. In the succeeding chapters I shall consider the principles involved in the style or composition of a sermon, the merits and defects of delivery, and those graces and qualifications that constitute a fine bearing and magnetic personality in a speaker.

CHAPTER VI.

KINDS OF SERMONS.

I.

DEVOTED TO THOSE WHO RIDICULE RHETORIC, ELOCUTION, AND KINDRED STUDIES.

In the series of chapters which has just closed, we have considered at length ten characteristics of good subjects for sermons. The thing next to consider is how to make good sermons out of good subjects. While no man can make a good suit out of poor cloth, it is by no means certain that he will make a good suit out of good cloth. Other things equal, the kind of suit he will make will depend entirely upon his ability to cut, fit, and make up. In like manner, other things equal, a sermon will be good, bad, or indifferent according to the preacher's ability to compose.

Meaning of Composition.—But composition as ordinarily used has so narrow a meaning that a few words in explanation seem necessary. I can, for instance, imagine some of my readers saying: "Well, I don't believe in composing sermons. That smacks too much of sectarianism. What is 'composing a sermon' but cutting and drying it and getting it all ready to speak like a piece?"

To such young men composition means the irksome task of transferring thought to paper. There is in this sense a painful farewell clinging to the word. It reminds them of school days when the agony of essay-writing recurred at stated intervals in connection with language work. Nor is this memory keen and hateful without good grounds. So wretched have been composition-methods in the past that I have known whole classes to look forward to the day with a dread not unlike that with which the victim of ague awaits the chills and fever.

"And so they want us to 'compose' our sermons now. Well, that lets me out. I don't want to preach, if that's the case. I don't think I could enjoy the Spirit if I had to 'compose.' Judging by past recollections, I am afraid I should breathe something bad into the Gospel."

Now, it has perhaps not occurred to such preachers that every thought they ever uttered is composition, and differs from the bugbear sentence-making of their school-boy memory, only in not being set down between the capital letter and the period. 'Compose' —why, you cannot escape it save by suicide. Every question you ask, every explanation you make, every story you tell, every sermon you preach, every prayer you utter—is composition. You have composed volumes already, and volumes remain yet for composition. One of these is undoubtedly a love story, more thrilling perhaps (to you) than anything Dickens ever penned.

Of course these volumes are not in black and white, which on the whole must be counted a blessed thing for humanity. I make this last remark deliberately: for the fact that you hate composition-writing is strong evidence that you do it poorly; and the reason you especially hate composing on paper is that you are made to gaze upon your own creations; whereas composing upon the air, i. e. preaching, relieves you from looking upon the deformities of the children of your brain. In the latter case the pleasure and agony are unjustly divided: you get the first, and your audience the last.

Now as regards ninety-nine per cent of the composition-work that Latterday Saint Elders must do in life I take no concern in this series other than to remark in passing that their success in any line will be commensurate with their ability to compose or express thought in that line; on the one subject of preaching, however, I am very much concerned; not only because it is the purpose of

PREACHING AND PUBLIC SPEAKING. 179

this book to be so concerned, but also because I shall listen to sermons, and the composition thereof will be to me a source of pleasure or pain according to the skill or want of skill of the preachers. The choosing of a subject has been discussed at some length, profitably it is hoped, and it will now be in order to consider the kinds of sermons, under what circumstances each kind is appropriate, and how to compose, on any given subject, the kind of sermon best suited for the occasion.

Elders that Sneer at Rhetoric and Elocution.—Before proceeding directly to this theme, let me indulge one more paragraph by way of preface. Many of our Elders speak sneeringly of rhetoric, elocution, and kindred studies in connection with preaching. If some Elder has delivered a particularly telling sermon they remark in describing it: "That was preaching which went to the heart—no display of rhetoric or elocution there." And thus they seek to convey the thought that these studies tend to artificiality—that they are trappings which a speaker wears as he may a fancy cloak, to be put on or laid aside as occasion may demand.

In the first place, it is quite safe to say that these critics have never looked inside a work on rhetoric; and in the second place, they probably base their estimate of these studies upon the vain struttings of amateurs whose rhetorical smattering has all run into vanity. People who make a vain show of oratory can scarcely be said to have studied rhetoric, save in the sense that Pat went through college; for against no other fault is rhetoric so severe in its condemnation as against the vapid, empty displays of would-be rhetoricians.

Real Meaning of Rhetoric and Elocution.—The fact is, rhetoric makes a business of studying whatever is effective in composition, and seeks to know why it is effective; and the same is true of elocution as regards delivery. The body of laws and principles presented by these sciences are the observations and deductions of ages as to the most effective way of communicating ideas;

and it is quite safe to say that no man ever excelled in the composition or the expression of thought, save as he did so by compliance with these laws and principles.

But what of this great writer and that great speaker—men who never took a single lesson in these arts? I repeat, their triumphs are due solely to their practical application of the principles and laws on which these arts are founded. They may not know that they are following laws of art, any more than does the flower-girl who arranges a bouquet to perfection, although she may not consciously know the first definition in the science of the harmony of colors. It is a mistake to suppose that the only rhetoricians are those who have studied rhetoric. It is equally a mistake for those who find themselves possessed of a natural literary taste to imagine that they do not need to cultivate language, or for those who find themselves naturally gifted with oratory to imagine they need not study elocution. And if these need to study the laws of composition and delivery, how much more do they need to do it who have no natural taste!

Let us then hear no more ridiculing of these important aids to self-culture. The man who indulges in such sneers exhibits simply his own stupidity. Let him rather surround himself with a number of first-class text-books on these neglected branches, and seek thereby to improve daily his oral and written expression.

II.

THE RELATIVE VALUE OF ORAL AND WRITTEN SERMONS.

My last chapter brings me to a point where I may remark upon the difficulties of writing a treatise on preaching. I am dealing with a very technical subject, which, to be treated in a scientific way, must presuppose a class of readers familiar with rhetorical principles and laws. But I cannot proceed on such an assumption.

PREACHING AND PUBLIC SPEAKING. 181

I must write for readers many of whom are unfamiliar even with grammar. As compensation for this deficiency they are, I believe, more than ordinarily gifted with native common sense. It is to this faculty I shall address my remarks on the composition and delivery of sermons. It remains to be seen whether I shall succeed in making the subject intelligible.

Variety of Sermons.—To begin, then, let me observe that the sermons or discourses we listen to in this Church differ widely from one another, not merely as regards degree of perfection, but as regards almost any other particular that may be used as a criterion. Perhaps there are but few of my readers who have not already made this observation. Manifestly then, before we shall be able to proceed intelligibly, it will be necessary to classify if possible these various methods of preaching.

It is a very important consideration to know the value and general tendency of each kind of sermon. A day or two ago I had occasion to witness the dexterity of a certain carpenter at work. He had a dozen tools about him that I had never seen before. Upon my remarking this fact he said: "Yes, I can get through as much work in a day as three ordinary carpenters with the old-time tools. You see each of these is adapted for a particular kind of work and does it better and faster than any possible combination of other tools." And I thought how effective preaching might be made if the preacher were but well acquainted with all his tools and knew exactly when and how to use each!

But to classify all the oral compositions that pass under the name of preaching is a most difficult thing to do. For instance, from what point of view shall they be judged? Perhaps we shall gain some useful hints, if we classify them in turn from various points of view.

Oral and Written Sermons.—One classification might be based on the method of composing—whether it be oral or written, and whether, if oral, it be studied or extemporaneous. On this head there is little to say. The oral method is the only one that obtains favor among the Latterday Saints—I might even say, the oral impromptu or unstudied. The low ebb to which our preaching has sunk is owing to this latter qualification. Oral composition may be good, but impromptu composition is generally bad. You perceive I am harping on my old complaint. We take no thought, but on the spur of the moment speak what happens to come into our heads. If I were a believer in chance creations, I might have a little hope that sermons logical and forceful would eventually grow out of this catch-as-catch-can method of preaching; but as it is, I have grave fears that each succeeding generation will grow more desultory and scatter-brained, if the method continues.

As to written sermons I have no desire to change the concurrent opinion of our people. I take this stand not because of the argument that the Spirit cannot inspire a written sermon as well as an oral one. Latterday Saints know better than this. It was by the written, not the oral sermon that the Presidency communicated with the Church during the raid. But I favor the oral because it is the natural, the untrammeled way to the human heart. The true preacher is the spiritual focus of his congregation. Their dumb wants and aspirations flow toward and converge in him, and he by the aid of the Spirit bends back the silent current, transmuting it into a golden stream of articulated truths. Now if he be not within the influence of such human heart-throbs while composing, he may indeed invent expressions for these truths, but will his inventions chime with the feelings of his hearers?

Sit Down and Write out a Dozen Sermons. —But while, on general principles, I should oppose the writing method of composing sermons, still if asked to prescribe the directest cure for the ills of Latterday Saint preaching, I should say to nine Elders out of ten: "Sit down and write out a dozen sermons!" Nor is there the least suggestion of irony in this advice, although I am well aware

PREACHING AND PUBLIC SPEAKING. 183

that I could take no keener vengeance on the rambling preacher than to make such a requirement of him.

"Reading," says Lord Bacon, "maketh a full man, conversation a ready man, and writing an exact man." Now exactness is one of the things we need most. Our thoughts, like little chickens, scatter aimlessly over the field of discussion. It needs the eagle eye of exactness hovering over to call them in and make them move to one common impulse. By the time the first sermon is written, these Elders will have been brought face to face with their vagueness, with their meaningless repetition of worn-out phrases, and with their aimless scattering of random thoughts. They will discover also that, as in the case of the chickens, their ideas hitherto spread out through an hour or more of desultory talk, can be brought together in a surprisingly small space.

If this knowledge could be brought home to our preachers, who can calculate the life and force that would come at once to our Sunday meetings? Writing out a few sermons will do it. I do not mean that these sermons are to be read after they are written. They are solely for the benefit of the preachers. I only urge that the doctor occasionally swallow his own pills, that he may properly judge of their effect upon his patients.

III.

SERMONS BASED ON THE NATURE OF THE CONGREGATION—
DOCTRINAL SERMONS.

A second classification of sermons might be based on the nature of the congregation addressed. Here we shall have to take into account the age and the general intelligence of the hearers, and the nature of the meeting. Let us consider first how age should make a difference in the sermon.

Nature of the Congregation.—Under this head we have to consider the nature of remarks appropriate for the Primary association, for Sunday school, for the M. I. associations, and for general Sabbath meetings. It is surely plain to all that age alone must make a difference in the kind of sermon suitable for these different associations. Not only must the delivery vary, but the subject-matter, and the manner of treating it, i. e., by narration, by description, by exposition, by argument, or by persuasion, must likewise be adapted to a different order of mind activity with each age. Clear as is this distinction in theory, I have seen very few Elders capable of observing it in practice. If called, for instance, to address a Sunday school, they begin in the stereotyped, grown-up fashion: "Brethren and sisters, we are living in momentous times, and it behooves us to be," etc.—talking quite over the heads of the children, who in the meanwhile wriggle and squirm as if their little bodies were built upon spiral coils.

It is of course impracticable in this connection to point out what should be the character of discourses suited to each of these ages. This will be treated in later chapters. Sufficient for my present purpose if the critical attention of my readers be directed to the problem. Let the Elder who is really in earnest to find out the best way, give his children at home an hour of his time each evening, and observe the varying effect of now this method now that upon the susceptible minds of the toddlers round his knee. I know of no better way to discover the true method of preaching, at least as regards instruction addressed to the young.

It will generally be found that the narrative method interests children and all adults whose minds have not grown with their bodies. The persuasive method, appealing as it does to the emotional faculties, which are generally awake even when intellectuality is quite asleep, comes next in the order of easy comprehension. The exposition or explanatory method, and the method of argumentation, dealing as they do with abstract principles, can be used to advantage only where the mentality is fairly well developed.

The Intelligence of the Audience Addressed must next be considered. He is a poor preacher indeed who leaves this out of account. Is it a congregation of outsiders or of church members? What is their general intelligence? From what countries came they? What are their traditions, their prejudices, their occupations, their social and domestic virtues and vices? Do they read? What? The answer to these and a score of similar questions will place the speaker on an eminence where he can make his remarks tell for good. He should not fall into the error of thinking that the mind is matured simply because the body is full grown. I verily believe that in a majority of congregations in Zion today most good can be done by methods adapted in composition to the minds of children; provided of course that they be disguised by trimmings to suit the minds of adults.

Sermons must also be adapted to the purpose of the meeting. What is appropriate for one occasion is manifestly out of place for another, yet we have some old larks among us that sing the same song in all weathers and in all seasons. Think of an Elder so wedded to a single subject that he will preach a whole hour on marriage when the occasion is a funeral! Yet this is an actual occurrence, and I could name the occasion and the man.

We have thus far classified sermons (1) with reference to the pains taken in composing, and (2) with reference to the nature of the congregation addressed; but these do not touch the inherent qualities of the discourse, consequently.

Nature and Purpose of Sermon Itself.—We shall base a third classification on the nature and purpose of the sermon itself. An ideal division under this head would be to consider sermons as addressed (a) to the understanding, (b) to the imagination, (c) to the emotions, and (d) to the will. But this arrangement would be more fanciful than practical, and Latterday Saint sermons are nothing if not practical. They are unique in that they defy the ordinary rules of rhetoric as applied to sacred composition. By this I mean that I can gain very little that is applicable to my purpose from a rhetorical study of sectarian sermons. If my divisions therefore be faulted as illogical, they will at least have the merit of being real, and of following the actual lines of our preaching; and the empiricism, if such there be, must be charged to the practice not to me, the mere recorder of the practice.

The Missionary Sermon.—The first class, then, that claims consideration is the missionary or doctrinal sermon. Its nature is argumentative and its purpose conviction. It aims by instructing the understanding and by controverting erroneous doctrines to convert the listener to the truth. Three books—Spencer's Letters, the Voice of Warning, and Orson Pratt's Works—have almost created this kind of preaching. The first is polemical and fairly bristles with the spirit of debate. The second is illustrative and proceeds on the principle of drawing comparisons. The third is argumentative—a closely woven network of theology from the meshes of which no man can escape who will admit the authority of the Scriptures.

But now consider for a moment the kind of minds toward which two of these books—Spencer's Letters and Orson Pratt's Works—are directed. Are they not minds resembling those of the authors—minds intellectually awake, capable of apperceiving principle in the abstract? How many such minds are there in the world who are still willing to turn their attention toward religion? Ninety-nine out of every hundred men and women among the masses are utterly concrete, basing their belief upon immediate and palpable example.

Argumentative discourses, requiring as they do an awakened intellectuality, are generally meaningless to men whose reasoning faculties slumber. Occasionally such people may be awakened through the emotion of combativeness, which is ever alert to a chance for debate. If they can but be induced to investigate, which is only another way of saying if their intellectual faculties can be aroused to these principles, the missionary or doctrinal sermon is very effective. But this is a rare thing in the fields where our Elders preach today. Congregations in the world are attracted by our hymns, and manifest a dumb astonishment at our prodigal quotation of Scripture, but they go away unstirred: they are not aroused to the point of intellectual investigation. And to me the reason is plain. This kind of sermon is directed to apartments of the mind in which these people do not live—chambers in which the dust and cobwebs of generations have accumulated.

The period when Elders Pratt and Spencer were active missionaries was an age of doctrinal polemics. A score of churches had their rise about this time, based upon different interpretations of Scripture. Numerous independent associations were formed to study the Bible. All sects appealed to this book as the end of argument. Christians so called everywhere reverenced the word of God, and made an intellectual effort to comprehend it. Religion had then to do with the head as well as with the heart. Under these circumstances no sermon could be more popular than that of which Orson Pratt's "Kingdom of God" is an example. The minds of the people were ripe for it. Their doctrinal controversies had prepared the way. Hundreds were converted and came into the Church in a day.

A Change has Come Over the People.—Sermons on doctrine are out of date. Creeds and creedal worship are denounced today in ten thousand pulpits as the trickery of priestcraft. Ordinances and sacraments are held to have no saving efficacy. They are looked upon as fences dividing the field of truth and keeping Christians apart; or as the praying machines of some heathen countries—mere artificial contrivances. Religion is now a sort of universal but vague and indefinable "spirit of Christianity" whose only specific characteristic, so far as I can conceive it, is a hatred of theological distinctions.

This I believe to be the rational explanation of why the doctrinal sermons of our Elders take with less and less favor in the world. The power of darkness soon discovered that there was no chance to cope successfully with the Latterday Saints on Scriptural grounds, so the evil one set about to discredit the method. And he has succeeded. There is now very little real faith or interest in the Bible, as we interpret its truths; but of course as interpreted by the new Christianity it has the same extravagant lip service as of old. One of the strongest reasons urged now for its divinity authenticity is that it is a mirror for all ages and peoples, in which the greatest light of every man is reflected back—with "divine effulgence." No human book, it is urged, could be at once the hope and solace of people so diverse in conviction and aspiration.

These are pretty words but what is the thought they disguise? Simply that the Bible is a vague old flatterer of every man's religious whim. But the real Bible, the Bible of Latterday Saints, the Bible that flatters no man's religious whim, but presents one consistent and undeviating plan of salvation—this Bible has few believers; nay, it is hated and despised in the persons of its advocates, Mormon Elders.

IV.

THE WEAKNESS OF THE DOCTRINAL SERMON.

Part of the last chapter was devoted to showing that the doctrinal sermon does not, in consequence of a want of intellectuality in the masses and a loss of faith in the Bible by the classes, carry the convincing power that it once did. But this is not altogether owing to the method. Much of the weakness lies in the inability of our Elders to use the method well. Given an intellectual audience and a cultured speaker, there can be no question that the closely-knit reasoning of an Orson Pratt concerning Church organization and the laws of adoption must arouse thought and investigation even in the face of the religious notions of the day that such organization and adoption are antiquated contrivances. But if these same things are advocated by preachers whose only basis of reasoning is memory, and to whose own minds many of the arguments so drawn from memory are not even intelligible, is it any wonder that thinking men and women refuse to entertain them?

Let us look ourselves squarely in the face and answer this question: If the young men whom we send on missions should begin their labors in our own settlements instead of going to the world, would we come out to hear them night after night? Would we come the second night? The first night—knowing what they are? And yet some of us will be very much disappointed if God does not visit condign punishment upon people in the world for not entertaining them and listening to their testimony! For my part, as I look back upon my first crude efforts at preaching, I am forced to admire the audiences that didn't come to hear me. I shall not turn accuser against them on the day of judgment.

The Doctrinal Sermon from Our Side.—Witness now from our side the chain of cause and effect with reference to the doctrinal sermon: Frequently, we select young men who know nothing about preaching and often very little about the Gospel; young men whose mental deficiencies I may best sum up by saying that they have not learned to think. Coming thus unprepared into the field, they are driven, by the necessity of having something to say, to load their minds with undigested passages of Scripture. These they fire upon their listeners with what aim they are capable of taking. But what with their embarrassment and ignorance of subject and audience, this aim, if aim it may be called, is wavering and uncertain indeed.

The first shots are few and scattering. But it is a beginning. Having no model to guide them, and unable to master more than one thing at a time, they content themselves by learning to fire first and to take aim afterward. Acquiring at length the ability to keep firing, one class become so pleased with themselves that it does not occur to them that they ought to learn how to take aim. Random shots rapidly made fill the room with sound and take up the time. What more is needed? If people can withstand such lung power, why—let them be damned. These are they that come back to the valleys of the mountains and talk and talk—the same garrulous class that have turned up in all these chapters.

The other class, less vain and more earnest, do not forget that they came to save souls. These seek constantly to better their aim before firing—by which I mean that they strive to arrange their thoughts in such logical sequence as to secure unity and force. To this class Orson Pratt's Works is a perfect mine of delight. But they become thereafter irrevocably committed to the doctrinal sermon, and when they return to Zion they are, for reasons which grow out of peculiar conditions in our midst, generally shelved, while the talkers are permitted to go ingloriously on.

From the Side of the World.—Let us next look at the chain of cause and effect on the other side. What of these first audiences, these victims, I was about to say, on whom young Elders practice preaching? It is safe to say that curiosity brought them together—curiosity of the worst type. Let us suppose the first to be an intelligent audience, biased indeed as are all so-called Christians, by the spirit of the age, and prejudiced, as it is sure to be, against the Mormons. Will this first meeting tend to remove, or will it tend to fasten that prejudice? Would it be natural for these Elders to find an opening here? Of course they do not make friends. How could they? Where is the basis for any affinity? The Gospel, you say. They have that to be sure—in their books—but what do they know of it?

After a number of such failures, they gravitate naturally away from educated centers; for there they feel continually conscious of being weighed in the balance. A double advantage is secured by this change of field: (1) the back woods people to whom they gravitate are incapable of measuring their mental acquirements; and (2) they are still imbued with something of the old-time reverence for the plain truths of the Bible.

Conversions in Spite of Doctrinal Sermons.—But if by such a change, something is gained to the Elder by reason of faith and humility in his hearers, much is lost to him on the score of their general intelligence. These minds are really not to be reached on the argumentative plan. The first audience might have been so reached had the speakers been finished reasoners, but these people are concrete, actuated by the influence of immediate things. They are to be interested and stirred by methods which would reach the hearts of children. Could Elders but realize this, and put the Gospel into narrative or persuasive form, using objects that appeal directly to the experience of the hearers, it would surely be easy to make an opening here. But no; they have learned but the one way to preach, and it must be this or nothing.

The converts made in such fields must not be credited to the doctrinal sermon. They are often made in spite of it—made by fireside conversations and narratives, and by the love which Elders inspire for themselves whenever they remain long enough to become intimately known. But the people thus reached by fireside methods are comparatively few, from sheer want of time to go round. Why not make more of these fireside methods in the pulpit?

Summary.—Let me sum up the points I have tried to make with reference to the doctrinal sermon. First, being abstract in its nature and somewhat artificial, it can be truly appreciated only by those of awakened intellects, which is always a small minority.

Second, the religious spirit of the age is set against its subject-matter, as being non-essential to salvation. To attempt to open a new field by a sermon on doctrine is, therefore, to invite defeat.

Third, our method of having preachers educate themselves

while "in the harness," makes it all but impossible to acquire any other than this method, the result being that our Elders instead of trying to adapt the sermon to the people, proceed on the Quixotic notion that the people can be made to adapt themselves to the sermon.

Fourth, owing to the fact that our Elders, from want of general culture, are excluded from circles where the argumentative method might be effective, and, on the other hand, have no other method to use in circles where it is not effective, it may be said in general that our converts are made rather in spite of it, than by it —that is to say, they are made more by incidental labors, than by formal preaching.

This is a severe arraignment of the doctrinal sermon. Has it no good points? It has, and they are very important, but space will not permit me to treat them in this chapter.

V.

MISSIONARY SERMONS—WHAT THEY SHOULD BE LIKE.

We have now discussed the kinds of sermons from two points of view, viz.: (1) sermons classified by the method of composition, as to whether they be oral impromptu, oral deliberated, or written; and (2) sermons determined by the nature of the occasion and the character of the congregation addressed. We began also a third classification based upon the nature of the subject matter used, and the faculties of mind appealed to. The doctrinal sermon came in for first consideration under the last head. It was shown, among other things, that this kind of sermon addresses itself almost purely to the calm, unemotional judgment or intellect, and presupposes faith in the prophecy, doctrine, and ritual set forth in the Bible— conditions seldom met today in our missionary fields.

In Opening New Fields of Labor.—From these considerations it would seem wise in opening new fields of labor not to emphasize argumentative discourse; that is, disputations about baptism, church organization, etc. For if people are unconverted to the need of salvation, they will scarcely be interested in the method of salvation. Who would think of discussing seriously before a band of Utes the relative value of one and two story brick cottages? Better persuade them first that any kind of house is good which cannot be attached to the back of a cayuse pony and trailed about. So with people in the world: the want of a saving religion—that is, the desire to be saved—must first be created. The learned, wise in their own conceit, commiserate in us what they deem the crude formalism of the past, and willingly trust their salvation to modern Christian universalism. The unlearned, not having the mind-power to assimilate abstract truths, are seldom interested in sermons requiring such mind-power. They readily flock, however, to preachers who take care to administer baby-food; that is, to preachers who carefully adapt their ideas to such mind-powers as they discover their audiences actually to possess. Would it not be well for Mormon missionaries to learn a lesson on this point?

Nature of Missionary Sermons.—What then shall be the nature of missionary sermons? This is a question very difficult to answer. If we were truly like clay in the potter's hand, the question would not need consideration. The Spirit would mould us as it listed. But we are far from being perfectly mixed and pliable clay. We are rather clods with sharp corners. When we get into our fields of labor it is God's first business to break us all up. Nor are we more than half-mixed by the time we are called home again. And then, I very much fear, most of us dry into clods again.

This much, however, may be said on the subject. The purpose of missionary sermons must be, first, to develop faith—develop it, not prove it out of the Bible. For there are sermons on faith just as objectionable for their cold, abstract argumentativeness, as any which turn on the mode of baptism. Doctrinal sermons do not create faith where it is not, however much they may confirm faith where it already is. We must have sermons that will awaken a loving faith in God as a living, warm-hearted, resurrected Father—the perfected man. Sermons that will draw men from the mystic, impersonal being of Christian and heathen conception, and lead them to the God of Abraham, Isaac, and Jacob. We must have sermons that will make men believe in the true Savior—our Elder Brother; in mankind as being really and truly the children of God—as belonging to the race of the Gods; in this earth as belonging to our Father—every drop of water and every grain of sand; in the right of God to rule what he has created; in the likelihood that he would concern himself in the welfare of his children—by showing them the way to become perfect as he is perfect; in the Bible and other revelations as containing that way. In short, to create a simple, child-like faith in God, in mankind, and in the plan of salvation—this must be the first aim of the missionary. But it cannot be accomplished by argumentative sermons on what faith is, its manifestations, historical instances of, etc. All this is purely intellectual, and may actually leave the soul barren. The need of a living faith must be brought home to these people by homely applications to their daily lives.

Must Create a Lively Desire.—The next purpose of such sermons must be to create a lively desire to find the true way of life; to discover what can be done today toward becoming like our Father in heaven. This is repentance. Here the preacher enters the domain of human conduct—a field boundless in extent and variety. Here the multitudinous questions of right and wrong, with their endless perspectives of cause and effect in shaping the destiny of man, are to be looked at afresh from the point of view of a newly-found faith. What a world of subjects for sermons is here if we will but open our eyes—subjects not to be treated in a harsh, dogmatic, Pharisaical way, nor in the analytical, argumentative way, but with kindness and charity and brotherly love! In this field of human joys and sufferings are to be found the concrete examples—the parables—that carry principles to the human heart, and arouse the emotions to deeds of righteousness.

The Method of Fiction-Writers.—Why should fiction-writers appropriate this field to themselves? They have truly learned the way to the human heart. Pity that they stir in it such fruitless emotions. What then? Is the method wrong? Then is the organization of man at fault, for God adjusted minds so as to be appealed to in this way. No, no; the use made of this method is sometimes wrong, and often leads men from the truth. But this is no fault of the method. Should we say the soil is poor because it produces a luxuriant crop of weeds? Is it not rather a certain proof that the soil is good?

Then, let our preachers learn to use this soil for harvests of righteousness. Our Savior set us the example. Let me repeat, he set us the example—he did not exhaust the method. "The poor ye have always with you"—the poor in intellect also; they whose minds if reached, whose hearts if touched, must be reached and touched by principle embodied in example; by a story, a parable, a narrative.

How much better this way than the usual dry, doctrinal sermon on repentance. After you have labored an hour by argument and quotation to prove the meaning of repentance—what then? You have performed an intellectual feat, nothing more. Your audience is as unrepentant as before. But if, like Christ, you choose some prodigal son or daughter to illustrate the principle—then you have made the doctrine clear, and started the work of reformation as well.

It seems quite clear then, that the missionary sermon must first develop a fervent, a wide, an all-embracing faith; a faith that shall give the convert a just conception of God, his being, his attributes, and his works; at least so much of a conception as shall start his growth toward God aright. Second, it must inspire in him the desire to put his own life in harmony with the laws of the universe,—for what is repentance but that? It is also clear that the method of accomplishing these purposes must be such as will actually succeed even though we be compelled to learn a lesson from the domain of fiction. Think what marvels will be acomplished when the Elder acquires the power to use the narrative as effectively to convey Gospel lessons, as the novelists use it to picture romance.

Let me not be understood as urging that sermons be substituted by complete stories with plot, counterplot, and denouement. As in the discourses of the Savior, narratives are to introduce principles not yet stated, or to illustrate principles already stated. I do not even urge that the characters be fictitious, though on this point there could be no objection, since Christ has set us the example.

VI.

THE NEED OF ADOPTING MORE POPULAR METHODS IN PREACHING.

Must Learn to Adapt Methods to Needs.—When sectarian ministers make a hundred converts in a certain section to our one, we usually say it is because men love fables rather than truth. I think we make a mistake; they love truth in fable, better than truth in cold argument. Indeed, so well do they love the fable or parable form that they willingly, or rather let me say unconsciously, accept error, if it be only dressed in this attractive garb. What a harvest there will be when we shall be able to adapt our methods of teaching truth, as sectarians adapt their methods of teaching error!

But before that time comes, we shall have to study more carefully the principles of truth or error that lie beneath every word or thought or deed of man and beneath man's interpretation of every fact or change in nature. We shall have to become a more thoughtful people; a people able to see the hand of God in all things, able to turn all things to account for his kingdom.

At present the natural method of appealing to man is used largely to teach what is often justly condemned as things unnatural —that is, in teaching fiction; and because it is so used, the very method shares in the condemnation. On the other hand, an unnatural method is used, because of this odium, to convey things natural—truth. Witness the result: for one person that turns naturally to religious things, a thousand turn to fiction. The good soil bears a thousand fold—of weeds; the sterile soil scarcely reproducing the good seed sown.

Now, in this matter of adapting method to the requirements of mind, sectarian preachers as above intimated, are far in advance of us. The absolute need of supplying by artificial stimulus the interest which among Latterday Saints is sustained by the Holy Ghost, has wonderfully sharpened their wits as to the best means of moving men. Let me not be misunderstood. I am not commending the stories they tell. I only recognize the effectiveness of their methods of conveying principles. This distinction it is well to keep in mind, otherwise we shall be so illogical as to condemn the method because of the use to which it is put. Even then it is difficult not to blame the method; for who can listen to the maudlin deathbed or graveyard scenes, told so often in a tearful voice to set the congregation sniveling, and not become prejudiced against the pathetic story as a means of conveying a Gospel lesson?

But all sectarians do not resort to sniveling stories; though so many do that one is tempted to believe it of all. If one would know how effective the narrative method may become in giving life to a discourse, let him read a few sermons of Henry Ward Beecher. He will there learn that the story is effective in arousing all shades of emotion.

Our Attitude the Effect of Prejudice.—One word now as to our attitude toward this method of conveying truth. I believe that a majority of our Elders condemn it. Nothing is more common than to hear: "Oh, he appealed to their feelings and of course he caught all the weak-headed ones." The implication is that to appeal to the feelings is contemptible. Can you see the sophistry? Suppose his purpose had been pure and holy; would it then have been contemptible to appeal to the feelings? Are not the feelings as God-given as the intellect? If men are spurred to all that is base by appeal to their feelings, are they not, on the other hand, encouraged to all that is exalted and heavenly by the same means?

The fact is, the feelings are simply channels by which to reach the soul. As to what reaches the soul, whether good or bad, depends upon that which is put into these channels. It may be remarked that if a preacher wishes to present a weak cause, or carry out a dastardly purpose, he invariably proceeds by lulling the intellect and arousing the passions. Our Elders have seen so many mobs raised by this method, that they are to be excused for condemning it. But still, it is very irrational to do so; for the same stimulus directed toward righteousness would have produced the opposite effects; not equal effects, of course, since the capacity for doing good has seldom been educated like the capacity for doing evil.

Our Tendency to Credit the Devil.—"But," says the Elder, "a tree is to be judged by its fruits. Is not this way the broad road that leads to damnation? Is not this method the very means Paul saw would be used to tickle the itching ears of sinners in the last days?" Now I am quite aware that these are the things we say about methods that "convert" hundreds in a day. I have said so myself. But I strongly suspect that our chief reason for saying so is the same that the fox had for calling the grapes sour: we are such blunderers in using these methods.

For as to crediting the devil wholly with the inspiration and methods of sectarians, I take very conservative grounds. I think it quite compatible with the Gospel to believe that God is directing his children all over the world to do the highest good they are capable of conceiving; and that wherever, in Christian or in heathen lands, anything is found in line with the Gospel, it comes from the Father of light. I cannot therefore credit the evil one with inventing or perfecting the method of appealing to the emotions. But even if I could say that this method is used almost exclusively by him, I should still have to defend it and say that the devil knows a good thing when he gets hold of it; and the reason he has almost completely dropped our way is, that he finds it so wretchedly ineffective.

Effectiveness of Narrative Methods.—Now as to exemplifications of the narrative and persuasive methods of preaching, they are very meagre among us—at least on the positive side—for the reason that our preaching has mostly been by the doctrinal method. I appeal, therefore, to the experience of every missionary as to whether the fireside narrations, the hymns, the pictures of Utah, and the stories connected with them, the esteem and friendship resulting from intimate acquaintance—all direct means of appealing to the emotions—did not do more to convert men than doctrinal preaching?

Among our tracts in the Southern States was one written by Elder Ben E. Rich on the "Kingdom of God." The people never tired of hearing us read it. Why? Because it was in narrative form. The plot was insignificant—merely a running conversation between a church of England pastor and a Mormon Elder, with a traveler for audience. But it was enough to lend a human interest to the abstract principles set forth. Our listeners loved to picture the effect upon the good old clergyman, as truth after truth was driven home to him. The "Faith-promoting Series" may be mentioned as having the same general tendency; also the splendid work being done by the Juvenile Instructor, and other home periodicals in the same line.

But on the negative side, we have no end of testimony to the insufficiency of the doctrinal method, and therefore to the need of the appeal to the feelings. Why are our Elders so unfitted to give the Gospel in a shape to be understood and appreciated by the world? They have not heard it that way at home. Nor do they hear it today. Our meeting houses, in spite of all our drumming up, are fearfully depleted in consequence of this lack. The old members who were converted by the doctrinal sermon still take pleasure in the doctrinal sermon, and are there every Sunday, like fixtures; but where is the majority of the generation that has grown up in Zion? Where, indeed? These are positively starving for the Gospel, and cannot get it, because, like people in the world, their minds demand it in concrete form.

VII.

THE REAL VALUE OF THE DOCTRINAL SERMON.—THE TOPICAL SERMON.

Having discussed at sufficient length the weakness of the doctrinal sermon, I am ready to consider its strong points. The doctrinal sermon bears the same relation to the promulgation of the Gospel, that the trunk and branches of a tree do to its foliage and fruit. Observe (1) that it is the trunk and branches which give definite form and stability to the tree; (2) that though it is the foliage that attracts our admiration and the fruit that gives us food, these would not be possible save for the nourishment of the branches; (3) that there may be a thousand apples and ten thousand leaves, yet there is but one tree; (4) that these leaves are but transient, and, detached from the tree, fly hither and thither and settle in the gutter; and the fruit being perishable must be eaten in

PREACHING AND PUBLIC SPEAKING.   201

the season thereof, otherwise it will rot; finally (5) the tree naked and leafless is not a pleasant object to look upon, and if it bears no fruit deserves no better treatment than to be hewn down and cast into the fire.

Danger of Popular Methods when Used Alone.—Permit me now to justify the analogies I have drawn. First, necessary as it is to use narrative and persuasive methods to arouse interest and move men to reform, there is danger of getting lost in the labyrinths of human hopes and fears, and of exciting activities that tend to divide men rather than unite them, unless those relations which form the warp and woof of doctrinal sermons be kept clearly in view. This is the case of Protestantism today. Having cut quite loose from doctrine, their sermons on emotional subjects, effective though they be for single occasions, lack the power of coherence, or of fitting into a definite, consistent scheme of salvation. Consequently, like toy balloons, they float in the sunlit air of speculation, exciting admiration, it may be, but leading men hither and thither as the wind of feeling blows, until the pretty baubles are out of mental sight, when each entranced worshipper returns to his own way with only a gilded memory.

The Catholics know better. They indeed employ all the devices known to composition, but always in view of some definite doctrine. Organization, tenets, rites, and ordinances—the materials for doctrinal sermons—are being discarded among Protestants because as taught by them they do not appeal to common sense; they are too much revered among Catholics to be permitted to appeal to common sense; but Latterday Saints need neither fear the result of examination of their ordinances, rites, and tenets, like the first; nor shroud them in impenetrable mystery, like the second. The search-light turned upon their doctrines can only reveal what must appeal alike to reason and admiration. Unity and stability in any system or organization are not possible without a rigid framework of well defined doctrine.

The Need of Underlying Doctrine. — Second, fruits of righteousness can grow only upon some branch of doctrine. The branch may be entirely hidden, and it is often better so. For instance, in a sermon designed to develop faith, the word faith may not occur at all. But the conscious purpose: "I wish to develop faith in this or this principle" must be behind all that is said. A sermon without such a purpose is exactly like leaves detached from the tree. This, indeed, is nothing else than what I have so oft criticised as aimless talk.

Let us now revert to point three in this analogy, viz.: that there may be a thousand apples and ten thousand leaves, yet there is but one tree. The Gospel tree is spreading its branches over all the earth. But nowhere can a leaf (sermon) hope to live and do its part in nourishing the tree, save as it grows out of or is attached to a twig (doctrine); nor can its fruit (converts) ever grow to maturity and ripen (gain salvation), save as it clings to the parent tree (church).

The Real Place of the Doctrinal Sermon.—Points four and five in this analogy as given above, will, I trust, convey the thought intended without further comment.

It is not that doctrinal preaching is bad that I speak of it as I do. In its place it is invaluable. But its place it to sum up or generalize. Its purpose is to extract the spiritual essence of our experiences, but it can never take the place of those experiences. To hope to make a man better by preaching doctrines into him is futile; we merely load his memory, and perhaps make him a hypocrite. He must taste the experiences himself— taste them in solution, as it were, and then the doctrine as it crystallizes in his mind will have some real meaning to him.

This question is not a new one by any means; at least not new to the teaching profession. Every teacher has discussed it over and over as applied to methods of instruction. I have purposely kept back the terms deductive and inductive, by which the opposite sides of the question are known. In doing so, I have followed the inductive plan—the only way to make knowledge real to beginners. Deductive preaching, like deductive teaching, may be a swift way to cover a subject. It is in fact often so swift that the speaker runs out of matter, and must spread over half a dozen subjects to fill out the time. But as compared with inductive preaching, the impressions conveyed are very superficial. The overland traveler may now cover territory in a few hours that required months for the Pioneers to travel, camping as they did night after night on an unbroken trail. But can his knowledge of the Rocky mountains be compared with theirs? His impressions have scarcely depth and coloring enough to last for one telling; theirs have become part of their very lives.

This must close the discussion on the doctrinal sermon. I trust I shall not be misunderstood. We need more than ever to be grounded in doctrine and principle. My contention is only that we must go at it in a more natural way. The grounding must be the result of finding out something—not of being told; of generalizing from concrete examples verified by experience; of inductive lessons as opposed to memory cramming.

The Topical Sermon.—The second kind of discourse to be considered in this classification may be called the topical sermon. I was almost tempted to name it the editorial sermon, so nearly does it resemble a collection of editorials. No better example of this kind can be found than the general epistles of the First Presidency to the Saints during the Raid. Such sermon-epistles we get at every conference, the difference being only that they are oral, and in many respects more elaborate.

The topical sermon is most admirably fitted for the purpose it is intended to fulfil, which is to bring before the people matters of general interest, to warn them of impending danger, and arouse them to the duties of the hour. Thus President Cannon during the last conference (October, 1894) spoke Sunday forenoon, as nearly as I can remember, on the following topics: 1. The attitude of the Church toward the Utah University. 2. The general disbelief of mankind in an overruling Providence. 3. The insidious spirit of text-books. 4. The need of more harmony in the home-circle. 5. The damnable sin of seeking to escape the responsibility of raising a family. Is not this an admirable list of editorial headings? In the afternoon, President Smith occupied the time, discussing another list quite as timely and germane to the occasion.

Its Range.—This kind of discourse has, it seems to me, but one proper range of subjects, viz.: things of immediate and pressing importance; things that can be disposed of in a few words because they are already in men's minds. The topical sermon is thus appropriate to all who preside—Apostles, Presidents of stakes, Bishops, superintendents, quorum leaders, heads of associations, and fathers of families. Care should of course be taken to speak at such times, and appeal to such feelings as will further not frustrate the object in view.

But subjects of only general importance, should not, it seems to me, be treated in this running fashion. When they are, I fear there is no way to distinguish the sermon from an aimless wandering talk. Certainly where there is not pressing need to speak on many subjects in one discourse, greater force will result from concentrating all the attention upon one subject for each meeting, amplifying and illustrating it till the thought cannot fail to be comprehended, and the purpose felt even by the simplest. Intension not Extension is what should be aimed at even in the topical sermon.

VIII.

THE EXHORTATION AND ITS CUMULATIVE MISERIES.—THE MISSIONARY REPORT.

A third kind of discourse common among us may be called the exhortation. We seldom have a sermon throughout of this character, however; for exhortation is like the weather: when we run short of other matter we sandwich it in. I might also add, to be quite candid, that its effect in edifying is about the same as that of the weather; and its effect in moving men is often not equal to that of the awkward silence it serves to relieve.

Weakness of the Exhortation.—Who does not instinctively fortify himself with a sort of listlessness and inattention the moment such phrases as these come within hearing: "We ought to be thankful that—etc.," "It is our duty to see that we—etc.," "We should be continually on our guard not to forget—etc.," "It behooves us as Latterday Saints to see that—etc.," "Let us always remember that—etc.," "It devolves upon us as members—etc."?

When these expressions occur in the summing up of a course of reasoning, or in drawing a moral from an illustration, they are quite in order. We could scarcely get along without them. But when we have a running series of "shoulds" and "oughts," and "behooves"—covering every duty in the catalogue without break or breathing spell between, and with no other order than as they happen to strike the speaker's memory—it is then that good advice becomes as cheap as oyster cans by the road side.

Three Degrees of Hortatory Misery.—In point of exasperation there are three degrees in this cumulative weariness of exhortation. The first degree is a mild pleading. This is quite tolerable when it comes from the heart; and even moves us when the exhorter is an exemplary man. But if these conditions be lacking, we simply remain indifferent.

The second degree is like nagging. It is here that indifference begins to take on the complexion of pain. As soon as the habitual nagger begins with his "oughts" and "shoulds," that "tired feeling" begins to settle down upon the congregation. Many is the unspoken wish that he would sit down.

The third degree is scolding. The scolding preacher is one that goes into the gutter during week-days to collect "don'ts" and "ought-nots" for Sunday. He is one that invariably belabors those that come to meeting for the sins of those that stay away. If he be a monotonous scold, with perhaps a nasal twang, then the exhortation method reaches its climax of exasperation. But often he is anything but monotonous. He gets excited, his voice takes a high key, his face grows red, his arms gesticulate wildly. This is a decided relief. The congregation is grateful—grateful that it can keep awake without the usual effort. "We got it in the neck today, didn't we?" is the jocular remark heard as the people leave the building.

But what good is accomplished? None. Scolding and nagging never do good but always do harm. How I am tempted to dash off a chapter on this theme! The good that scolding and nagging seem to accomplish at times may be set down as the price men are willing to pay to escape torture. This good is only seeming, it is not real. But the bad aroused beneath this cloak of seeming good is alas! only too real.

The Fault and the Remedy.—What then is the matter with exhortation as we usually hear it? This must be our next enquiry. Let me quote a passage from James:

"If a brother or sister be naked and destitute of daily food and one of you say unto them: 'Depart in peace; be ye warmed and filled'—notwithstanding ye give them not those things which are needful to the body; what doth it profit!"

Now let us paraphrase this passage:

"If a brother or sister be slack in faith and lack interest in the Gospel, and one of you say unto them: 'Have faith, be prayerful, be honest, be virtuous, attend your meetings, pay your tithing, cultivate brotherly love'—notwithstanding ye give them nothing but your naked advice by which to stir up their hearts to righteousness: what doth your exhortation profit?"

This is the key to the whole matter. Can we say to a man: "Be sad—be merry—now laugh—now cry"—and expect these emotions to respond? Then why should we look for results when we say to other emotions: "Be humble—be prayerful—be chaste"? And if we repeat these commands or entreaties for an hour together will our hearers be better or worse for it? Are the doors to the emotions so flimsy that they may be battered down by much knocking?

The fact is, we seek to reap where we have not sown. We look for effects when there are no causes. We must bear in mind that if we would stir up a feeling in the human heart, we must present an adequate cause for that feeling and present it skillfully. If the feeling seems to be stirred without an adequate cause, depend upon it, it is sheer hypocrisy, or perhaps self-stultification.

It will thus be seen that the fault in our method of exhortation is exactly the same as that found in our doctrinal preaching. It does not take into account the organization of the human mind, but imagines that words projected into the air will imbed themselves, germinate, and bear fruit without any care being taken as to preparation of the soil and nourishing of the growing plant. Is there anything that man may expect to do well without studying 'how' to do it? Why should preaching be an exception?

The Mission Report —A fourth kind of discourse very familiar to Latterday Saints may be called mission reports. As we believe ours to be the true Church of God, it must follow that its growth and development is of prime importance to every Latterday Saint.

Hence the labors of missionaries should be of absorbing interest to every member, and generally they are. More than the ordinary number of people turn out to hear the returned Elder relate his experiences. The interest manifested may fairly be accounted for by the fact that the sermon is largely narrative, and deals immediately with the concerns of human beings.

As mission reports have in them much power for good, they will probably always have a place in our Sabbath gatherings, and therefore deserve study for their own sake. But as I shall fully discuss narrative composition in some later chapter, I will only remark here, that these sermons, like nearly all others, seem often to be given "without taking thought" as to what shall or shall not be said. Frequently they are without perspective, disconnected and bewildering. Quite as often the perspective depends only upon a daily chronology, as, "Then we took breakfast, after which we retired to the woods to pray; after which——after which——after which——," etc., giving details too trifling even for a diary. In such cases there seems to be no power to separate the essential from the non-essential.

Some Elders again make it a point to dwell only upon the novel or sensational. They thereby give wrong impressions. For instance, the Southern States, one of the best missions in the world, has by such reports gotten the name of being particularly dangerous by reason of mob violence.

As most of these faults occur through the Elder's taking no thought till he is called to the stand I suggest to returning missionaries that they make a careful analysis of their labors, keeping in mind the question: What will be alike interesting and instructive to the people at home? Then write down every word, observing the principles of narration, without which no story arouses interest. The report, which of course is not to be read, will thus crystallize into definite and logical shape by the time it is to be delivered. Such a story would often be valuable for publication. And even if it were not, what better monument of an Elder's missionary labors could he hand down to his posterity?

The Unclassified Three-fourths —This finishes my classification and yet three-fourths of the sermons we listen to in Zion remain unclassified, and, as I may say, unclassifiable. Some Sundays ago I was taking minutes after a certain speaker, and had tried in vain for half an hour to find something logical and consistent to put into the record. At last, in despair, I turned to my seat-mate and asked:

"What report can I make of such a sermon as that?"

"Oh, simply say Brother ——— made a series of desultory remarks on the Gospel."

Now, that is it, in a nutshell. These are desultory sermons. It is a pity that the bulk of our preaching must be so classified; and I am sure we all unite in hoping it may not much longer be so.

CHAPTER VII.

METHODS OF COMMUNICATING THOUGHT.

I.

ESSENTIAL CHARACTERISTICS OF A SERMON.

Kinds of Discourses.—We have just finished a series of chapters relative to the kinds of sermons preached by Mormon Elders. We have also taken occasion to glance at the merits and defects in the composition of each variety. But it has not been possible to give in connection therewith many practical hints as to how to proceed in composing any given kind of discourse. This, then, is the question before us now.

There are five ways in which we communicate thought, viz: by narrative, by description, by exposition, by argumentation, and by persuasion. While any one of these may be the predominating style, it would be rare indeed for a sermon to proceed with one alone. A discourse is much more likely to use them all in varying order as the exegency of the thought shall demand. It will therefore be well for the young preacher to become acquainted with all the essential characteristics of thought communication, that he may not have to stumble along his path like one in the dark. Accordingly, I shall treat in turn each of these methods of conveying ideas.

The first, and perhaps most important, is narration. I call it the most important because it is almost the only avenue to the awakening intelligence of children, and to the undisciplined minds of adults. The narrative not only conveys truth on its own account, but is constantly called upon to enforce truths conveyed by other methods. In no kind of popular composition can thought long escape prosiness, if story, anecdote, incident, or illustration be absent. It is therefore of the utmost importance that the Elder discover what is effective and what is not effective in narration.

Must Seem Important.—The first consideration is to make the narrative seem important. Witness how the successful story teller gets his hearers ready for the anecdote he is about to relate. There is a light in his countenance which plainly shows that his mind has stumbled upon something rich. His introductory remarks go all around it, as if it were too good to give away. His very voice causes us to prick up our ears and lay down our papers. When expectation has in this manner been aroused to the proper pitch, the story is given in the most picturesque way; and we are pleased even though the substance of it be too flimsy to bear repetition.

Contrast with such a one the man in the same circle who is "reminded of a similar incident." By the time he reaches the point of his story we are deeply interested again in our papers, all save the unlucky wight on whom the narrator keeps his eye. His story may actually be better, or rather have better material, than the first. Why then such a difference in its reception? He does not make it seem important. His face wears a timid apologetic air; his voice hastens as if conscious of taking up valuable time; then he laughs at points where we see nothing to laugh at. Poor fellow, he is fast whittling out. When the point is reached his only auditor responds with a huh! through the nose.

Must have a Purpose.—But if the successful story-teller is first careful to create an appetite that is sauce to his narrative, he is likewise skillful in the construction of his plot and the elaboration of his materials. A good story must begin with some definite purpose in view,—as, to please, to instruct, or to illustrate—otherwise it cannot have unity. And not to have unity is to leave an uncertain impression, which is equivalent to no impression; in other words, the story will have no point, and a pointless story affects us in the same way as so much time spent in trying to fit together the fragments of a beautiful jar that has been broken; we feel that much time and effort have been wasted—the result being neither useful nor ornamental, though had a little care been taken it might have been both.

Must have but One Purpose.—But what does unity in the story mean? It means that a story must seek to realize one purpose and but one. It means that every sentence and every paragraph shall bend to this purpose—help to realize it by so much. No incident, no allusion, no word nor phrase must be introduced, however brilliant in itself, if it tends to arouse thought at a tangent with the object in view. Between the introduction and the climax the story must take the shortest route consistent with the purpose.

But this is most difficult to do. Every idea has a net-work of associations. To choose the one link which will lengthen out the thought in the desired direction and reject all the others without so much as a recognition, requires great powers of self-denial. Indeed I know no better criterion of the cultured mind than this ability to seize unerringly upon what is relevant and reject what is irrelevant.

Temptation to Wander.—The difficulty of holding to the thread of a story varies with the audience. In the case of children or of audiences with child-minds the narrator is often obliged to halt and impress by explanation or illustration some setting of the narrative, which by a more cultured audience is intuitively seen. Unusual skill is required to bring the minds of the listeners back to the point of departure with unabated interest and imagination properly stimulated to appreciate what follows. The difficulty is still increased when the excursus is indulged in at the suggestion, or in answer to the questions, of children. Teachers that thus give way to the rambling phantasies of their audience, will find themselves taking a course as erratic as the will-o-the-wisp. The story will be haphazard and pointless.

Completeness.—A narrative should be complete. This does not mean that the story must be lengthy. Nor are we to infer that incompleteness will invariably occur at the latter end. It may be incomplete in the introduction, or in any paragraph along the line. Wherever the purpose fails in whole or in part, there is the incompleteness. If the effect is flat, the work should be re-scanned. It may thus be found that the setting or frame-work is indistinct, and the mind of the hearer has consequently not been put in the proper attitude. A descriptive touch may be necessary here to hit off this character, or a flight of fancy needed there to paint more vividly that incident. Fulness without prolixity should constantly be aimed at.

Brevity.—It is not less important that the narrative should be brief; that is, it should be told in as few words as may be consistent with completeness. It is in this respect that imagination can do its finest work. Words are but the open sesame of stored-up experiences. He who has the art to choose the proper word or phrase will arouse a train of associations in the reader's or hearer's mind that a hundred other words might fail to produce. And even if a hundred words could supply the information which the one well-chosen epithet starts into consciousness, the pleasure derived from the many is small compared with that resulting from the one; since in the first case the mind being passive merely receives the picture, while in the second it is made active, and so creates it.

II.

ESSENTIAL QUALITIES OF A PLOT.

The last chapter discussed some of the essential qualities of the narrative; pointing out that (1) it should seem important, (2) it should have a purpose, (3) it should have unity, (4) it should be complete, and (5) it should be brief. This is like enumerating the finishing touches that make a house beautiful and comfortable. Now beneath and quite hidden by the garnishing which gives us a sense of comfort and beauty, there lies that without which all finishing touches were vain—the skeleton or frame-work of the building.

The skeleton or frame-work of a narrative is the plot; and other things equal, the story will be good, bad, or indifferent according to the nature of the plot. A well-constructed plot resembles the drainage system of one of our deep canyons: every brook and rivulet, no matter how winding its course, is fast approaching the central stream; and once gathered, the whole body of water plunges over a waterfall, or rushes perchance down deep-gorged cataracts, or quietly spreads out into some mountain lake. A story without a plot—if such a thing were possible—resembles a water-shed—an expanse so flat and uncertain that lazy streams move in various directions only to end at last in fens and stagnant pools.

Naturalness of the Plot.—The first requisite of a good plot is that it must seem probable. Causes must be made to seem adequate to effects, and both causes and effects must be such and only such as come within the range of common observation. It is by this principle that trashy fiction is most easily detected. Dime novels are usually a net-work of glaring improbabilities. Think for instance of the heroism (?) of Diamond Dick, the New York "Kid," out on the great Plains, killing fourteen Indians in one encounter and finishing the day's exploits by stabbing a grizzly and pushing it over a precipice!

But leaving yellow-back literature out of the question, three-fourths of the stories that are widely read by average society people, should be condemned, for being false; false in the only particular in which a novel can really be false, viz: in that they are improbable, untrue to life. Compare, for instance, the extreme simplicity and naturalness of the characters and incidents on which George

Eliot's novels turn with the impossible situations of the Charlotte Braeme, "Dutchess," "Ouida," or Mary J. Holmes' type of stories. It may be added, though not strictly pertinent to my theme, that while we do well to condemn three-fourths of the works of fiction that flood the land, we should not forget that among the remaining fourth are works not one whit behind the best authentic literature in true character-formation.

The principle that a plot should be probable admits of exceptions in the case of myths, fables, and fairy tales; which make no other claim to reality than that of fancy, and do not, therefore, impose even upon the credulity of children. As to all other forms of fictitious narrative, there is no excuse for improbable characters and situations; and we may add that there is no explanation either, save ignorance of real life, or a culpable disregard for truth in the writers or inventors. Certainly our Elders should be the last to weaken the integrity of their listeners by such impositions.

A Story should Excite Suspense.—A plot should be so constructed as to arouse curiosity and create suspense. It is chiefly this characteristic that chains the attention and arouses interest. The anxiety to know how a thing comes out, is one of the most constant of man's native powers. Not to make use of this power, in any form of composition where it can be made available, argues want of tact in writer or speaker. How shall curiosity and suspense be kindled and kept aflame?

The answer is not easy, but we may approach it in a general way. Consider for a moment what it is that arouses one's interest in the ordinary affairs of life. It is not that of which we know nothing but suddenly learn something. Such facts or happenings do not even create surprise; for surprise argues contrary anticipation, and certainly anticipation of any kind is not possible where something new and unknown is sprung upon us. Nor is suspense created where we know so much of the trend of an affair that we can forecast the result. The anxiety which should characterize the unraveling of a plot lies, therefore, between two extremes: between the sudden springing of the unknown upon the reader or listener, on the one hand, and, on the other, the telling so much of an affair that he is no longer doubtful as to the outcome.

Let the Elder who is interested in mastering this essential of the successful story, pay analytical attention to the next plot that arouses his anxiety. He will discover that every important turn of the narrative has been foreshadowed or is in some meagre way connected with what has preceded. Figuratively it is the kindling of a new torch of interest and insight along the dark highway of the plot. The effect is to make us read just our conceptions of what has been told, and enable us dimly to penetrate the mysteries of what is to come.

Plots are usually defective by reason of inability to create and manage suspense. The bungling story-teller will give no hint of the advent of a new character or the coming of a striking event; and so, when the effect is flat, as it is sure to be, he must deliver a short lecture to explain the connection of the new with the old; when as a matter of fact this connection should be intuitively seen, and the seeing it should give the pleasure. Or he will tell so much of the story that the end is foreseen, and consequently the truths which he expected to teach—truths which, had the story been properly told, could not have escaped attention—he must now ram down their throats by way of exhortation.

The Story Must Move.—A plot must be so constructed that the story will continually present a conscious forward movement. A narrative might be called an excursion of the imagination. Certainly no small part of the pleasure comes from the sense that we are moving. Especially is this true of children and people whose reflective faculties are meagrely developed. Such an audience is impatient of delays. Readers of the unreflective kind skip scores of pages devoted here and there to philosophy, sentiment, or description, in their eager haste to follow the fortunes of the characters.

PREACHING AND PUBLIC SPEAKING.   217

The narrator who would be listened to with wrapt attention must ever keep this weakness of his listeners in mind.

And yet never to expatiate on the passing beauties of thought and sentiment, is not to get the best results of the narrative form of conveying truth. Rather the contrary; for the story, especially in the hands of the preacher, should come freighted with all the generalized truths of life that its current can carry. To revert to a comparison used in the opening of this chapter, a mountain stream may be interesting and even beautiful as it meanders beneath the shade of birch and willow, or plunges swiftly down narrow gorges of adamant; but it becomes truly useful to mankind only when it spreads out o'er the fertile but parched soil, and makes meadow, field, and garden smile forth out of the thirsty desert.

As to when the movement of a story should be fast, when slow, let this illustration help to make clear: while the thought moves among the barren, rocky common-places of existence, the narrative may imitate the swiftness of the stream; but when it reaches the fertile valley of human action, let it linger and spread out to develop the richness of the soil and paint the landscape of life with living beauty.

Must Reach a Climax.—The last but by no means the least essential of a good plot is a climax, or denouement, as the French have it. "Kindly inform me when to laugh," is a just criticism of the story without a point. Of course when the narrative is authentic, it may consist in the relation of a series of connected events that do not rise in climacteric order. In such a case the motive running through the successive items must furnish the desired point; or perhaps the climax may come from their cumulated effect, either real or imagined, upon the actor or the narrator; or the narrator at a given point may be reminded of some other circumstance which by contrast or illustration will give the finishing touch. Certain it is, if the story is told for its value in conveying truth, it must be so constructed as to reach a climax, and the climax should, if possible, close the story. Again, I can do no better than to urge Elders to observe the art employed in the next good story they read, and thus see how the climax is attained. For giving a point to what would otherwise be a pointless story, no publication excels the Youth's Companion; this paper is so remarkable for its power in retouching anecdotes and incidents, that it is scarcely too much to say that its marvelous popularity is owing mainly to this characteristic.

III.

ESSENTIAL CHARACTERISTICS OF THE DESCRIPTION.

Next to narrative description is perhaps of the most value for the preacher's purpose. I say for the preacher's purpose it stands next to narrative; but taking into account the whole field of thought, it stands pre-eminently first among all forms of communication. Description might be called the mother of literature, since it is the form in which all our percepts are recorded; and certainly there could be no concepts and consequently no judgments or reasoning without percepts.

Relation of Narration and Description. — Narration can least of all proceed without the aid of description; so much are the two interwoven that one might be called warp and the other woof. A story is narrative while in motion, but mainly descriptive when it halts and spreads out. And it is very essential that a story shall halt and spread out: here to paint a landscape, there to depict a character. Our best novelists, among whom are Dickens and George Eliot, excel in description. Take from Hawthorne his pre-eminence in descriptive portrayal, and what would be left of his narratives? Merely connecting links without anything to connect. Whoever has read the "House of Seven Gables" will know what

PREACHING AND PUBLIC SPEAKING. 219

I mean. He cannot fail to remember the strongest chapter in the book, and for aught I know, the strongest chapter in all literature, the description of Judge Pyncheon's last sleep in the old arm chair. All great novels are likewise filled with descriptive scenes. What would "Les Miserables" be without Victor Hugo's masterly descriptions?

If descriptive powers be so essential to the communication of thought, I need scarcely stop to urge the preacher to make a careful study of the principles which make it effective.

By way of preliminary it may be well to make a distinction between descriptive which aims primarily to instruct, and description whose primary aim is to please. The first collects and classifies facts in such a way as to make what we call our sciences; as, botany, zoology, chemistry, and counts no detail too trivial for record. The second carefully avoids detail, and seizes upon those bold characteristics of the thing by which all people instantly recognize it, the purpose being only to make use of the emotions which seeing the thing would naturally arouse.

Respecting description whose purpose is to convey information I have only this to say: clearness and accuracy should be aimed at, leaving the elements of pleasure to the reader's or hearer's own extraction. To an audience interested in the information conveyed the last quality will not fail if the first two be present.

To be clear a description must keep the 'whole' before the mind while each detail is being added. For if from the start we do not see the whole, how shall we note the changes as the description progresses? What difference is there then, it may be asked, between the whole at the beginning and the whole at the end? The one is a vague crude outline, the other is that outline filled in to the minutest detail.

Clearness depends next upon the order in which these details are filled in. This order should be the natural, not the intellectual one; that is to say, it must be the order that would attract the attention of the people to whom the description is given, provided they were actually looking upon the thing described.

Suppose a man to be the subject of description. Intellectually the details might come as, age, size, color, head, ears, eyes, nose, mouth, beard, then body, limbs, dress, etc., in a mere enumeration. But this might by no means be the natural order. What would be the natural order? This must be determined by looking at the man. Perhaps the first detail would be the nose, if this member were so prominent as first to attract attention. In another instance it might be the feet. A smile perhaps or a frown might be a starting point in another case. Some women for instance lose themselves so completely in finery that the dress would first come under attention, and gradually the animated dummy beneath it would be discovered. Whatever be the starting point, other details are to be given, not in the order of contiguity, but in the order in which they would actually strike the eye or ear of the observer.

A good test of clearness is to shut the eyes, and then in imagination try to see the thing described. If the picture is clear we should ask, "Can the reader, from the outlines and details given, see what I see?" By this means, we shall perhaps discover that we see the thing mainly by reason of details not yet given, that the latter, should he construct a picture from the facts furnished would get a false impression. In this way then we shall be able to transfer the picture from our minds to that of our audience, and to do this with exactness is to be clear in description.

Importance of Clearness and Accuracy.—Clearness and accuracy of description are what make information valuable, hence these are the main characteristics of scientific description. Clearness depends upon ability to see within one's head; accuracy, upon the training of one's senses, and upon one's native love and respect for truth. All these qualities—the constructive imagination, the well-trained observation, and the love of truth—are powers already made or marred in the preacher, to a greater or less extent, according to his previous training. Should he find himself deficient in descriptive power the only remedy is to educate the faculties that make clearness and accuracy possible.

Description Must Have a Purpose.—The first requisite of description, as of all other forms of composition, is that it shall have a purpose. It is the purpose which determines the nature of the whole work. Let a mountain or a river be the subject of description and let the purpose in one case be such as a railroad engineer might have, in another that of a poet or writer of fiction, and in a third that of a sawyer—and it is obvious that we should have three very different descriptions of the same object. Not only is the character but also the length and elaborateness of a description determined by the purpose in view. For the sake of an illustration the Rocky Mountains may be described in two bold strokes, while for the purposes of geography, geology, mineralogy, etc., they may require a score of volumes.

Poetic Description.—Now, the main use that a preacher will have for description is in so far as it lends itself to the enforcement of moral truths. Consequently enough has been said of the other kind—the kind which seeks only the direct purpose of conveying facts concerning works of nature or art. We are now to discuss the kind whose object is indirect, such, for instance, as the rousing of the emotions in view of some hoped for decision or action. J. B. Gough painted the drunkard's home, not to add to our stock of knowledge, but save men from drunkards' graves. The revivalist gives reins to his fancy in depicting heaven and hell for a similar reason. Indeed, outside of text books and catalogues, so accustomed are we to have our descriptions illustrate or enforce some ulterior truth, that we hardly have patience to read through a description which exists simply for description's sake.

Need of Unity.—Our next consideration is that no matter what be our purpose, we must adhere to it undeviatingly. No detail however beautiful or striking in itself must be introduced if it would serve to distract attention from the object in view, or arouse emotions not in harmony with the purpose. To put it technically, the description must preserve 'unity.' In other fields of invention the "eternal fitness of things" is ever present, and there is very little temptation, to violate unity. The milliner, in building a hat, is not tempted to put this flower or that bird into the trimming simply because she has them at hand, and they are beautiful in themselves. They might destroy the general effect. Think what wonderful colors, forms, textures, and designs might enter into the making of a dress, the building of a house, or the decoration of a parlor, did not a sense of unity and harmony forbid!

What we need is to get the same severe taste in literary invention that we display when we make combinations of material things. It may be added in this connection that until we get such taste, we shall make poor headway in appealing to mankind; and this for a reason similar to that which causes us to be held in a kind of contempt if we manifest a crude and ridiculous taste in dress and the social amenities. It is with truth as with good clothes, whether it shall please or displease mankind depends very largely upon the cutting and fitting.

Must be Saturated with the Human Element.—A description ought always, if possible, to keep in touch with the human element. The beauty of a sunset in print does not appeal to us unless it is made to affect some soul whose aspirations are akin to our own. The magnificence of mountain scenery is cold and unattractive until we put human figures into it. An old house does not interest us as a house, but as a home of human beings of our kind. The turbulence of a river, which in one author we pass by with scarcely a thought, becomes by the description of another so deeply impressed upon our imagination that we see it in our dreams; simply because the latter contrived to have a boat-load of our friends overturned into the raging flood. Jules Verne has perhaps woven into popular literature more dry facts and statistics on scientific subjects than any other author; and this by the admirable way in which he mingles the human element in his narrative, descriptions, and expositions.

Completeness and Brevity.—The remaining general qualties of description are that it should be complete and should be brief. It is complete when the purpose is fulfiled, if it occupy only two lines. Conversely it is incomplete when the purpose fails—if it fail on this account—even though ten chapters be devoted to it.

To read and visualize a description requires greater mental energy than to follow in imagination the characters and events of a narrative. Hence the greater need of studying brevity in descriptive portrayal. How to do this successfully will be mainly the theme of the next chapter.

Brevity and suggestiveness are the most invariable qualities of the best literature in any language. It is not what Shakespeare says so much as what he makes us think, that gives us pleasure. I know of no better way to become master of a suggestive style—and such a style is invaluable not only in description, but in every other form of composition—than to make a careful analytical study of the English classics. As an illustration of how a choice of words may enable the writer to be brief without sacrificing completeness, let the reader follow out the suggestions aroused by almost every word and phrase in Coleridge's "Ancient Mariner;" a poem which though it does not devote a single line to description, nevertheless flashes upon the mind pictures which a volume of conscious descriptive effort would fail to portray.

IV.

THE PROCESS OF DESCRIBING.

Eyes or no Eyes.—A few years ago there appeared in one of our home magazines a description of Fish Lake and vicinity, which is without doubt one of the most picturesque summer resorts on the continent. Many friends of the writer took occasion to thank him for the pleasure they had felt in seeing the scenery, as it were, through his eyes, and declared their purpose to take the first opportunity of enjoying it for themselves. Some of them did so the following summer and one or two expressed a disappointment.

This is by no means an unusual experience. So far from descriptions not doing justice to scenes or characters, the opposite is more generally true. If Pecksniff or Uriah Heep were daily to walk before us should we see as much in them as we learn from Dickens? If we were to gaze upon the scenes depicted in "Views Afoot," should be disappointed? Very likely, unless we should happen to be Bayard Taylors. What is the explanation of our failure to see in a landscape or other object what others are able to see?

Effect of Seeing too Much.—The fault may lie in our eye or in the powers behind the eye. Perhaps we are tired or hungry, or heartsore, or loaded down with business cares. Perhaps the day is not propitious—sunshine makes a vast difference. Any one or all of these causes might produce the disappointment. But there is something in the nature of description itself that will account for our feeling. When the writer before mentioned made his portrayal of Fish Lake he selected just those details which he thought would make a clear and attractive picture in the reader's imagination and slurred or left out the thousand and one common-places which would interfere with the unity of such a picture. Now, unless the tourist has the same faculty—the faculty of refusing to see what is common-place, how shall he discover the unity or harmony of a scene in nature? Happily this faculty is capable of cultivation. But the majority of sight-seers get hopelessly lost in the complexity of details. As Lowell puts it, because of the trees they fail to see the forest.

Effect of the Point of View.—He who would successfully put a picture into words, must begin by doing precisely what he does who would put it into colors; that is, he must choose a point of view, and maintain it till the work is done. He must not attempt to describe things as they are, but only as they appear. A mountain will be rugged and precipitous if it is near, or shadowy and mist-veiled, if far. Viewed from its bank, a river may be a muddy, trubulent flood, but from the neighboring mountain top it is a "silver thread winding in and out amid the velvety green of the valley." A human figure near by is Old Mother Hobarty, a little way off it is an old woman with a cane, still farther, a woman merely, then a human being, and lastly a moving object. The laws of perspective can no more be dispensed with in a description than in a painting.

But let us not make the mistake of supposing that the point of view must always be a point in space. It is often only an attitude of mind. For instance, a murder has been committed and the accused is placed behind the bars. Here two reporters face him and draw his portrait in words, the one from the point of view, "He is innocent," the other from the conviction, "He is guilty." Both will be more or less exact descriptions, but how different in outcome! Of course, in such a case the point of view should be, "He may or may not be guilty."

Grouping an Act of the Mind.—Contrary to the usual conception, things do not exist in nature already grouped and unified for description. True, there are crude divisions and classifications such as we observe in passing from zone to zone, or in ascending to higher altitudes—classifications made by the uniform and persistent forces of nature. But these divisions are only as the great limbs of a tree. After that so far as the purposes of man are concerned, her products and forces are more or less jumbled together, haphazard. I say, for man's purposes they are so jumbled; for if we could look at them from God's point of view, we should perhaps find orderly and inevitable arrangement clear to the uttermost twig and leaf of creation.

But for man's puny purposes, this natural classification is on too wide and infinite a scale. He must recombine it by taking here a little and there a little. His subject-matter lies spread out before him like the uncut material of a milliner store; and the constructing of a description does not differ essentially in principle from the putting together of a hat; a certain unity is conceived in the imagination, and then the forms, colors, and textures are chosen here and there as needed to make real the conception. But on nature's shelves the details are so multitudinous, diverse, and complicated that it requires a discrimination more keen and far-reaching to describe well than to trim hats well.

The Problem of Selection. — From the foregoing it will be seen that the problem for the descriptive writer is not so much one of finding as selecting. It is not the enumeration but the exclusion of details that will tax his artistic powers. Think, for instance, how long and tedious would be the description of even the most beautiful building if all its details were given. While this might be necessary in an architect's design, yet for the purpose of arousing the emotion of beauty, only a few bold, characteristic strokes dare be trusted; and just how many details and which details to give constitute the whole art of picture-making by words. When too many particulars are furnished the tedium and common-place of the catalogue settle over the spirits of the reader; and when too few are given the object remains so hazy and indistinct in the imagination as not to excite interest.

Which Details Should be Given.—As to which details should be furnished only this general principle can be given. Supposing the outlines already drawn, furnish the reader with just those facts which will stimulate the imagination to creative fervor, and at the same time guide it in forming a true conception. As a rule these will be characteristic details; that is, they will be marks which enable us to distinguish the thing itself from other members of its class. For instance, let us suppose that one hundred details would be an exhaustive description of a human being. Then fifty of them would apply to all human beings alike; twenty-five more to the sex to which he belongs; ten would be characteristic of his nationality; ten more would be true of all in the same station and occupation in life. There would remain then only five details characteristic of himself. And he would perhaps have to be a very strongly marked individual to have such a proportion of distinguishing characteristics.

Now, our knowledge concerning any man becomes indistinct precisely in the direction in which these figures grow smaller, and the same principle holds true respecting other objects of description. Plainly, then, the rule which should guide us in selecting and rejecting details might be thus stated: "Of details classified acording to their generalness, draw most largely upon the smallest division, and least largely upon the greatest division." Or to put the idea more tersely. "Draw upon facts in the inverse proportion to their generalness." This principle applied to the illustration used above would lead to something like the following choice of details: four out of the five facts peculiar to the man himself; three out of the ten peculiar to his station and environments; two from the ten characteristic of his nationality; one from the twenty-five relating to his sex; and no other fact than the name human being from the fifty details true of all mankind.

Word-Painting.—The highest art in selection consists in choosing the one word or phrase which flashes the whole picture upon the reader's imagination. For instance, if some one should exclaim: "Here comes an eye glass and a cane!" we should not only see the whole dude, but have aroused, as well, all the slumbering contempt we may feel for this variety of the biped. Great writers are noted for their ability thus to "take off" a character or a scene in a word. Literature is full of examples. Read, for instance, Goldsmith's satirical pen pictures of the famous coffee house club of whom Dr. Johnson was the pompous autocrat.

Effect of Arrangement.—But it is not by selection alone that the reader of description is assisted to just mental pictures. Quite as much depends upon grouping. By one arrangement, details obscure each other's light, by another they enhance it. Who has not been surprised at the difference of effect in, say, the same goods in a store, or the same furnishings of a room, simply by appropriate changes in the grouping!

Now, grouping in description is only another name for classifying or making appropriate divisions in a theme, and this question is exhaustively discussed elsewhere in this treatise. (See Chapter Eight, Section IX, X, and XI.) I cannot refrain, however, from quoting a fine example of it as applied to description.

"In studying any interesting scene, let your mind look carefully at all the details. You will then become conscious of one or more effects or impressions that have been made upon you. Discover what these impressions are Then group and describe in order the details which tend to produce each of the impressions. You will then find that you have comprised in your description all the important details of the scene.

"As an instance, let us suppose that a writer is out in the country on a morning toward the end of May, and wishes to describe the multitudinous objects which delight his senses. First of all, he ascertains that the general impressions produced on his mind are 'luxuriance,' 'brightness,' and 'joy.' He then proceeds to describe in these groups the details which produce these impressions.

"He first takes up the 'luxuriant' features: the springing young crops of grain, completely hiding the red soil; the rich, living carpet of grass and flowers covering the meadow; the hedge-rows on each side of the way, in their bright summer green; the trees, bending gracefully under the full weight of their foliage; and the wild plants, those waifs of nature, flourishing everywhere, smothering the woodland brook, filling up each scaur and crevice in the rock, and making a rich fringe along every highway and foot path.

"He then descants upon the 'brightness' of the landscape: the golden sunshine; the pearly dew-drop hanging on the tip of every blade of grass, and sparkling in the morning rays; the clusters of daisies dappling the pasture-land; the dandelion glowing under the very foot of the traveler, the chest-nut trees, like great candelabra, stuck all over with white lights, lighting up the woodland; and lilacs, laburnums, and hawthorns, in full flower, making the farmer's garden one mass of variegated blossoms.

"Last of all he can dwell upon the 'joy' that is abroad on the face of the earth: the little birds, so full of one feeling that they can only trill it forth in the same delicious monotone; the lark, bounding into the air, as if eager and quivering to proclaim his joy to the whole world; the humble-bee, humming his satisfaction as he revels among the flowers; and the myriads of insects floating in the air, and poising and darting with drowsy buzz through the floods of golden sunshine. Thus, we see that by this habit of generalizing, the mind can grasp the details of almost any scene."

The Need of Using Comparisons.— We speak of conveying information. But, really, nothing is more impossible than this, taken in the sense of transferring a fact from one mind to another, as we might convey a letter or a parcel from hand to hand. What we convey are signs, not ideas. If these signs have the same significance for others that they do for us, they arouse into consciousness ideas and thoughts similar to ours. Now, it continually happens that he who is describing uses signs that do not arouse corresponding ideas or thoughts in the minds of his listeners, and this for the simple reason that there are no such ideas or thoughts to arouse. The listeners do not explain their confusion in the way I have: they merely assert that they do not understand.

"Let me see," says the speaker, thoughtfully, "have you seen" —and here he names something 'like' the thing not understood. Being assured that they have, he proceeds to say that the thing is like that in this and this respect, but differs thus and so. By this means an adequate picture is at length lodged, or rather created in the imagination.

There is no other way. It is for this reason that descriptive writing especially is so full of metaphor and comparison. The primary aim in the use of figurative language should be, as in this case, to render an idea clear and accurate. When it does not do this, it is affectation to employ it. But it cannot make thought perspicuous without doing more: without adding force and beauty as well as clearness to the idea. I shall not add illustrations of the value of figures in description. Every chapter in this book will furnish examples of metaphor and simile, more or less apt and useful, and the subject is fully treated elsewhere under the head of "Imagery and Illustration."

Dynamic Description.—Homer has successfully imposed upon the world the conviction that Helen of Troy was the most beautiful woman that has ever lived. Yet if every reader of the Iliad were called upon to give form and life to the impressions he has received of the world's beauty, she would be found to co-incide with his own ideal, and therefore not differ essentially from the woman he loves. We should have Helens of every conceived type of beauty: tall, medium, short; light, and dark; stout and lean;

sad and gay; sentimental and practical; esthetic and matter-of-fact.

Now, Homer could have produced so wonderful an effect only in one way—by description; but it is description of a peculiar kind, viz: that which gives effects and leaves the reader to create the causes. The most striking conceptions gained from literature are produced in this way. What mere grouping of descriptive details concerning Banquo's ghost, could make us feel the terror inspired by witnessing the quaking form and horror-stricken face of Macbeth at the banquet scene? Here is a passage from the Book of Job which also describes by noting effects:

"In thoughts from the visions of the night, when deep sleep falleth on men, fear came upon me, and trembling, which made all my bones to shake. Then a spirit passed before my face, and the hair of my flesh stood up. It stood still, but I could not discern the form thereof; an image was before mine eyes, there was silence, and I heard a voice saying, shall mortal man be more just than God? Shall a man be more pure than his Maker?"

What cause, we ask ourselves, could be adequate to such an effect? As we sense the deep stillness, the intense darkness, and see a spirit—or rather know than see that it is there—then picture the fear, and trembling of the old man, and his hair standing on end, a terror siezes us, too, that verges upon the sublime.

These examples enable us to understand the merits and defects of description which proceeds by noting effects. So far as the vividness of the emotion aroused is concerned the method is more forceful than direct description; but so far as furnishing the mind with a true picture or conception of the thing producing the effect it is utterly unreliable; since, being a self-creation entirely, such picture or conception would not be exactly the same in any two minds, but would in fact differ as the minds differed.

V

ESSENTIAL CHARACTERISTICS OF THE EXPOSITION.

Prominence has been given, in the foregoing chapters, to Narration and Description, partly because our Elders neglect these forms of communication, but mainly because of their intrinsic importance in preaching or teaching. It may be well, by way of introduction to our present theme, to show the connection between these forms and the form known as Exposition.

Relationship of Narration and Description to Exposition. —A narrative has to do with particular dates, particular persons, and particular events; that is to say, the objects are concrete, not abstract. It is for this reason that it is so easily understood by the lower grade of intelligence. The same is true of the description: it is the individual thing, not the class notion, about which we give details; and each detail, moreover, is a particular fact or idea. Minds incapable of grasping abstractions or generalizations readily take hold of the facts and events out of which such abstractions or generalizations grow, and the preacher (and teacher) will do well to remember that it is for just such minds that he exists.

But the only purpose of narration or description is to culminate in some such abstraction or generalization. Let me try to make this plain by analogy. You are sitting down to breakfast. Let your eye rest for a moment on the variety of good things before you. Each object is a generalization—the culminating point of a long series of narration and description. The well-browned rolls have a recent history in the kitchen, another in the mill, another in the harvest field, still another in the fertile soil. Then think what descriptions of sunshine, and rain, and wind, and changes of form, size, shape, color, and quality, are to be found

PREACHING AND PUBLIC SPEAKING.   233

and known at each step in the narrations. Is it plain to you, now, that bread is the 'abstraction,' or combined sum of all these processes? Do you appreciate likewise that this combined generalization is the result of many smaller generalizations? The story of sprouting—a most interesting story—culminates in a spear of wheat; the story of growing, in the ripened head, the story of garnering in the well-filled bin; the story of milling, in the snowy flour; the story of cooking in the steaming roll. In each case the product so differs in form as almost to be called a new thing. All narratives or descriptions should thus culminate in some general truth or principle which we call knowledge or wisdom.

Meaning of Exposition.—Now in casting about us for subject-matter, we come oftener across the finished product—the generalization—than upon narratives and descriptions—forms whose tendency is toward such a product. To minds familiar with the generalizing process, in any case, it is sufficient merely to name the generalization; but to minds unfamiliar, one of two methods must be followed; the generalizing process—narration or description—must be taken through in order that the result may be seen; or the generalization must be torn apart and spread out, as it were, that its elements may be examined. This latter is exposition.

The first is the more natural way, and the truths when gained are more vivid and forceful, but it is a long process. It leads to the modern primary school and to the so-called laboratory methods in higher education. The second method, though its information, like the back-water of a stream, lacks sparkle and freshness, is indispensable because it is a short way to get at facts. It leads to the compiling of dictionaries, cyclopedias, and to the writing of essays, treatises, on every conceivable subject. This book is an attempt at exposition of the ideas "Preaching and Public Speaking."

Synthesis vs Analysis.—Remember that spreading out and exposing to view the inner parts of a subject is the very essence of exposition. If the millions of rain-drops falling on the canyon slopes represent the concrete sources of ideas (synthesis) then the stream represents the generalization; and the taking out and spreading of the stream upon the land (analysis), represents exposition. Reverting to my former illustration of the source of bread, it may here be pointed out that the information gradually conveyed by the 'converging' incidents of a narrative, is in the process of exposition somewhat abruptly conveyed by the 'radiating' facts of the essay, e. g.

I. Bread: 1. What it is; 2. Ingredients; 3. How combined; 4. How cooked. II. Flour: 1. What it is; 2. Chemical constituents; 3. How made; 4. Kinds. III. Wheat: 1. Kinds and grades; 2. How stored; 3. How threshed; 4. How harvested. IV. Growing grain: 1. Time required; 2. Necessary conditions; 3. Dangers; 4. Steps in the growth. V. Germination: 1. Meaning; 2. Conditions; 3. Chemical changes; 4. Physical changes. Each of these heads would have an appropriate series of sub-heads.

The latter method is analysis, the former synthesis. They are opposite in procedure, but each gives us adequate ideas respecting a generalization.

Definition, Classification, Partition.—The spreading out or exposition of a term may take two directions: it may enumerate the qualities of the thing, in which case it is a Definition; or it may name the various varieties of the thing, in which case it is a Classification. Were this an exact treatise, I should elaborate upon this distinction, which is very important both from a logical and a rhetorical point of view. But for the practical purposes of the Latterday Saint Elder it is sufficient to divide the subject as illustrated in the last paragraph, into just those sub-heads, whether of qualities or varieties, or both, which the demand for information calls for, and such a division is called Partition, and is exhaustively treated elsewhere. (See Chapter Eight, Sections IX, X, and XI.)

The need for exposition lies in two facts. First, the circle of knowledge is constantly expanding, and every strip of territory snatched from the frontier of the unknown, brings with it facts and generalizations for which names must be invented. Botany, zoology, chemistry, physics, astronomy, and a score of similar sciences, are pushing their conquests further and further into the present world; history, by means of an equal number of sciences, is probing the past; so too the future is made vaguely to yield its treasures by the development of man's prophetic sense. Each branch of thought-activity is piling up a nomenclature, locked up in which is the accumulated knowledge of the race. To come at this piled-up information by synthetic methods would require a lifetime equal in length to the combined lives of those who piled it up; but by analytic or expository methods it is mastered in a few years, and the student is himself at the frontier of knowledge, ready to extend the territory of truth. The coral polyp lives and builds upon the roof of a million successive tombs of his ancestors; man does the same thing, with this difference: his mental life may extend more or less perfectly along the entire series from bottom to top—all which should teach us what we owe to exposition as a method of imparting information.

Fodder, Beef, and Essence (of Thought).—The second fact necessitating exposition is to be found in the very nature of the human mind. The more intensely a man thinks, the more he compresses his thoughts in their expression. Thus, from Cooper, whose diffuse tales contain thought as fodder contains beef, down—or up —to Shakespeare, whose thought-compression can scarcely be compared to beef, but rather to the essence of beef, we have in different authors a hundred ratios between the weight of the thought and the volume of its expression; and the reason that literary works of such varying merit remain popular is simply that there are minds corresponding to each variety.

While it is true, that the less wood in a work of literature, the more nearly, in this respect at least, it approaches the classics, it does not follow that it becomes likewise the more useful. Because iron is not gold is no evidence that it is not as useful as gold. The fact is, all grades of literature are useful, and any grade may be useless. The ripest scholar begins by feeding on fodder, even though he ends by reveling in essence. At any stage in the growth of his mind, he can look back on writings that he disdains because of their tedious diffuseness; and forward upon writings that make him fall asleep in his chair, because they are "too hard to understand;" that is, because they are too much condensed for mental digestion.

Now, it is to aid us in moving from one stage of mental growth to another that we need a teacher. He must make a choice of the best methods of bringing home to our minds the deeper generalizations. Where time will permit he will choose synthetic methods; that is, he will lead us to discover the truth in the same way as did he who recorded it. But life is too short for this method, save only as it is necessary to train our minds to a vigorous inventive activity; for the most part, he must rely upon exposition to lead us from the diffuse to the concise.

Mistakes in Exposition.—The question is sometimes asked: Can children be made to understand Shakespeare? The answer is, yes, if you make a thin enough soup of him; if by exposition you carry the essence of his thought, through half a dozen transformations, to the primitive herbage whence it was first gathered; or to vary the figure, if you expand his apothegms into the volumes of mythology, romance, history, travels, biography, theology, natural history, etc., out of which they have been boiled down. The answer applies equally well to attempts at teaching children the writings of St. Paul, or of other abstruse thinkers.

It may be done, I repeat, but it never is; for no teacher has the time for so extended an exposition, nor has any child the endurance to listen to it. The attempt to do it ends, therefore, by piling into the memory a lot of indigestible facts and generalizations that act upon the mind in the same way that filling the stomach with marbles would act upon the body. Paul's principle of exposition is the natural one: Milk for babes, meat for strong men; essence, we may add, for the gods, the intellectual giants among men. Let parents, teachers and preachers, when requested to explain anything, ask themselves this question: Is the thing enquired about just now crowding itself upon the enquirer's horizon of knowledge, or is it anywhere near the circle of that horizon? If so, explain it. But if it is very remote, refuse to explain it. An exposition of something far out of its relations, even if it does not stultify the mind, is likely to create wrong impressions; for between telling directly what is false, and telling the truth out of joint, there is often no difference save in motive. Explain rather what book should be read, or what time should elapse, or what circumstances should take place, ere the thing enquired about can be understood in its true relations. Occasionally a thing may be brought from far to one's mental horizon; but a safer rule of knowledge-growth, is to wait till the natural expansion of the horizon takes in the thing.

VI.

METHODS OF EXPOSITION.

Methods of Exposition.—Having discussed some of the principal facts concerning Exposition, its relation to Narration and Description, the conditions making it a necessity, its importance, and the general principle which should determine the choice of subject-matter, we shall do well to examine a few of the ways in which thought is amplified or spread out for better comprehension.

Re-scanning Particulars.—Since every general truth may be regarded as made up of a number of particular truths, the most natural way to impress the reader with it, is to spread out those particulars before him. Suppose the general truth to be the oft-repeated statement that the Latterday Saints have made the desert to blossom as the rose. The amplification might begin: "When they came here they found the country a desert, indeed," and here such particulars would be given as would make plain and vivid the meaning of the word 'desert.' Next a few characteristic facts concerning the 'manner' in which the transformation took place, would be given, and lastly a series of apt contrasts between what was and what is would make the exposition complete.

Sometimes the general truth can best be amplified by examples, e. g. "Truth crushed to earth will rise again." Here history must be drawn upon, and no end of illustrations present themselves to the thoughtful reader. Lectures are made in this way.

But general and particular truths are in fact reciprocal, and quite as often the latter are made forcible by illustration from the former. Especially is this the case where the general truth is axiomatic, e. g. We are tempted to buy when we can scarcely afford to do so, but conquer the temptation by remembering Poor Richard's advice: "Pause a long while before a big penny's worth." Or we are about to decide a matter which under the heat of emotion looks clear as day; but we hesitate remembering our infallible maxim: "Trust not thy judgment in anger." Or we are about to act a deceitful part, persuaded that the "End justifies the means," when we remember that this maxim is safe only when placed along side of another: "It is never right to do wrong." In each of these cases some particular thought or act is made plainer in its bearings or consequences by being looked at in the light of a general truth. It may be added, as a wider illustration of the same principle, that statute law, representing the particular enactments, receives its interpretation from common law, representing the general conclusions of jurisprudence.

Exposition by Repetition. — Frequently a general notion needs no other treatment than to be given time to impress itself. How to keep it before the mind long enough to burn its lines into the consciousness becomes then the problem. The orator makes a pause before and after the important idea, the first to clear the mind of other notions, the second to give the idea time to be realized. This is the key to exposition by delay. Prepare the attention by some remark leading toward the idea, next give the idea, then keep it before the mind by repetition. Care must of course be taken not to offend the verbal ear by sameness in sound or construction. Clothe the idea successively in a new dress and each time let it march in, as it were, by a different door. Put a question embodying the thought and if this does not fix it, exclaim at the unlikliness of the opposite idea. The notion, which if boldly stated would have been lost, is by such a process of delay made to record its full weight of meaning upon the mind. I shall not stop to illustrate this kind of expansion. This book is full of such "tautology," which is defensible only on the ground that I am ever keeping in mind the young Elder whose opportunities have not given him quick and keen verbal penetration.

Re-clothing the Skeleton. — A fourth way in which amplification makes thought more vividly comprehensible is by re-clothing in flesh and blood and life, the dry bones of narration, description, and definition. Most of the narratives in the Bible, for instance, are mere skeletons, often not complete as skeletons. This is no criticism upon the sacred writers. The necessity for condensation precluded the recording of all those life-like details which alone can make a story real. What then? Cuvier from a single fossil reconstructed one of the monsters of the prehistoric world. The subsequent discovery of a complete skeleton proved his judgment correct. So we are to take the literary fragments which reach us by a hundred different channels and from them recreate in imagination the original scenes or transactions. Without such realization, history and literature are at best only cut and dried fodder.

There is a kind of moss, sometimes for curiosity's sake kept in so dried and shriveled a state that it crumbles and almost changes to dust at the touch; but placed in water it regains its pristine life and coloring almost under the glance of the observer. Such a transformation the imagination should make upon all things taken into the mind. The student capable of doing this needs no teacher, but is himself pre-eminently fitted to be a teacher. And as nine people out of ten are not able, or but feebly able thus to recreate for themselves, the preacher, of all men, should most assiduously cultivate this power.

Example of Amplification.—Perhaps an example of this kind of amplification will be of assistance. Suppose it be the purpose of the preacher to impress upon his hearers the moral greatness of our Savior, and he has chosen a scene from the crucifixion. It is not enough to say, for instance, "Christ was an exemplar of his own teachings respecting love for one's enemies; his dying prayer was, 'Father, forgive them: they know not what they do.'" For although the supreme fact in this scene is thus set forth, it reaches only the intellect: we know but do not feel that it is so. Somehow we must fire the imagination and awaken the emotions. For instance, we might say: "The Savior of the world had been nailed to the cross. The cruel spikes had been driven through the quivering flesh, and now he hung upon the torn and ragged nerves of his hands and feet. Streams of blood had clotted and dried and then flowed afresh with every movement. The crown of thorns had pierced his brow and drops of blood mingled with the dew-damp of approaching death. Overhead was a burning sun. He was athirst, but they gave him gall to drink.

"What must have been his suffering! The thieves who hung by his side were coarse in texture, and the sluggish nervous system which had dulled their interpretation of the joys of life, now made them insensible to the pains of death. But he whose physical organization, more delicate than the aeolian harp, had been attuned to all the harmonics of the universe—what must have been the torture, how exquisite the agony, that accompanied the tearing asunder of the fibres of such a life! How long must it last? Each minute is

PREACHING AND PUBLIC SPEAKING.   241

an age, yet as a sheep before her shearers is dumb, so openeth he not his mouth; but from his pores come drops of blood!

"But physical suffering is the least of his agony. Beneath him in mocking groups are his enemies, their stony eyes, and bony fingers turned upon him in derisive triumph; the brutal soldiery savagely glad at witnessing a spectacle; the fickle multitude who had lately been fed at his hands now emptying their small souls upon the air; and the spotless priests, those whited-sepulchers, those fiends incarnate in the robes of sanctity, taunting him with their victory and his defeat, mocking his suffering, and calling upon him to come down and thereby prove to them that he is the Christ. Must he endure all this? Why does not the earth open and engulf this godless multitude? Swift annihilation should be their punishment. But no; that would be too easy: their dying should be lengthened out to eternities.

"Alas, these are our thoughts, not his. As far above vengeance as the sun above mists, sits his soul even in this ordeal; but still is it true that his physical pain is the least of his suffering. He is dumb with unutterable sorrow for the sins of his brethren, children of the same Father and Mother in Heaven. These are the men who have falsely accused him, persecuted him, scourged him, smitten him upon the cheek, spit upon him, and now doomed him to the slow, lingering death of a felon, whose ignominy they seek to increase by their mockery. Vengeance hangs in the heavens over their heads. He has but to say the word and it falls upon them. But he does not say the word. He endures and pities and loves. He is a man of sorrows and acquainted with grief. Betrayed, mocked, scourged, spit upon, crucified, in the supremest moment of his agony, he lifts his eyes to heaven, and from his bosom, like the breaking of a heart come the words: "Father, forgive them, they know not what they do."

"It was not a man that spoke—it was a God!"

The foregoing is an instance where narrative is aided by description. The Bible is full of situations where such expansion is necessary to a full realization of the thought; as for instance, Simeon blessing the infant Jesus, the flight into Egypt, the youthful Christ with the learned doctors, and many similar passages which barely record the naked facts in half a dozen words. For an example of a definition expanded, turn to Chapter Eight, Section I, II, and III of this treatise, which are amplifications of Cicero's statement as to the purpose of the introduction, viz: "Reddere auditores benevolos, attentos, et dociles."

VII.

METHODS OF EXEGESIS.

Perhaps the method of exposition which would be of the most immediate value to the preacher is that technically known as exegesis. As applied to holy writ, it is the enlarging of any scriptural passage so as to exhibit all its bearings and connections.

Need of Exegesis in the Missionary Field.—Young Elders are often lamentably deficient in the analytical power necessary to vigorous exegesis. I remember listening, meeting after meeting, to the five minute talk of a raw missionary companion of mine, during which time faith would be defined in Paul's words as the substance of things hoped for the evidence of things not seen. At last as we were in the woods one day I said:

"Brother D——, what do you mean by these words?"

"Mean? Why, I mean just what the Bible means."

"Well, what is that? Make it plain to me. I confess I don't get a single idea from merely hearing you quote the passage."

He was unable to answer. The passage was an uncracked nut to him, which had lain for years undigested in his mental stomach. When the meaning was demanded he was utterly helpless.

How to Acquire the Power.—We proceeded then to spend the next two hours in amplifying the thought. First the idea "substance (assurance) of things hoped for" was taken up. I made this young man name a dozen things that he ardently hoped for, and then we examined the ground or assurance for the hope in each case. Thus he was made to see that the assurance resting in our minds that we will get the things we hope for, constitutes our faith.

In the same way the words, "evidence of things not seen" were taken through. A score of objects in history and geography —objects that the Elder could not possibly have seen—were singly examined and the evidence that they exist or existed, questioned. In this way it was discovered that nine tenths of all the things we say we know, are only the "evidence of things not seen," or rather our faith that things exist which we have not seen.

The principle thus laid bare beneath these oft-quoted words was next applied to spiritual matters. It was, for instance, shown to be as natural to have faith in a resurrection, as in some earthly, hoped-for contingency, and as easy to believe that the Savior existed and performed his miracles, and was raised from the dead, as to believe that Moses was saved in the ark, and afterwards delivered the Israelites, or that Napoleon rose, and reigned, and fell.

An Example of Exegesis.—All of Paul's writings need thus to be expanded in order to be comprehended. Even Peter realized this when he spoke of things hard to be understood in the epistles of his fellow Apostle. But of this the reader may be certain: when these condensed and sometimes mystical sayings are amplified, they will present perfect revelations of truth. Take this passage for instance: "The righteousness of God is revealed from faith to faith: as it is written, The just shall live by faith."

The exposition in this case turns upon the exegesis of the words "righteousness of God," "revealed," "from faith to faith" "the just" and "live by faith." By way of illustrating this kind of amplification, let us attend briefly to the meaning of these expressions.

Righteousness is the quality of being righteous, and righteous is the attribute of being right and doing right. "The righteousness of God" stands, therefore, for the perfection of God, i. e., the state our Father has reached in the scale of eternal progress.

This perfection is to be "revealed" to man. Now, "revealed" cannot possibly signify merely "exhibited" as in a vision, for it is to come from "faith to faith." It evidently includes the idea "bestowed upon," or "given to," man. In this sense then, man is endowed with the righteousness or perfection of God from "faith to faith."

It is by "faith" that we get the first glimpse of the perfection of God. It is not until we "do" what we "see," and thus endow ourselves with this first perceived perfection, that we are able to get a greater "faith," and in turn a higher conception of Deity, and thus reach a nobler standard in ourselves. It is thus "from faith to faith" that we grow upward to God.

Paul next proclaims it a law that the "just shall live by faith." The "just" here must stand for those who are justified by God, i. e., those who grow as he would have them grow. When it is said they shall live by faith, the implication is, they are not to live by sight. Three questions arise: (1) Is this way of getting knowledge the actual way in this life? (2) If so, what is the purpose of God in so shaping our destiny? (3) Will the next life present any change in this system of mental growth?

It would be interesting indeed to write a lecture discussing these questions. But it would require too much space for this treatise; for it would involve some of the most vital questions of the science of teaching, as well as the deepest questions of theology.

Orson Pratt's Works.—Many fine examples of exegesis are to be found in Orson Pratt's tract on "Divine Authority, or Was Joseph Smith Sent of God?" Take for instance his exposition of the blessing on the head of Joseph: "Joseph is a fruitful bough, even a fruitful bough by a well, whose branches run over the wall. * * * The blessings of thy Father have prevailed above the blessings of my progenitors unto the utmost bounds of the everlasting hills." Each point in this prophecy is discussed separately and its bearings pointed out at great length. Unless Elders thus get into the habit of giving the closest analytical scrutiny to words and phrases in the scriptures, they will miss the strongest evidences of Mormonism.

Method of Mind-Association.—Exposition or amplification grows out of a desire to make thought plain and comprehensible. In the language of psychology, this means the interweaving of the new knowledge with the old by as many bonds of associations as can conveniently be made. The tendrils of the new idea, to speak figuratively, are drawn out, and made to penetrate the mind and intertwine themselves as deeply and intricately as possible among the tendrils of ideas already growing there. The methods of association are not difficult to classify. They are contiguity, similarity, contrast, analogy, and correlation.

Association by contiguity is the lowest and crudest form of mind-activity. It is said that the Chinese teacher, after he has stated what he regards as an important fact, will give one of his pupils a sound thrashing, turn a summersault, or perform some other striking feat, that the fact may sink into their minds and be easily recalled. This happens according to the law that impressions made upon the mind at the same time tend to recall each other. With children and people of a low grade of intelligence this is often the only effective way. The history of mission-work among the Indians and other savage races is full of examples of this method. What, in fact, are all the paraphernalia of the Salvation Army but means of impressing truth by mere contiguity, or juxta-position of unrelated things?

Association by similarity is the name given to the tendency to see likenesses between things—likenesses of form, size, color, weight, texture, or any other quality that an object may possess. This is one step above the arbitrariness of contiguity, and leads to the enlargement of thought by examples, illustrations, comparisons. It is a very effective way of impressing the mind.

Association by contrast is the obverse of association by similarity. It is the seizing upon the 'difference' between things. It is frequently as effective to tell what a thing is not as to tell what it is. The Elder will do well to get into the habit of asking himself what would be the effect of the opposite of the thing maintained. He whose mind is keenly alert to likenesses and contrasts will seldom lack material for exposition.

Association by analogy is the ability to perceive spiritual likenesses. It is the source of all our poetry. Gibralter lashed by the angry ocean, ceases to be a mere mountain, and becomes a symbol of firmness. A river typifies life and a thousand relationships of life. Every object in nature calls to mind its analogy in the mind-world, and becomes thereby a means of portraying truth.

Correlation is a general name for a multitude of associations which the mind is able to perceive between things; as cause and effect, or vice-versa, part and whole, instrument and user of instrument, sign or symbol and the thing symbolized, material and the thing made of it, etc. It is hardly too much to say that the material civilization of the nineteenth century is owing largely to our sharpened perception of the correlation of things. It is a species of mind-association that the preacher cannot afford to neglect.

Condensation and Elaboration.—This finishes my discussion of exposition. But no sooner am I done with urging the Elder to amplify and spread out thought, that I am seized with a desire to write a chapter urging him to condense; for he is quite as much at fault in respect of the latter idea as of the former. Where he now elaborates—on the mere trimmings of thought, things which an audience cannot escape understanding by the slight allus-

PREACHING AND PUBLIC SPEAKING. 247

ion—I would have him condense; and where he condenses, or rather repeats mere general statements, I would have him elaborate. But all this he will do instinctively, as soon as he learns to think.

VIII.

PRINCIPLES AND METHODS OF ARGUMENTATION.

Consider as a subject for a sermon the proverb, "The fear of the Lord is the beginning of wisdom." It is composed of two terms, viz., (1) 'the fear of the Lord.' (2) 'the beginning of wisdom,' and of the copulative verb 'is.' What is meant by 'fear of the Lord' and 'beginning of wisdom?' The answer leads to exposition. Now, after these terms are exactly defined and agreed upon, there remains the verb 'is,' which asserts that the first of these terms is included in the second. Is this a truth? The answer leads to argumentation.

All controversial subjects—subjects about which there are differences of opinion—can be settled only by argument. This is not saying that there must be a particular form of procedure. All the other forms of discourse—narration, description, exposition, persuasion—may be called into requisition to solve doubts; in fact are called, and combined as the exegency of the case may require. But aside from this use of the word it stands for a special forensic kind of discourse, some of the principles of which, I now proceed to discuss.

Three kinds of Arguments.—There can of course be no argument without a definite proposition about which to take sides. This point is discussed at length in a later part of this work. (See Chapter Eight, Section VII and VIII.) There may be many ways, as above intimated, of presenting the proof of this proposition, after the facts of that proof are collected; but as respects the directions from which we collect such facts there are but three. Facts proving a thing are taken (1) from circumstances prior to the thing—that is, they are "a priori" facts;—which are held forth as causes; or (2) they are taken from circumstances resulting from the thing,—that is, "a posteriori" facts—which are regarded as effects; or (3) they are taken from circumstances connected with the thing, but presenting points of resemblance which are regarded as "examples" tending to prove the thing.

Rhetoricians give various names to these arguments. My constant aim has been to keep technicalities out of this work, but right here I really see no way clear of adopting one of these classifications. We shall accordingly call the first class, arguments from 'antecedent probability;' the second, arguments from 'sign;' and the third, arguments from 'example.' In illustrating each variety, I shall draw my examples as much as possible from arguments used to establish Mormonism.

Argument from Example.—The undeviating constancy of the laws of nature leads us to believe that like causes will produce like effects. And as the God of nature is equally the God of revelation, we are led to expect equal consistency in the spiritual world. The scriptures confirm us in this view, by assuring us that God is the same yesterday, today, and forever. In view of this principle, let us consider briefly the arguments in support of one of the foremost doctrines of Mormonism, viz:

Continuous Revelation is Essential to the Existence of the True Church of Christ.

Orson Pratt, in treating this proposition first clears the way by showing that in every scriptural age there has been continuous revelation, from the days of Adam to the days of Christ; whence he draws the conclusion that it is reasonable to expect revelation in this dispensation also. This is purely an argument from example.

Argument from Antecedent Probability.—He next proceeds to prove that to expect continuous revelation is not unscriptural, i. e., there is no antecedent probability 'against' the proposition. Then he proves the converse, viz: that to expect continuous revelation is scriptural, i. e., that antecedent probability favors the proposition. To quote prophecies in past revelation to the effect that God will reveal himself in our day, is not to show forth the cause of new revelation, but only to present antecedent probability in favor of new revelation.

Argument from Sign.—Thus it is seen that the first and third classes of argument can be used in support of this proposition. Will the second also assist? Let us see. What are the 'signs' or results of new revelation? How do these signs support the proposition? Under this head the fact will be set forth that when new revelation came it cleared up all the difficulties in the Bible which have led to such a division of Christian sects, that it re-established the Church of Christ in organization, in doctrine, and ordinances; that with us also the "signs follow the believer;" lastly that every faithful member gets a direct testimony from God that the new revelation is from him. These are all effects, direct or indirect, and as such are adequate to show a cause, viz: the truth set forth in the proposition. This last is an argument from 'sign.' A proposition becomes remarkably well fortified when it draws support from all sides of it, i. e., from antecedent probability, from effects or signs, and from examples.

The Disproof of a Proposition proceeds by the same methods as the proof of it. Let the proposition be the reiterated assertion:

Mormonism thrives only on ignorance.

As 'antecedent probability' against this slander, we quote our belief that the "Glory of God is intelligence," and that man is saved and exalted only in the degree that he becomes like his Father in heaven. We also quote Joseph Smith's declaration: "No man can be saved in ignorance," and also: "A man is saved no faster than he gains intelligence." Is it likely, we ask, that a people ardently looking forward to a future life, will neglect the only means which, according to their faith, will make secure that future life?

We should next draw arguments from sign. Do we find the marks of ignorance in Mormon communities? The percent of illiteracy is lower than that in four fifths of the states of the Union, including Massachusetts. What of the neatly-kept lawns, flower-gardens, and orchards that distinguish Mormon homes? What of the public buildings, from the humble meeting houses and school-buildings, the first rude architectural plants of the desert, to the magnificent temples, which express the loftier conception, that of beauty united with utility? What of the absence of poor-houses, of the unbuilt and disused jails and reformatories, of the rare instances of Mormons keepings saloons, of the low percentage of Mormon inmates of the penitentiary? What of the thrift and industry which make Mormon emigrants welcome in surrounding states and territories? Are these the marks or signs of ignorance?

We may next draw arguments from example. This brings us to an actual investigation of the schools and all other agencies which tend to spread culture and intelligence among the people, e. g., the Mutual Improvement associations, the Primary associations, the Relief societies, the Sunday schools, the Quorum organizations, etc., all of which have, or aim to have, free libraries. Upon this showing we challenge comparison with any other people or community on earth. Is it ignorance, then, on which Mormonism thrives?*

Negative and Positive Arguments.—Note the fact that it is of as much importance in arguments of the first class, to look for negative as for positive probabilities. That is, it will often strengthen a cause quite as much to show that there are no facts making against it as to show that there are many facts making for

---

*Strictly speaking, in so far as the argument in this paragraph presents causes of which the general effect is intelligence, it is an *a priori* argument, and belongs to the first class But in respect of the facts that schools, etc., are counted evidence in other communities of a hatred of ignorance, it is adduced to prove that the same fact is claimed among us, whence it becomes an argument from an example.

it. It is the observance of this principle especially that makes Orson Pratt's argument so invulnerable. It is, in effect, sweeping the field of causes and tendencies with the eye of your adversary as well as with your own eye. It inspires confidence to give to the opposition as full and fair a hearing as it can possibly claim, and then prove the point held in spite of such concessions.

To Overthrow an Argument drawn from antecedent probability, one must show that effects are being claimed which the tendencies in question would not produce; or that granted the tendencies are toward such effects, something else intervenes and destroys the tendencies, so far at least as the given effects are concerned. In no other kind of argument is there more opportunity for intellect to strike fire against intellect than in this balancing of tendencies with counter-tendencies. Exact information and a keen power to forecast results and weave a close web of cause and effect, are the requisites of 'a priori' reasoning.

Evidence of Witnesses.—Under the head of argument from sign comes the consideration of testimony, or the evidence of witnesses. As set forth in the foregoing it is the purpose of arguments from sign to gather from a circle of effects what the thing was which produced the effect. Now when the thing set up as cause involves sounds and actions, no effects are stored up unless an intelligent eye and ear are within range of the cause. It is this stored-up effect or sign; which of course can be used only by consent of the mind in which it is locked, that constitutes human testimony. It is valid as a basis for reasoning according to the 'veracity' and 'integrity' of the mind that gives it up.

Respecting the first of these conditions, space will permit no discussion, other than to point out the lamentable fact that there is constant danger that facts may be colored from the lightest shades to the blackest hues by wilful falsehood. We must know much of any witness ere we will believe what he tells us. Rarely, indeed, do we have the same confidence in effects drawn from the human mind that we should show for similar testimony could it be drawn from a camera obscura or a phonograph.

Incapacity of the Human Mind.—Respecting the second condition, 'integrity' of mind, we must recognize that honesty alone is not sufficient evidence of truth. Honest minds are often self-deceived, so many are the tricks played us by imagination. The untrained eye does not always see in the same occurrence what the trained eye sees. A hundred different mariners testify to having seen the sea-serpent, ("or something like it" we feel like adding). Yet a single photograph of the monster climbing over the waves, would settle the fact of its existence forever. Such is man's comparative estimate of the integrity of the human mind. And we may as well add that it is a well-ordered distrust, and leads to weighing all the conditions under which a thing is seen or heard at the same time that we weigh the testimony itself.

The Need of More than One Witness.—It is from the last circumstance that we instinctively feel the need of more than one witness. Elder Benj. Cluff, on a recent visit to Harvard university, got into conversation with Prof. James, the eminent psychologist, on the origin of Mormonism. "Professor," said a listening student, "what is your theory of Joseph Smith's vision of the angel and the golden plates?"

"It is purely a case of hallucination. I can quite believe that Smith was absolutely honest in his assertions, but still the fact remains he was probably deceived by his own senses. All the circumstances go to show he was laboring under mental aberration: filled with intense religious excitement, alone—"

"Pardon me," said Elder Cluff. "There you are mis-informed. The vision was seen by three besides himself, and afterwards by eight others. Permit me to read their testimonies."

After the reading Prof. James remarked: "Such testimony

PREACHING AND PUBLIC SPEAKING. 253

must be accounted for by other means than hallucination." God wisely ordained that human evidence must be sustained by the "mouths of two or three witness."

IX.

PRINCIPLES AND METHODS OF ARGUMENTATION, CONTINUED.

Authority.—Of all the arguments drawn from signs or effects, that which is substantiated by authority is perhaps most familiar to our Elders. Authority may be defined as the crystalized judgment or opinion of men respecting the inter-relation of causes and effects. Thus, when our Savior said: "Except a man be born of the water and the Spirit he cannot enter into the kingdom of God," we believe he generalized from a multitude of effects that were within his range of vision, all of which proclaimed the same common cause. Authority is based upon experience. Its value depends upon the thoroughness of the sifting. Hence the greater the number who, by sifting, have reached the same result, the more reliable the authority drawn from it. Nine-tenths of all the principles which guide us in life are perhaps derived from this source. It is right that the remaining one-tenth should be left for experiment, for by no other way could we get accretions to our knowledge and wisdom.

Refusal to Accept Authority.—When we refuse to accept the dictum of experience, that is, authority, there is no other way for us to learn than by having the experience ourselves. This is often unfortunate, even though it be inevitable. One of Zion's brightest daughters confided to me the other day her intention of marrying a "man of the world," a man in the worst sense of that word. In vain I reasoned from the 'a priori' grounds that the moral principles which were the fabric of her mind, would find no sympathy or support from him; in vain did I invoke the example of unhappy marriages of this character; in vain urged the wisdom drawn from the accumulated suffering and misery of such mis-alliances. She remained obdurate.

"My case is not theirs. I cannot feel that I shall fail. I cannot believe but that there must be some way of avoiding such misery on earth; and as to the hereafter, I believe God is a just God, and will look at my honesty and purity of intention. And if my marriage is a success in this life, such as I mean to make it, it will hold for eternity—much more likely to than many a Temple marriage which entails a life of misery."

"But," said I, "what do you make of God's positive declaration to the contrary? You refused just now to take the experience of women like yourself who have suffered through such a mis-step—refused because you thought them incapable of drawing the proper conclusion. Will you impute the same incompetency to your Father in heaven? For what are laws but the generalizations of exeprience?"

It was no use. Her love was greater than the universe. "If I had your faith in God," said she, "I should probably be guided by his word. But not having that faith, what can I do, but learn by experience?"

She was absolutely right. There is no other way for him or her that is unwilling to be guided by authority. All she would promise me was time—time to prove whether deep conviction or transient emotion swayed her.

Value of Argument from Authority.—This incident enables us to see just wherein authority is valuable in preaching, viz: where there is unshaken faith in the source thereof. The Bible has been our great tower of strength in the past. It is not so any longer. Not that it has ceased to be true, but that it has ceased to be believed. Our work in converting the world is now similar to

Paul's: we must lay anew the foundation. Nor will the methods Paul used avail us in the nineteenth century. We must resolutely enter the arena of specific thought, and show that Mormonism is so great a truth that it encompasses all other truths.

Defects of Arguments from Example.—The argument from example while extremely serviceable in making reasoning clear, and therefore in producing conviction, is very liable to abuse. It is hardly too much to say that most of the disputes which render political questions so rancorous arise from the application of examples. Because two things agree in this or that particular, they may or may not agree in a third. But the party interested declares they do and bolsters his assertion by sophistry, thereby inviting ridicule, which his partisan soul, now thoroughly energized, returns with interest.

Watch the next pair. Observe one of them lay down a principle of economics, that is to say, a generalization from thousands of cases. Observe the other adduce a similar example directly in opposition to the law. It is a case of his own experience of what has happened in the neighborhood, and he appeals to by-standers for corroboration. They chime in and he thinks he has "floored" his adversary. But the latter has caught up with him by this time and brings forward several examples supporting his proposition. Then begins the squabble. The one cannot afford to lose his triumph, so clings doggedly to his contrary instance; the other insists that it is an exception, and therefore does not disprove the rule. It takes only three minutes of such jangling to arouse partisanship, then— well, let no self-respecting man stay to witness the end of it. Let him rather adjourn to a dog-fight if his soul stands in need of a counter-irritant.

Sectarian Sophistry.—But it is not alone in politics that strife is raised by reason of examples. Wherever in any kind of argument a general principle or law is brought forward it would be remarkable indeed not to find a single instance in opposition. Being concrete, the example appeals to the ignorant more forcibly than does the law. Thus, our Savior's declaration that baptism is essential to salvation is set aside by thousands of professed Christians, from a false interpretation of his remark to the penitent thief: "Today shalt thou be with me in Paradise." Every Elder in the mission field has encountered this sort of opposition on nearly all the principles of the Gospel. While therefore argument from example will continue to remain one of the most potent factors for conveying truth, it is almost as potent a means of maintaining error. The difficulty lies in the inability of the ordinary mind to keep in view any other aspect of the example than the one immediately claiming attention.

Source of the Difficulty.—This weakness, says Mill, is "the characteristic intellectual vice of those whose imaginations are barren, either from want of exercise, from natural defect, or from the narrowness of their range of ideas. * * * To such minds objects present themselves clothed in but few properties; and as, therefore, few analogies between one object and another occur to them, they almost invariably overrate the degree of importance of those few; while one whose fancy takes in a wider range perceives and remembers so many analogies tending to conflicting conclusions that he is much less likely to lay undue stress on any of them. We always find that those are the greatest slaves to metaphorical language who have but one set of metaphors."

Examples of False Reasoning.—Here are a few examples illustrating the tendency to wrong conclusions by reason of false analogy. They are taken from Prof. A. S. Hill's Rhetoric, pp. 210-217.

There is an instance in a tale of Cumberland's, intended to prove the advantage of a public over a private education. He represents two brothers, educated on the two plans respectively, the former turning out very well, and the latter very ill. And had the whole been matter of fact, a sufficient number of such instances would have had weight as an argument; but as it is a fiction, and no reason is shown why the results should be such as represented, except the supposed superiority of a public education, the argument involves a manifest petitio principii and resembles the appeal made in the well known fable, to the picture of a man conquering a lion —a result which might just as easily have been reversed, and which would have been so, had lions been painters.—Whately.

"If," they say, "free competition is a good thing in trade, it must be a good thing in education. The supply of other commodities of sugar for example—is left to adjust itself to the demand; and the consequence is, we are better supplied with sugar than if the government undertook to supply us. Why, then should we doubt that the supply of instruction will, without the intervention of government, be found equal to the demand?"

Never was there a more false analogy. Whether a man is well supplied with sugar is a matter which concerns himself alone. But whether he is well supplied with instruction is a matter which concerns his neighbors and the State. If he cannot afford to pay for sugar he must go without sugar. But it is by no means fit that, because he cannot afford to pay for education, he should go without education. Between the rich and their instructors there may, as Adam Smith says, be free trade. The supply of music masters and Italian masters may be left to adjust itself to the demand. But what is to become of the millions who are too poor to procure without assistance the services of a decent school master?—Macaulay.

It is argued that "a great and permanent diminution in the quality of some useful article, such as corn, or coal, or iron, throughout the world would be a serious and lasting loss; and that if the fields and coal mines yielded regularly double quantities, with the same labor, we should be so much the richer; hence it might be inferred that, if the quantity of gold and silver in the world were diminished one-half, or were doubled, like results would follow, the utility of these metals, for the purposes of coin, being very great. Now there are many points of resemblance and many of difference, between the precious metals on the one hand, and corn, coal, etc., on the other; but the important circumstance to the supposed argument is that the utility of gold and silver (as coin, which is far the chief) depends on their value which is regulated by their scarcity —or rather, to speak strictly, by the difficulty of obtaining them; whereas, if corn and coal were ten times more abundant (i. e. more easily obtained) a bushel of either would still be as useful as now. But if it were twice as easy to procure gold as it is, a sovereign would be twice as large; if only half as easy, it would be the size of a half-sovereign: [It would remain the same size, I think, but would purchase half the goods in one case, and double the goods in the other. N. L. N.] and this (besides the trifling circumstance of the cheapness or dearness of gold ornaments) would be all the difference. The analogy, therefore, fails in the point essential to the argument.—Whately.

Because a just analogy has been discerned between the metropolis of the country and the heart of an animal body, it has been sometimes contended that its increased size is a disease—that it may impede some of its most important functions, or even be the cause of its dissolution.—Copleston.

Another example is the not uncommon dictum that bodies politic have youth, maturity, old age, and death, like bodies natural; that after a certain duration of prosperity they tend spontaneously to decay. This also is a false analogy, because the decay in the vital powers of the animal body can be distinctly traced to the natural progress of those very changes of structure, which, in their earlier stages, constitute its growth to maturity; while in the body politic the progress of those changes cannot, generally speaking, have any effect other than the still further continuance of growth: it is the stoppage of that progress, and the commencement of retrogression, that alone would constitute decay. Bodies politic die, but it is of disease, or violent death; they have no old age.—Mill.

A false analogy has been made the basis of an argument in favor of despotic government. It has been likened to the government exercised by a father over his children; a government which it resembles only in its irresponsibility; that is, in the fact that it is a despotism: whereas the beneficial working of paternal government depends, when real, not on its irresponsibility, "but on two other circumstances of the case—the affection of the parent for the children, and the superiority of the parent in wisdom and experience." The argument from this false analogy is usually summed up in the convenient phrase, "paternal government,"—the fallacy lurking in the word paternal, a word which may refer to the power of a father, or to his power judiciously exercised; it may mean like a father, or like a good and wise father.—Hill.

This want of discrimination between analogies which are arguments and analogies which are mere illustrations—analogies like that which Butler so ably pointed out between natural and revealed religion; from analogies like that which Addison discovered between the series of Grecian gods, carved by Phidias and the series of English kings painted by Meller—has lead to many strange speculations. Sir William Temple deduced a theory of government from the properties of the pyramid. Mr. Southey's whole system of finance is grounded on the phenomena of evaporation and rain. In theology this perverted ingenuity has made still wilder work. From the time of Irenaeus and Origen, down to the present day there has not been a single generation in which great divines have not been led into the most absurd expositions of Scripture by mere incapacity to distinguish analogies proper (to use the scholastic phrase) from analogies metaphorical.—Macaulay.

X.

THE CONDUCT OF A DISCUSSION.

There can be no argument as such without an opposing side either actual or assumed. This fact must be my excuse for introducing another chapter on argumentation. My purpose shall be to consider definitely relationships between the parties to any controversy.

Value of Debates.—Debating societies are occasionally discountenanced, on the ground that the partisanship engendered too often becomes so intense as largely to eclipse respect for truth. Now, respect for truth is of such transcendent importance that every thing dear to man, even life itself, should if necessary, be made to go down before it. While I deliberately take such a stand, I am not quite ready utterly to condemn debating,—

First, because there seems to me no good reason why this method of education should be singled out for proscription. Every form of communication between man and man is liable to engender feelings that tend to obscure truth. Business transactions are rife with such temptations. Love and courtship are not free from them. Married life is often a tissue of shams and make-believes. Prayers are sometimes eloquent with rhetorical falsehoods. Respect for truth may be, and is, assailed on every hand. As Burns says—

"Some books are lies frae end to end,
And some great lies hae ne'er been penned;
E'en ministers they hae been kenned,
Wi' holy rapture,
At times a rousing whid to vend,
An' nail't wi' Scripture."

Men do not hesitate to trade, love, marry, preach, and pray because these activities are ocasionally associated with loss of respect for truth. And, since the temptation to make and love and defend a lie is incident to almost every necessary condition in life, why become especially frightened at such a tendency in one of these conditions? Shall we refuse to sow wheat for fear of smut?

Secondly, because the mind-power gained through debating, or similar mental encounters, is essential to the successful maintenance of truth. How shall our Elders break down and dislodge the fortresses of error if not by grappling hand to hand with its defenders? The latter are skilled in all the arts of sophistry and trickery of debate. How shall men who have scorned to learn how to thrust and parry, hold their own with such antagonists? One of the most pitiable spectacles in the missionary field is to see a young preacher filled with the conviction that a certain attitude is right, and yet feel overcome with the consciousness that he is helpless to maintain it.

PREACHING AND PUBLIC SPEAKING.   261

It only shifts the question to say that it is the Elder's duty to preach the Gospel and avoid such encounters. He cannot avoid them. He may indeed escape formal debates, and perhaps will do well to do so; but encounters with error intrenched behind prejudice, he cannot escape save by silence. For, what is a successful sermon but truth arrayed at every point against error? That error is not always up in arms, i. e., that the Elder does not always have an active opponent, is no reason why truth should not be on guard against every species of attack. Whoever advocates or maintains any principle or doctrine talks to an opponent either real or assumed, if he talks to any purpose at all.

Thirdly, not to have the training gained from attrition with opposing minds often leaves a man so warped and partisan, not to say egotistical, that he cannot comprehend truth. If a man be possessed of correct principles, debating will marshal them into definite order, clear them of doubtful conditions, and fix them in his mind. If his principles be incorrect, the chances are favorable, provided he is an honest man, that the errors will be weeded out. Under any circumstances, the conceit will be knocked out of him and this is always a big point gained. Now, to urge that an Elder can be equipped for the aggressive and defensive warfare of truth, without aggressive and defensive training, that is to say, by being educated as it were, in a calm, is in my opinion to advocate an absurdity. As well attempt to produce a champion to meet a Corbett or a Sullivan by feeding a man liberally on beaf-steak and oat-meal.

One other remark may be ventured in this connection. The dangers from debating result, not so much from the mental opposition encountered, as from unwise choice of subjects. When questions of faith are selected, or principles of religion depending mainly upon spiritual intuitions, a fruitless wrangle, leading perhaps to permanent bias, will often result. This will be true also of purely intellectual questions, the relationship of which are beyond the grasp of the contestants. It is like wrestling in water over your head; the danger is not so much from overthrowing or from being overthrown, as from drowning.

In choosing an appropriate subject the first enquiry should be, "Are the facts such as are likely to yield to exposition and argumentation?" and the second should be, "Are the contestants resonably familiar with the bearings of the question?" These things satisfactorily settled, let them go ahead and take their exercise. It will not only be good mental discipline, but will prove a valuable lesson in self-control.

The conclusion seems irresistible, therefore, that debating is to be treated like all other methods of education; its use should, under favorable circumstances, be encouraged, and its abuse strongly guarded against. There may be instances where it should be entirely prohibited; though, we may safely venture the remark that where minds need such extreme protection, it is doubtful whether there is any mental integrity either to save or to spoil!

Burden of Proof and Presumption.—But the principles I am about to call attention to, apply as well to the argument that proceeds without an opponent (the speech or discussion), as to that which proceeds with an opponent (the debate). The first general principle to be kept in view is that the 'burden of proof' lies with him who attacks any existing order of things; in other words, the 'presumption' is always, that things which are, have a right to be; or as Pope puts it: "Whatever is, is right." We may actually know that whatever is, is not right, in any given case. It is our business then to attack, and the business of our opponents merely to defend. If we succeed, and maintain the point established till it be sanctioned by custom and usage, then the conditions are reversed: our opponents must attack—we have only to defend.

What would be thought of an army secure behind a fortress, if it moved out and risked a battle in the open plain? Time enough for that when it has been dislodged. Until then all that can be expected of it is to defend and fortify.

Now, just as this mistake has been made time and again in history, from a Quixotic sense of honor and fairness, so the young Elder, with more zeal than wisdom, often throws away the advantage with which presumption surrounds him and wastes his strength in trying to tear down what his adversary has really not yet succeeded in building. The army, if sorely pressed, may fall again behind its stronghold: not so with the man who leaves his fortress of thought: to forsake it is to destroy it; to disregard a presumption in one's favor is virtually to confess a doubt as to the rightfulness of the thing defended, and consequently to place it on an equality of merit with the thing opposing it.

Arguments illustrative of this principle will readily occur to the reader. For instance, what we can clearly prove from the Scriptures respecting the Church Christ set up in his day—as, for example, its organization, its laws of adoption, its gifts and blessings,—we may justly claim as a presumption in favor of similar conditions in the Church of today, and the burden of proof is upon all the churches which have departed from the original pattern; but what we cannot so distinctly prove, as perhaps polygamy, tithing, temple-building, stake and ward organizations, M. I. associations, the Book of Mormon, etc.—these it becomes our duty to establish, —to the extent at least that they cannot be distinctly proved from the Bible. The question of burden of proof and presumption is one that cannot be lost sight of at any stage of a discussion. It applies as well to the uttermost twigs of an argument as to the branches or trunk. One division of a theme may require aggressive treatment, and the next merely defensive. To know exactly when to attack and when to defend, constitutes a prime qualification of anyone who would enter the arena of thought.

Fairness to an Opponent.—Other principles of discussion

turn upon the disposition to be made of the arguments of the opposing side. The first requisite is to state them correctly and allow them their full weight and pertinency. You thus gain a reputation for fairness, and inspire confidence in the counter-arguments which you are about to present. These must be very strong, your hearers argue, or else you could not afford to be so liberal with your opponent. To garble or misrepresent your opponent's arguments will for similar reasons produce the opposite effect.

When and How to Refute.—A second requisite is to decide when to take up for rebuttal the opposing arguments. Refutation may come at the beginning, in the middle, or at the end of one's own presentation of the case, or a refutation of each individual point may parallel the respective opposing argument. Conditions in each discussion must determine this matter. If the impression produced by one's opponent be strong, it may be necessary to attack and refute his arguments at once, in order to gain respectful consideration for what one has to say on his side of the question. For similar reasons, if the impression has been weak, it is best not to refer to them at all, lest one drag from oblivion arguments which the hearers would otherwise not have been led to think about again. At any rate, "if the persons addressed do not have the opposing arguments in mind, it is obviously injudicious to suggest them until one's own case has been (partly at least) made out. If, however, an opponent is to follow, it is impolitic to state his case for him after getting through with your own, for this would leave him master of the field.

"Generally speaking, then, the 'refutation of objections' should be near the middle of the argument, so that the argument refuted may not make either the first or the last impression. The beginning and the end of an argument, as of a dramatic composition, are the most important parts.*

---

*A. S. Hill, Principles of Rhetoric, p. 233

As the reasoner grows in experience he will learn to let some arguments of his adversary severely alone, from an intuition that he cannot overthrow them, for to try and fail, in such a case, is worse than not to try at all. He will learn, too, that sometimes it is advantageous to acknowledge frankly that the position of his opponent is impregnable. Trust him also for acquiring the trick of promising to refute at a later part of the discussion, and then conveniently forgetting, and causing his hearers to forget his promise.

Order of Presenting Proof.—Lastly it is of importance to consider the most effective order of one's own arguments. This is treated in a general way further on under the head of divisions of the theme. Here it will be necessary to note a few specific points relative to argumentation.

"In arranging his proof," says Prof. Hill, "a reasoner does well to follow the natural order—that is, the order in which arguments would naturally occur to the mind—even where that order is, in itself, considered, less effective than an artificial order would be. Any departure from the obvious arrangement is likely to suggest the idea of artifice; and the suggestion of artifice excites suspicion of sophistry—what may be merely a fault of form being imputed to substance.

"If, however, in consequence of following the natural order, an author or a speaker is obliged to present his weakest arguments last, he will do well to recapitulate them at the end in the reverse order; for the principle of climax applies to reasoning as fully as to style.

"In many cases, the most natural order as well as the most effective order is that which places argument from Antecedent Probability first; those from Sign second, and those from Example last. The arguments from Antecedent Probability raise a presumption in favor of the proposition in hand; the arguments from Sign adduce evidence tending to strengthen that presumption, by showing that a thing which was likely to occur, did occur; and the arguments from Example strengthen it still further by evidence concerning similar occurrences. The first proves the principle which is applicable to the case; the second proves that the principle actually applies to the case; the third furnishes instances of its application in other cases."

XI.

PRINCIPLES UNDERLYING PERSUASION.

Meaning of the Term.—Persuasion is not the name of a particular method of composition, as is the case with Description and Narration. It is rather the name for a particular use or purpose to which any one of the methods may contribute. Thus John B. Gough, in his vivid delineations of drunkenness; John Howard in his strong portrayal of prison life; George Kennan, in his graphic account of the horrors of exile life in Siberia—all sought by description to enlist the sympathies and activities of mankind to the accomplishment of some definite purpose. Harriet Beecher Stowe, in Uncle Tom's Cabin; Dickens, in Nicholas Nickleby and other novels; and Ignatius Donnelly, in Caesar's Column—each attempted by narration to stir men to rise up and make right certain crying social wrongs. Whatever appeals to man's emotions in a way to take hold of his will belongs to Persuasion, in its widest signification. But in the narrower sense—the sense in which it is used in the following chapters—Persuasion stands for those means and devices which a speaker may use to arouse the feelings of his audience to the sticking point of conviction or action; and it is therefore synonymous with oratory in the most restricted meaning of that word.

Importance of Persuasion.—A little reflection will enable the reader to sense the transcendent importance which attaches to this field of thought-communication. Exposition may furnish the mind with facts; argument may win the intellect to view these facts in a definite relation; but it requires persuasion to give dynamic effect to such facts and relations—to release those activities of mind and muscle which shall work out the preconceived changes. Think for a moment of what work there is for persuasion to do in the world: the countless strokes of brain and brawn to gain a livelihood from mother earth; the millions of wrongs, social, political, and individual, that are to be righted; the daily encounter of truth and error in every human soul—all those operations of mind which involve changes in thought and feeling and action are directly or indirectly dependent upon forces set in motion by persuasion. What steam is to the machinery of the world, nay, what the sun is to the operations of nature—that persuasion in its widest sense is to the evolution of the human race. We can conceive motors to exist without power, the sun without light and heat, and intelligence without incentive; but to do so is to conceive a universal paralysis.

Sequence of Mental Activity.—In order to come to close quarters with our theme let us briefly consider the relationships growing out of the three well-marked operations of the human mind, viz: 'knowing,' 'feeling,' and 'willing.' Let our first enquiry be as to the sequence of activity of these powers.

Strictly speaking, we must 'know' something of the nature of an impulse ere it can affect our feelings. The simplest proof of this fact is that were we to listen to a recital of the most blood-curdling atrocity, given in a language not understood by us, our feelings would remain undisturbed, providing the narrator were calm. If he actively felt the horror, we should perhaps by contagion feel the same in a mild degree without knowing why. There is then ordinarily no getting at the feelings save through the gate-way of the intellect, contrary as this fact may seem to the popular notion that we may talk directly to the feelings.

It is next to be noted that the will cannot be stirred save as the impulse reaches it from the feelings. To make this fact clear, suppose all feeling-power were dead, and knowing and willing power normally active. Then suppose your child being scalped and flayed alive by an Indian right before your eyes. Every movement, every sound, of the otherwise heart-rending tragedy would be registered in your intellect; but having no feeling, you would stand by unconcerned and see the end of it. Physically you could have prevented it, but why should you? It was a matter of indifference. You could not get up enough interest to raise your finger by way of interference. You were powerless—like a dead locomotive on the track. Perfect in its machinery, and filled properly with coal and water, it lacks one thing—fire. Now what fire is to the locomotive, feeling is to will.

The will thus seems to be the innermost sanctum of the soul. Between it and the intellect there would be an impassable gulf, were the feelings taken away. The sequence of any rational mental activity resulting from thought-communication is therefore first knowing, second feeling, and third willing. Now, while we may affirm with much certainty that any will-impulse resulting from an outward communication, must have passed successively the intellect and the feelings, we cannot say of any impulse just starting that it will continue till it reaches the will. It may spend its force in the intellect; or it may go no further than the feelings; or it may pass both these portals, enter the will, and be reflected in some overt act. Reasons for this fact will be seen as we proceed.

Relative Strength of Mental Powers.—Our next question is as to the relative strength or degree of development of knowing, feeling, and willing. For the sake of clearness, let us suppose that 1000 represents the degree of perfection possible of attainment in each of these powers during life. And for brevity, let A stand for knowing-power, B for feeling-power, and C for willing-power. It is then pretty safe to say that no human being, unless it be our

PREACHING AND PUBLIC SPEAKING. 269

Savior, has ever had a perfectly developed and perfectly balanced mind, such as would be represented by A—1000, B—1000, C—1000. Take Aristotle, who is counted the greatest mental giant of the race, and his ratio might probably be: A—900, B—300, C—400. Human beings differ in mind according to the difference in ratio of intellect, feeling, and will. If the scale which I have arbitrarily chosen, were correct, then we should be able to have as many varieties of character as the product of 1000x1000x1000, or one billion types. To the eye of Omniscience there is perhaps even a greater number of differences than this in the characters of men and women on the earth.

Examples.—Take out a pencil and set down the estimated ratios in the characters of your friends and acquaintances, using 10 instead of 1000. You will be surprised at the results. Let us try a few ratios, and discuss the characters probably corresponding thereto. (1), A—3, B—8, C—9. This character acts first, then thinks afterward, or does not think at all. It is a character admirably fitted to lead a mob. It may also be a wife-beater, or even a murderer. Every impulse is carried into action, and whether the action be good or bad depends much more upon the "color" of the feelings than upon any restraining influence of the judgment. The more ignorant the community, the more likely is it that an audience will be made up of this kind. From Elder Bean's account of the inhabitants of Kane Creek, Tennessee, as also from the fact that they shot down Mormon Elders at the instigation of a red-hot revivalist, I should judge them to be of this class. Such characters are undesirable in any relationship of life.

(2), A—8, B—3, C—2. This is also an extremely ill-balanced character, but quite the opposite of the last. We have here a book-worm; a mind that takes in forever, but seldom 'gives out;' full of theories, but impractical to the last degree; a mind filled with knowledge of science, of mathematics, of history, of dead languages, or of whatever may be its peculiar bent—as full as a bin is filled with wheat, or a pit with potatoes; but the knowledge is quite out of relation with the conditions that would make it a power for good in the world. Socially there is no more juice in such a one than in a mummy, and the little will he has is practically useless if taken out of the grooves in which it has been accustomed to work.

(3), A—3, B—8, C—3. Here is another extreme—a character that feels much, but thinks little, and is too timid to act. Her sentimentality, maudlin to a nauseating degree, wastes itself on creatures of the imagination, or perhaps on pugs or poodles. Robust literature, such as would call into play reasoning or judgment, bores her to death, when compelled to listen to it; and she generally escapes with a pretty toss of her curls and a naive declaration that it makes her head ache. But novels—and especially romances—she devours by the score; and it is while reclining on a lounge, yellow-back in hand, or in her bed, near the midnight lamp, that she weeps for the sorrows of mankind, and visits the widows and fatherless in their distress.

These casts may be extreme types, but between each one and the other two are almost infinite varieties of ability to know, to feel, and to will. It is the business of the educator to equalize these powers. But the point I am seeking to make is, that unless a speaker have some general estimate of the ratio of these powers in his audience, he lacks the first element of success in persuasion; for what would fire an audience like case number one, would disgust an audience like case number two. The orator feels by instinct what this ratio is, but he did not always feel it; if he is an orator in the truest sense, he perhaps began with much intuitive discerning-power which he perfected by conscious study of the kind of minds he had before him to influence. The young man for whom I write this treatise, may not begin his career as preacher with such natural

PREACHING AND PUBLIC SPEAKING. 271

intuitive power; but the germ at least is there and cultivation will develop it like any other capability.

Knowledge Needed to Read an Audience.—It is not my intention to write a chapter on how to begin such an investigation. For, to study the knowing, feeling, and willing power of an audience, is to make a profound study of their physical, social, intellectual, moral, and spiritual environment. To know these forces is to be acquainted, 'a priori,' with the causes of the mental conditions; to read an audience is to read 'a posteriori,' the written results of these causes; for every audience may be regarded as the summed-up effects of past and present environments. These faces—what are they but a living canvas on which the soul paints the thoughts and emotions dominant within? The form and movement and voice and dress and toilet—what are they all but indexes of the manner of man that sits before us, if we are only able to interpret such signs; and with this knowledge, persuasion is merely a question of adapting the thought that we have to express to the condition of the being to be moved, in order to reach the desired result. The following from the pen of Henry Ward Beecher, will illustrate the value of knowledge of this kind.

"I see a man with a small brow and big in the lower part of his head, like a bull, and I know that man is not likely to be a Saint. All the reasoning in the world would not convince me of the contrary; but I would say of such a man, that he had very intense ideas, and would bellow and push like a bull of Bashan. Now, practically, do you suppose I would commence to treat with such a man by flaunting a red rag in his face? My first instinct in regard to him is what a man would have if he found himself in a field with a wild bull, which would be to put himself on good manners and use means of conciliation, if possible.

"On the other hand, if I see a man whose forehead is high and large, but who is thin in the back of the head, and with a small neck and trunk, I say to myself, That this is a man probably whose friends are always talking about how much there is in him, but who never does anything. He is a man who has great organs but nothing to drive them. He is like a splendid locomotive without a boiler.

"Again you will see a man with a little bullet-head, having accomplished more than the big-headed man, who ought to have been a strong giant and a great genius. The bullet-headed man has outstripped the broad-browed man in everything he undertook; and people say, 'Where is your phrenology?' In reply I say, 'Look at that bullet-headed man, and see what he has to drive his bullet head with.' His stomach gives evidence that he has natural forces to carry forward his purposes. Then look at the big-headed man. He can't make a spoonful of blood in twenty-four hours, and what he does make is poor and thin. Phrenology classifies the brain regions well enough, but you must understand its relations to physiology, and the dependence of brain-work upon the quantity and quality of blood that the man's body makes.

"You may ask, 'What is the use of knowing these things?' All the use in the world. If a person comes to me with dark, coarse hair, I know he is tough and enduring, and I know that, if it is necessary, I can hit him a rap to arouse him; but if I see a person who has fine silky hair, and a light complexion, I know that he is of an excitable temperament, and must be dealt with soothingly. Again, if I see one with a large blue, watery eye, and its accompanying complexion, I say to myself that all Mt. Sinai could not wake that man up. I have seen men of that stamp whom you could no more stimulate than you could a lump of dough by blowing a resurrection trump over it."

XII.

ESSENTIAL CONDITIONS OF PERSUASION.

Understanding the relationships of the knowing, feeling, and willing powers of an audience, is a question outside this treatise —a question to be answered by a systematic study of psychology, physiology, phrenology, and kindred sciences; but adapting methods to secure the purpose in view, after such understanding is secured, is quite within the purview of a work on preaching; for preaching more than any other form of oratory depends for its effectiveness upon persuasion.

Ratio of Brain-energy.—The underlying principle of successful oratory is to remember that every human being has but a limited amount of energy with which to operate the mind. In most people it is very small. This may be because there is but little in the body; or because little has been accustomed to flow to the brain. But, little or much, it differs in amount with every being, and if we suppose the minimum, above idiocy, to be 5, and the maximum to be 100, then minds, it will be seen, range in power, all the way from stupidity to brilliancy, from another cause than simply degree or kind of development. Let the mental energy of an audience be what it may, it is with this that an orator must produce his effects. Part of it will be expended by the intellect, in the effort to understand; part by the feelings, in the effort to realize; and what is left, by the will, in the endeavor to act.

Mistakes in Distribution of Energy.—When the purpose is to instruct, the speaker will try to turn the whole stream on the intellect; but when the desire is to excite to conviction or action, he will use as little here as possible, in order that more may be left for the feelings. The orator, whose aim is mainly persuasion, always makes a mistake when he uses up all his fire on the threshhold of the feelings. This blunder occurs in two ways: When he presents thoughts beyond the grasp of his hearers, and when he is abstruse or obscure in his expressions.

The first fault, that of presenting abstract or philosophical ideas, violates the essential conditions of an oration, making it a lecture. The second, that of using terms difficult to understand, proves equally fatal so far as the feelings are concerned. To illustrate, let the ordinary audience try to sense the ideas hid away in these words: "Corruscate, corruscate, diminutive stellar orb!" Now, if we suppose the mental energy to be ten, then nine at least will go to extract the meaning, and there is but one left to appreciate it when squeezed out. Put the same thought in these words: "Twinkle, twinkle, little star!" and this ratio is reversed.

Effect of Intellectual Obscurities.—Let it not be understood that thought intended to persuade must not appeal to the intellect: it must do this very thing ere it can appeal to the feelings; for to leave the intellect unsatisfied is to put the judgment on guard against the emotions. But care must be taken to introduce only such ideas as, like the illustration given above, pass through the understanding into the domain of feeling, without drawing appreciably upon the mental energy. This principle is violated by considerations that are subtile or far-fetched; by allusions to obscure myths or to characters and events of history or literature not familiar to the hearers; by using a style and diction alien to their ways of thinking; by adopting a higher moral tone than is likely to be appreciated or understood; and in general by using imagery, phraseology, and rythm, too rich and exquisite for the mental appetite of the audience. Such things may create a kind of dumb wonder, or at best stimulate a desire to understand; but, lacking the touch that makes the world akin, they arouse no emotion.

Need of Perspicuity.—When it is remembered that an audience has but the present instant in which to catch the meaning of a word or phrase, it will be recognized that the first requisite of persuasion is perspicuity; for without this essential all other good qualities are as truly covered up as the shining pebbles and speckled trout of a brook if its waters be turbid. The clearness needed for the purposes of persuasion depends upon two things: concreteness of subject-matter, and simplicity in its presentation.

Respecting the first, it must not be forgotten that oratory presupposes a popular assembly, which means generally an uncultured assembly. Here and there may be found an educated listener—one capable of following a train of abstractions; but for the most part such an audience will be made up of men and women whose lives rarely rise far above the objects of sense. To reach their feelings a speaker must make use of the images stored up in their minds— the experiences gained in the home-circle, on the street, at social gatherings, on the farm, or wherever outward or inward sensations meet and act upon their consciousness.

The second condition of clearness, the use of simple language, grows out of the same necessity as the first; for words are but symbols of ideas, and to use simple language is mainly to speak of concrete things in the way a child might speak of them. Each grade of culture has its own vocabulary. The unlettered speak of common things in a common way; the falsely educated or little-learned, speak of the same things in a lofty way. To the latter a house becomes a domicile, a plow an agricultural implement, a family row a domestic infelicity, and so on, throughout the whole range of words. It is when a speaker tries to reach the hearts of people by poking at them words like these, coined in the frigid zone of abstraction, that a dismal failure takes place.

Value of Detail and Individual Instance.—Akin in value to the effect of concrete objects and simple language upon the feelings, is the employment of detail and individual instance. Our lives are so nearly alike in the essential conditions of existence, that you cannot relate the thrilling experience of one without arousing by sympathy similar emotions in others. Witness with what breathless interest an audience listens to some incident illustrative of a principle, and how the breathing goes on again and the attention relaxes, when the argument is resumed. The generalization to be made from such an incident might have been stated in one sentence; and were the purpose merely to furnish the mind with an additional fact, it would have been economy of time so to state it: but one would no more expect to awaken feeling thereby than to rekindle a fire from ashes.

Futility of Exhortation.—Yet this last impossibility is sometimes attempted. It is attempted in nine cases out of ten, when resort is had to exhortation. The tenth case is redeemed from failure and made to exert an influence upon us by reason of the respect and esteem in which we hold the exhorter, not by any intrinsic merit in his method. Men do not ordinarily expect fruit without a tree or without giving the tree time to bear and ripen; yet they do often speak as though, for instance, generosity could be aroused by saying: Be generous; or prayerfulness, by saying: Remember to pray always; or charity, by saying: Do not forget your duty to the poor. When these emotions are normally active such reminders may serve to stimulate their activity; but so far from creating emotion by such appeals, you might as well try to conjure with stones.

How to Arouse Emotion.—The true way to arouse emotion is to give the causes of feeling, or to exhibit the effects of such causes, that is the feeling itself; but, never merely to state the generalized intellectual product of such feeling. The latter may be necessary as a crystalization of the feeling, but it can never be made to produce the effect resulting from the feeling in solution.

The emotions of an audience will be stirred by a strong portrayal of causes, even though their effect on the speaker be weak; or by a weak or general presentation of causes, provided their reaction upon the speaker be strong: but a more pronounced sensation will follow a vivid portrayal of causes coupled with equally vivid effects.

The strongest result of all follows a vivid portrayal of causes accompanied by a realization on the part of the audience that the speaker is making strong efforts to suppress in his own feelings effects which would otherwise burst all bounds.

Interchangeableness of Emotions.—It is a curious fact that closely-related emotions are largely interchangeable when it comes to the practical objects of persuasion. The lesson to be gained from this fact is never to despair because the way to some definite emotion seems hedged and barred. Try the gateways of its nearest neighbors. Thus, Shakespeare teaches that pity may sometimes lead to the same consequences as love; and certainly many a lover has won a nuptial couch by persistence after repeated failures by more direct methods. Self-interest and love, though somewhat opposite feelings, are nearly universal incentives—rival keys to almost every human emotion, good or bad.

"What strings can I pull on?" is the vulgar way of looking for avenues to the attainment of a certain purpose. When we who are behind the scenes witness the deliberate efforts of the revivalist to awaken religious fervor through the medium of death-bed scenes and grave-yard farewells, we are disgusted—but many who do not suspect the artifice are deeply moved, and readily permit the preacher to transmute their sorrow for the dead into the wildest paroxysms of spiritual excitement.

This trick of arousing one emotion and then making use of it to subserve the purposes of another, seems, in the light of the last example, to be sordid and hypocritical; but it is only what we all do to gain our ends, from the three-year-old urchin who waits till his papa has cuddled him, to ask for a nickle, or the pretty wife who provides an unusually good dinner for her lord and master before mentioning the new dress or bonnet, right down to the criminal lawyer who engineers all sorts of expert devices to snatch the murderer from the gibbet. On the whole, therefore, it must be counted a legitimate means of persuasion. If aynone objects that it is so often used for evil purposes, let him resolve to bring it into better repute by using it only for good purposes.

Direct Address Necessary.—A few remarks on the style of composition and delivery as it affects persuasion must close this chapter. It surely needs no argument to show that direct address is one of the prime essentials. Reading from manuscript may suffice for the lecture, which aims only to instruct. But for persuasion, whose purpose is to convince and arouse, the speaker must be untrammeled—free to respond to the surging waves of psychic influences which react upon him from the audience, else how can he control these feelings and guide them to the destined goal?

A Swift, Sententious Style.—It is almost equally obvious that a persuasive style must be a swift, sententious style. There must be no equivocation, for this compels a pause to judge of alternatives, and fritters away the energy ere it reaches the feelings. So, too, the sentences must be free as possible from adjectives, adverbs, and phrase and clause modifiers. These may contribute exactness of meaning but it is at the expense of force; for with the addition of each qualification the mind must readjust its first conception, the result being that the mental energy is absorbed mainly by the intellect, e. g.: It is more forcible to say, "Jesus wept," than to say "The Savior of mankind as he stood gazing upon the Holy City, doomed to so swift a destruction, was overcome by his emotions and gave way to tears."

Variety of Construction.—Lastly, it is important that the speaker rest his audience as much as possible. Nothing is more wearying than monotony. To avoid it his main resource, so far as style is concerned, is variety of sentential structure. The declarative sentence is assertive and dogmatic, and appeals mainly to the intellect. It should frequently be relieved by the interrogative, which tends to change the mind from passive to active receptivity, and by the exclamatory, which addresses itself immediately to the feelings.

PREACHING AND PUBLIC SPEAKING. 279

Space precludes the giving of passages to illustrate the foregoing principles. The real student will seek exemplification in every effective speech or sermon with which he comes in contact.

XIII.

QUALIFICATIONS OF AN ORATOR.

Any speaker that carefully follows the principles and methods set forth in the preceding chapters should be as successful in persuasion as any other speaker providing all other things be equal. But all other things are seldom equal: there is a strong personal element in successful oratory. It will be the purpose of the present chapter to discuss those qualities of a speaker which make for or against his efforts as an orator.

He should have a Fine Personal Bearing.—It is of great advantage for a speaker to have a fine physique and a commanding presence. Attention is thereby immediately gained, and admiration prepares the way for conviction. On the other hand, the "singed cat," as an unprepossessing speaker who happily disappoints expectation is sometimes called, begins with a strong opposition to overcome,—the aesthetic disapproval of his audience. If he overcomes it, the reaction in his favor often more than counterbalances the negative tendency set in motion by his appearance; but it is not often that he overcomes it.

Now, while it is given to few to have the commanding presence of a Bryan, it is within the reach of every young Elder to have a well-formed body and a graceful bearing. In a later part of this work will be found a chapter devoted to the physical culture necessary to accomplish these results. At this point, let me take time merely to urge that it is folly to neglect personal appearance under fear that to walk gracefully and stand erect may be mistaken for vanity. Attention to toilet and deportment may be the indication of pride only skin deep, but it is equally the sign of the pride of self-respect. Unsupported by deeper qualities such care may serve merely to class a young man among dudes; but re-enforced by a well-stored mind and a sterling character it may, among other useful functions, subserve the holiest purposes of religion.

He Should be Sincere.—It was said of Christ that he spoke as one having authority, and not as the Scribes and Pharisees. This is perhaps the most important qualification of an orator—power to impress an audience that he speaks with authority. It involves a combination of many qualities, the staple of which is sincerity. One who speaks from his head merely, may convey facts and furnish the understanding; but one who speaks from head and heart, warms while he enlightens. And is this not the very essence of sincerity?

The sincere voice is the voice with heart-tones vibrating in it; the sincere countenance is that which lights up with the glow of the emotions. Sincerity is the expression of the whole being—the combined product of intellect, feeling, and will. It is the perception of this truth that leads us to say of a sincere person, that he is 'whole-souled.' And the persuasive power of sincerity lies in the fact that we feel willing to trust that which has produced so strong a conviction in a being of equal intelligence with ourselves. Conversely, we distrust instinctively what does not develop earnestness in the speaker himself. For, we reason, if he who knows all about a thing is not moved, how can he expect to move us who know nothing of it? There can be no persuasion without sincerity, or a counterfeit of it skilful enough to pass for the true coin.

He Must Have Good Judgment.—But sincerity is not enough. The world is full of beings whose sincerity we pity. We must feel that intellectual qualities of a high order gave consent to the conviction which dominates the man. The stronger these qualities the more are we impressed with the principles that subdue and regulate them. In every-day terms, the more we have reason to respect the judgment, the more forcibly does the sincerity appeal to us, and vice versa.

Now, the first requisite of good judgment is knowledge. We cannot be wise in that concerning which we know little or nothing. It becomes plain, then, that in order to persuade, a speaker must be master of his subject in all its bearings, and must, moreover, impress his audience that he is master. In the case of most people this is enough, so prone are men to shirk investigation on their own account, and to base their convictions and actions on the authority of others.
of others. Persons wielding such power in a community are called men or women of influence.

People are not influenced by an ignoramus, nor by a speaker whom they believe to have only a smattering of information concerning the subject about which he speaks. It follows, therefore, that to become an effective preacher, an Elder must work early and late to acquire a reputation for knowledge and good judgment. And I may add, that in this particular case a reputation can grow only as it is rooted in fact. Get the knowledge and wisdom therefore and do not hide them under a bushel.

He Must be Honest and Moral.—If a speaker has a reputation for knowledge and wisdom, and thrills with sincerity while he speaks, he is likely to lull any suspicions that may arise as to his honesty or morality. Yet these latter qualifications are vital to the orator, as will best be realized by considering them absent. We may be entertained by the eloquent hypocrite or even the confessed rascal; but as we look upon him we are thinking too much of Mephistopheles to be persuaded to acts of virtue. All the proverbs in the language, such as stealing the livery of heaven to serve the devil in, come to our mind as such a man tries to move us; and the consequence is, we are not moved more than for the instant. I need not urge that the preacher must be an exemplar of the moral virtues.

He Must not Seem Above His Audience.—Another important qualification of a speaker is a certain democratic courtesy and ease that shall make the audience feel by instinct, "He is one of us." Any stiffness, aloofness, "aboveness," or condescension, are sure to arouse resentment, and then all opportunity to persuade is lost. "I always assume," said Abraham Lincoln in explanation of his phenomenal success as a public speaker, "that my audience are in many respects wiser than I am, and I say the most sensible thing I can to them. I never found that they did not understand me."

Says Professor Genung: "Such alliance [between speaker and audience] goes more deeply than mere intellectual agreement. In order to persuade men, the speaker must make them tacitly recogognize him as one to be trusted, so far as the issue before them requires trust, as one who has earnestly at heart their intersets as well as his own cause. The first relation to be established between speaker and hearer, a relation without which no real progress can be made in persuasion, is the relation of mutual trust and respect.

He Must be Frank and Manly.—"Of such trust and respect the initiative must be taken by the speaker. Not with cringing or flattery, not with any brow-beating air of superiority; but with a manly, self-respecting frankness, he is to approach his audience as men occupying a common ground with himself, as having rights, abilities, opinions, that are to be respected and conciliated. Let them once recognize this as his genuine attitude toward them, and he has their ear, not only for things agreeable, but for sharp and searching, even reproving things; he can declare to them his whole counsel; and count on its being at least fairly weighed, which is surely the first requisite to its being followed.

"To the establishment of such friendly relation the most effectual bar perhaps, is the appearance of any kind of artifice. If such is detected by the audience, the speaker's efforts are as good as futile; it is such artifice, such tricks of flattery and argument, that have given an unjust reproach to the rhetorical art in general.

The hearers are looking for a man; if they find but a persuading machine laying arts to entrap their sympathies and their wills, they are embittered not only against his cause but his whole profession. After all, it is only genuine character and sincere conviction that can be safely relied on before an audience."

He Must be Self-possessed.—From the preceding chapter it will be concluded that the speaker who aspires to influence the opinoins and actions of his fellow-men, must be a tireless student of human nature, else he is liable to bring his thoughts to the wrong market or, to be more exact, bring to market the wrong thoughts. He must also be a man of self-possession, and of fertility of expedient. It is related of McDonald, the Canadian Premier, that once when pitted against a brilliant young lawyer in a political debate, he came forward to speak in a beastly state of intoxication. He had hitherto always been able to sail clear of all difficulties no matter how many sheets he had in the wind; so his friends were quite easy on this occasion in spite of his condition. But owing to the unusual jam the air had been hot and foul so that when the wily old politician staggered forward to greet the audience he hesitated—choked —then—well, his introduction was a surprise, to put it mildly.

Here was a dilemma. The countenances of his political sympathizers fell. The election would surely be lost. How could their champion retrieve the loss of respect that would ensue? But McDonald was equal to the occasion. Leaning for a moment against a chair to steady himself, he put on a face of disgust and brazenly turned to his audience: "Ladies and gentlemen," he said, "I never did listen (hic) to that man," pointing to his political rival who had just sat down, "without (hic) wanting to vom—hic, and now its come at last!" The audience—so goes the story—went wild with laughter and applause. His self-possession and ready wit had saved the day.

While no Elder will ever have occasion to duplicate such an experience (let us hope), still every audience presents contingencies which the speaker must manage and turn to account. It is not least of Bryan's oratorical accomplishments that he was able to do something of this kind on nearly every occasion during his silver campaign. One day a crowded meeting was being held in a grove; many of his auditors had climbed into the trees, and one man broke the limb on which he sat, and of course came to the ground, amid the laughter of the audience: "This man," observed Bryan, "does at least not belong to the gold-bugs; for they are trying hard to saw off the limb on which they sit."

He Must not be Vain.—It may be well to conclude this chapter by noting a few qualities in a speaker which are adverse to persuasion. Foremost of these is vanity. And vanity is, moreover, peculiarly a weakness of the orator. It is perhaps the wish to be thought well of more than a burning desire to shape the destinies of mankind that causes most men to study oratory. When success comes, it is so sweet and nectar-like that the winner must stop to sip it, and too often the sipping is done before the audience. When we see this, we do not refuse to listen nor to give in return the nectar on which he feeds; but deep down in our hearts, we refuse to believe in the praise we bestow.

"It is a peculiarity of the rhetorical art," says Whately, "that in it, more than in any other, vanity has a direct and immediate tendency to interfere with the proposed object. Excessive vanity may indeed in various ways prove an impediment to success in other pursuits; but in the endeavor to persuade, all wish to appear excellent in that art operates as a hindrance.

He Should Avoid Getting a Reputation for Eloquence. —Akin to vanity and standing second to it in defeating the purposes of persuasion, is a reputation for eloquence. All flock to hear such a speaker, but they study his methods more than his thoughts. They are continually moved to admiration, but seldom to conviction or action. Whately on this point justly observes: "A poet, a statesman, a general, though extreme covetousness of applause may mislead them, will, however, attain their respective ends certainly not the less for being admired in poetry, politics, or war; but the orator attains his ends the better the less he is regarded as an orator. If he can make the hearers believe that he is not only a stranger to all unfair artifice, but even destitute of all persuasive skill whatever, he will persuade them the more effectually, and if there ever could be an absolutely perfect orator, no one would, at the time at least, discover that he was so."

He May be Humorous but not Funny.—The funny man can seldom persuade us to do anything more serious than to laugh. No matter how earnest he tries to be, we only laugh the harder. It is a most pathetic situation. Whoever consents to play buffoon will never get rid of the cap and bells. What I say here is true of the Bill Nye or Artemus Ward variety of humor, not of the Dickens or Irving kind. The latter, which is sometimes only one step removed from pathos, is often the strongest weapon of persuasion—strongest because it brings the genuine whole-souled emotions out from their covering of reserve; and once they are made dynamic, they may be transmuted as the orator wills. Not so with the low wit or drollery which tickles our fancy by ludicrous conceits. This serves rather to seal up our feelings as being too sacred and dignified for such company; and therefore least of all can we open our emotions to him who ordinarily is the occasion of our closing them.

CHAPTER VIII.

ANALYSIS OF THE SERMON.

I.

INTRODUCTION; THE EFFECT OF PERSONALITY.

It becomes necessary now to analyze the structure of the sermon, and thereby determine the meaning and purpose of each part; also to discover if possible whether the ordinary sermons of our Elders can be improved in these respects.

Ancient rhetoricians divided the discourse into six parts, viz: (1) the Exordium, (2) the Division, (3) the Statement, (4) the Reasoning, (5) the Appeal to the feelings, (6) the Peroration. This was the order followed by the great orators of Greece and Rome. Modern rhetoricians have varied somewhat from this analysis; chiefly, however, in giving new names to old things, and including under one head what is given above under two or more.

A noted recent writer on homiletics, Dr. Austin Phelps, makes a sermon consist of seven parts: viz: the Text, the Explanation, the Introduction, the Proposition, the Division, the Development, and the Conclusion.

Too Artificial for Latterday Saints.—But our Elders will hardly tolerate so much art. Fancy a congregation of Latterday Saints nodding wisely at intervals as if to say: "Now he is beginning the Explanation. How will he manage that text? Well done —a very neat exegesis. * * * Now comes the Introduction. * * * Good! What will be his theme? * * * Ah, that was a neatly stated Proposition. * * * What Divisions will he make of it? * * * Splendid! * * * Now, let us settle back and enjoy the Development. * * * What keen analysis! * * * Now comes the Conclusion, the peroration, the appeal to the feelings. * * * He begins it well," etc.!

Most of our Elders are plain, blunt speakers, who do not dream that the sermons they preach have definite parts: men who despise artificiality so much that they would give themselves up to random remarks rather than arouse the faintest suspicion that they were trying to imitate sermons which too often are constructed to "tickle itching ears."

Far be it from me to criticise this earnest unconventionality. It will be a sad day for Mormonism when art shall supplant heart in our sermons. But, it may be asked, need art supplant heart? May not earnestness co-exist with culture? Let us not despise the method because of the use to which it is sometimes put; but rather agree that the method which accomplishes so much without earnestness and sincerity, will accomplish infinitely more when accompanied by these virtues.

Beginning, Middle, and End.—However, the division of the sectarian sermon is, I am quite convinced, too cumbrous and artificial for Latterday Saint preaching. I shall therefore adopt the simplest analysis possible, and say that a sermon must have a beginning, a middle, and an end. Can you conceive of a sermon that has not these three parts? Hardly, in the ordinary acceptation of the terms.

But if the beginning is what it should be, it is an Introdution; if the middle is what it should be, it is a Discussion; and if the end is what is should be, it is a Conclusion. Now, if it be asked whether our sermons always have an introduction, a discussion, and a conclusion, I must say no. Some of them continue to begin till the time is up; others discuss and discuss, but never reach a conclusion; still others are ready to stop every minute during a whole hour. Such lop-sidedness is possible only because our preachers wilfully neglect to take thought concerning the construction of a discourse. It will never be otherwise as long as the only rule of preaching is "Let it talk." Surely there is need of reform in this respect. Let us then proceed to consider in turn the three essential parts of a sermon.

The prime purpose of the introduction is to arouse interest in the discussion about to begin. If it fails in this respect, it would better have been omitted entirely. For not to arouse interest does not by any means argue that the audience is left fresh as it was. It means rather that the preacher has from the start drawn upon the patience of his congregation. If his hearers be Latterday Saints he is safe. There is still abundance of charity left. Nowhere else in the wide world are religious gatherings so generous and long-suffering, a circumstance that may be explained by the fact that we have no paid ministry and each listener feels that it may possibly be his turn next. But let a lecturer or a political speaker begin as lamely as preachers often do and the patience of his audience will not last till the discussion begins. His discourse is lost.

Effect of a Faulty Introduction.—But even though the preacher whose preliminary remarks are trite and wearisome, may count on respectful attention when at length the discussion begins, he has placed the odds against himself. He has perhaps done himself an irreparable injury; for he who makes a blunder in the opening, will rarely be possessed of the tact and versatility necessary to retrieve it in the body, of the discourse. Having missed the one opportunity of placing his hearers "en rapport" with himself, he is doomed to deliver his sermon to a cold audience; at best to an audience patiently striving by faith and prayer to warm itself up to the subject; and at worst to an audience impatiently waiting for him to get through.

Now, which of the two conditions last named is the severer reflection upon the abilities of a speaker? There can be no question

PREACHING AND PUBLIC SPEAKING. 289

as to which audience represents the better class of Latterday Saints. But even on this point, let me raise a question. Is this superabundance of charity for the crudities of preaching an unmixed good? Do not these very crudities grow ranker daily by the indulgences they receive? In many wards they have gone to seed more than once. I mean, that we have two or three generations of such preachers within the walls of the same assembly. In such cases, of what avail are the efforts of one or two in uprooting the evil? Nothing but a concerted movement will rid the field of these products of indolence and carelessness. In the meanwhile, let no Elder need to fear any other criticism more than this, viz.: that his congregations cultivate patience while he is talking.

Cicero's Definition.—Redders Auditores Benevoles.—But what does it mean to arouse interest in a congregation? Cicero, who in keenness of analysis and compactness of statement can seldom be improved, declares this to be the purpose of the introduction, viz: reddere auditores benevoles, attentos, et dociles, which may be freely translated: to render an audience favorably disposed toward the speaker, keenly alert to the discussion, and warmly in sympathy with the views about to be advanced. Let us briefly consider each of these conditions.

The purpose of the introduction is, first, to render the audience favorably disposed toward the speaker.

It surely needs but little argument to show that the acceptance of truth depends largely upon the bearer of it. Mankind too generally prefer dull water in a sparkling cup to sparkling water in a dull cup. How often it happens that Elder so and so sets the multitude agog by some insipid remark—accompanied of course by the graces of oratory—while you and I—plodders that we are from an elocutionary point of view—have told the same truth in brilliant apothegm without causing a ripple!

Effect of Personal Bearing.—Shall an Elder then seek power over a congregation on account of his personal bearing?

Most certainly. His usefulness in God's service depends largely upon his personality. No more fatal mistake can be made than the don't-care, rough-and-ready attitude of many preachers respecting this point; preachers that argue: "What difference does it make to the truth who bears it? If the devil tells a truth, is it not a truth?" Certainly, but even a Saint will hesitate to swallow a truth that he imagines bears the smutty finger marks of his Satanic Majesty. Grant that in point of fact it is only a fancy that truth can be smirched by the fingers of its bearer—the difficulty remains: you and I and all the world share the fancy; and the preacher, if he would reach the head, must take into account the failings of the heart.

Some of the requisites for securing the power of personality will be discussed under the head of 'essential characteristics' of the introduction. Suffice it to say here that a score of things enter into the judgment of a congregation on this point. The size, form, personal appearance of a preacher, his dress, the condition of his hair and beard, his gait, his attitude—these are points intuitively seized upon in sizing him up. If his previous life be known, it is there with him in the pulpit. Perhaps it is a dead weight upon his head, crushing him down. Perhaps it is a shining pedestal under his feet elevating him to view. Perhaps it is a dull, mediocre shroud neutralizing all tints of interest. Whatever be his personal history, there it is, and his sermon cannot escape the influence of it.

Unconscious Attitude of Audience.—All these things are integral parts of his introduction, though as yet he has not uttered a word. The moment his voice is heard it becomes instantly a powerful addition to these intuitive factors that go to make up the general estimate in which he is held. Perhaps not one person in ten has made a conscious effort at analysis of the speaker; yet if the inner life of the congregation could be laid bare, it would be found that every spirit whose attention is now bent upon him, has taken a definite attitude toward him. These intuitive facts of eye

PREACHING AND PUBLIC SPEAKING. 291

and ear are like so many winds of influence blowing from different directions. The mental attitude they give rise to is the critical line of direction—a line which results from the summation of psychic forces.

The moment he begins to advance ideas there begins a conscious modification of this attitude. Here is his grand opportunity. How will he use it? Ere he has spoken five minutes some such verdict as this will be consciously or unconsciously registered against him in every mind: "He is dull—he is brilliant; shallow—profound; ignorant—cultured; his ideas are muddy—his thoughts are clear; he speaks at random—he has given thought to the subject; to be here is a waste of time—he is well worth listening to," etc.

This early verdict may be changed later, but the chances are against it; for if the verdict be generally negative, it will be a psychic opposition which genius can scarcely break down; and if the verdict be positive, it will be a psychic support that will bear even mediocrity triumphantly along. Let no Elder then neglect any means of gaining the good will of his congregation.

II.

RENDERING AN AUDIENCE KEENLY ALERT INTELLECTUALLY

While it is desirable for an audience to become favorably disposed toward a speaker, this sentiment may easily go too far. It goes too far, for instance, when the speaker's accomplishments attract attention to themselves. To have an audience say or think: "What a fine presence! How rich and powerful that voice! What a gift of eloquence!"—and so on, is strong evidence that the speaker is rather a declaimer than an orator; for the real orator does not give his hearers time or opportunity for such observations. So entrancingly absorbed are they in his theme, that they quite forget the man, for the time being. It is only as an after-thought that they pronounce upon his merits as a speaker; hence it will be well for the preacher to bear in mind—

Reddere Auditores Attentos.—The purpose of an introduction is, secondly, 'to render the audience keenly alert to the discussion.'

Have you ever on coming home from your work smelled the delicious savors of roast beef afar off? What a keen appetite you suddenly became aware of! Do you know what caused it? The gastric juices, intoxicated by the flavor, could not be longer restrained, but poured from their glands in anticipation of a feast. Finding none, they commenced gnawing the walls of the stomach. This is hunger. But these juices were not alone in their anticipation. Your teeth seemed to grow the fractional part of an inch longer, and your "mouth watered"—that is, the saliva prepared to do its part in digestion. A loaded cannon could hardly have kept you from that tempting supper, visions of which came to you through the medium of your nose, (if I may venture so mixed a figure).

Now, it is this same keen edge that an introduction should put upon the mental appetite of a congregation. "Blessed are they that do hunger and thirst after righteousness." This is the way the Lord looked upon intellectual alertness when he was upon the earth. Examine any part of Christ's ministry, and you will find that it was his first care to stimulate the mental appetite. "Master, what does this saying mean?" was the invariable question of his followers.

Hunger the Best Condition for Digestion.—It is easy to understand why they who hunger for truth may be called blest: "for they shall be filled." We may say that it is only they who do thus hunger that can receive this blessing. In the case of physical food, hunger is the best condition for digestion; but in the case of mental food it is the only condition. Souls may come together on the Sabbath day starving for the word of God—starving but not conscious of what it is that makes them weak in the faith; starving without any feeling of hunger. Now, unless their spiritual appetite can be sharpened; unless the gastric juices of the mind can be made to flow; unless the mental teeth grow keen for exercise—these souls will go home faint and pale as they came.

Plainly, then, it is the preacher's first duty to beget in his hearers "a hunger and thirst after righteousness;" an attitude of expectancy that shall permit no truth to escape; an alertness of all the faculties which are necessary to a complete assimilation of the ideas advanced. This condition can best be realized during the opening remarks; and if it be not realized here, the case is generally hopeless; for there are advantages when the introduction begins that no longer exist when the discussion is entered upon. The minds of all are fresh, and most are filled with a curiosity eager to be turned to interest if the slightest encouragement be given. But if curiosity be not deepened to interest by the time the discussion begins, then it has been changed to ennui, and nothing but patience remains for the listener to fall back upon.

Creating Mental Appetite.—An Example.—How shall the mental appetite be whetted? This is a most difficult question to discuss. The manner of arousing interest will vary with almost every sermon and every speaker. What I have to say upon it in a general sense, will be found under another head of this discussion. The remark I wish to make in this connection I shall have to preface by an illustration.

Suppose my little boy, four years old, climbs upon my knee and begs for a story. I conclude to tell him of Daniel thrown into the lion's den. Before I can proceed I must prepare his mind in many particulars. First, I must make him feel as strongly as he can the sentiment that it is better to lose one's life than not do God's will. This effect I can produce only by a preliminary story in some way applicable to himself. Next, I must make him sense —also by a story—how ferocious and cruel lions are. Then it is desirable that he have some conception of the dismal horrors of a lion pit (if indeed, it is wise to tell the story of Daniel at all to one so young).

All this is general introduction only, and may occupy more than one evening. Before the Bible story actually begins, there is a special introduction the purpose of which is to create sympathy for Daniel and hatred for the senseless worship of idols. I now venture the story, cautiously feeling my way, so as to be certain that every object used carries its quota of emotional effect. For all this round-about work, I have the pleasure of witnessing the gradual deepening of an impression that time can never efface.

Deductions.—Observe, first, that this method of introducing a subject is peculiarly rich in its power to educate the mind to grasp relations, as of cause, effect, contiguity, similarity, contrast, and so on; in other words, it stimulates the intellectual faculties to vigorous activity—renders an audience keenly alert to the discussion. Note also that each of these relations is made to arouse its appropriate emotion; as, courage, pity, horror, hatred, disgust, justice, mercy, love—thereby keeping a balance between head and heart.

Observe, secondly, that it was only when I began to cast about me as to what back-ground of mind was necessary for the proper effect of the story, that I was led to question the wisdom of telling it. Thus, introductions, by compelling us to foretaste the effect upon an audience of what we have to say, are a powerful aid to the just selection of subject-matter.

Observe, thirdly, that without an introduction, the objects used would not have been comprehended and the moral would have been lost. Nay, more, the story might even have been fruitful of wrong ideas. It is related that a certain teacher once told this story to her Sunday school class. Having finished, she invited comment, but was horrified to hear one bright little fellow say: "Poor lions! they didn't get any dinner, then, did they?" This innocent remark has often been quoted in proof of the doctrine of total depravity; but it proves nothing more than that the teacher did not pave the way for her story; unless it be the further fact that the child was true to his own emotions rather than to hers. She had probably explained that the lion is like a big dog. Now, if the boy were the owner of a big dog, it is easy to understand why the hunger of the lions should draw most strongly upon his sympathies.

Observe, fourthly, that though the preliminary explanations made it necessary to talk all around the story, care had to be taken not to break in upon the unity of the narrative; that is, the point of the story must not be given away. Such a blunder would have defeated one of the very objects in view—the exciting of curiosity. It is the management of this feature of an introduction that requires the greatest art.

The Example Applied to Preaching.—Now, the subject-matter of a sermon stands in the same relation to a congregation that this story does to the mind of a child. It may be objected that these are not child-minds—but minds mature, and well filled with experiences whereby to apperceive or assimilate the new ideas. This is often not completely true. It is then the business of the introduction to supply the elements lacking. But when it is true, there is none the less need of an introduction. This back-ground of experience is out of memory or else cold and inert, and needs warming and reworking in order that the new ideas may properly cohere.

The 'how,' then, of making an introduction arouse the faculties to alertness must depend practically upon the answers to the following questions: First, what facts must be known to my hearers in order that this subject may be comprehended, and what emotions must be active in order that the result I aim at may be accomplished? Second, are these facts in the minds of my hearers, and are these emotions active in their hearts? He who can answer these questions correctly will know intuitively what should be the nature of the introduction.

But, it may be urged, who is able to say what his hearers know or what emotions may be stirring or asleep in their hearts? I answer, any Elder may know this, who wants to know it. By "wanting to know it," I mean having the thoughtfulness to ask these questions, and to bend the mind toward seeking the answer, not forgetting to make it a matter of prayer.

III.

PLACING THE AUDIENCE IN SYMPATHY WITH THE VIEWS ABOUT TO BE ADVANCED.

Two Kinds of Men.—To find out what an audience may know or may not know respecting a certain theme—which knowledge is so necessary to enable a speaker to supply just those facts which shall prepare their minds fully to comprehend the discussion—this is the work of the Spirit of truth, which is ever ready to help the Elder that tries to help himself. Is it sensible to believe our part is done, when we have exerted ourselves only to the extent of asking the Holy Spirit to guide us in our remarks? Will the Elder who leans like a dead weight on the Lord discover what the congregation needs to awaken it to mental activity? Hardly. His obsequious indolence scarcely imposes even upon us. We may well believe, therefore, that God recognizes him as a sponge, and is too good a teacher to reward his confiding laziness by furnishing spiritual intuitions for him to suck up and squeeze out again.

No, it is the man who prayerfully and resolutely attacks these problems, determined to think them out, that gets aid from the Spirit of truth. I say 'resolutely' and 'determines to think,' because these are the only marks in a preacher that give evidence of true faith—the faith that is exhibited by works.

A Spurious Kind of Faith.—I speak thus emphatically for I feel that the notion still clings to us that only the goody-good, insipid man, is full of faith—the man that prays much and thinks little; the man who, too timid and indolent to produce results by launching into a bold strain of thought, seeks to maintain his prestige by a parade of humility. Such is the sectarian idea of the man of great faith, and this is frequently the leaven still working in our bones. I have called such a man a sponge, for though he differs in quality, he does not differ in kind, from the toady who waits the nod and beck of the great man—the man at whose board he fares without other equivalent than acting the servile role of audience and echo.

When such a one arises to speak, we need not expect the introduction to open the eyes and ears of the congregation. If we did, it would imply that he had made a careful study of the people before him—of their physical, social, intellectual, moral, and religious status; that he had gone over in his mind from beginning to end the truths he desired to say to them; and that he had mentally fitted his thoughts to the varying conditions of his hearers, and had thus discovered what preliminaries he needed to explain in order to make his discourse tell for good.

But all this means hard mental work; and work he will not: he will only pray. The result is inevitable. He will give the dry, hackneyed, tasteless introduction that we have heard Sunday after Sunday, month after month, year after year; and once more we will wait with patience for the dreary platitudes and apologies to be done with, in the hope that something fresh may turn up.

Another Kind of Faith.—Let not my readers misjudge me. Preachers must first of all be humble and prayerful, but not of the kind that are constantly aware that they are humble and prayerful. What vanity is more contemptible than that which prides itself on not being vain—which cloaks itself in humility? The prime quality of a true faith is "go-aheadness." We want a prayerfulness and humility that will give a man no time to compare his godliness with some one else's godliness. To such a one God will reveal whole discourses; that is, he will be enabled to think them out logically, part by part, and will often be surprised at the vigor of his thinking power. His introduction will come to him as if by oratorical instinct. But let us not call it by this name. It is the Spirit of God guiding his thought unerringly to what is appropriate for creating a hunger and thirst after righteousness. It is the spirit of inspiration, which all Elders pray for, but which only those get who are willing to think as well as pray.

Reddere Auditores Dociles.—The purpose of an introduction is, thirdly, 'to render the audience warmly in sympathy with the views advanced.'

When Paul the Apostle got an opportunity to address the cultured Athenians assembled on Mars Hill, he did not bring against them a railing accusation. "I perceive," said he, in substance, "that in all things ye are much given to the worship of the gods. Among your countless altars, I find one to the unknown God. Whom therefore ye worship as an unknown Being, him declare I unto you."

For the assembly and the occasion this must be counted a pattern introduction. Nothing could be more graceful in allusion nor more conciliating in tone. I have softened one or two of the expressions in the King James' translation, satisfied that they are not quite in harmony with Paul's purpose, expressed as it was in the aesthetic phraseology of the original Greek.

What was this purpose? To gain a respectful hearing for the Gospel of Christ. The fact that he succeeded is the strongest evidence of the fitness of the introduction. Paul was probably the most cultured of the Apostles, yet even he must have failed had not the Spirit restrained the natural vehemence of his temper. Paul's spirit, we are told, "was stirred within him, when he found the city wholly given up to idolatry." Did he let this impatience break out in denunciation? Oh, no; he was too wise for that. He knew how futile is a discourse that does not at the start gain the sympathy of the audience.

"Use a Little Guile."—The very brevity of this introduction was an indirect compliment to the quick intelligence of his hearers. Then, instead of showing vexation, he began with praise; a quality as sweet to the palates of the artistic Athenians as to the mouths of the prosaic inhabitants of today. This is evidently an example of what Paul meant by the words: "Use a little guile." That the opening sentence, alluding to their worship of many gods, was from Paul's point of view a reproach, cuts no figure: Paul knew that the Athenians would count it a compliment. He also knew, perhaps, that no more telling a compliment could be paid them than to praise their piety. By this master stroke he accomplished the first purpose of the introduction: he rendered his audience favorably disposed toward himself. Intellectual alertness, the second condition, was aroused by appealing to their curiosity; and as to sympathy, the third condition, we can readily imagine each venerable Areopagite exclaiming inwardly: "Silence! Room for the Jew! It is concerning one of our own gods that he would speak."

Managing the Emotions.—The question of rendering an audience sympathetic toward the principles about to be advanced is a question of managing the emotions. It ought not to be difficult to any one that makes a careful study of his hearers. When such a monster as Enoch Davis * can excite widespread sympathy, it is pretty evident that there is an abundance of this quality lying around ready to respond to any cause good, bad, or indifferent; provided only that he who would draft it into service has the tact and delicacy to approach it from the right side—which means, at least

---

*Enoch Davis was convicted, during the year 1894, of having murdered a sick and helpless wife in her bed, horribly mutilating her body with a hatchet, and afterward wrapping it into an old blanket and burning it in a potato cellar. The details were most revolting, yet many prominent ladies interested themselves in circulating petitions for his pardon.

in the case of an unholy cause, the side not guarded by reason and judgment.

He is counted a poor mariner who cannot sail in the teeth of the gale. The good sailor makes use of every wind. So must he be counted a bungler in preaching who gains no sympathy for the ideas he is about to advance; for the orator moves the multitude hither and thither as he lists. It is not a question of what is just and right, but of what is dramatically made to appear just and right, that tells with an audience. In the case of the bungling preacher, the cause is pleaded before the poorly developed intellect, and is lost through the feebleness of an apathetic judge. In the case of the orator, it is tried before the all-dominant emotions, and is won through the decisiveness of an impressionable jury.

The arguments for any cause are certainly not less adjustable than the sails of a ship. There is then no reason from the speaker's side why they should appear in this way rather than in that way. The question as to which way they are to be adjusted must depend upon a predetermination of what winds of emotion are in the air. It is because the orator feels these winds by instinct, and adjusts his sails by instinct, that he is called an orator. Now, because you and I are not thus endowed, shall we shut our eyes, and with blind rage face the blizzard? The germ at least of this instinct is within us and careful observation and thought will soon develop it.

Letting it Talk.—These words bring me to the very seat of all the difficulty; we have never given careful observation and thought to the effect of this method or that method of preaching; we have simply shut our eyes, so to speak, and let it talk. If it were not so, how could an Elder use the same introduction Sunday after Sunday for twenty-five years? Have you, my dear fellow-preacher, ever calculated the amount of weariness produced by the one way you have of approaching all your subjects? Well, I do not single you out because you are unique in this respect. We are a big company and are more or less alike in our sins of omission and commission.

But is it not time we were waking up? We are about at a stand-still. Let us honestly confess, that the effects we produce are feeble. It was only last Sunday that I listened to four speakers, not one of whom, so far as I could discern, stirred any emotion in the congregation save that of patience. This, in the case of two of them, was stirred to impatience. We must awaken. We must get "method" and "fire" into our discourses—which will never happen so long as we "take no thought about what we shall say."

IV.

AS TO THE LENGTH OF AN INTRODUCTION.

It seems almost like overdoing matters to write more on so small a portion of the sermon as the introduction; especially so in view of the fact that, as preachers, we have hardly begun to consider what an introduction means, least of all determined to make use of this device in our discourses. But as I confidently believe that the time will come for each Elder when the tasteless little talk whereby he now seeks to steady his nerves will no longer be indulged in, by reason of an ardent desire to arouse in his hearers a high pitch of interest for the message which he feels burning within his bosom—believing, I say, that our Elders will shortly feel all this in a definite way, I venture to open the subject again.

Thus far I have sought primarily to discover 'what' are the purposes of an introduction, and reduced them to three, viz., (1) to dispose an audience favorably toward the speaker; (2) to arouse intellectual alertness; and (3) to gain sympathy for the views about to be advanced. In the chapters which follow I desire to discuss especially 'how' these objects are to be accomplished.

An Introduction should be Short.—Just as it is the main purpose of an introduction to excite curiosity, so it should be the chief care to turn this curiosity into genuine interest, ere suspense and weariness have made it flat. The behavior of yeast furnishes me a fine simile here. Every housekeeper knows that under favorable circumstances the vinous fermentation progresses rapidly, but if continued too long, the acetous fermentation begins; or, to put it in Anglo-Saxon, if the yeast works too fast, and too long, it turns sour. Let me carry this illustration a little further. A scattering individual here and there has tasted bread made from sour yeast; but all of us, without exception, have tasted sermons that have been soured by the introduction. This observation leads me further to remark that the sisters manage their bread better than the brethren do their sermons; a circumstance explained perhaps, by the trifling fact that some attention is usually given to bread-making.

Principles Governing Length of Introduction.—A long introduction occasionally holds the attention of an audience. But in such cases, we may be pretty certain that it is failing in its real purpose. Instead of exciting interest for what is to follow, it is drawing attention to itself. To fail in this manner is to leave it without an excuse for taking up time; but it is even then better than the introduction, whose length, not so relieved, makes it flat and wearisome. Long introductions under the most favorable circumstances, are offensive to the mental eye as being out of proportion. They remind you of those curious houses which have very gaudy and pretentious fronts, but which fall rapidly into insignificance by one lean-to after another, until the series closes—appropriately, let us say—in a coal-shed or dog-kennel.

Undue length is not the only thing that sours an introduction; it may fall flat from a number of other causes which will be touched upon shortly. But this one is perhaps the most prominent cause of

PREACHING AND PUBLIC SPEAKING. 303

sourness or flatness. This leads to the enquiry: What is undue length in an introduction?

In answering this question let us fall back upon our illustration. If yeast be placed, say in the cellar where the temperature is low, it works slowly; but if brought near the stove, it goes with a gallop, so to speak. Now every audience has a certain emotional temperature which rises quickly or slowly, partly in accordance with the previous culture of the people, partly by the magnetic force and imaginativeness of the speaker. For instance, take an audience of children. Here the introduction must be excursive, and each separate point be made an object-lesson designed to excite interest on its own account. Without such preparation the ulterior lesson cannot be attained. An uncultured grown-up audience have in many respects child-minds, and must be treated in the same way —without seeming to be so treated, however. Milk is actually what both minds need, but you cannot give it to the bearded boys and wrinkled girls with a spoon.

Bearded Boys and Wrinkled Girls. —I said, 'in many respects' the uncultured adult mind resembles that of the child. One of these is the want in both minds of collateral facts and ideas whereby to 'apperceive' the thought to be presented. This missing basis of knowledge must be supplied, as well with an adult audience as with children, if the principles of the sermon are to be assimilated. But in the case of the adult, no matter how meagre his information, the very exigencies of life will have given him a power not possessed by the child, of reasoning to conclusions; an ability to "catch the drift" of a sermon, to feel the force and bearing of facts, and to see the end towards which those facts are converging.

If now the general principle be kept in view, that the secret of interest is giving the mind something to do, there should be no difficulty in deciding in what respects introductions for children and for uncultured adults should be alike and in what unlike. They should be alike in being elaborate and graphic; in giving all the facts necessary to flux, as it were, the ore of the sermon. This means that they must be long, quite too long for the patience of the few here and there who do not need this information.

They are unlike in that with children the relationships arising out of the introductory facts must be woven so finely—must be made so gauze-like—as barely to veil the truth in which we seek to arouse interest. This is a most delicate point to reach without accident. One word wrongly put may spoil all by "giving away the story." When their little eyes sparkle with restless anxiety, as if to say: "Is it this, or is it that? Oh, dear, I wish I knew," then must the introduction end and the discussion begin.

But long ere this pitch of interest is reached with the child, the man, with his quicker grasp of relationships, has seen through it all. To persist explaining after this has happened is to make him conscious that you are trying to feed him with a spoon, (and to make yourself aware by the contempt he manifests for your efforts that he is a big ungrateful boy).

Don't Chew for Others.—I stated a short time ago that the secret of interest is giving the mind something to do. This 'something' I may add here, must be original work, not work on matter which you have chewed fine first. Let this be a hint to those delightful (?) people who want to tell it all. We are interested when we begin to discover relations for ourselves, not when relations are pointed out. The cause of the interest is our uncertainty as to whether we are right; which makes us eager to hear more, in order that we may verify our forecasts. The speaker who has not the power to cause us to make forecasts draws upon our patience. He who spoils our forecasts by a blundering tongue draws upon our disgust.

Length and elaborateness of introduction must depend, then, upon (1) the nature of the subject, (2) the nature of the occasion, and (3) the degree of mental activity manifested by the audience. Frequently no introduction is necessary, especially where the objects of the meeting are definite and well-known. When it is given, it is better to err on the side of shortness than length. Five minutes is ample for preliminary remarks. This will give the speaker time for five hundred words, which is ten per cent of what should be the limit of a long sermon, five thousand words. When the minds of the audience are finely poised, it will be well to make the introduction as short as was Paul's before the Athenians.

A Spiritual Thermometer. — It will be seen therefore that as regards length or elaborateness of introduction, no rules can be given that do not take into account the conditions of the audience. To know these conditions is the great art or rather the great inspiration of the preacher. This, I think, is the meaning of the gift of discerning of spirits. It is a sort of spiritual thermometer that detects instantly the religious warmth or coldness in the room, thereby enabling the speaker to adapt his remarks to meet the conditions. Speakers that ramble from start to finish seem not to have this delicate mental perception. The habit of talking to a room full of air in which human figures happen to sit, rather than to throbbing hearts and beaming eyes, has dulled their sensibility alike to the warmth and the coldness of the spiritual climate. Such speakers get their pleasure solely by the vanity of standing before an audience; and gather their inspiration, such as it is, by the sound of their own voices. Could they at some given moment be made keenly sensible of the feelings they have aroused in their hearers, what a collapse there would be in this fluent march of empty sounds!

V.

THE INTRODUCTION SHOULD BE SIMPLE, DIRECT, AND SUGGESTIVE.

Observe people in a fair. They are not all interested in the same things. Among the medley of sights and sounds clamoring for attention, each looks at and listens to what interests him. But what is the secret of this interest? Familiarity. What he knows something about, he is anxious to know more about. Let the speaker take note of this human characteristic.

The Introduction should be Simple, Direct, and Suggestive.—By the word "simple," I mean that it should contain no word or form of expression that will not yield its kernel of thought without a severe mental effort. It must be borne in mind that the audience has as yet attained no intellectual momentum: the wheels of thought are just beginning to move. To load them down at the start is to stop or balk the machinery. Simplicity is lost, as before intimated, by the use of unfamiliar words, by involved constructions, and by haziness of thought. The last is the most common as well as the worst fault. Too often preachers act as if the time allotted for the introduction were for their particular benefit and not for the benefit of the audience. Instead of coming forward with ideas clear and definite, they practice blindly on their hearers for a time, till the muddiness of their brain has settled and their thoughts clarify. The audience in the meanwhile is called upon for a severe mental effort at the start in order to get coherency out of this jumble and tangle of ideas: and when it fails, as it must fail, all three aims of the introduction are frustrated: respect for the speaker is lost, intellectual alertness blunted, and sympathy for the object of the sermon not aroused.

Want of naturalness in the introduction from whatever cause is a fault analogous to want of simplicity. The speaker that exhibits undue feeling on the start, forgets that his audience is cold and impassionate, and can have no sympathy with such an outburst. I call to mind a preacher who began so vehemently that in less than five minutes the tears were streaming down his cheeks. The causes of this sudden feeling were, I suppose, quite adequate—to him; but he forgot that these causes had not been presented to the audience. The result was, he cried alone for us all, while we hung our heads in pity, or shame, or disgust—I scarcely know which—for him.

A calm, deliberate beginning followed by a gradually increasing warmth—an emotion that transfers heat so subtly to the audience as to seem itself rather more cool than the occasion demands—is the best plan in nine cases out of ten. The tenth case is where the audience is already in a state of excitement, perhaps through the efforts of a previous speaker, perhaps through the influence of circumstances or happenings felt alike by all. The unimpassioned introduction is manifestly out of place in such a case. A fine general rule as regards simplicity is always to begin on the intellectual and emotional level of the audience, whatever that may be. This again brings forward the fact that the preacher exists for the congregation, not the congregation for the preacher.

Striving for Effect.—In saying that the introduction should be "direct," I have special reference to the avoidance of a "showy" beginning. For instance, nothing is more common in the first essays of the student than attempts at "fine writing." Effect is sought by elaborate phrases, inverted construction, climacteric and periodic sentences, rich displays of metaphor and simile—in all which the feeble thought, if thought there be at all, is over-shadowed like the daisy in the tropics. Now, although, when such essays are read, the uncultured multitude exclaims: "How beautiful!" it is not such surface approbation that preachers must aim at.

I quite foresee, however, that when our young Elders shall give conscious attention to the construction of the sermon, the first mistake they will make will be in this same striving after effect by the mere ornaments of style. I wish therefore to call attention here to the fact that the safest rule for the introduction, as indeed, for the discussion also, is: "Talk to the point and stop when you reach it." Utility, not ornament, must decide the choice of every word and phrase. The charm of Joseph Smith's preaching lay in the fact that he took the shortest route to the hearts of his hearers —often it would seem, to the serious disturbance of a strait-laced brother or sister here and there, who had been accustomed to the "firstly," "secondly," "thirdly," etc., of elaborate discourses.

Directness is oftenest violated by want of unity. In such cases, no single purpose has been kept in view and the result is an introduction so loosely constructed as to serve equally well for each of a dozen sermons; which means that it would serve none of them well. Directness does not exclude diversity of material. It simply insists that a single purpose shall co-ordinate and subordinate it all, and also that no matter shall be included which does not bring the introduction nearer the discussion. For that species of mental vagrancy which sets off at a right angle to illustrate some thought, then straightway forgets the thought and sets out at another right angle to illustrate the illustration, and so on ad infinitum—there is no cure save a vigorous course of study that shall tend to mind concentration. Such minds cannot afford to indulge in the slightest digressions; for there is danger that they will not come back. Let all such follow the trail while it is hot, allowing no smaller thoughts starting from the sides to tempt them from pursuit of the original purpose.

Begin Within Hailing Distance.—Directness implies that the introduction must begin within hailing distance of the discussion; as near indeed, as the audience happens to be. This is to remind certain Elders that it is not necessary, nor always desirable, to preface every sermon by a synopsis of the history of the Church. Such a going back for a beginning reminds us of the Dutchman, who, thinking a certain stream too broad to jump, took a two-mile start from the top of a hill, but found on reaching the bank that it was necessary to pause awhile to recover breath, before attempting the leap. So the Elder who takes his hearers on a useless preliminary excursion in the hope of arousing interest, will find them too weary to appreciate his discussion when at length it begins.

Not only should the thoughts composing the introduction spring up from a radius near the discussion, but like good soldiers, they should move by orderly and swift advances toward the scene of action. What can inspire more courage in a speaker and more confidence in an audience than the exhilarating effect of such a rapid forward movement? The speaker whose thoughts thus converge and "pitch right into" the subject, arouses expectation. "He means business; if we are to follow him we must keep our wits about us."

An Introduction Should be "Suggestive;" that is, it should not only excite expectation, but it should excite expectation concerning the subject in hand. It should be of the same quality of cloth as the discussion, and should differ in color, only as trimmings may differ. Where expectations have been aroused which the discussion fails to satisfy, the audience feels balked. If the speaker has done this so adroitly as to make his hearers acknowledge themselves outwitted, then something of the eagerness shown by the reader who has been thrown off the scent of a detective story, will attach to the next step in the sermon. But how rarely would all circumstances combine to make an audience admit this! Oftener the preacher will be charged, and justly, too, with blundering and haphazard talk. "What has all this, that he has just been telling us, got to do with the subject now being treated?" And the answer in most cases must be: "Nothing whatever, save as it enabled him to whet his dullness upon our patience." Thus, the objects of the introduction are frustrated, especially in respect of sympathy for the principles to be advanced.

But not too Suggestive.—But, while the introduction should be suggestive, care must be taken to make it only suggestive; that is, it must not steal thunder from the discussion. He is a poor story-teller that "gives away" his plot at the opening. So is he a poor preacher that instead of making use of curiosity throughout his sermon, satisfies it at a single gulp, and is thereafter compelled to ram all his doctrines down unwilling throats by the unaided force of his spiritual dogmatism. Chickens are fattened for market by this ramming process, but I very much fear that souls are made leaner by it.

This adjustment between the introduction and the discussion, is, as remarked in the last chapter, the most delicate point in the whole business of sermon-making. On the one hand nothing should be left out of the introduction that can place the mind in a better attitude toward the subject-matter; yet, on the other, there is the greatest danger that too much will be said; that the discussion will be so stripped of its richest coloring as to seem, when it comes, like a series of thread-bare repetitions. But difficult as is this adjustment, it can be successfully accomplished by every Elder that will give it sufficient thought. Witness how skilfully Nathan the Prophet prepared the mind of King David for God's judgment upon him for the double crime of adultery and murder. His parable of the ewe-lamb was suggestive, without being too suggestive. Would his purpose have been accomplished as well had he blundered in the introduction?

VI.

MODERATION AND MODESTY IN THE INTRODUCTION.

In no other place can a man so ill afford to promise what he is unable to fulfil as when he stands before an audience. To excite expectations by a splendid introduction is quite the proper thing—for the man who is able to gratify such expectations. But for the man of ordinary talent, it is better to lead the audience to expect little than much, so that the interest may rise rather than fall as the sermon progresses. The language is full of phrases expressive of failures in respect of promising too much. "He came out of the little end of the horn" is a familiar way of putting it. Another, which however smells rather too strongly of tobacco, has it, "He bit off more than he could chew." A building started on too large a scale and left unfinished is invariably denominated So and So's "folly." Anti-climax in any form appeals rather to ridicule than to respect. The preacher cannot afford to run this risk. The next qualification of the introduction will therefore be self-evident, viz.:

The Introduction Should be Moderate and Modest.— But there is in fact little need of cautioning our Elders on this point. If they indulge any vanity it is much more likely to be the opposite one—that of excessive self-depreciation. This leads me to discuss the prime quality of the introduction—as also indeed of the entire discourse—viz: modesty.

Modesty, in the first place, forbids the parading of self before the audience. I say 'parading,' for such conduct does not deserve a more gentle word. There are two forms of this species of intrusion. The first is where the speaker either directly or indirectly holds himself up as an object of praise or adoration. Fortunately this form is rare among Latterday Saints, though it crops out occasionally. It is very much to be feared that, ere these views on preaching shall be interpreted as I would have them, the pendulum will swing high to this species of vanity. The other form is all but universal among us now. I refer to the tiresome, long-drawn-out apologies about the unexpectedness of the call, and about being unprepared, etc., etc., with which we deem it necessary to preface our remarks. Occasionally a speaker throws in an extra paragraph or two on his physical ailments! There may be instances wherein allusions to self in a discourse are quite proper. But our sermons would be vastly improved if preachers regarded such instances as exceptional, and would follow the general rule not to exhibit themselves either for exaltation on the one hand, or for stultification on the other.

Excuses and Excuse-making.—One word as to excuses and excuse-making. Next to the student that habitually shirks, stands the student who has the habit of making excuses. The first is lazy, the second is weak; both are ciphers so far as real progress in this world is concerned. The first fails through want of desire, the second through want of will. The excuse-maker may have the desire, but he lacks the force to carry it through. Instead of his controlling circumstances, circumstances control him.

Often, however, he is weak by carelessness rather than by want of force. Dr. Maeser well knew this characteristic of human nature. The first excuse would perhaps be accepted with a reassuring smile, the second with a look of surprise, the third with some stern reproof like this: "Young man, this is the last excuse I want to hear from you this term. I hate excuses. They are generally a sign of weakness. 'Sickness?' Don't get sick, that's all I can say. It is high time you were learning to make things bend to some supreme purpose of life."

And strange as it may appear, excuses generally ceased to

come. The student somehow learned to deny himself of parties, sociables, and frivolities, and to place duty above them all.

Now apply this little moral to the ten thousand preachers among the Latterday Saints. If those who preside would treat shiftless Elders as Brother Maeser treated shiftless students, there would soon be an end of the excuse-making apologies which, it is scarcely too harsh to say, are now a disgrace to our preaching. What business have Elders in Israel to be making excuses?

Respect for the Feelings of an Audience.—Modesty in the presentation of a discourse demands, in the second place, every possible courtesy and consideration for the feelings of an audience. A speaker will not indulge airs of superiority or of condescension in the presence of his hearers if he hopes to get them favorably disposed toward himself, or in sympathy with his views. On the contrary, he will, if he is wise, manifest toward them a spirit of genial, democratic frankness that shall make them say: "He is one of us." I am just now thinking of one of the Apostles whose chiefest charm this is. So warmly does the quality attach people to him, that he can say the severest things—and he seldom fails to give iron-clad reproof wherever it is needed—without making his hearers love him any the less.

Respect for an audience is best shown by a proper self-respect. The sloven in dress or speech need not expect much sympathy even though his hearers be themselves largely of that class. It is related of Patrick Henry that, wishing to win the voters of a certain remote district, he dressed in homely garb and spoke to them in their own peculiar dialect. It was a piece of bad judgment on his part. These backwoods farmers were insulted. They knew too well that the greatest orator of America was not in the habit of dressing like a tobacco planter, nor of electrifying his audiences by the lingo of the plantation.

Aiming as Related to Firing.—In conclusion let me urge that time and thought put upon the opening remarks of a sermon are not wasted. When it is considered that the purpose of preaching is not to gratify the vanity of the preacher but to persuade men to a better life, then any detail, be it ever so trifling, which helps to insure the fulfilment of his purpose is important. The sight is one of the smallest things about a gun. It is moreover quite unnecessary to the man who shoots merely for the fun of hearing the sound and seeing the smoke. But the man who fires every time to some purpose counts it of the supremest importance, and would not think of getting along without it. When the young Elder gets beyond the novelty of "holding" an audience, and past the vanity of being pleased with his own voice, he will begin to appreciate the value of a sight to his gun.

This does not conclude the subject of the introduction, though it must end further discussion of it here. It would be quite in order, did space permit, to devote a chapter to examples illustrating the principles set forth. In lieu thereof I must urge the reader to be on the look-out for examples of introduction. He will find them in all species of writing and speaking. In this treatise, for instance, there is not only an introductory chapter to the whole work, but a paragraph or more of introduction to each chapter. I point them out with no little fear and trembling; for the chances are that the majority of them will not fit the rules I have laid down. It is easier, as Shaksepeare puts it, to give advice to twenty men than be one of the twenty to follow that advice.

VII.

THE DISCUSSION—MEANING OF THE TERM—A DEFINITE PROPOSITION NECESSARY.

From what has been said respecting the introduction it must be evident that this part of the sermon, as its name implies, exists only for the discussion: that if it fails to smooth the way for the real subject-matter, it fails utterly and has no excuse for taking up time. From this circumstance, it will be seen that though the introduction is the first to be spoken, it should be the last to be thought of; for the discussion must at least be outlined in the mind, before the speaker is made aware of what is necessary to introduce it. In all formal composition, especially that which is committed to paper, both introduction and discussion should be carefully thought out before delivery; but the former, being only a device to make the latter more effective, can rarely first occupy attention to advantage.

Do you insist, then, asks the reader, that preparation for a sermon shall consist in going over in the mind the points of the discussion before it is presented? I may answer 'yes' and 'no.' A lecture is not worthy the name, that has not thus been thought out, part by part; and he is a poor teacher who comes before his class without having definitely considered what he is going to teach and how he will teach it. The sermon among Latterday Saints differs from the lesson or the lecture in that it is not prepared for a definite occasion. But prepared it must be, not only by much thought, but by much definitely arranged thought, if it is to be worthy the name of sermon. Elders who come before the people in the capacity of preachers must form the habit of daily mental discussion of subjects appropriate for sermons. In no other way can the clay be kept mixed and pliable to the potter's hand. This mixing can be done while following the plow, while resting at noon, while doing any one of a hundred things that require only muscular attention. What I insist upon is that we should think—think logically and consecutively—then when we arise to speak, our thoughts will naturally follow a line.

What is the meaning of discussion as here used? A successful discussion, it may be replied, must be a clear realization of these two propositions: 1. What do I wish to accomplish? 2. How shall I accomplish it? That is to say, a discussion is (1) the knowing definitely what doctrine is to be proved, what principle maintained, what lesson to be enforced; and (2) the finding of arguments and persuasions suitable thus to prove, maintain, or enforce the truth in question. Let us proceed to consider in its order the first of these propositions.

Vagueness of Purpose.—No fault is more common to preachers, nor more fatal to their sermons, than vagueness of purpose. Dr. Holmes tells of a clergyman who wrote a book entitled, "Thoughts on the Universe." Think what must be the quality of one of these thoughts! You would have to sniff all the ether this side of the Pleiades just to get a smell of it. And yet had there been a bigger place in which to spread out thought, this misty divine would probably have chosen it!

Vagueness, my observation leads me to believe, is much more common among Latterday Saint preachers than among sectarians. And the reason is not far to seek. Sectarians make a business of preaching, and spend the week days elaborating their sermons. Nothing else tends to definiteness so much as writing. "Reading maketh a full man, conversation a ready man, and writing an exact man," says Lord Bacon. Now, exactness these preachers generally have, however else they may fail in presenting divine truth. Mormon Elders, on the other hand, "taking no thought," but relying, as they generally do, for inspiration upon the spur of the occasion, sail out upon the sea of thought without rudder or compass, and often have not the faintest idea where they will land.

This want of clearness and definiteness has already been touched upon under the general head of subject-matter. Here it is necessary to consider it in its relation to the discussion. Imagine a teacher coming before his class with no other preparation than a vague idea that his subject is to be something on science—that is, he is certain it is not on history. What will he be able to say? No doubt he will succeed in filling up the hour, but his lesson will be as scattering and disappointing as would be the talk of the man who should try to give his opinion of "things in general."

An Example.—Yet just such vagueness as this is rather the rule than the exception. Ask the average preacher among us what he will preach about today. The answer will be "The Gospel."

What do you wish to say concerning the "Gospel?"

"Oh, something—whatever I shall be led to say."

Well, have you no definite truth—a truth deeply affecting mankind—that you desire to maintain concerning the Gospel?

"I don't understand you."

Surely you cannot preach upon the Gospel as a whole: it is too broad and vague.

"Oh, as to that I shall select some part of it, say faith."

Well, what do you wish to maintain as to faith?

"Why, I'll 'talk' about faith. Faith is my subject."

Certainly, but why do you choose it? What do you expect to accomplish by talking on this subject? What do you wish to prove?

"Oh, as to that, I'll wait to see how my mind is led."

But the result will prove that such a mind is the last to permit itself to be led. The mind that refuses to tie itself down to some definite thing can neither be led nor driven. It will take a zig-zag course, keep on the move, but get nowhere. Tramps, we say, are beings out of 'human' relation—floating specks on the stream of humanity which collect over night in police eddies, then scatter again. There are minds which open on occasions just like police stations—turning loose whole beggarly hosts of tramp ideas—ideas out of 'rational' relation. But this is not discussion, it is mere twaddle.

Definite Proposition Necessary.—There can be no discussion unless it turn upon some definite proposition. It is therefore of the supremest importance that the speaker ask himself, "What do I wish to accomplish? What purpose do I have in view in taking up the time?" If he is wise, he will let the wants of the congregation decide the answer to these questions. He is there for their sakes, not they for his sake. However, let him answer the question as he will, be it from his point of view or theirs, if his answer be exact, he will have something to talk to—something that will make his sermon a unit, and therefore compel thoughtful attention.

What is a proposition? Something to be proved or maintained. Honesty, truth, virtue, charity—these are not propositions; for there is nothing about them to be proved or maintained. No man can talk intelligently upon ideas embodied in single words. They cannot be the subjects of discussion. The man who would begin a sermon on so vague a subject as "Truth," ought in order to be consistent with himself, to respond with equal alacrity to such a summons as this: "Run quickly and fetch me something from somewhere."

Yet sermons begun on just such vague subjects turn out to be intelligent occasionally. Why? Because the preacher stumbles upon some proposition respecting them. But this stumbling is accidental, and does not always happen. When it does, the proposition is a happy one only by luck. But it ought not to need to happen. Preaching has passed the stage of such rude experimentation. The man that has not wit enough to make a proposition respecting a subject—not merely a proposition, let me say, but the proposition which the occasion requires—ought not to be permitted to waste the time of a congregation.

Meaning of Proposition.—The words, honesty, truth, virtue, charity, are terms merely. Terms become propositions when we assert something in respect to them, as: (1) Honesty is profitable—not only from a financial, but also from a physical, a mental, a moral, and a religious point of view. (2) Truths, like good seeds, require cultivation; errors, like weeds, grow of themselves. (3) It is better to be virtuous than merely innocent. (4) Charity, when not guided by wisdom, does more harm than good.

These propositions may or may not be maintained: it is the business of the discussion to determine this. But certainly they present something definite for the mind to grapple with. Both speaker and hearer enter with zest upon a discussion when it turns upon a proposition about which there may be an honest difference. A well stated proposition bristles with suggestion, and thus has power to direct the mind into channels of thought undreamed of before. Even though the subject respecting which the proposition is made, be trite, yet the new aspect in which it is presented by a well chosen theme, will lend interest and attention.

Examples of Proposition.—Here are a few suggestive propositions for sermons on faith. An hour in which to treat each of them would be limited time indeed: (1) The impulse to believe in a supreme Being is inherent in the human race. (2) It is only when this impulse is guided by correct knowledge respecting God, his being, his attributes, and his works, that we can term it true faith. (3) Without the attribute of mind called faith, the simplest form of society is impossible, let alone the complex form called civilization. (4) Is faith a "sargasso sea," as asserted by Colonel Ingersoll? (5) Faith which leaves out the element of reason is superstition. (6) No man can have true faith and remain unrepentant. (7) That faith is most pleasing to God which resembles the confidence of the child in its parent. (8) Why Satan first attacks faith in God. (9) Faith considered as a mechanical power. (10) Why God ordained that we should walk by faith and not by sight.

These are aspects of faith that present themselves in less than five minutes' reflection. The list might readily be swelled to a hundred or a thousand, all of which would vitally touch the interests of mankind. Into sermons on these subjects could be woven history, biography, the lessons of fiction, the achievements of science and art, daily experiences, the hopes and aspirations that stir the soul like zephyrs from an unseen world—everything that can instruct and elevate mankind. And so of all other principles of our religion. Whenever our Elders shall set themselves to be guided by propositions, instead of trusting to the vagaries of mere terms, trite preaching will have had its day among us. The question will then be, not how shall I get a fresh interesting subject, but rather which of this multitude of fresh subjects shall I choose.

A Proposition Aids the Speaker.—Note that a clearly stated proposition aids the speaker in two ways: (1) It stimulates mind-activity by putting him in the attitude of instructing his hearers or of attacking or defending some principle believed in by mankind. (2) It directs this mind-activity into a definite channel, thus preventing him from getting lost in the mazes of his own thought.

Take for instance the proposition, "It is better to be virtuous than merely innocent." Here the mind is first directed to the distinction between virtue and innocence, viz.: that innocence is a primal state, and virtue is innocence tested and tried. This distinction will be widely illustrated, not only by the Adam and Eve of the garden of Eden as contrasted with the Adam and Eve bowed low with trials and tribulations and old age, but also by examples drawn from the experience of living men and women. The reasonableness of the proposition having been demonstrated, it will be further strengthened by scriptural quotation.

The enquiry will next be how does mankind act with reference to this truth. The mind will here be directed to the fact that more than half of Christianity practically reverse this conception in belief, and a very large number do so in actual practice. Roman Catholics must maintain that innocence is the state most acceptable to heaven, else why should they withdraw from the world and enter cloister and convent? Examples may be drawn from other religions, as for instance those of India. Nor need we go to such general cases only. Illustrations may be found in the peculiar customs and habits of all people. Where does the opposition to the co-education of the sexes come from, save from the belief that innocence is better than virtue?

The third enquiry is most important of all. How do we as a people act with reference to the principle? In the education of our children do we spend our time in warding off temptation, or in fortifying their minds against it? How many of our sons and daughters fall because parents have sought to maintain their purity through keeping them in ignorance! Shall temptations be set before children, then? No. Shall children be shielded absolutely from temptation? No. What is the principle that shall guide us, then? The same that guides God's providence: temper the wind to the shorn lamb. See that temptations are never greater than can be resisted.

Such would be the framework of a discourse on the proposition, "It is better to be virtuous than merely innocent." This framework, be it noted, can be filled in by anything and everything that will appeal to intelligence and help to enforce the purpose in view. Now, if you would know how the speaker has been assisted, picture him on the other hand left to flounder through an hour's talk with nothing but the vague idea of "virtue" to guide him. The cruelest thing a man can set his faculties to do is this same chasing of some phantom word through the heights and depths of the universe.

I trust that my point is established, viz: the necessity of a definite proposition as a backbone for discussion. If further proof were needed it might be drawn from a consideration of the uniform practice of successful secular orators. The lecturer knows the end from the beginning by reason of his analysis or "diagram" of the subject; which is equivalent to the proposition, divisions, and proof of the preacher. The lawyer never fails to "state" his case to the jury before beginning his plea. The legislator speaks to some resolution or to some definite portion of a bill. All these "talk to the point," because they have a point to talk to, and because no other kind of talking would be tolerated. That vagueness is tolerated in preachers is a pity; were they compelled, equally with their secular brethren, to swallow wholesome doses of merciless criticism, the Lord's work would be better done. That they permit themselves to stop at "good enough" because no lash is raised above their heads is only another instance where the cloak of holiness is used to shield abuses.

VIII.

SHOULD THE PROPOSITION BE STATED TO THE AUDIENCE.

Reasons for Stating the Proposition.—Having established the need of a proposition in a discussion, we may next ask the question: Is it necessary to state the proposition to the audience? Usage on this point is divided, though reasons are strongly in favor of doing so. First, a proposition clearly stated becomes a bond of common understanding between speaker and hearer—a sort of contract for a certain, definite kind of thought which the party of the first part agrees to deliver conscientiously, and the party of the second part, to pay for by close attention. This understanding is beneficial on both sides: the speaker, conscious that he has given his hearers a criterion by which to judge his remarks, and feeling that no defect in his sermon will remain undetected, no merit undiscovered, is stimulated to do his best, and do it coherently. The hearers, in addition to the stimulation they receive from being made intelligent listeners, have an interest in the outcome of the sermon on their own account; for are they not led to think upon and develop the same theme? Thus the attention of the audience reacts upon the speaker, making him more lucid and eloquent; and his added clearness and force again stimulate the audience. Consequently both attention and interest demand that the proposition should be given.

PREACHING AND PUBLIC SPEAKING. 323

Second, the proposition is a kind of key to the discourse. Sometimes, but not always, the drift of the sermon can be gained from the context; but it is always by the expenditure of mental energy that might be more profitably given to the theme, were the theme known. Whenever a hearer is led to ask: "What is the speaker driving at?" it is plain that he is losing what he ought not to lose. It is often too late to give the key to the discourse in the conclusion; for then the thoughts that needed unlocking are past and forgotten, or but dimly called to mind. As the first aim in preaching is to be understood, so the proposition whenever it adds clearness should be stated.

When to Leave it Unstated.—But occasions arise when the proposition would better be left unstated. In the speaker's mind it should be present at every instant of the discussion, whether stated or unstated, else he must invariably beat about in the fog of incoherency; but when the stating of it would serve to arouse opposition, he will do well to approach his conclusions under cover. Often the individual arguments of a theme arouse no antipathy, but are on the contrary well-received. It is only when these arguments are placed in juxta-position, so as to prove an unlooked-for proposition, that prejudice gets the upper hand of reason and judgment. In order, therefore, that a series of arguments may have fair consideration, it is often necessary, especially in the missionary field, to keep the ultimate purpose concealed.

A case in point was my first sermon in the Southern States. More full of zeal than wisdom, I faced the cold stare of an audience out of whose eyes projected texts concerning false prophets, and boldly announced that I should prove from scripture that Joseph Smith was a prophet sent by God. Imagine the effect of this proposition. It was one of those narrow, straight-laced sects who try to follow the letter of the word, but do not dream of its spirit; long-haired and fanatical to the last degree; men who believe that the earth and stars and the powers of heaven revolve about a few scriptural discoveries that they have happened to make. I am now convinced that the hundred odd Dunkers I addressed that day, counted themselves reserved from the depths of eternity, to come forth in these last days just to show the world how false prophets and wolves in sheep's clothing should be treated. At the time, however, I could only stand amazed at the first step in the program, which was taken immediately upon the announcement of my theme. These valiant few in this big world of sinners, whose holy locks were squarely cropped near the shoulders, turned their backs upon me and rested their grizzly chins upon their fists. There I stood and poured scripture for one hour—upon their rear. Quite useless; as well might the gentle rains of heaven try to soften the hearts of the moss-backed boulders of the forest; which, by the by, these "steadfast brethren" resembled in more ways than one.

Here was an audience whose continual boast was that they followed the teachings of scripture in the minutest details. Yet so hateful was the proposition I had made that they would not believe holy writ in support of it, even if an angel of heaven should proclaim it unto them. I saw, when it was too late, that much of this unlucky discussion might have received respectful consideration had the ultimate purpose been concealed. As it was, the last hope we had of opening a field in this locality was crushed. I sincerely trust that the Lord will forgive our Elders for the many fields they utterly spoil by their first crude efforts at Gospel planting and sowing!

The Modified Proposition.—Observe, however, that even in so extreme a case as the one just cited, it is not necessary to proceed without giving the audience some form of proposition. For nearly every theme is capable of subdivisions, each of which should have its proposition. And even where it is not so divisible, the proposition may be stated in so general a form as not to arouse opposition, and yet preserve that concentration of the minds of an audience, so necessary to a successful discussion. Indeed, where the desire is to approach a conclusion under cover, the very best cover is just such a general proposition. To have no proposition, or rather studiously to avoid making a proposition, is apt to arouse suspicion of something hidden, something to be sprung upon the audience in the conclusion. And in this case every hearer instinctively fortifies himself against the surprise, by refusing to admit anything.

It will be seen therefore that the need of with-holding the statement of the theme for fear of opposition is more apparent than real. The specific proposition may need to be so with-held till the way has been paved by argument, but it is generally best to give as a substitute some mild form of it that would not be objectionable.

A more real occasion for with-holding the proposition is the case of the inductive sermon—especially the narrative form of it. Here the very art of the preacher centers in keeping the "point" hidden, and the interest of the congregation hinges on the discovery of it from the examples and illustrations given. In this kind of sermon the purpose should be kept more rigidly than ever in view by the speaker; for the work should be so well done as not to need the announcement of the purpose even in the conclusion. He is but a dauber who needs to say of two pictures which he has just painted: "This is a man, and this is a horse."

Substance and Form of Propositions.—A few words now in conclusion, as to the substance and form of the proposition. It goes without saying that the statement of the theme should be calm and impassionate. No matter how vehement may be the filling-in matter, the proposition must address itself purely to the intellect. Let all exhibition of feeling be reserved for its proper place—the conclusion. Here is an example of this fault as taken from a red-hot sectarian sermon:

"Man until regenerated by the spirit of almighty God, is ab

solutely sinful; wholly an enemy of God; in all the faculties of his being, distorted, depraved, guilty, and corrupt. So that no remnant of spiritual life remains in him, but he is dead in trespasses and sin, and an object of God's utter abhorrence."

Such propositions, even aside from their objectionable length, remind one of the old flint-locks which would often spit fire so long at the priming vent that half the force of the charge was spent ere it went off.

Should be Simple and Direct.—It is equally obvious that the proposition should be simple and direct. Clearness and definiteness are what both speaker and hearer demand. What—exactly—do I wish to maintain? This must first be settled, else clearness of discussion is impossible. Now, clearness and definiteness are more likely to be present where the words of the proposition are simple, and where the construction is direct; just as ambiguity and obscurity are most likely to lurk in words so long that they throw a shadow, and in constructions so involved as to be full of labyrinths. Here as elsewhere obscurity is often mistaken for profundity. Whenever a theme does not admit of absolutely lucid statement, the first business of the discussion should be to mark its limitations. "It is this I desire to maintain, not that." Otherwise confusion will result to speaker or hearer, perhaps to both.

One Leading Thought.—Unity demands that one leading thought shall run through the proposition, and but one. Nor must it be uncertain, among the multitude of suggestions that may cling about the theme, which that leading thought is. For instance, take the proposition. "Blessed are they that do hunger and thirst after righteousness." Here suggestions spring from almost every word: "Blessed"—by whom? How? "are"—or will be—which? "Hunger and thirst"—how? Why should they? What circumstance in life should lead the mind to hunger and thirst? Give examples. "Righteousness"—what does it mean? Do all men agree as to what righteousness is? If not, how shall we tell what it is? What is it in the parent? In the child ? In the brother? In the friend? In the citizen? In the ruler? Is our conscience a guide as to righteousness? Is the Indian's? These are not a tithe of the suggested thoughts that indirectly must find their way into the discussion; but the leading thought is: They shall be blessed. It is this that makes the proposition a unit. This is the thought which the speaker must maintain and prove. To do this well, he will need to follow the life of a man who thus hungers and thirsts—follow it through the vicissitudes of this life and point out the connection between cause" and effect, between the 'hungering' and God's blessings to him; follow it to the promise of another world; and at every step draw a contrast between such a man and one who does not 'hunger and thirst after righteousness.' Where such a leading thought is not prominent in the proposition, even the speaker is led into ambiguity.

Should Contain but one Hour's Talk.—Unity next demands that a proposition shall be so restricted as actually not to include more than an hour's discourse can reasonably exhaust. Some propositions, that thoughtless preachers enter upon, would require ten quarto volumes to treat. What can be done by a preacher in such a case? The utmost he can do is to drive a few stakes and drag a stone here and there into line for a foundation: as to building the house—well, it is a cold place to leave an audience, and they never fail to absorb its coldness. This attempting to speak upon subjects too broad is a common failing among Latterday Saint preachers. As before observed nothing can be crueler or more maddening to the mind than such a task. Set a man to plucking apples from a tree and some pleasure comes from his work; but bid him pluck the stars from the blue vault of heaven—supposing that he would act as blindly in such a matter as he does in preaching—and his best directed efforts would yield him no more satisfaction than would a frantic beating of the air.

Declarative or Interrogative Form.—One other question

deserves consideration, viz.: the form of the proposition. Shall it be a declarative sentence or a question? This depends upon the method of discussion pursued. For argument and persuasion the declaration is the better; for exposition, the question. Space will not permit me to amplify this distinction. Observe, however, that the question creates the more mental activity in the audience, since it invites every hearer to be a co-investigator; whereas the declaration tends to make the audience mere witnesses of the investigation

If I have by this time succeeded in showing that a discussion needs primarily a back bone—that is a definite proposition—my next chapter will be devoted to illustrating how this back-bone needs body and limbs; in other words, I shall discuss the principles underlying the 'division' of a theme.

IX.

THE NEED AND VALUE OF DIVISIONS IN THE DISCUSSION.

The last two chapters were devoted to showing the need of a definite purpose to talk to in the discussion; a purpose, the statement of which must be a clear and complete answer to the speaker's question: "What do I wish to accomplish?" Judging by the quailty of their sermons one would say that the question is not asked by our Elders as often as it should be. For if it be asked in faith, the Spirit will not fail to reveal the answer. But will the answer be given when it is not asked? Hardly. God is not in the habit of bestowing gifts unsought. The Elder so little concerned about results as not to ask this question will not get the aid of inspiration. He will more likely be permitted to talk right on from the plenitude of his own vacuity. Let us not credit inspiration with his sermon, lest we thereby credit the Spirit of truth with utterances whose disjointedness is a reproach to mere human intelligence.

PREACHING AND PUBLIC SPEAKING.   329

Granted, however, that the speaker has asked the question and that the purpose of his sermon is clear to his mind—his first question then must be: " 'How' shall I accomplish it?" This is my present theme—how to proceed with a discussion in the most effective way.

Trusting to Chance.—My first care must be to impress the preacher with the need of definitely marked divisions in the discourse. Surely, says the reader, so obvious a fact cannot need to be impressed. Let us not be too certain. If the need of divisions be so obvious, why do speakers among us so seldom adopt them? The fact is that while no sermon can proceed—move forward—without divisions, most speakers trust to the drift of their ideas for finding them.

But this is trusting to the merest chance. In the case of all wandering talks, divisions definitely related to one another, are not found at all; hence the aimlessness of the preaching. Where divisions are stumbled upon, there is no assurance that they will occur in the order most effective to the purpose; or that all the divisions essential to the purpose will be found; or that those found will be essential. Some may be germane to the proposition, others only incidental to it; others, again, though perhaps good in themselves, may serve only to distract attention from the point under discussion.

It is this blind trusting to the drift of ideas for those changes of topic so necessary to an all-sided discussion of a theme, that I am inveighing against. Such a course is nothing but a painful exhibition of mental vagrancy. When desultory habits of mind are manifested in any other occupation than preaching, the person is said to be thriftless and improvident. Such, for instance, is the farmer with no other plan of work than the day forces upon him; and such also is the day laborer who lives a hand-to-mouth existence, always waiting for something to turn up; but the preacher—?

A sermon is a structure. It is made up of parts definitely related. It is therefore just as subject to laws of construction as is a house. There is no need to trust to the drift of ideas to determine the shape of it. What would be thought of an architect who modified his plans each day just as the masons happened to build? What I contend for is that the plan should determine the sermon, not the sermon, the plan. Our Elders should be architects capable of keeping the whole structure in view while building any part; not mere bricklayers, blind to everything save trowel and plummet.

Some Objections Considered.—It seems like wasting breath to argue that a thing made up of parts must be built by parts, and that he who would construct the whole must not leave the cutting and fitting of the parts to mere guess-work. What conditions have prevented our Elders generally from applying to preaching this simple reasoning—reasoning which is so obvious when applied to everything else they do? Perhaps the fact that putting conscious attention upon the manner of preaching has by many been counted irreverent, must largely answer for sermons that proceed without definite order. But there is another cause. The impression is general among Latterday Saints that this plan of pre-arranging divisions in a discourse is one of the glaring artificialities of sectarian preaching.

Nor is this prejudice unfounded, for the plan of proceeding by topics is not without its abuses. If a tree have but little foliage it should have but few branches, otherwise its unfruitfulness becomes glaring. Where a sermon on some meagre theme is spun out to the "forty-fifthly" point, an exactly similar impression is conveyed to the audience. The skeleton, although so essential to the beauty of symmetry in man, is a most hideous thing to look upon when divested of its fleshly covering. In like manner the sermon whose frame-work protrudes at every joint, give us the impression of something withered and dried up.

What then? Can we have human beings without skeletons?

"Skin and bones" will always be an unpleasant object to contemplate whether in the human being or the sermon. The remedy, however, is not to take out the bones, which in the case of the sermon would result in the hash-talk so common now—a dead thing in which no spirit can reside; but in clothing this frame-work till it reach the point of beauty and symmetry, and above all, in breathing into it the breath of life.

Angularity in Preaching is not always due, however, to poverty of clothing material. More often it results from carelessness on the part of the preacher in not concealing the scaffolding. That a frame-work is necessary to support his thought, is no excuse for thrusting this frame-work upon a congregation. Preachers who thus offend good taste, seem to imagine that what is good to guide the speaker must be good to guide the listener. It is perhaps this thought which leads sectarian divines to mark their divisions "firstly," "secondly," "tenthly," etc., to the disgust of our Elders, who cannot tolerate any show of artificiality. But suppose this ostentatious show of numbering the items were not openly indulged in, would the sermon not be better for the careful analysis which makes such numbering possible?

A more real objection to successive topics in the plan of a discourse, is where the divisions become cast-iron in their exactness. In such a case, there is no opportunity to take advantage of thoughts which the inspiration of the occasion may suggest. The remedy is not to do away with divisions, but to make them flexible enough to include all contemporaneous ideas likely to aid the sermon.

It is hardly profitable to continue in this strain, answering objections that have never been made. Few of the Elders whom I hope to benefit by this discussion have thought enough about sermon-making to urge an argument for or against the purpose of my present theme. To discuss difficulties which cannot be understood because not yet encountered, is like setting up straw men and knocking them down again. But as it is desirable that Elders should become judges in this matter by reason of actual trial, following further considerations are urged, for adopting divisions in the discourse.

The Argument for Divisions. — 1. — Divisions promote perspicuity. Perspicuity is clearness from the point of view of the audience. No quality is more important; for on it hinges all other qualities. A hearer has but one chance to get the thought of a speaker. He cannot, like the reader, go back and re-read a passage whose drift he fails to catch. Any device, therefore, which aids him to understand a sermon as fast as it is uttered, is of prime importance. Divisions are clearly such a device, if followed logically One sees more clearly the flight of an arrow when the target is in view.

2.—Divisions promote comprehensiveness. It is not possible to treat a subject from all its sides if the speaker relies simply upon the drift of thought for change of topic; for there is no more certainty that thought turned loose will cut the proper channel than that a river will. But by a conscious pre-arrangement of topics, all the necessary aspects of a theme will be likely to come in for discussion in their proper order.

3.—Divisions promote unity of discussion. Topics will of course be arranged with reference to the development of some one leading thought. This thought could not be made to tie the sermon together without such a pre-arrangement; setting off one argument against another, emphasizing this aspect, shading that, as the nature of the theme may demand. Can a complex machine be constructed to work as a unit, unless the size, shape, and adjustment of each separate part be fully understood? No more can a sermon.

4.—Divisions promote progress. One of the essentials of a sermon is that is shall move forward. Nothing is more exasperating than preaching which merely beats time or moves round and round and gets nowhere. Topics successively arranged for treat-

PREACHING AND PUBLIC SPEAKING. 333

ment not only help the speaker to avoid repetition, but like milestones along a dreary road, they give a congregation an exhilarating idea that they are getting somewhere.

5.—Divisions promote brevity and conciseness. Just as articles of various shapes and sizes can be packed into a much smaller space when properly classified, so ideas definitely and logically arranged take much less time in the telling.

6.—Divisions promote interest. Whatever gives a sense of clearness, order, unity, and progress cannot fail to arouse interest. We are interested in that which we understand, in that which shows evidence of design, and in that which we perceive is moving forward. The opposite of these qualities: obscurity, confusion, movement without progress, tends to dissipate attention and interest.

7.—Divisions promote permanence of impression. Memory is dependent (1) upon intensity of impression and (2) upon systematic association. A well classified theme insures both these results; the first, by reason of interest; the second, by reason of logical arrangement. We fail to remember detached bits of knowledge. Fragmentary sermons, if they leave impressions at all, do so by reason of our minds' doing the neglected work of classifying or associating the truths thrown out. But how much time or inclination is there to do this work during the progress of a rambling talk?

X.

FACTORS THAT GO TO DETERMINE WHAT DIVISIONS MUST BE MADE.

Basis of Experience Lacking.—Now begins the most difficult part of this discussion. For if I have succeeded in making it seem desirable that the proposition should be followed by well arranged divisions, the question, how to proceed in arranging such divisions, is at once raised. The difficulty lies in want of power by many of my readers to apperceive what is necessary for me to say in answer to the question. A majority of the young Elders for whom I write—the very ones that most need this information—are not familiar with the principles underlying composition; that is, they have never studied grammar or rhetoric. Accustomed to "talk right on," they have stored up but few experiences that can be appealed to by way of making clear this or that method of dividing a subject. If they, in speaking, pass from one division to another, they are perhaps unconscious of it, and feel by retrospect only a vague notion that this was the best thing to do to prove the point under consideration. If successful in a sermon they are content to say simply, "It was the Spirit that spoke," when they should note carefully how the Spirit led them to speak. If conscious of a failure they are content to feel badly over it in a dumb way, when they should carefully analyze the failure so as to discover, if possible, the causes of it. Thus these Elders have no basis of knowledge for the apperception of what must be said on this subject. It will therefore be necessary for me to furnish both warp and woof in the discussion that follows.

The Desire to Make Divisions.—It might be remarked as a preliminary that with no other guide than an earnest desire, an Elder will not fail to find some way to divide a subject so as to admit of more or less intelligent and effective discussion. Native common sense will guide him. Indeed, this must guide him under any circumstances, theory or no theory. He, therefore, who consciously puts to himself the question, "How shall I divide this subject?" will find a way, and as a result make a discussion far more complete and comprehensive than he who simply "goes it blind."

It might also be added in the same connection, that it would be much easier for me to suggest divisions in a given subject than to formulate rules to guide the speaker in dividing subjects in general.

Factors that Determine Divisions.—However, to make a beginning, let us consider first the factors that determine what shall be the nature of our divisions. These are: 1.—The qualifications of the hearers. Are they cultured or uncultured? Are they capable of prolonged attention? Are they in the habit of giving voluntary attention, or must attention be excited solely by arousing interest? If the latter, what will arouse interest? That is, what emotions are active? Divisions will be modified just as these questions are answered.

2.—The ability of the speaker. Is he a thinker or a thought-gatherer? What is the range of his information? Manifestly what a man has to say on a subject must determine what he can set for himself to say. He will not put in a division of which he knows nothing, however necessary, intrinsically, this division may be to the completeness of the sermon. From this circumstance it will be seen that every preacher must divide his own theme. A poorly made shoe that actually fits the foot is more serviceable than a perfectly constructed boot a mile too large.

3.—The nature of the theme. As I cannot here take into account the complexion of individual congregations or of individual preachers, and as that which I shall have to say in a general way as to the influence of these two factors, belongs under another head, I take up the third factor at once, viz.: divisions as influenced by the nature of the theme.

The Natural Order.—It must be plain that all subjects will not admit of being divided by the same general principle, just as it is evident that no one key will unlock all doors. A sermon should, above all things, unfold in a natural order, if we can discover what that is. No two trees in an orchard have an identical arrangement of limbs and branches. Nevertheless, each species conforms to general laws of division, else we should be unable to distinguish one kind from another. Sometimes the distinction is very marked, as between the poplar and the apple; in other cases trifling, as between the peach and apricot. Similar likenesses and differences we should undoubtedly find in the natural evolution of sermons, did we but study them with half the attention given to horticulture. Only a few of these varieties can be noticed in this article.

Divisions by Logical Necessity.—The order of divisions may often need to be determined by Logical Necessity. That is, one topic of a theme cannot be touched till some other topic has paved the way for it. Such a logical order is recognized as running through the entire scheme of salvation. Gradation in any study depends upon this principle. Milk before strong meat, was Paul's way of putting it. Missionaries who do not keep this principle of division in view, are apt to make fatal errors. A Methodist preacher in Virginia poisoned several counties against myself and companions by publishing extracts from the revelations given to the Prophet Joseph Smith. A truth out of joint is often mistaken for a lie. Too much sunshine may affect a bed of flowers in quite the same way as an untimely frost. How many Latterday Saints, think you, could keep their faith unblighted were they suddenly permitted to read the Doctrine and Covenants as angels read it? We have great need of making more than we do of the principle of taking the first round in the ladder before presuming to take the second or third.

A single instance will suffice to illustrate the division which turns upon logical consequence. Let the proposition be: What constitutes true repentance? This theme is then appropriately treated under these five heads: 1.—Recognition. 2.—Regret. 3.—Resolution. 4.—Restitution. 5.—Reformation. It must be plain that there can be no repentance unless there be first a 'recognition' of sin. So the recognition of a wasted life can hardly escape being followed by 'regret,' or godly sorrow, as Paul puts it.

The next logical step must as surely be a 'resolution' to sin no more. But "the road to hell is paved with good resolutions." To be genuine and fruitful, repentance must seek to restore or make 'restitution' as far as is in the sinner's power. The last step—and this is the work of a life-time if not of an eternity—is 'reformation,' or a gradual growth toward the likeness of God.

One word here as to the striving for uniqueness in the statement of divisions. The above arrangement of five R's is, if I mistake not, by Professor G. H. Brimhall and Dr. M. H. Hardy, both of whom are remarkable for verbal devices to aid the memory. When, as in this case, the distinctions actually turn upon thought, alliteration and similar artifices must be commended as assisting both speaker and hearer, not only in the clearness with which thought may be developed, but also in the readiness with which it may be recalled. But the constant danger of such classification is artificiality—a tendency to base distinctions on sound rather than sense. Only the keenest of thinkers should trust to this process of double association in the naming of topics.

Division by Cause and Effect.—The order of discussion will often turn upon the principle of Cause and Effect, or of Effect and Cause. Themes that fall under this head may generally be treated in either of these orders. When causes are discussed before effects the sermon is generally analytical or deductive. When effects are discussed and the causes afterward traced, the sermon becomes synthetic or inductive. The latter is especially valuable in the narrative form of preaching.

Let the proposition be the familiar proverb: "An idle mind is the devil's workshop." By the first method the theme divides itself perhaps as follows: I.—Causes. (1) Which are the forms of idleness? (a) Physical vagrancy, as street loitering, all play and no work, downright laziness; (b) mental vagrancy, as fireside moping, listlessness in school, skimming in reading, and inattention to work in hand; (c) social vagrancy, as time given to improper companions, late hours, vicious amusement, poisonous literature; (d) moral and religious vagrancy, as neglected training in respect and reverence for parents and love of home, habitual unwillingness to take part in family prayer, refusal to attend religious meetings or read religious books, the growth of dishonesty under the name of smartness, and of revengefulness under the name of manhood. Idleness as here used is simply neglect or refusal to take the exercise necessary to the proper development of any power of mind or body. II.—Effects. (2) What results when these forms of idleness become habits? (a) Ignorance, physically, mentally, socially, morally, religiously, and consequently an inability to enjoy life. (b) Animal passions and appetites; as drinking, smoking, carousing, debauchery. (c) Pauperism, a hand to mouth existence. (d) Crime and misery. Not all these perhaps, but any of them, may result from idleness.

Instead of giving all the causes first and effects afterwards, each separate cause and effect may be matched. In the second method, the effects are studied first, and the causes traced in the lives of people exhibiting such effects.

Cause and effect themes have to do with the most vital concerns of our lives. The dealings of God with man, rewards and punishments whether in this life or in the next, all come under this head. A very little thought as to divisions will swell any theme, as in the case cited, quite beyond the limits of an hour's discourse; and the matter will generally be practical and to the point.

XI.

ILLUSTRATIONS OF VARIOUS METHODS OF DIVISIONS.

Who ever has learned to divide his theme by the principle of Logical Necessity, or by the principle of Cause and Effect, will never lack for something effective to say, or an effective way of saying it; the subject-matter which yields to these methods of division is practically exhaustless. Nevertheless, he could not treat all subjects so; hence it will be well to consider other methods.

Division by Genus and Species.—Some subjects admit of discussion under the order of Genus and Species or vice versa. Where the intention is mainly to convey clear-cut, useful information, this is perhaps the best division. This was a favorite method of our Savior, as witness these three examples:

(1) Genus: Sowing of the Gospel seed. Species: (a) The seed that fell by the wayside; (b) the seed that fell on stony places; (c) the seed that fell among thorns; (d) the seed that fell in good soil.

(2) Genus: The spirit of the Ten Commandments. Species: (a) Thou shalt love the Lord thy God with all thy heart, mind, and strength; (b) thou shalt love thy neighbor as thyself.

(3) Genus: People that shall be blessed. Species: (a) The poor in spirit; (b) they that mourn; (c) the meek; (d) they that hunger and thirst after righteousness; (e) the merciful; (f) the pure in heart; (g) the peacemakers; (h) they who are persecuted for righteousness' sake.

The method of Statement and Illustration comes under this order of treatment. Every statement is a genus, and the examples educed in support of it are the species. This is the method by which science proceeds—the method of classification. It is, therefore, peculiarly adapted to the lecture, which aims at instruction by enlarging the horizon of knowledge.

The M. I. Manual.—In this connection let me call attention to the commendable outlines of study prepared for the M. I. Manual by Assistant General Superintendents M. H. Hardy and G. H. Brimhall. The analysis of lectures there set forth cannot fail, wherever followed out, to teach clearness and consecutiveness of thought. Take this syllabus for example:

Theme: The History of the Gadianton Robbers. Divisions: (1) The origin. (2) The organization: (a) its nature (b) its object;

(c) the social condition of the community at the time; (d) the arch-conspirators; (e) the operators; (f) the supporters; (g) temporary banishment from the Lamanites; (h) its encouragement and popularity among the Nephites, especially in political circles; (i) the extinction of the organization and the burial of the secret oaths. (3) The re-organization in the mountain retreat. (4) The raid upon the citizens. (5) The second robber war. (6) The surrender of the robbers.

Now, who could ask for a more admirable plan than this—for a book about the Gadianton Robbers? Its very clearness and definiteness invite thought and study. The mind has something to grapple with at every step. Compare the logical development of the lecture which proceeds under this plan with the wandering talk about Gadianton Robbers which must result from having no plan. You will then be prepared to appreciate the advice I am about to give, which is this: Let the Elders whose aimlessness I have scored so unmercifully, set to work and prepare the lectures blocked out in the M. I. Manual, and deliver them also if they can find an audience. I know of no discipline more likely to benefit mind-wandering.

Having said so much by way of commendation, I can afford a single adverse criticism. One feels like indulging a smile when remembering that these are ten-minute lecture plans. The one I have quoted covers a very moderate patch of ground, indeed, as compared with some of them, which occupy a whole column of the Manual. There are plans in this course which it would puzzle the authors themselves to get through with in ten hours.

But even here let me be quite just. These lectures were probably planned not so much for the short time allotted to their delivery as for the pressing need of systematic and exhaustive private study. The latter object, by far the more important for beginners, cannot fail of happy realization, if the course laid down be followed carefully. As to the former, the art of speaking, one of two things will happen with such extensive plans. (1) If the speaker tries to cover the ground, he can touch only surface relations, and is, therefore, in danger of contracting the hop, skip, and jump habit so prevalent among preachers who gather thought rather than think it. Or (2) if his mind be given to intension rather than extension, that is, if he be a thinker, he will scarcely have finished a single division when his time is up. The foundations of an immense structure have thus scarcely been laid, when out of very necessity the work must be left to the elements.

This talking at the edge of a subject, as one might nibble at an iceberg, tends to develop the habit of being satisfied with disproportioned work; the habit of starting and not concluding, or of hastily forcing a conclusion in much the same way as the half-finished walls of a building are sometimes roofed by canvas when a storm threatens. A plan for a sermon ought never to include more matter than can be elaborated within the time set for it.

Divisions on a Psychological Basis.—Almost every subject is divisible upon a Psychological Basis. The mind has but three general capabilities. These are knowing, feeling, and willing. He who is familiar with mind-activity, will find no difficulty in dividing on this plan. The success of a teacher depends upon this very thing—ability to fit the knowledge to the child's stage of mind-growth and activity; a condition which varies with age. Let the preacher ask himself what will be the effect of this topic given first, and how will it leave the mind to receive the next division, and the practical knowledge which he has picked up concerning the laws of the mind, will enable him to make approximately correct divisions on this principle.

The Chronological Order.—Many subjects admit of clearest treatment by the Chronological Order. Such are travels, mission reports, biographies, histories, narratives, etc. Care should be taken to group facts and events about some person or date easily kept in mind. This leads naturally to discussion by "periods" or "epochs"—stretches of time during which one series of events continues to act. No method of discussion can more dismally fail to impress an audience than that in which a multitude of dates and events follow one another without respect to the weakness of the nineteenth century memory. Yet this is the very sort of jumble we must often listen to in mission reports and other sermons that adopt the historical arrangement. If there is one kind of literature more trying to the reader than another it is that in which ideas are tied together by endless expressions like, "followed by," "after which," "and then," "succeeded by," etc. This order of movement is perhaps tolerable in minutes, though the minute-taker might often spare his readers if he would. But when it occurs in the sermon, there is but one arrangement beyond it in producing weariness. That is the "we find" sermon.

The Order of Rhetorical Force.—In argumentative discourse the order of division should be that of Rhetorical Force. Arguments will seldom be of equal weight. The necessity of climax demands that the lighter shall precede the heavier. Thus negative arguments will pave the way for positive, presumptive for probable, and proximate for conclusive. The finest examples of this arrangement will be found in the pleas of skilful lawyers before a jury. The method is, however, equally valuable before a congregation; for what is a congregation but a jury on a larger scale?

General Requirements.—In general, divisions must be contrived so as to secure a constantly increasing interest on the part of hearers. This can be done by starting in with the remote and ending with the near; treating first the general aspects of a subject, then gradually narrowing it, till it touch the confines of what is direct and personal. All good sermons, let them begin where they may, must end in the concrete; must enter the domain of our daily thoughts and experiences—bringing thither, from the eternal heights of revelation, pure, sparkling rivulets of truth to refresh our lives and invigorate our withering purposes. For it is not enough that a sermon shall refresh us. It must stimulate us—make us feel that we, not our neighbors, are the people that should live purer lives. As in Nathan's parable, there must be no mistaking the conclusion: "Thou art the man."

XII.

ESSENTIAL CHARACTERISTICS OF THE CONCLUSION.

Meaning of the Term.—In a preceding chapter it was maintained that the first requisite of a discussion is a definite proposition, which shall be an answer to the question: "What do I wish to accomplish?" The next requisite, it was pointed out, is a division of that proposition into appropriate topics, in answer to the question: "How shall I best accomplish it?" This plan, carefully followed results in a logical and complete exposition of the theme. But the sermon is not finished yet: the discussion needs to be clinched.

Clinching the discussion is what is meant by the conclusion. When the preacher is done with his last topic he naturally asks the question: "Have I accomplished the thing I set out to accomplish?" If the answer be yes the next question will be: "Do my hearers realize that I have accomplished it?" The answer will generally be no. Then they must be made to realize it.

Parts of the Conclusion.—The question naturally following is 'how.' It will first be necessary to re-state the theme or proposition. Then each point made under the subdivisions will be named or the argument for it briefly repeated. By such a synopsis the intellect is convinced. This is recapitulation. But there may be conviction without realization. The truths set forth in the sermon have some application to the lives of the people addressed. What application? How shall it be made? What incentives can be appealed to? What emotions are active at the time, and available for the purposes of persuasion? The answer to these questions leads to an appeal to the feelings, whereby the will is aroused to decide or to act according to the conviction of the judgment.

Importance.—Elsewhere in this treatise a sermon was compared to a house, of which the introduction may be likened to the excavation, the theme to the foundation and the discussion to the partition of the rooms and the building of the walls. The conclusion, in so far at least as it affects conviction, may be likened to the roof. There remains, then, the application, the appeal to the feelings, the interweaving of the truths of the sermon with the hopes and aspirations of the hearers. This resembles the garniture of the house, the house-warming, the occupancy of it by living beings.

I repeat this illustration to call attention to the importance of the conclusion. It would be difficult to impress the unity of a sermon upon a congregation without it. So many diverse thoughts and illustrations have grown out of the discussion that unless something be said to tie them together and thus show that they have a common end in view, none but the most acute minds will see their application; just as the walls of a house tend to disintegrate and fall apart if not roofed in. Then, there is the aesthetic sense which is as much offended at a chopped-off sermon as at an unroofed building. The preacher, who would persuade to a better life cannot afford to leave anything for which he expects his hearers to show charity. The very ability to detect flaws calling for the exercise of charity shows that the intellect rather than the heart is engaged. Whereas an audience should be so carried away with the thought as to be quite unconscious whether the method be good or bad.

Nor is the conclusion important only as a means of creating unity of impression. It is here that the speaker leaves the common ground of generalization and enters the specific domain of individual responsibility. Nathan's parable would never have been a sermon to David without the application, "Thou are the man." We are entertained and instructed by the discussion of moral principles; but unless the preacher strikes home in his conclusion, we are likely to think of people that ought to have been at the meeting to hear it, rather than of ourselves as standing in need of it.

It is in the conclusion that exhortation has its proper place. This is owing to the fact that the minds of the audience have been prepared for it by the discussion. Their convictions bear testimony to the efforts of the preacher to arouse feeling and will. But it is almost the only place where exhortation is effective. For, the legitimate function of exhortation is to urge upon the will that which is already understood and approved by the intellect, and partly realized at least, by the feelings.

Kinds of Conclusions.—The conclusion will differ in form according to the kind of composition that precedes it. A narrative is usually closed by a culmination of the plot. If well constructed it will clear up all the obscurities and adjust all the equities in one supreme climax. A description may fitly be closed by noting the effects upon the feelings of the thing witnessed, and by general reflections as to the lesson taught by it.

"In discourse of the intellectual type," says Prof. Genung, "the conclusion is generally a summary of the preceding arguments and facts. This summary is made, where the individual arguments are important and distinct, by a recapitulation, sometimes in the same order in which they were given, sometimes in the inverse order. In other cases the last argument or division may form the conclusion; but only when it gathers into itself the force and significance of all that has gone before. The ideal way, no doubt, is to construct the discourse in such climax or augmenting interest that its very momentum shall bear it onward to a natural, not labored or artificial, conclusion.

"In the impassioned type, the conclusion gathers into itself more of the spirit of the discourse, or its significance as related to life and conduct. In summarizing or recapitulating arguments, it takes them up by their practical application, aiming to leave the impression of appeal. Or some new application, kept in view but not mentioned before, may hold up the thought in an unexpected light, and thus form the culmination of the discourse."

Style of the Conclusion. — Respecting its style, Dr. Phelps says: "A conclusion may involve any or all of the radical processes of composition. It may explain, illustrate, prove, persuade, or all combined and intertwined. It may be the most complicated process in the whole structure of a sermon. It is susceptible of the most varied and ingenious methods of procedure. The culmination of a preacher's power may often be seen in these few closing paragraphs. Your utmost force of character as a man may use here, unconsciously to you, your utmost skill as an orator, and the richest treasures of your scholarship. The ancient orators proved themselves masters of many of the very same resources which the pulpit needs, when they put the supreme strain of their personal force into the out-pouring of their perorations."

Place for the Conclusion.—Perhaps the most ideal and artistic place for a conclusion is where ancient orators gave their peroration—at the end of the discourse. And I may add that those who prefer a reputation for eloquence to the dissemination of truth will perhaps do well to follow the rhetoricians closely on this point. But for those who see in preaching only a means of reaching and rescuing souls, a better plan will be to clinch a truth whenever and wherever it is driven home. By this rule the conclusion will be distributed throughout the sermon in the form of applications and exhortations at the end of topics or arguments. This certainly seems to be the natural way. The principles set forth in the foregoing will, however, apply equally well to distributed as to final conclusions.

The Endless Conclusion.—It will perhaps be in order now to speak of some of the mistakes people fall into in respect of this part of the sermon. The first is the conclusion that keeps trying and can't. Of all devices to test the patience of an already weary audience, this is perhaps the chief.

"It may be worth while," says Dr. Whately, "to remark that it is a common fault of an extempore speaker to be tempted, by finding himself listened to with attention and approbation, to go on adding another and another sentence (what is called in the homely language of the jest, "more last words") after he had intended, and announced his intention to bring his discourse to a close, till at length, the audience becoming manifestly weary and impatient, he is forced to conclude in a feeble and spiritless manner, like a half-extinguished candle going out in smoke. Let the speaker * * * resolve that whatever liberty he may reserve to himself of expanding and contracting other parts of his speech, according as he finds the hearers more or less interested, he will strictly adhere to his original design in respect of what he has fixed on for his conclusion; and that whenever he shall see fit to arrive at that, nothing shall tempt him to expand it beyond what he had determined on, or to add anything else beyond it."

The Illogical Conclusion.—Another mistake is to draw a wrong conclusion, or to urge considerations not heard of in the discussion, as if they had been discussed and fully agreed to. Foisting bad logic upon an audience never helps to persuade it, even in a good cause. My Sunday school teacher, when I was a boy, told a story to her class of a man who, finding he had no matches, took a paper out of his vest pocket, lighted it at a stove and thereby conveyed fire to his pipe. The paper proved to be a five dollar bill. From this she drew the conclusion how wicked and expensive a habit it is to smoke! Her exhortation fell flat, however, for young as we were, we were able to draw the real conclusion: how expensive it sometimes is to be absent-minded!

Irrelevant and Hackneyed Conclusions.—Where the sermon is irrelevant the conclusion must of course be irrelevant. It is too late to mend a scatter-brained discussion by a show of logical summing up. Better be honest and acknowledge that your talk has been so desultory that there is nothing to draw from it by way of conclusion, and that the only way to conclude is to sit down. Closing remarks of this kind will be mended when the rambling talks which they close, are mended. But there are sermons started on so vast a scale that they are only half finished when the time is up, and the speaker makes no attempt to close, or draws only the hackneyed conclusion with which we are all so painfully familiar, and which is rivaled in power to produce weariness, only its twin barbarism, the hackneyed introduction. Let us have done with things dead and cured in preaching.

CHAPTER IX.

RHETORICAL AND ELOCUTIONARY EMBELLISHMENTS.

I.

THE ACQUISITION AND USE OF WORDS.

It is said that a certain Greek philosopher, who had a house to sell detached a brick from the wall and carried it in his pocket to show to buyers. The folly of the thing is what is usually held up to view; but may not the man have been something better than a fool after all? The design of the house and its interior arrangement, he could describe, but the quality of the material could better be realized by ocular demonstration.

Importance of Diction.—How many of us, when we look upon a mansion, stop to reflect how much its comfort, beauty, and durability depend upon the collective units of which it is built? Let the brick be of different sizes, shapes, colors, or hardness, and it would still be possible to make a house of them, but what kind of house would it be? Such a thing seldom happens in the architecture of material, but it is very frequent in the architecture of thought. The design of a sermon, a poem, a story, or a drama, may be faultless, and yet the composition fail because of a wretched choice of words in which to execute it; for good taste will no more tolerate slovenly detail in a literary invention, than in a mechanical or architectural invention.

Do we fully sense the fact that all verbal communication between man and man, whether it be the most common-place thought, or the sublimest conception of the poet, is dependent upon words? Perhaps we do; but just how much of its clearness, force, and beauty depends upon this choice rather than that, can be known only to him who has labored to perfect it.

Value of Style.—In literature every inventor must be his own mechanic. The general design of his work, and the finding of thought to embody it, show the master-mind; the collecting and choosing of words, and their arrangement into phrases and sentences, show the master-workman. And the former is practically at the mercy of the latter. The best authors spend perhaps one-tenth of their time in gaining ideas and nine-tenths in dressing them; for it is the dress even more than the thought that gives a work of literature life and immortality. The Egyptians embalmed their dead bodies, while the Greeks embalmed their thoughts; both survive the ravages of time; but while the latter delight and instruct us in all their pristine beauty and freshness, the former are dragged from musty catacombs only to furnish fuel for engines and locomotives.

Now, this dressing or embalming of thought is called style. It depends upon two things, the choice of words, and the arrangement of words. The importance of style lies in the fact that recognition of thought by mankind is in the ratio of the artistic taste with which this choice and arrangement have been made.

A Man's Vocabulary is the list of words at his instant command. As every man has a different range of ideas, and a different conception of individual objects within this range, it follows that no two minds have the same vocabulary. It is only in those particulars in which these lists of words agree in meaning that ideas may be conveyed with exactness. Truth is thus at the mercy of its hearers' vocabularies. This may acount for a hundred different versions of something that was said on a particular occasion. As one values truth, so he should daily consult a first-class dictionary; for a dictionary is a kind of common ground where the ideas of men may be trimmed and pruned so as to agree with one another.

It would be impossible for me to note in a single chapter all the merits and faults of an Elder's vocabulary. I shall discuss the subject only from three aspects: (1) as to its fullness; (2) as to its exactness; (3) as to its purity.

More Ideas than Words.—In respect of fullness there is first the man with more ideas than words. When he arises to speak he stumbles along as if he walked on stilts. He is as helpless as a carpenter with only a saw, a hammer, and a jackknife. He is constantly hinting to the audience what good things they might get from him, if he only had words to convey the thoughts that arise in him. No doubt he could better lay bare the contents of his mind, if his range of words were wider; but as to his being a thinker, let him not so deceive himself. Thoughts exist in his mind only as rain-drops exist in the clouds. They are perhaps ready to form, but they never will, till he sets to work to find words. He either does not know how to do this or is too indolent and lazy to set about it. He is thus driven to the alternative of being silent or expressing himself in stock phrases or downright slang.

This man has been to school but very little, and has perhaps never read a book through in his life; or if he has been to school, he probably studied mathematics and, in general, was content to have ideas pumped into his head. It is safe to say that he hated all those studies which required the expression of what he was learning day by day.

The shortest route to an improvement in his vocabulary is a careful word-for-word study of a dictionary, especially a dictionary of synoyms; for the better half of words, the meaning, is already in his mind, and is eager to be joined to the other half, the symbol.

More Words than Ideas.—The second case is where a man has many words, but very few ideas. This is the opposite of the last, and is, if anything, more distressing and hopeless—distressing to his hearers, and hopeless of cure. Such a speaker loves to preach. He talks, talks, talks, yet seldom says anything. People say he has the gift of gab, and this is perhaps the best description of him. Words lie in his mind like empty shells; or if not empty, then with very shriveled meanings in them.

He is a product of the cramming system of education. His bent of mind began by his being compelled to memorize words without reference to their definitions. His mental energy was thus first directed to verbal memory; and regions, like reason, judgment, and imagination, which are engaged with the meanings of words, were left arid and barren. The result is that ever after, in whatever he hears or reads, his mind is caught by the verbal aspects of the subject, and pays little heed to the underlying thought.

The cure for this man is more difficult than for the other, simply from the fact that he believes himself learned. Superficiality is his disease He needs to take each one of his words, let out the wind from it, then refill it with living thought. He will never do this of himself, for he is a thought-gatherer in so far as he gets thought; and if he goes to the dictionary, the very definition will only give him more word-shells. The only way to cure him is to "pin him down" and make him think out the relationship between words.

Exactness in the Use of Words is an evidence of close, clear thinking and vice versa. Want of exactness occurs both where the vocabulary is meagre, as in the first example above, and also where it is full, as in the last. It is always a source of misunderstanding. Inexactness comes from the same spirit of carelessness which results in slovenliness of dress and toilet, and is cured by the same means, viz., by careful attention to the niceties of distinction in propriety and precision. Here are a few examples. Substitute the words in parenthesis:

He is worthy of praise for his observation (observance) of filial duty. He disperses (dispenses) ..:vors on all sides. I guess (suppose) you intend to speak respectably (respectfully) to your seniors. Those scandals have robbed him of his character (reputation). He demeaned (lowered) himself by scandalizing (speaking evil of) his friends. It is aggravating (annoying) to have a couple of (two) colds in succession. I have suffered remorse (regret) ever since I sold my violin. Rectify (amend) bad habits and amend (rectify) mistakes. Self-degradation (self-abasement) is the first essential of a religious spirit.

Big Words with Little Meanings.—Whenever you hear some one using big words ("pretentious vocables," as such a one would say) where simple, direct expressions answer better, depend upon it, his mind is a verbal junk-house, his words are of the shell-kind, and his feeble thought rattles in them. I once heard an Elder, in opening a meeting, "invoke the beneficent influence" of "divine grace" upon the "assemblage of worshiping souls," and in spite of the "paucity of our numbers" "besought the omniscient Father" to "vouchsafe the effluence" of the Holy Ghost, and to "make bare the arm of his omnipotence," and enable us to feel the "omnipresence" of his spirit, etc. Even while he was praying I thought of the hymn which says, "Prayer is the simplest form of speech which infant lips can try," and reflected that the very bulkiness of these words would keep whatever little devotion there might be in them, from raising above the earth.

A preacher especially should weed from his vocabulary long, high-sounding words and phrases. Let him get his diction from the people rather than from books. Here are parallel examples showing the difference between the two:

To be obligated to perform the same action incessantly or to be kept for a protracted period at any one species of occupation, however pleasant it may have been at the commencement, seems to us the acme of irksome drudgery.

To be obliged to do the same thing over and over, or to be kept for any length of time at the same kind of work, however pleasant it may have been to begin with, seems to us the height of irksome drudgery.

Inexactness is best overcome by carefully studying some good work on synonyms, such as Smith's "Synonyms Discriminated," or Crabb's "Synonyms," and then carefully guarding one's speech against the use of words that do not convey the very shade of meaning we desire to express.

Violation of Purity.—A few Sundays ago a speaker in the Provo Tabernacle used this sentence: "There are many sects that believe and practice the first principles of the Gospel as far as faith, repentance, and baptism, but when it comes to the laying on of hands for the reception of the Holy Ghost, they're not "in it." Just think of it! The expression grates upon one's ears even in connection with a political speech; and how an Elder, supposed to be guided by the Spirit of truth, could, on the Sabbath day, and in connection with so sacred a subject, descend to such vile slang is inexplicable on any other theory than that "we first endure, then pity, then embrace."

The purity of English is violated by the use of obsolete words, foreign words, technical words, newly-coined words, and provincialisms. The first three are mistakes of the learned, hence they need no further reference in this work. Of the fourth, I shall notice only the coinage of ignorance or depravity—slang.

Origin of Slang.—As before pointed out, whenever a person with a vocabulary more limited than his ideas, is driven to his wits ends to find an expression, he must either coin a word, or use an old word or phrase in a new sense. It is rarely the case that words thus farthered are legitimized, though "crank" is an instance. The reason for this is not so much that the word is strange and intractable as that no sooner is it born than it is beaten, and mauled, and ridden to death.

Take the slang above noted, for instance, and can you find a single action or situation in life to which it could not be applied? If a man is too late for his dinner, he is "not in it." If a young lady jilts her lover, straight-way he ceases to be "in it." But the young man who cut him out is "strictly in it." A thousand examples would not exhaust the possibilities of this wretched phrase. And so with the expression, "No flies on," e. g.: No flies on that tie," "No flies on your wit," "No flies on that poodle," "No flies on his honor," "No flies on her beauty"—heaven save the mark!

The Effects of Slang.—It will next be pertinent to inquire what effect slang has upon the mind of the user. From the examples given it will readily be seen that fifty slang expressions will do duty for a thousand words, so far as the purposes of ordinary society are concerned. It follows then that the user of slang will take no pains to add that thousand words to his vocabulary. And yet in the ordinary social circle, such an ignoramus will shine to better advantage than one who disdains thus to soil his mouth,—so low has our moral standard of words fallen. I have often enjoyed picturing the dilemma these people would be in, should a second decree of Babel blot from their memories all slang expressions. What a squawking, gibbering menagerie of fashionable creatures we should have turned into the schools to learn their native tongue! —people brim-full of ideas but with no words, or but very few words, in which to give vent to their pent up thoughts and feelings.

But preventing the acquirement of a rich vocabulary is by no means the worst effect of slang. It reacts upon the user in a moral way. Slang can never be definite and clear, since what fits every case indifferently can fit no case well. To use slang is to think slang, and soon the mind becomes unfitted for vigorous and specific thought.

A Provincialism is, as its name would indicate, an expression peculiar to a certain section. It is not vicious like slang, but is rather the embodiment of the spirit or flavor of the region where it occurs. Every canton in Europe is distinguished by certain turns of expression natural to it alone. So also in America. The delightfulness of the Bigelow Papers comes largely from Mr. Lowell's apt expression of New England provincialisms. Our Elders are perhaps most struck by the peculiarities in the Southern dialect. But while we smile at the mistakes of others, let us not be too certain that we are free. For instance, the Southerners say "I reckon," and in our superior way, we correct it, "I guess," but the latter is quite as provincial as the former.

A provincialism may, in the region where it belongs, be used in conversation, but it is not dignified enough for composition, unless, of course, it is used to hit off a character. To introduce the provincialisms of other sections is no better than to introduce slang. This is for the benefit of those Elders who enrich (?) their vocabularies with peculiarities like "tote," "right smart," and so on, while abroad, and then try to get credit for wit by setting them into circulation at home.

The Conclusion of this chapter is, that it is the duty of every Elder to widen the range of his vocabulary and to make it daily more exact and pure. To do this it will be well to note down, in a vest pocket book kept for that purpose, all the new words, or old words used in a new sense, that he may come across from books, papers, magazines, lectures, sermons, or casual encounters. Then at the first opportunity, go to Webster's International, or some equally good authority, and search out the meaning of the whole list. This advice is good for all; but for those who have time, it is well, in addition, never to cease making a formal study of words.

II.

SENTENCE AND SENTENCE MAKING.

Result of Neglecting the Sentence.—Next in importance to choosing proper words is putting them into proper places—that is constructing good sentences of them. It seems a simple thing—this making a sentence; so simple in fact that he who knows least of grammar is most confident that he can do it well. In no other art does a "little learning" lead so quickly to self-sufficiency. The sentence—simple, complex, and compound; its subject, predicate, and modifiers; its punctuation, with capital letter and period:—surely, says he, the secret of good literature cannot lie in such transparent principles. He rushes into the intricacies of grammar and rhetoric; then plunges into the mysteries of literature, and saturates himself with the opinions of critics.

His self-sufficiency swells in the mean time to alarming proportions. At length it bursts into an essay, a poem, or a story which is no sooner received by the publisher than it goes flying into the waste-basket or is returned with stereotyped thanks. He tries again with less vanity but no more success. He now begins to class himself with great but neglected authors, and talks about Shakespeare as one who would be unable to get a market were he alive today.

Importance of the Sentence.—At length he comes back to the unit of composition, to the one thing which seemed so easy that he needed to give it little or no attention—he comes back to the sentence; that is, if he is ever afterward heard of outside of MSS. In some way, no matter how, his eyes have been opened to the importance of the sentence as foundation-work; and he begins to see beauties and graces unperceived before. He turns his newly-found specs upon the old familiar authors, reading this time through his own eyes rather than through the eyes of a critic; and thus a true literary taste is begun. At a venture he dips into his neglected manuscripts. A page or two is enough. He is disgusted with his former self, and the whole bundle of lumbering sentence-work goes headlong into the fire. This is the beginning of his literary career, if he is to have one.

Is a realization of the meaning of sentential structure so important as this? asks the reader. It is all-important. Classic literature is only another name for successive sentences so constructed and arranged as to be individually and collectively perfect, or nearly so. Whoever can write a good sentence every time he tries can write classic English. No wonder that authors spend years in the study of the sentence.

The Need of Studying Grammar.—But it is not my purpose to enter into an elaborate discussion of this subject; the reader must go to first-class text-books in grammar and rhetoric for that. I only wish to call attention to a few principles which any Elder, no matter how unlearned, may put into practice—must put into practice if he would succeed as a preacher.

Perhaps the most glaring fault in the sentence-making of the Mormon preacher is his bad grammar. He is not ignorant—only illiterate. He is quite capable of instructing, if he could get men to listen. Unfortunately, as soon as cultured people discover that he murders the English language, their sensibilities are wounded, and they close their ears. They at once apply to him, reasoning that is usually true of mankind in general, viz.: "Illiterate men are ignorant men, and we can gain nothing by listening to them." In pioneer communities and in backwoods districts, where mountain-grammar is common, men are measured by a more substantial rule. This is one reason why our Elders naturally gravitate to such centres.

No Elder is too old, in my opinion, to take up a work on

PREACHING AND PUBLIC SPEAKING. 359

grammar and master its contents. This is what I should strongly urge. Here, I can only point out a few of the worst mistakes.

Mistakes in Verbs.—For instance, no one would say, 'They is,' 'You is,' or 'Is you,' 'Is They?' Then why say, "They was,' 'You was,' or 'Was you?' 'Was they?' Just as he would say "They are,' 'You are,' etc., so let him say, 'You were,' 'They were,' and 'Were you?' 'Were they?' A big advance will be made if this correction is secured. But do not say, 'I were,' 'He were,' etc., no more than you would say, 'I are,' 'He are,' etc. For one mistake in over-doing counts worse than ten in neglecting to do.

In the following sentences examine carefully the words in single quotations (subjects) and compare them with the words in parenthesis, (verbs).

The 'men' was (say were) found hiding. Was (say were) the 'horses' fed? Great 'pains' needs (say need) to be taken with these exercises. The 'cars' has (say have) stopped just in time. The 'mechanism' of clocks and watches were (say was) entirely unknown a few centuries ago. There goes (say go) two 'men.' Was (say were) the reports true?

The rule is that when the thing spoken about (the subject) is plural, then the word making a statement about it (the verb) must be plural also; that is, "A verb must agree with its subject in number." Now, every sentence has a subject and a predicate (or verb), and if they are always made to agree, a long list of mistakes will be avoided.

Mistakes in Pronouns.—No one would say 'Me will go,' 'Him will go,' yet when they are coupled together we seem to think it correct to say, 'Me and him will go.' Say 'he and I.' Do not say 'meself' for myself, 'hisself' for himself, 'theirselves' for themselves. If we speak of one person we may say, I saw 'him;' if of two or more, I saw 'them.' This is the proper use of these words. Now, if I could speak of 'them' horses, when I should say those horses, then by the same rule I could speak of 'him' horse, when I mean that horse. Do you see the absurdity of using 'them' instead of 'those' in pointing out objects?

Here is a list of very common errors: If 'anybody' wants a place to stay they (say he) must tell the committee. Let every 'one' take care of their (say his) own affairs. If any 'one' comes tell them (say him) I am not at home. Every 'man' can do what they (say he) please (pleases). 'Each' of the candidates gave their (say his) word of honor.

It will be observed that the words in parenthesis (pronouns) stand for the words in single quotations (antecedents). The rule is "Pronouns must agree in number with their antecedents." There is much room for improvement under this rule.

Mistakes in Tense.—Another list of errors creep in through wrong use of 'tense.' Tense means time. For instance, present tense, 'He goes;' past, 'He went;' present perfect, 'He has gone.' Every verb has these three principle parts: e. g., 'go, went, gone;' 'do, did, done;' 'write, wrote, written;' 'see, saw, seen,' etc. Note that the third in each of these series, the past participle, can be used only in connection with some helping verb, as 'has gone,' 'is done,' 'was written,' 'had seen,' 'may have done,' 'might have been seen,' etc. Then it is plain that to say 'He has went,' 'He has wrote,' etc., is wrong. It is equally wrong to use the third in place of the second, e. g. 'He done (say did) it for I seen (say saw) him do it.' You might just as well say, 'He written it,' as 'He done it;' and 'He gone,' as 'He seen.' Here are a few of the worst faults in tense.

She has just 'sang' (say sung) a song. I've 'drank' (say drunk) my last glass. He 'slang' (say slung) a stone against the window He's 'ran' (say run) until he's tired. He had just 'give' (say given) me to understand. You have 'took' (say taken) my seat. I 'see' (say saw) him as soon as he came. When he had 'spoke' (say spoken) for half an hour, etc. The wind 'blowed' (say blew) hard. The tree 'growed' (say grew) tall. He 'eat' (say ate) his breakfast early. He 'drawed' (say drew) a bucket of water. He has 'rode' (say ridden) more horses than you. He has 'drove' (say driven) right through the garden. The bird had 'flew' (say flown) away. His ax had 'fell' (say fallen) into the stream. John 'come' (say came) home late. I meant to 'have written' (say to write) you yesterday.

Transitive and Intransitive Verbs.—A series of ridiculous mistakes results from confounding the verbs, lie, lay; lay, laid; lying, laying; lain, laid; rise, rose, raised; rising, raising; risen, raised; sit, set; sitting, setting; sat, set. Space will not permit me to distinguish them further than to say that he first of each pair, being an intransitive verb, is complete in itself, while the second always requires an object to complete its meaning, e. g.: to 'lie on the sofa,' to 'lay the child' on the sofa; he 'rose from his bed' and 'raised the window;' the court 'is sitting' for the purpose of 'setting the date' of the next trial.

There are many other varieties of error, some of them the mistakes of men who have made a shallow study of grammar, such as, "between you and I (say me)," "It is the duty of he (say him) who has the care of the Church," etc. "This was bought of Jones —he (say him) who keeps the bargain counter." But these for the most part will annoy only the grammarian; so that if our Elders would free their speech from the kind of errors I have pointed out, they would pass muster with ordinary audiences.

Importance of Clearness.—Elsewhere in this work I have treated clearness or perspicuity at some length. This quality is dependent partly upon fulness of exposition and proper sequence in the arrangement of divisions, but mainly upon the choice of words and the structure of the sentence. The safest general rule to follow is to make short sentences. We have one prominent Elder among us whose sentences are so long, that before he is done with them he has often forgotten what he started to talk about.

Want of clearness often results from neglecting to use small and apparently insignificant words. Note how much clearer the sense becomes in the following sentences by using the words in parenthesis:

He has tried the old and (the) new method of cure. (Though) walking on a slippery place the other day, I managed, with these patent heel corks, to escape unhurt. He forgets the gratitude that he owes to those that helped all his companions, and (to) his uncle in particular. I think he likes me better than (he likes) you. Pleasure and excitement had more attraction for him than (for) his friend. He was (at) home. Nothing prevented him (from) going. This happened (in) some other place. It is (of) no use. The saving (of) my life. He ate a little (piece of) pie. You don't seem to like anything I do (say like). Have you heard how old (of what age) Mrs. J. is? (Or, how the old lady, Mrs. J., is?.)

Confusion often arises through the careless use of pronouns. e. g.: "John's father, Mr. Brown, told him to go into the pasture and get his horse as he had to use him that day to drive his mother to the city." Change to the direct address, thus: "John, my boy," said Mr. Brown, "go to the pasture and get my horse, as I have to use him today to drive your mother to the city." When the ambiguity is between two plural pronouns, clearness results by making one of them singular: Men (man) look (looks) with an evil eye upon the good that is in others and think (thinks) that their reputation obscures them (him) and that their commendable qualities do stand in their (his) light; and therefore they (he) do (does) what they (he) can to cast a cloud over them, that the bright shining of their virtues may not obscure them (him).

Funny mistakes occur frequently through not placing words and phrases near the words they modify: The woodshed and contents of Mr. A. was burned last night. Lost: a cow belonging to a colored lady with a white face and long horns. He said that the mosquitoes would climb up on the trees and bark; and that he had no doubt a great many of them would weigh a pound. The captain of the steamer was drowned, and so was his daughter. She was laden with tropical fruit, and her loss is estimated at eighty thousand.

Value of Transition.—Clearness is promoted to a wonderful degree by attention to transition. Thought should be so closely knit, that one sentence grows visibly out of another, like branch out of branch. Paragraphs should in the same way be connected with each other like the larger limbs to the trunk. But thought may be so related in fact, without seeming to be so on the surface. The reader cannot be relied upon to discover this relation, and should he fail to do so, the unity of the impression is broken. It is therefore the duty of the writer or speaker so to construct sentences and paragraphs that they will, figuratively speaking, glance backward over their shoulders at what has been said before. This subtle turn of phrase, or allusion couched in adjective, or antithesis, or direct synoptical reference, is called transition. For examples you should be able to dip into this book, and be rewarded now and then, if keeping theory constantly in view can be relied upon to crystalize occasionally in practice.

Importance of Force.—But it is not enough that sentences be clear: they must stir as well as instruct. The stirring quality of a sentence is called force. Apply to sentence-making the lesson taught by this illustration: Take a number of objects in the hand, say a cork, a marble, a bean, a kernel of wheat, and a bullet, and throw them at once: which goes the farthest or does the greatest execution? Observe that it is not because the bullet is smallest, but because it is most compact, that it has the greatest force. So in a sentence, the more compact, the thought can be made, provided it remain clear, the greater will be its power to stir the feelings.

The most common violation of this principle in the speech of our Elders, and indeed in most of our home literature, is what might be called leaving dead wood in the sentence. Think of a tree with strips of life along its trunk and a living branch here and there, and you have by analogy exactly what I mean. Cant phrases, stock-expressions, worn-out comparisons, hackneyed scraps of scripture, and cut-and-dried "remarks," make up this dead wood of sermons. I should urge Elders to guard their speech against such empty, lifeless expressions, but this would reach only the external symptoms. The real cure is to learn to think intensely. Words coined at a white heat cannot fail to be free from verbal scum and scoria.

The Need of Unity.—But want of force frequently comes from introducing into the sentence elements that distract attention. Unity of impression is quite as essential in the sentence as in the paragraph or the theme. And to have unity a sentence must contain but one leading thought. This thought must be like the track of a lantern in the dark, clear and onward-tending. Ideas obtruding themselves endwise on each side of the light should rarely be noticed at all. Ideas running parallel to the track, may if near enough, receive notice, but only in such a way as to indicate their proper degree of dimness, never in such a way as to steal light from the direct path, e. g.: "When 'we' were about to go, 'they' put into my hands a bundle of books, and when 'I' undid them 'they' proved to be exactly what 'I' wanted. Here there is no leading thought though "bundle of books" seems the most important. If all the other ideas be properly subordinated to this one, the sentence will read: "On our departure, a bundle of books was put into my hands. When opened they proved to be exactly what I wanted." 'We,' 'they,' and the first 'I,' illustrate what I meant above by "ideas obtruding themselves endwise." They are left out or properly subordinated in the corrected sentence.

In the two sentences following, the passages in single quotations serve only to detract attention and should be left out, or made the subject of new sentences. "I received the letter you wrote from Chicago yesterday, and, without a moment's delay or waiting for dinner, proceeded at once to Dr. Bunsby's office, though it was raining at the time, 'and the clerk said he had just telegraphed his acceptance.'" "Tillotson died in this year. He was exceedingly beloved both by King William and Queen Mary, 'who nominated Dr. Tenison, Bishop of Lincoln, to succeed him.' "

Value of Harmony.—Before we can be persuaded we must first be pleased; therefore whatever in the language of a sentence grates upon our sensibilities detracts from the force of the thought. Clumsiness in anything offends the aesthetic sense and though it may be condoned in preaching (among us), it must not be forgotten that audiences which pity, are in but little better frame of mind to be persuaded, than audiences which condemn. Sentences should therefore be made as smooth and agreeable to the ear as possible. Repetitions though sometimes necessary to clearness or force, are always unpleasant; but frequent repetitions of the same word, or of similar words or sounds becomes painful; hence whenever an idea is referred to the second or third time, it should be under a new name; and this name should exhibit the spirit or color of the thought in connection with which it is used. Thus, in a narrative it would be monotonous always to refer to the leading character as Jenkins. In one paragraph he may be the "old farmer," in the next, the "rural visitor," and so on the "unsophisticated old plowboy," the "irascible old gent," the "honest old man," the "white-haired son of toil," etc., the allusion in each instance taking color from the thought to be conveyed.

The Climax and the Period.—Force is secured by arranging ideas in the order of climax, e. g.: "It is an outrage to bind a Roman citizen; to scourge him is an atrocious crime; to put him to death is almost parricide; but to crucify him—what shall I call it?" So it is conducive to closer attention if ideas be so arranged that the main thought is suspended till the close of the sentence. This is called the periodic structure, e. g.: "If you look about you and consider the lives of others as well as your own; if you think how few are born with honor, and how many die without name or children; how little beauty we see, and how few friends we hear of; how many diseases and how much poverty there is in the world—you will fall down upon your knees, and, instead of repining at your afflictions will admire so many blessings which you have received at the hand of God."

It has not been possible to make this chapter clear and complete as it might have been made, could I have relied upon my readers' having a knowledge of grammar and rhetoric; but such as it is, I trust it will be of some assistance, if in no other respect than to encourage the young Elder to a more exhaustive study of the sentence, in text-books specially written for that purpose.

III.

IMAGERY AND ILLUSTRATION—EXAMPLES.

Figures of Orthography.—So arbitrary and difficult is English spelling that most people cherish a secret revenge against it. Hence we smile when its absurdities are burlesqued. For instance:

> Once a young lady of *Worcester*
> Was sent to catch the old *rorcester*
> His perch was too high, but her lover was nigh,
> So she kindly asked him to *borcester*.

This is called a figure of orthography. It is from the anomalies in our system of spelling that certain "phunny" writers, like Artemus Ward and Josh Billings, draw much of their humor. The peculiarity of this figure is that it can be enjoyed only through the eye.

Figures of Etymology.—The pronounciation of English is almost as varied as the spelling, with this difference, that it falls into more or less well-defined dialects, according to locality and nationality. Thus we have English tinctured respectively with the twang of German, Italian, Scotch, Irish, Danish, and many other tongues. And even where English is the native tongue, we have characteristic pronunciations. Every shire in England has its peculiar "lingo," and in America the dialect of New England and of the Southern States are each well marked. No doubt dialect writing is carried on to an extreme, yet it would be difficult to hit off character without giving effect to this peculiarity.

Figures of Syntax.—Mountain-grammar is by no means confined to mountain districts: wherever English is spoken by the uncultured masses, its syntax suffers more or less. As with figures of etymology, so also with figures of syntax—they are often necessary to give truth and vividness to character-portrayal. Had Will Carleton made the three "good district fathers" grumble about the new-fangled methods of the school in faultless grammar they would have seemed mere puppets, and all the realistic effect would have been lost. As it is, they are made to stand before us, tousle-headed, grizzly-bearded, bony-fisted, and nasal-twanged—just as they probably were—mostly by the refrain: "Them 'ere's my sentiments, tew."

Figures of orthography can be of no service to the preacher, since they cannot be made to appear in sound, but figures of etymology and of syntax will often heighten the effect of a narrative told in illustration of some principle. It will not be harmful for our Elders to keep their eyes and ears open to the customs and dialects of the people among whom they travel, provided they can keep their own speech and habits separate and apart. But to forget that such peculiarities are peculiarities, and use them unconciously, makes their acquirement a serious matter. For while some credit may attach to the happy use of dialect in character-sketching, the habitual and unconscious use of it always stamps the user as illiterate and uncultured.

Figures of Rhetoric.—The figures thus far considered are such as touch only the surface of thought; that is, its expression. We are now to discuss a class that spring out of the very source of thought. Figures of rhetoric are of two kinds, viz.: figures that leave a picture or image upon the imagination, and are called from this circumstance, "Figures of Intuition" (from Latin 'intueor,' I see); and figures which aim, by contrast or exaggeration, to increase the force of what is said, and so are called "Figures of Emphasis."

The Use of Figurative Language is by no means a peculiarity of the learned. On the contrary, the fewer the words in a man's vocabulary the more likely is he to use this method to make himself understood. The Indian tongues, for instance, are almost exclusively a language of comparisons and signs. But, of course, the more cultured the mind, the more apt and graceful the figure used is likely to be. And it is on this point that a few remarks will, I think, be most profitable.

Language has been called a dictionary of faded metaphors. To realize the truth of this remark one may take almost any word that has ceased to carry a figurative sense and dwell upon it long enough to make its original color stand out vividly again. For instance, to say a man has good understanding once meant what it now means to say, he stands on firm ground, i. e., his judgment is unassailable. The difference between the poet and the ordinary man is that the former sees words bristling with all their pristine beauty and color, while to the latter they are mostly gray-coated.

Learning to use Imagery.—Now, whoever would succeed in illustrating his ideas with figures must develop the imaginative power of the poet. There are many ways of doing this. Let him first form the habit of seeking analogies from every object or action that presents itself to his senses. He picks up a pebble. It is round and smooth. What made it so? Just so the ruggedness of our character is worn off by society. He throws it into a pond. Thus does individual man sink out of sight by death. The circle widens till tiny ripples reach the shores. Thus does his life affect mankind even to the verge of eternity. The matter-of-fact man sees ten objects without stumbling upon a single analogy, but the poet finds ten analogies clinging round every object.

If it is good for the poet to cultivate the matter-of-fact side of his nature, it is much more necessary for the matter-of-fact man to cultivate the poetical side of his nature, especially if he sets up for teacher or preacher. This habit of double observation soon becomes a delight beside which carnal pleasures seem coarse and vulgar. To begin the habit there is perhaps no better way than to read poetry and imaginative literature, taking care to analyze every conceit, image every figure, and follow every suggestion to the idea that exhales it. Soon instead of the intellect, the narrow workings of which often fill the man with a foolish boast of his "common sense," the whole brain is energized, and the mind made alive in all its faculties. It is easy for such a mind to speak in figures, simply because it thinks in figures.

Scripture Full of Imagery.—The Bible is largely incomprehensible to a mind untrained to grapple with metaphorical language. Job, the Psalms, Proverbs, and nearly all the prophets can hardly be said to use plain language at all. The thought is couched in the highly-colored imagery of the orient—an imagery difficult at first to the prosaic western mind, but capable of yielding exquisite delight, when fully comprehended. Let the missionary, whose exclusive library is the Bible, resolutely set himself to understand and assimilate the poetry of Israel, and the mental exercise gained thereby will re-act beneficially upon his choice and use of imagery and illustration.

The Simile.—Of the figure of intuition the most common is the comparison or simile. It is also the most useful, at least to the preacher, whose aim above all things is to make truth clear, attractive, and forcible; and no other figure can do this so well for uncultured audiences, such as our Elders are most likely to meet with. Teaching by comparison is an attempt to get at the meaning of the unknown, through the medium of the known. People are constantly storing their minds with the experiences they meet with every day. The speaker who has the art to realize these experiences, and make use of them as illustrations of his ideas, will be rewarded by earnest attention and quick comprehension.*

The Metaphor is a shortened comparison. Instead of saying, "He is like an oak," we may say, "He is an oak." Here is another example: Comparison: "Happiness is like sunshine; it is made up of very little beams." Metaphor: "The sunshine of life is made up of very little beams." In the following paragraph the metaphors are printed in single quotations:

Kindness is the 'golden chain' by which society is 'bound together.'—What is pride? A 'whizzing rocket that would emulate a star.'—We cannot all be 'cabin passengers in the voyage of life.' Some must be 'before the mast.'—Aloft on sky and mountain 'wall are God's great' pictures hung.'—Silently,one by one, in the 'infinite meadows' of heaven, 'blossomed' the lovely stars, the 'forget-me-nots of the angels.'—A certain amount of opposition is a great help to a man: 'Kites rise against and not with the wind.'—Spare moments are 'the gold-dust' of time.—He worked hard 'to keep the wolf from the door.'—Time is the 'warp' of life. Oh, tell the young, the gay the fair, to 'weave it' well.

IV.

IMAGERY AND ILLUSTRATION—CONTINUED.

The Pleasure of the Metaphor and the comparison lie in our perception of a parallel between otherwise unlike ideas. For instance, take the simile: "It is with words as with sunbeams—the more they are condensed the deeper they burn." And we have—

IDEA: Words— . . . . . x x
ILLUSTRATION: Sunbeams—condensed—burn.

The pleasure comes the instant we perceive the hidden ideas marked 'x.' Sometimes a bungler in the use of imagery will give

---

*I need scarcely give examples of the simile, since they can be found on nearly every page of this book. For somewhat extended illustrations see the opening paragraphs of Sec. I, IV, and V, of Chapter II.

us a figure which leaves no 'x' for the mind to discover Such a comparison is said to walk on all fours. We are bored by it, and feel as though the speaker had thought it all out for us like one who distrusted our intelligence.

Nevertheless this very thing must sometimes be done with children and audiences of so little intuitive power that they fail to perceive the analogy unless pointed out with a stick. But generally speaking the keener the power of imagination the greater the number of 'x's' necessary to give pleasure. It is for this reason that the metaphor is more forcible to cultured imaginations than is the comparison, e. g.: "Condensed thoughts burn." These three words tell all that is contained in the above simile, and the sentence is therefore more forcible to minds capable of seizing its analogies and suggestions.

Personification is the name of a particular kind of metaphor, which represents inanimate things, or beings of a lower order, as human or as possessing human traits. In the following paragraph the words which indicate personification are placed in single quotations:—

Kind Fancy plays 'the fairy godmother.'—'Scowling' turrets and 'frowning' battlements.—Our bugles 'sang' truce.—Hope enchanted 'smiled.'—Violet, sweet violet! 'Thine eyes are full of tears.' Fair Science 'frowned' not on his humble birth, and Melancholy 'marked' him for 'her own.'—Creaking with 'laughter' swings the old barn door, at little 'winking' seeds upon the floor, dropped from four 'hungry' barrels in a row.—Joy and Temperance and Repose 'slam the door' on the doctor's nose.—All day the sea waves 'sobbed with sorrow.'—Marbles 'forget their message' to mankind.

The Allegory is a form of writing in which only the illustrative half of a succession of thoughts is given and the reader's imagination is trusted to supply the thoughts themselves. Any metaphor indefinitely extended in its particulars, becomes an allegory. The finest example in the language, perhaps, is the "Pilgrim's

Progress." Our Savior's parables are splendid instances of short allegories. So also are Aesop's fables. A common illustration of this figure will be found in the first chapter of this book.

Metonymy is the name of a figure in which some relationship of an idea is used to convey the idea. Its value lies in the vividness of impression which results from singling out some one aspect of an object for the imagination to dwell upon:—

Gray hairs (age) should be respected.—Streaming grief (tears) his faded cheek bedewed.—He addressed the chair (chairman).—The bench (judges), the bar (lawyers), the pulpit (preachers).—His steel (sword) gleamed on high.—The kettle (water) boils. —The drunkard loves his bottle (whisky).—They have Moses and the Prophets (their writings); let them hear them.—He deserves the palm (victory, which among the Greeks was signified by the palm).

The Synecdoche is a species of metonymy in which the part of an object is placed for the whole, and a definite number for an indefinite, or vice versa, e.g.:—

Give us this day our daily bread (all things needful for us).—The world (part of the world) knows his worth.—We have tea (supper) at six o'clock.—He employs twenty hands (men).—I will not be paid in paltry gold (money).—The Assyrian (an innumerable host) came down like a wolf on the fold.—The cattle upon ten thousand hills (very many hills).—A maiden of sixteen summers (years).—The canvas (picture) exhibited by this artist is a marvelous product.—She bestowed her hand and heart (her whole being) upon a worthy man.

The Apostrophe consists in addressing the absent and inanimate as if human and present, e. g.: "O death, where is thy sting? O grave, where is thy victory?" "O Jerusalem, Jerusalem, thou that slayest the prophets, how often would I have gathered you as a hen gathers her chickens, but ye would not!" "Toll toll, thou bell by billows swung." "Go, little book, whose pages hold those garnered years in loving trust." It is a very effective figure in fervid discourse, but is quite out of place in dispassionate discussion. (See next chapter.)

Vision is also a very effective figure. It consists in a panoramic presentation of thought, the past being represented as present or future, the future as present or past, and sometimes the present as past or future. A good instance is the fifty-third chapter of Isaiah, where the life and sufferings of our Savior are depicted as having already taken place. Here also is a short example: "I see the pyramids building; I hear the shoutings of the army of Alexander; I feel the ground shake beneath the march of Cambyses. I sit as in a theatre,—the stage is time, the play is the world." Vision is especially valuable in descriptions. By its means the speaker becomes a guide for his hearers, who, by means of imagination, are made to see the scenes depicted as if they were visible to the natural eye.

Interrogation and Exclamation.—Of the figuers of Emphasis, the interrogation and the exclamation have already been discussed under the head of Persuasion, and also in the chapter on Sentences. Their value is to enliven thought and rest the flagging attention by relieving the monotony of declarative sentences. Exclamation does this by appealing directly to the emotions, and interrogation by putting us in the attitude of active participants in the thought advanced. Here are some examples:—

EXCLAMATION:—"A horse! a horse! my kingdom for a horse!—Farewell, a long farewell, to all my greatness!—O strong hearts and true! Not one went back in the Mayflower!—Oh, what a tangled web we weave, when first we practice to deceive." INTERROGATION:—"Hath a dog money?—Is it possible a cur can lend three thousand ducats?—Am I my brother's keeper?—Who is not proud to be an American?—Can the Ethiopean change his skin or the leopard his spots?—Shall mortal man be more just than God?—Is life so dear, or peace so sweet as to be purchased at the price of chains and slavery?"

Antithesis and Epigram.—Contrast is one of the keenest o the delights of children, and it never ceases to be a pleasure to adults. This difference, however, is noticeable: with children (or barbarians) the contrast must be so wide as to be practically a contradiction; but with adults (or cultured people) the pleasure grows in exquisiteness as the contrast approaches harmony. A deep law of human development underlies this phase of mind. Antithesis is the name given to a contrast of ideas, and epigram, to a hiden harmony lurking beneath an apparent contradiction, e. g.:—

ANTITHESIS:—"The shallows murmur while the deeps are dumb.—Deeds show what we are; words, what we should be.—Better to reign in hell than serve in heaven.—Fools rush in where angels fear to tread.—God made the country, and man made the town.—Silence is deep as Eternity; speech is shallow as time." EPIGRAM:—"The child is father of the man.—Verbosity is cured by a wide vocabulary.—Beauty, when unadorned, adorned the most.—The fastest colors are those that won't run.—A new way to contract debts—pay them off!—Beneath this stone my wife doth lie; she's at peace and so am I."

The Hyperbole exaggerates an idea for the sake of empahsis, e. g.: "Waves mountain high broke over the reef." "They were swifter than eagles; they were stronger than lions." "The tumult reached the stars." "Rivers of water run down my eyes because they keep not thy law." "Here [at Concord] once the embattled farmers stood, and fired the shot heard round the world." Hyperbole is admissible when dignified, but it detracts from the respect felt for a speaker when it is trivial, e. g.: "I'll kill you, if you don't mind." "An awful good time," "tired to death," "tickled to pieces," "an exquisitely lovely pug dog," "a divine moustache," etc.

Irony and Sarcasm.—Wit and humor are acceptable sauce to almost any kind of literary dish; but of these elements as qualities of style I have nothing to say here. There are distinctly occasions, however, when no other figure of emphasis is so timely as irony or sarcasm—figures which may be regarded as gypsy cousins of wit and humor. Irony pokes fun under the guise of saying something quite proper or complimentary: "Cry aloud," said Elijah to the discomfited priests of Baal. "Cry aloud: for he is a god; either he is talking, or he is pursuing, or he is in a journey, or peradventure he sleepeth, and must be waked!" Sarcasm directly aims to wound the feelings and consequently employs the most cutting words in the language. Humor is usually playful and therefore in its sallies there is a laughing with, not a laughing at. Now, add to this delightful quality the slightest tincture of worm-wood, and we shall have irony. To produce sarcasm—a word which in Greek signifies to tear flesh—we take wit, which is itself merciless, and dip it into gall. It then becomes a most dangerous tool—one to be used only as the surgeon's knife is used—when heroic treatment is demanded.

V.

IMAGERY AND ILLUSTRATION—FAULTS.

The foregoing is a brief consideration of the meaning and use of the principal figures of speech. It remains now to note, briefly, also, the most common mistakes..

Worn-out Verbal Finery.—If a person never pretends to dress in any other than a plain way, he will never invite adverse comment even though he does not excite admiration. But he who strives for prestige in apparel and is able to wear only tawdry goods and cheap finery, will get contempt from the cultured, whatever be the estimate in which he is held by the vulgar. It is exactly so in the fashion of composition. Gaudiness is always associated with cheapness and vulgarity. He who has not a severe taste in the selection and use of figures, will do well to employ them sparingly.

But this is exactly what the neophite in composition will not do. As his imagination awakens to analogies, he becomes intoxicated with his perceptions. Time, for instance, he discerns as a river down which float our barks of life to the ocean of eternity. Or life is a ship, with helm, masts, ropes, and sails—each typified by some quality or attribute; while captain, helmsman, crew, and passengers find their parallels in man's associates; and wind and wave and breaker each contribute their resemblances to the enchanting picture. Hope becomes a star, friendship a golden band, wisdom a fountain, sorrow a drooping flower, passion a tempest, and so on, through all the trite and worn out metaphors in the language.

Not least of the agony to the listener is the insufferable vanity with which this bedraggled verbal finery is brought forth. The face of the speaker glows with all the joy of first discovery; and you are certainly expected to praise these ancient conceits, at the risk of being counted jealous if you do not.

Poor simpleton! What gives him such keen pleasure, ought, he thinks, to give the whole world pleasure, not realizing that obvious resemblances like these are seen by everybody, and have found their way into composition ten thousand times since Adam's day.

Inappropriate and Obscure Figures.—Figures are often used which add neither beauty, clearness, nor force to the thought. Thus the description of a volcano gains nothing by being compared to a forge in which God's hand blows the bellows. One of our local poets has tried to convey some idea of the magnificence at night of the electric arch at Saltair by comparing it to the coronet of an Eastern princess. "Our prayers and God's mercy," exclaimed a devout preacher, "are like two buckets in a well: while the one ascends the other descends." He probably did not reflect that the descending bucket is always empty.

In order that figures may add clearness to the thought—and without clearness there could be neither beauty nor force—it is necessary that the object used for illustration be better understood than the thought to be illustrated. These conditions are often reversed: we get the thought, but are compelled to search dictionary or encyclopedia to understand the figure. References to obscure places or characters in mythology, history, or fiction, and metaphors drawn from technical science and philosophy, or from the trades and professions, can be understood only by the limited number of people who happen to be familiar with the area of thought whence they are drawn. They are therefore for the most part wasted in sermons, which are meant to convey thought to the masses.

Imagery should be used for the sake of the audience rather

than for the sake of the subject. "I wasted half my lecture," said a popular speaker, on his return from a provincial town, "before I discovered just where the people lived. It was not until I began drawing my illustrations from the gutter that I was able to reach their understanding or appeal to their sympathies."

Obscuring by too much Light.—A comman fault of inexperienced Elders, and one which I often had occasion to notice in the mission field, is the opposite of that discussed under the last heading. This fault, if it results from thinking at all (which is doubtful), comes from a belief that the audience is utterly ignorant of the source of the illustration about to be used, and consequently must be instructed, before the application can be made. Thus, instead of saying, "'Today shalt thou be with me in paradise,' said Christ to the penitent thief," and then going on with the trend of thought, the Elder stops to narrate all the circumstances under which Christ used the words, with the result that both speaker and audience often forget what the interruption was made for.

To illustrate well, care must be taken to make prominent the single aspect of the illustration, which makes the idea clear or forcible, and to subordinate those aspects which have only an indirect bearing upon it. The ability to do this well is evidence of that intensity of thought which never for an instant loses sight of the unity of the subject discussed.

Mixed Metaphors.—Figures of intuition grow out of the imagination, and only out of the imagination. He who uses them must image them in detail or he is likely to fall into the error of incongruity. Here is an example of a metaphor evidently drawn from memory: "Mr. President, I smell a rat, I see it floating in the air, but mark me, sir, I'll nip it in the bud." We can guess at the idea meant to be conveyed by this mixture of slang and trite metaphor. But had the speaker actually seen a rat in imagination, he would not have located it in the air, nor would he have thought it possible to "nip it in the bud." The fact is, these diverse figures had been lodged in his verbal memory, each with a certain vague meaning, but with no vestige of an image; hence when occasion demanded the particular combination of ideas for which they stood in his mind, he brought them out as he would any plain series of words or phrases. Here are other examples:

"Jonas, my son, you are entering upon your life; before you the 'doors' of the future open wide, and, 'like a young squirrel escaping from his cage,' you go forth to 'navigate' the sea of life upon your own 'wings.' [The passages in single quotation are trivial as well as "mixed."]—We thank thee, Lord, for this 'spark' of grace; and we devoutly ask thee to 'water' it.—The little church at Jonesville is once more 'tossed' upon the 'waves,' a 'sheep' without a shepherd. He alone can manage the storm-tossed 'ship' of state on its 'march.'"

Bombast.—I now invite attention to passages from a most remarkable product of overdone imagery, submitted for criticism as a graduating address. It is needless to say that it was rejected.

"Ladies and Gentlemen, be patient while I now condense the story of a student's life, as he, step by step, emerges from the spangled parlors of blissful nescience, where the youthful guests are fed from the platter of praise. There is a period in the life of man when the privilege and the power are his to purchase and procure [Note the alliteration—five p's.] the crown and coronate himself, or bow his neck the yoke of servitude to wear."

Surely there is need of patience. What are the "spangled parlors of blissful nescience;" the "crown;" the "yoke of servitude?" The passage probably means: "Permit me to give you a few facts in the life of a student. Every man is given an opportunity to determine what his future shall be."

"The unclaimed coffers of Time, teeming with the golden days that God has coined at the mint of eternity, are his if he will seize them. A genuine sight-draft on the solvent firm of vigorous manhood is his, if he will present it. A check on the First Natural Bank of Character and Reputation belongs to him if he will only cash it. Will he seize the coffers? Will he present the draft? Will he cash the check? And what will he purchase? * * *

PREACHING AND PUBLIC SPEAKING. 379

"If he be an abducted child borne away in the deceiving arm of Ignorance, let the signs of rescue be inscribed on every roadside rock, carved on the trees of the forest, penciled on the plains of the prairie, written along the river's banks, scooped in the sands of the desert, marked along the margin of the lakes, painted on the peaks of the mountains, colored in the field and flowers, and reflected in the floating clouds of heaven; that wherever his barbarous abductor shall bear him, his eye cannot fail to catch the inscription: 'Escape by way of the school.'"

—All of which probably means: "Let us hope that the youth starting out upon life will choose to get a good education." But the writer is so in love with his metaphors that he begins the same thought over again in a new series:

"Just now I see a child of love fall victim to that nescient witch. Some gaudy-colored veil hangs down to screen her face from the innocent eye of her captive; and that gem of affection, mistaking the witch for its mother's caress, is carried away with a smile. Ere long its little arms are clasped around Temptation's neck, and its ruby lips have learned to kiss the uncovered cheek of crime. Wearied at last, it slumbers in the arm of Treachery and dreams of a trusty cradle home. Evening after evening the child forgets that he once was rocked in the lap of learning and put to sleep by the lullaby songs of love. Now he lies on the lounge of Ignorance, soothed into dreams by the charming voice of Vanity. The nursing breast of knowledge has been cruelly with-held, and the bottle of conceit has been his only stimulant to growth. * * * At last he sees those signs of rescue * * * and bravely resolves on a noble and honest escape."

The asterisks in this passage stand for two pages of MS. descriptive of the emotions necessary to call out the resolve. He next reaches the school by three pages of MS., begins his studies by two more, and then is attacked with that disease so prevalent among students, the tendency to get the big head, and this is how the latter idea is set forth:

"That amorphous Angel of Temptation, emboldened by the darkness of the hour, remembering well how once her imperious neck was encircled by the arms of the youth, comes again arrayed in her silks of sorcery, her rosy cheeks painted with the powder of pride, her hair bespangled with the silver of sin, and the hyacinth of hypocrisy pinned upon her breast. He sees upon her wrists the popular bracelets of fashion, as she offers him the alluring goblet of ruin. Diamonds of deceit are glistening from their jeweled chambers, and the tinkling bells of blasphemy are ringing on her feet as she glides before that undecided mind."

Undress the staveling ideas hidden beneath this gorgeous clothing, and your most careful collection will hardly give this much sense: "A little learning tends to make the student vain." —a thought so trivial and hackneyed that it scarcely deserves jeans, let alone silk, satin, and lace. But the writer evidently loses sight of his beribboned weaklings, and imagines something dreadful is going to happen to the subject of his theme. He goes into apostrophes, in his eagerness to prevent the calamity:

"O strangers to that bewitching siren; ye whose eyes are charmed not with her jeweled beauty, and whose ears are aliens to her flattering voice—pause here and pour your oily tears upon the fierce, tempestuous wave. Go wake the slumbering Master—the better self of that tried soul, and he will rise, rebuke the wind, and bid the waves be still. * * * * *

"Again the trial has been met and Victory crowns his potent will. Hope, smiling hope, blessed joyous hope!—appears again and lures him on to realization."

Let no one suppose that this was designed as a burlesque. The student who prepared it was fairly charmed with its poetical worth, and was much disappointed at not being permitted to deliver it. For, mind you, had he been permitted to deliver it, he would have become the hero of the hour—among the lovers of spangles and cheap tinsel. Many a time I have sat writhing through such a performance, only to hear the plaudits, "beautiful," "glorious," etc., ad nauseam, when the meeting closed. The thoughtless multitude have, in literary matters, very little more taste than do savages

PREACHING AND PUBLIC SPEAKING. 381

in matters of dress; who wear rings in ears and nose, on fingers and toes, and fasten a gilded band wherever it will shine, and a bell wherever it will tinkle.

A few times in my life I have heard Mormon Elders deliver themselves of such gilded rubbish, but as a rule, they sin in the opposite direction. Our young ladies, however, so far as I have been able to judge of them through the effusions of their M. I. manuscript papers, have the metaphorical disease bad. The very names of these papers attest this vulgar taste for verbal finery.*

But if our young men seldom soar in this way it is because they have no wings, not because they love to move along the mundane level. And if I am particularly severe in holding such flights up to ridicule it is because I fear that, when our Elders shall make the careful study of preaching which has been so strongly urged in this book, their first acquirements will be just such verbal volatility.

Let me make it most emphatic here that this kind of preaching is what 'not' to indulge in. Examine the passages which I have quoted: they violate every principle of unity, propriety, and proportion; but the worst fault of all is that the subject-matter is so weak and shrivelled that if the figures be taken away the thought will evaporate.

---

*Here is a list of the names of such papers, the genuineness of which I am ready to vouch for. "*The Young Ladies' Gem;*" "*The M. I. A. Garland;*" "*The Diadem;*" "*The Coronet.*" These are better: "*The Pathway;*" "*The Encourager;*" "*The Advance;*" "*The Busy Bee;*" "*The Intelligencer.*" Two of the latter are young men's papers, to which I may add two more that have still less of the sickish-sweet about them, viz: "*The Lazy Bee*" and "*The Gopher.*"

VI.

PERSONAL BEARING—HOW TO CULTIVATE A FINE PERSONALITY.

Our Father in Heaven the Pattern.—"Stand up erect, thou hast the form and likeness of thy God." So says the poet, and there is so much truth and good advice in the words that I would they might ring in the ears of every Elder each time he is in the act of rising upon his feet. If we could always keep the fact before us that we are children of God, what a difference it would make in our physical, mental, moral, and spiritual bearing! How, with such a Father before our eyes, we should scorn to do anything low or mean! With what noble pride of ancestry we should rise above the petty bickering and strifes of the human herd!

Dr. Maeser used to tell his students in theology that if they should be privileged to see our Father, or our Elder Brother, they would behold the personification of the perfect gentleman; that if from the entire race, they should cull lofty attributes to make an ideal man, it would be but a faint conception of the being whose perfection we are exhorted to emulate; yet it would be a conception which we might hope to realize in this life, and by that time we should conceive a being still nearer the divine model. It is with a single aspect of the ideal man, viz: personal bearing, that this chapter concerns itself.

Conduct and Behavior.—In the widest application, personal bearing includes conduct and behavior; or all that is usually treated under etiquette. Good breeding distinguishes the gentleman of culture, and is a passport into any society. The Elder most of all needs the prestige of polite manners; and where, as is often the case, missionaries are called from occupations that keep men away from cultured society, i. e., where their lives have largely been spent "roughing it," they will do well to make themselves familiar with the simple rules of behavior which the social amenities demand compliance with; lest their crude manners become a stumbling block to good people who might otherwise be led to investigate the message they bear.

Dress and Toilet.—So, too, with respect to dress and toilet, which may also be considered under personal bearing. No one seriously questions the fact that an Elder can be honest, humble, and full of faith, in ill-fitting or antiquated garments, unblacked shoes, untrimmed beard, and dishevelled hair. The trouble is that frequently none but the angels know the good qualities of his mind and heart, or care to find out; whereas it is the man's duty to be useful as well as good: and useful he cannot be if he persists in offending the sensibilities of people whose good-will he should cultivate. Let the Elder therefore pay careful attention to dress and toilet; let him divide by two the qualities that make a dude contemptible, and the quotient will be that which may save himself from being an object of contempt.

General Want of Dignity.—But worse than boorish manners and outlandish clothes is a certain servile, apologetic air with which missionaries sometimes meet people in the world. Phrenologists would call it want of self-esteem; it is really a sort of moral cowardice. Such faint-hearted preachers have not yet learned to prize the message they bear. The Gospel, having come to them cheaply, it is held cheaply; and when they ask for a night's lodging, they are fearful lest, being without purse or scrip, they should be classed among tramps and vagabonds. And yet the Savior said: "Into whatsoever city or town ye shall enter, inquire who in it is worthy; and there abide until ye go thence." And he further said that if the house was worthy they should let their peace rest upon it, otherwise their peace should return unto them. It is not till they have passed through sore trials that they learn the true dignity of an ambassador of Christ. But when they do, they read with a new meaning the passage which promises great reward to him who gives even a cup of cold water to a disciple of Christ, in the name of a disciple. Thereafter they realize that by partaking of a man's hospitality they honor him and confer blessings upon his house, beyond his power to recompense in this life.

President Cannon, in his first mission to the Sandwich Islands, presents a fine example of the self-respect and dignity with which a missionary should deport himself. A company of Elders had just landed in Honolulu, and were without a place in which to preach. Many of the older brethren were for seeking openings in the humbler quarters of the city; but Elder Cannon, though a mere stripling, believed that the best place in the kingdom was not too good for the Gospel of Christ. Accordingly he applied to the highest officials of the government, and obtained the state house in which to open the mission. Had one of the half-hearted Elders of whom I have spoken been in charge, he would probably have felt too small to approach the official dignitaries and ask so great a favor.

In such matters it is well to bear in mind that people—and especially those with whom we are not acquainted—are likely to take us at our own estimate. If an Elder shows by his bearing that his religion is of more importance to him than are the opinions of men, he will gain respect both for himself and for his message.

Psychic Effect of Posture.—It is not, however, of manners, and dress, and self-esteem that this chapter is designed particularly to treat; but rather of the personality—the physical form and attitude—of the preacher; especially while he is before an audience. "Stand up erect," is what many Elders fail to do, and the failure tells seriously against their preaching. The reason is not so apparent as the fact is certain, that a weak attitude begets want of confidence and respect. The influence of posture is probably psychic; for children in a school-room, who are not old enough to draw inferences from observation, assume unconsciously the relation of respect and obedience, or the opposite, even before the teacher opens his mouth; and so also, we may be pretty sure, of an audience with respect to a preacher.

Psychic Effect of Timidity.—It will hardly go to the root of the difficulty to tell Elders to "straighten up." Let us first consider some of the causes of slovenliness in bearing and posture. These are both mental and physical. The first of the mental causes is timidity. The body responds almost instantly to the domination of the mind. Want of self-confidence is reflected to the muscles of the head, shoulders, chest, and lower limbs, resulting in want of firmness. But if the body is influenced by the mind, the mind is also influenced by the body; and it is here that the Elder can take himself in hand to the best advantage. Let a brave man assume a cowardly attitude and he will soon begin to feel fear. Conversely, let the fearful man assume a brave attitude, and his fears will soon depart.

It is said of Colonel Francis Parker, the great educator, that at first he failed in his lectures from want of confidence. His wife, who at that time was a teacher of elocution, induced him to try the experiment of putting on a brave front by sheer force of will. He was surprised and delighted at the result. Not only did he feel brave and self-confident, but his audience came to his assistance by wrapt attention. And now it would be difficult to find a speaker who carries his hearers by storm more effectually than he. I recommend a similar course to timid Elders.

Servility Mistaken for Humility.—The second mental cause of weak attitude is a mistaken notion of humility. Many Elders seem to think that because pride and worldliness walk erect and keep up with fashion, that therefore humility, being the opposite of these in feeling, must be the opposite in expression. It was this delusion that led St. Antony to live in a cave, and never to wash himself for sixty years, nor change a shred of his clothing, save as it dropped off him; and so of the millions of ascetics that burrowed under the skin of the earth after his time. It is the same false reasoning which today leads certain sects, like the Dunkers, to milder forms of asceticism in dress and manners.

People who thus "crucify the flesh" no doubt believe sincerely that they are effectually crushing pride; but do they not in fact exhibit a vanity more contemptible than that which they seek to crush? No one reading the life of Antony can escape the conviction that the old monk was really as vain of his grimy skin, and dirty breech-clouts, as any village coquette is of her tinsel. Whenever a sense of humility leads a man to slovenliness in personal bearing, depend upon it, there is a suspicious ingredient in his holiness. Let us give up such foolish notions, and believe that he serves the Lord best, who develops his body as well as his spirit to the highest beauty and perfection of which it is capable.

Standing Upon the Heels.—The most common type of weak attitude is that in which the head croons forward, the shoulders rounding, the chest is hollow, and the abdomen protrudes. There are three main physical causes for this condition, all growing out of a single mental root, viz: carelessness, or want of proper self-respect. The first and primary cause is standing hibitually on the heels rather than on the balls of the feet. It makes ordinarily not more than six inches difference in the line of the center of gravity, but this is enough to cause an entire readjustment of the body.

The reader will of course understand that the line of gravity is an imaginary line running through the body,—an axis round which there must always be equal weight in every direction in order to maintain equilibrium. Whatever posture we take, the muscles adjust the weight in this way instantly, otherwise we should fall.

What adjustment, it may be asked, takes place naturally, when this line runs through the heel? First, the hips are thrown backward; to counteract this, the abdomen is thrown forward; then to get more weight back of the line, the chest sinks, making the body bend backward at the shoulders to equal the forward bend of the abdomen; lastly, the head drops forward in front of the line, completing the weakest and most ungraceful attitude known to art. I ask the reader to observe men in his own community who fit this description, then examine the heels of their shoes to verify my conclusions.

Standing upon the Balls of the Feet.—Standing habitually on the balls of the feet makes a complete transformation. The abdomen is drawn in, the chest is raised and thrown forward, and the head is drawn back and held upright. An attitude is thus secured which represents all that is best in man. The other is negative; this is positive. That stands for weakness of purpose, indecision, fear and cowardice, carelessness, and dishonesty; this, for strength, ambition, decisiveness, sturdy convictions, courage, and loftiness of purpose. Surely it is worth striving for. And the law of gravitation makes it the most natural adjustment, when the center of gravity is at the ball of the foot. All other things equal, therefore, a man would have a perfect bearing if he observed this simple law of standing.

But other things are seldom equal. The Creator provided for this simple law by making the ball more prominent than the heel. Then came the shoe-maker. In his wise way, he saw at a glance that the Lord had left a place for him to put a few extra tops of sole-leather; since which time man has stood on his skeleton—the bony connection which begins with the heel and ends in the head—instead of on the elastic covering of that skeleton.

To point out what must be done is one thing; to do it, even though simple, is quite another. Let a man be thoroughly convinced of the mistake of resting upon the heels, and it may still be years before he can make the change, so tenacious is an old habit, and so diffiult a new one. Most people would feel decidedly uncomfortable if the heels of their shoes suddenly came off. And yet this is the very problem we must solve—learning to feel comfortable and natural under such circumstances, and uncomfortable under conditions where we now feel comfortable—before we shall have permanently fixed the new habit.

The first requisite, therefore, is to wear shoes without heels or with very low heels; the next, to keep in mind that there are eggshells under our heels which we must not crush; the third is to dip the toe while walking so as to aim to strike the ball first. There are exercises in physical culture to hasten the fixing of the new habit, but of these I canont speak here. I will only point out that dancing is directly beneficial, since by requiring us to use the ball of the foot exclusively it develops a set of muscles long neglected in consequence of high heels. Again I ask the reader to verify my conclusions by comparing the personal bearing of people who dance with that of the lubbers and wall-flowers who mope during a party.

While standing on the heel has been the constant cause operating to produce slovenliness in attitude, it does not follow that standing on the ball of the foot will restore erectness and dignity. The utmost that can be claimed for it is, that it will facilitate the return; for muscles which have become set, do not yield to a steady, mild influence, but must be corrected by special exercises.

The Hollow Chest.—The first muscle to claim attention is the diaphragm, or midriff as it is popularly called; a muscle which divides the contents of the chest from the contents of the abdomen. In its normal state, and while at rest, it is arched upward like a hemisphere. The heart and lungs are thereby held high, and there is a fulness of the chest just below the neck. But owing to the radical defect in standing above criticised, a constant influence operates to cause this arch to sag, the consequence being (1) the hollow upper chest, which is so unmanly in man, and so unwomanly in woman; and (2) the increased weight on the stomach and bowels which tends to cause that vulgar prominence of the abdomen before noted.

The Crescent Shoulders.—The chest may be regarded as the main support of the shoulders. You will rarely find a full-chested man with round shoulders. But let the contents of the chest fall, and the shoulders soon follow. Vain attempts are often made to bring back the shoulders by calisthenic jerkings; equally futile is the use of shoulder-braces. As well try by means of a derrick to hold up the side of a house when the foundation has caved in. The real cure is to elevate the chest. Then see how naturally the shoulders take their places.

I have thus far referred to but one muscle—the diaphragm. But of course there are many others that assist. There are several sets in front of the body whose function is to draw in the abdomen and help raise the chest. Then there is an important set attached to the shoulders and spread out over the back. All these must be strengthened by appropriate exercise in connection with the diaphragm.

Raising the Chest.—Perhaps the best exercise for the latter muscle and those others which assist it in breathing, is to place one hand upon the abdomen and the other upon the chest. Then let each alternately rise and fall, assisting if need by pressure of the hand. This should last for five minutes, at the end of which time the chest should be raised to the highest point and held there by sheer force of will. At first it can be held but a short time, for the muscles are weak; but the time increases with each exercise, and at last the muscles hold the chest in place without any effort of will. Deep-breathing exercises are wonderful aids in this connection, but of this I shall speak in the next chapter.

Straightening the Shoulders.—To make the work of the chest-muscles easier, the shoulder muscles should also be strengthened. This is best done by raising the arms in front to a level with the shoulders, then bringing them back horizontally, with great force. This exercise may be varied by swinging the arms in a complete circle with the shoulders as centers. Exercises with the Indian clubs are especially to be recommended in this connection.

Raising the Head.—There remains lastly the crooning of the neck. Let us first realize exactly what has happened. Between each pair of the seven vertebrae of the neck is a pad of cartilage, which under normal circumstances is of equal thickness on all sides. But the weight having been put on the front side and taken off behind, it is left unequal, the front being thin and the back thick. To straighten up the neck is to equalize these pads of cartilage. Physicians have recommended walking with a sack of shot (twenty-five pounds) on the head while it is held erect. This places the weight exactly where it should be, and is no doubt the quickest way to effect a correction. But it is impracticable. The best exercise is to extend the chin in front as far as possible, then bring the head back with all the force you can command, making an effort to energize the muscles half way down the back. Vary this by rolling the head in a circle.

Lastly, bear in mind at all times the quotation with which this chapter opened: "Stand up erect, thou hast the form and likeness of thy God."

VII.

BREATHING AND VOICE DEVELOPMENT.

While it is personal bearing that makes the first impression upon an audience—an impression the more vivid because it is first—yet ere their feelings have had time to take a definite bias, they are modified for good or for bad by the speaker's tone of voice. If to a slovenly bearing he adds a hard, stiff voice, he loads himself with such an amount of psychic opposition that nothing short of very brilliant ideas will relieve him. And brilliant it is hardly likely that he will be, even though he have the quality in him; for ideas refuse to scintillate under such circumstances. As well expect sparks from striking flint against lead.

Importance of the Voice.—Need I say anything further

on the importance of preserving and developing the voice? James Edward Murdock, the great actor, and teacher of elocution, declared himself more and more convinced that the foundation of greatness in his art lies in voice culture. All the emotions of the human heart are, in a sense, at the mercy of the vocal organs for their expression. If this does not respond, making the voice low or high, soft or harsh, tremulous or firm, pure or husky, how shall we succeed in making our words mean what they say?

As a matter of fact, every human being whose feelings have had full play in childhood and youth, has been unconsciously cultivating his range of vocal power. But too often, there comes a time when dull routine takes possession of the voice as of the body, and then all its more delicate machinery falls first into disuse then into decay, leaving it capable of but one grating tune. Let every man with a tolerable voice beware. In nothing is the law of the talents more true; the voice that is unused will be taken away.

Kinds of Breathing.—Before we shall be able to discuss the voice intelligently, we shall need to understand something of breathing, which furnishes the motive power. There are three methods of supplying the lungs with breath. 1. We may raise and lower the shoulders, thereby increasing and decreasing the chest cavity, and causing a corresponding inhalation and exhalation of air; 2. We may expand and contract the rib-cage, by means of the chest muscles, and thus breathe somewhat more freely; or, 3. We may cause the diaphragm to contract and expand, and this is the easiest and most beneficial method of all.

Watch the ease with which a baby breathes, ere its muscles have been interfered with by clothing. Its diaphragm contracts, and pressing upon the stomach causes the abdomen to rise with every inhalation; then expands, causing it to fall with every exhalation. This is natural breathing. Women lose this power as soon as they begin to wear corsets. Thereafter they must rely upon the other two methods to get air. Men also frequently lose this power, not so much, perhaps, because of clothing as by reason of carelessness in breathing, whereby the habit of short breaths becomes fixed.

Effects of Improper Breathing.—Whatever be the cause the loss of abdominal, or deep breathing is a serious detriment to the production of the voice, and a positive danger to health. Let me discuss the latter idea first, with this single observation in passing: I am quite aware that the health aspect of breathing has no pertinency to the theme of this chapter save only as a realization of it may be an added stimulus to the acquirement of good lungs, which are the basis of good voice, as well as of good health.

If the human body renews itself completely every seven years, as physiologists tell us, then in each organ of the body fibres are breaking at every instant. Perfect health depends upon the speedy removal of these broken cells of flesh and nerve matter, and the building of new cells to take their places. The material for rebuilding is dependent upon wholesome food, but the work of removing worn-out tissues and other waste matter, depends mainly upon the oxygen supplied in breathing. The problem of health is therefore the problem of thoroughly oxygenating the blood.

Oxygen and Health.—The arrangement by which the oxygen of the air is absorbed by the blood, and by which at the same time, the carbon dioxide of the blood passes into the breath, is one of the marvels of science. Between the air-cells and blood-cells of the lungs is a very thin tissue, through which the life-giving gas enters and the poisonous gas escapes. The process is called osmosis. In order that osmosis may be full and complete, the entire lung area should be used; and this is possible only by abdominal breathing, or better still, by abdominal combined with chest breathing.

In the ordinary breathing of eighteen to twenty-four inspirations per minute, only the upper parts of the lungs are aerated, the consequence being that the blood gets very little oxygen, and does not get rid of its poisonous substances fast enough to give glowing health. Under such circumstances, weak organs of the body, here and there, having but little power of resistance, often give way, resulting in disease and death.

An Experiment in Breathing.—In order to realize the principles above set forth, let the Elder perform the following experiment. Let him elevate the chest, and inflate the lungs to their full capacity; then imagine there is a belt around the chest which he must try to burst by stretching the lungs. Let the pressure be gradual, increasing while he mentally counts up to eight, and decreasing in the same way. Let him do this for five minutes, and thrills of warmth will pass to the very extremities of his body.

This increase of temperature means simply that the oxygen is attacking unsound tissue and burning it up. An unusual qantity of the invigorating fluid is being absorbed, by reason of the fact that every air-cell in the lungs is full of air, and the partition tissues are distended so as to facilitate osmosis. Let an Elder follow this practice many times a day for a few months and he will be surprised at the vigor of health which will come to him.

Breathing and Voice Production.—But while health may in fact be the more important consideration it is only an incidental question so far as this chapter is concerned. Our present purpose is to urge the development of strong lung and correct breathing in order to furnish a good basis for voice production.

A good voice is full-toned, smooth, steady, and evenly sustained. To be the first there must be sufficient volume of air to give roundness and resonance to the tone; to be the last three, the pressure behind the air must be made with the least possible friction. Shoulder and chest breathing insure neither of these requisites, but abdominal breathing insures both: volume because the lungs are filled at every inspiration, and smoothness, because the pressure is due to the diaphragm, a muscle so free and flexible that it may almost be said to float.

The practical lesson to be gained from these considerations of health and voice is a determination to break up defective habits of breathing, and establish the correct one. The way to proceed has partly been indicated in the chapter on personal bearing. The chest should be carried high, frequent exercises indulged in to strengthen the diaphragm, and long, deep inhalations taken, until it becomes a habit to breathe deeply. When the Elder has nothing urgent to do, let him take out his watch and begin by inhaling five seconds, then exhale five seconds. Next let him increase the time to ten or even fifteen seconds. Or, if he is walking, let him inhale for ten steps, then exhale for ten steps—but always through the nostrils. He should aim to breathe about six instead of eighteen times per minute; and when he succeeds in doing this unconsciously he may be pretty sure that abdominal breathing has become a habit. If the Elder's sister or sweetheart would enjoy the same advantages she must of course first adopt natural clothing.

But there may be correct breathing without good voice. Other things equal, the proper management of the vocal organs is what gives the rare beauty and pleasing variety of the cultivated voice. It is not possible here to go into technical details respecting vocal culture. The brief hints I shall be able to give will be considered under the respective heads of articulation, pronunciation, and general management of the voice.

The Larynx or Voice Box.—But first it may be well to become briefly acquainted with the organs of speech and their uses. The larynx or voice-box is at the top of the wind pipe immediately above and behind the enlargement called "Adam's Apple." Across the mouth of it are stretched two white ligaments called vocal chords. It is these that produce the sound. In breathing they open to an oval, but in voice production they close so that a knife blade could scarcely be inserted between them. Upon the flexibility of these chords depends the vibratory power of the voice. It is this quality that makes the difference between the hard, stiff voice of the clod-hopper and the thrilling tones of a Jeny Lind. Flexibility is capable of indefinite development; but in the absence of a teacher, the best thing the Elder can do is to read much aloud, especially of emotional literature, seeking to make the voice express the feeling. Then, too, if the choir will tolerate him, let him join it by all means.

Other Organs of Speech.—Though the voice is produced by the larynx, it is moulded into articulate sounds by the other organs, viz., the nose, the palate, the mouth, the tongue, the teeth, and the lips. Talking through the nose, means really that the nasal cavity is closed or obstructed so as to offer no adequate resounding chamber to the voice. Talking "thick," means that the tongue is clumsy, and needs cultivation for flexibility. Often the teeth are closed in speaking, or but slightly opened, and then the sound approaches a snarl. Exercises should be taken to give more agility to the jaws. Then there is what might be called board lips—lips that scarcely touch in articulation, or touch as two boards might. This stiffness, and want of firmness in contact, are habits probably due to the same cause—sore lips and the habit of favoring them in speaking. The lips have need to be the most flexible of all the organs of speech. Any exercise that will make them so, is a valuable aid to sound production.

VIII.

ARTICULATION, PRONUNCIATION, AND ACCENTUATION—COMMON FAULTS AND HOW REMEDIED.

Articulation is that element of voice production which enables us to distinguish words from mere sounds. Clear articulation makes every word distinct to the ear, while poor articulation runs words into one common blotch of sound. Since the primary purpose of speaking is to be understood, it follows that good articulation is the basis of good delivery.

"In just articulation," says Dr. Gilbert Austin, "the words are not hurried over, nor precipitated, syllable over syllable; nor, as it were, melted together in a mass of confusion; they are neither abridged nor prolonged, nor swallowed, nor forced, nor, if I may so express myself, shot from the mouth; they are not trailed or drawled, nor let slip out carelessly, so as to drop unfinished. They are delivered out from the lips, as beautiful coins newly issued from the mint, deeply and accurately impressed, and perfectly finished."

Relationship of Vowels and Consonants.—While the vowel elements give rythm and melody to words, it is the consonants that give character and distinctiveness. And curiously enough, one may judge of the character of a speaker by the relative attention which he pays to these elements. The positive, strongly-individualized man will lay great stress upon consonants; the easy-going, don't-care-a-cent man will be noted mainly for the smoothness of his vowel combinations. If words were trees, the vowel elements would be comparable to the leaves and blossoms, and the consonants, to the woody skeleton which makes the symmetry and beauty of the foliage possible. Or if words were bricks, the vowels would be the body of the material, but the consonants would be the geometrical angles by virtue of which such material is called bricks. Now it is well to keep in mind that what a tree becomes without branches or twigs, and what a brick would be with its angles destroyed, that a word becomes when its consonant elements are neglected.

Cause of Faulty Articulation.—But what does it mean to neglect the consonant elements? This question brings us to the physical basis of articulation. Strictly speaking, there is no difference in principle between poor articulation and slovenly work of the hands—both are due to carelessness and laziness. Faulty articulation, while it usually passes without censure, where the cause is unknown, is particularly trying to one who realizes that it is due to sheer indolence. Such a one is tempted to say, "wake up, and get some vim about you!"

"Strength of contact and quickness of release," is Prof. Trueblood's statement of the law of articulation. Strength of contact signifies firmness of pressure of the organs used to mould articulate sound; as for instance, the lips in words containing b, p, m, f, and v; the tongue and roof of the mouth in words containing r, l, t, d, s, k, ch, sh, and so on. Want of firmness may come immediately from weakness of the muscles involved in articulation; but this only shifts the question: for this weakness results usually from want of vigorous exercise, or to be plain, from laziness.

The Remedy.—If I were compelled to give in one sentence the remedy for poor articulation, I should say, make more work of talking or reading; bring the organs of speech more vigorously into play. But this advice might result in wasting much energy, to say nothing of making an unseemly face. It requires really but very little energy, provided this little touch the right spot and nowhere else. In clean articulation all the voice energy is moulded into words, and no sound spills over. But ere this happy consummation is reached, much effort will be wasted in the endeavor to be distinct and clear. It is the case over again, of learning to write. Very little muscular power is necessary to wield a pen. But I have seen young men, Herculean in physique, perspiring at every pore with the work of learning to direct properly the very little energy required.

Developing the Organs of Speech.—It becomes an important question, then, what exercises to take in order to make it natural to articulate properly. One thing is clear on the start: the muscles controlling the organs of speech must be given, (1,) strength or firmness, so that they will close upon the sound with vigor, and (2,) flexibility, that they may release the moulded word without the accompaniment of loose noises. Pronouncing difficult words while keeping these two points in view, will develop the organs, but not so certainly and effectually as drilling upon elements, individually and in difficult combinations. For instance, compare the pronunciation of b in 'boy' with b (not be) standing alone. In the latter instance you can put ten-fold more vigor into the organs, with a correspondingly greater effect in development of strength. I have found that articulating a single consonant forcibly and quickly many times in succession, as, b-b-b-b-b-b, d-d-d-d-d-d, then alternately, as b-d-b-d-b-d, then in combinations of three, as b-d-k, b-d-k, and so on, using all the elements in turn—has produced the most speedy results.

The Neglected Chapter on Phonics.—Many other useful hints might be given did space permit. As it is, I can only urge the Elder to get some work on elocution and the most generally serviceable treatise on this subject, will be that universally neglected chapter on phonics in the school readers. Why no more attention is paid by teachers to this important foundation-work for reading and speaking, I am able to explain only on the theory that they are ignorant of its value, or have not the courage to brook the general dislike for drill of any kind. However, as most of our Elders are self-made men in respect of other requirements, let them not fear to tackle this question also.

Pronunciation.—Articulation, though so important that I have treated it by itself, is usually considered part of Pronunciation. The other divisions are (1) right quality of vowels, (2) correct syllabication and (3) proper accent. I shall now proceed to consider briefly each of these subdivisions in its turn.

All vowels are unobstructed sounds, that is, there is an open passage outward from the larnyx. This passage differs in length, breadth, and depth, with each element; indeed, it is owing to this very circumstance that sounds differ in quality. Observe the position of the organs in producing e long, as in eve; then change them for a in heart; next adjust them to oo in loose; and you have the three extreme types of vowel productions: the first, thin and long like a knife-blade; the second, round like a sphere; and the third, long and barrel-shaped.

Prof. Bell's Vowel Table.—Prof. Bell has arranged a chart showing how each sound gradually merges into the next, the series closing in oo. The following words will show this gradation: ell-ill-ale--eel-shall-carl-ask-ark-up-on-Paul-pole-pull-pool,—fourteen sounds in all. These together with four dipthongs, (isle-owl-mute-oil—sounds each made up of two simple vowels,) make eighteen vowel elements in the language. This is the simplest classification I know of, and therefore the most practical. Into one or other of these vocal elements, every sound in the English language is capable of being fitted. Correct use of English vowels means (1) the use of no other sounds than these, and (2) the use of these properly.

Common Faults in Pronunciation.—As a matter of fact, both these conditions are constantly violated. Sounds peculiar to other tongues are often introduced; but this is a trifling fault compared with the tendency to substitute one sound for another. It would of course be impracticable to discuss this subject at length in the few paragraphs left of this chapter. I shall therefore confine my remarks to some of the most common faults.

The teacher of singing is constantly urging his pupils to open their mouths. The music of speech demands the same condition. Especially is this advice good for the preacher. "What a wonderful voice. I could sit an hour listening to it, even though I did not understand a word." This is the remark one hears after a certain Elder among us has spoken. You may be sure that a voice obstructed by tongue, teeth, and nose, will never get a compliment like that. On the theory, then, that when people are pleased they are more easily convinced, Elders should learn to give all the music posible to words, and music lies mainly in vowel elements. Freedom obstructing sound depends upon flexibility in the movements of the jaw.

Wrong Vowel Sounds.—A long list of faults would be corrected if Elders would be careful as to the ending of words. The suffix 'ing' is often shortened to 'in' as, walkin', talkin', preachin', eatin'; 'ed' is given 'id,' as, departid, agid, interestid; 'es' is given 'is' or 'us,' as agus, churchis, boxus; 'ent,' 'ant,' 'ence,' and 'ance,' are given through the nose in sounds like 'unt,' 'unce,' as, contentmunt, attendunt, reverunce.

The sound called Italian 'a' is perhaps the most beautiful in the language. It occurs in words like the following: father, heart, arm, dark, mar, car, calm, psalm. Yet we hear it vulgarly broadened thus: fother, hort, orm, dork, mor, cor, colm, psolm. Let the Elder practice on these combinations: form-farm, lord-lard, until his ear clearly distinguishes between the two sounds.

The sound 'u' in mute, is also wrongly pronounced. Instead of duty, tune, student, due, duke, nude, institute, news, we hear constantly dooty, toon, stoodent, doo, dook, nood, institoot, and noos.

Provincialisms.—In English, words are not pronounced as they are spelled. 'Again' is to be pronounced 'agen'; courtesy, 'curtesy'; 'heart, 'hart;' Sergeant,' 'sargent;' 'pretty,' 'pritty'; 'draught', 'draft'; 'raillery', 'rallery'; and so on. To pronounce such words as they are spelled, is to advertise yourself a bumpkin. There is of course no excuse for pronunciations like these: Tobaccer, piller, medder, (meadow), pooty, (pretty), nigger, Injun, jine, instid, set (sit), yit, (yet), jist, (just), Izrul, (Israel), kittle, kag, (keg), libery, (library), rense, (rinse), ribit (rivet), redieule, (ridicule), yaller,—the list might be indefinitely extended. Such pronunciations are invariably taken as marks of illiteracy.

Syllabication.—Very little need be said under this head. Avoid the vulgar haste which drops syllables in words, as in ev'ry, hist'ry, hon'rably; so also avoid the pedantry which takes pains to pronounce every syllable with mathematical exactness. In syllables preceded by l, m, n, r, there is a tendency to give two impulses of the voice instead of one; as, spu-ring (spring), su-lain (slain), bu-less (bless), su-mote (smote), su-nare (snare), etc. Another remark that may be of assistance is the caution not to neglect unaccented syllables. Yet nothing is more common with careless speakers. For instance, in the word 'authority,' the audience gets only "thority,' the first syllable having received so little stress as hardly to be heard ten feet away.

Accentuation.—English is perhaps the most omniverous language known to man. Words from every possible source, high or low, far or near, it takes into its capacious maw and in due time masticates and digests. But for a long time, and in some cases for all time, such words retain some distinctive characteristic of their origin. In most instances this is the accent. There is a peculiar English accent which words have a tendency to assume; but until they become Anglicized, each retains its own, and there is no knowing what this may be, save by examination in each case. From these circumstances comes the importance of accentuation in English pronunciation.

On this point very little can be said to advantage further than to urge constant reference to standard authorities whenever someone else's accent differs from our own. A vest pocket dictionary is valuable for this purpose. Mispronunciation is perhaps more common through wrong accent than by all other methods combined. Sometimes mistakes are amusing. A man who made a point of collecting and using large words was asked his reason for such stilted language. "Oh," said he, "I want to improve my vocabul-ary." (Accent on bul.)

By way of conclusion let me say that the very best assurance of ultimately getting a good voice, and one trained to articulate and pronounce well, is to feel a constant anxiety that not a word of one's speech shall be lost on even a single hearer.

IX.

STYLES OF DELIVERY AND FORMS OF VOICE.

*'Tis not enough the voice be sound and clear—
'Tis modulation that must charm the ear.*

The last chapter was devoted to the development of the voice, its relation to breathing, and its use in articulation and pronunciation. It is the purpose of the present to discuss those changes in sound-production which enable us to express the ever-varying emotions of the soul.

It is a most difficult chapter to write, for in it I must sift and condense what usually fills a good-sized volume on elocution. I cannot hope to satisfy enquiry respecting the management of the voice, nor would I if I could. My design is merely to furnish such an outline as shall enable the Elder to investigate intelligently his own vocal delivery, and perchance arouse in him the desire to study a manual devoted especially to this subject.

Styles of Delivery—Conversational.—To begin, then, at the broadest point we may note that the various styles of delivery fall conveniently into three general divisions, viz.: the conversational, the oratorical, and the dramatic. The first named is the most natural and therefore, all other things equal, the most effective way of reaching an audience. As the name implies, conversational delivery proceeds with a multitude of people as if it were a single being. If the reader will make a careful study of tone-production in conversation, he will discover that its chief charm lies in modulation—in a constantly varying inflection to suit the most delicate shades of meaning. He who can do this with an entire congregation, will not fail to awaken sparkling attention—the attention in which each mind becomes an active participant in the ideas set forth; in which each listener is ready and eager to contribute his rill to the advancing stream, should the opportunity afford.

Such a speaker does not overwhelm his hearers—leaving their faculties paralyzed save only as they have power to gape with eyes ears, and mouth, and to exclaim, "How sublime!" On the contrary he wakes up all their sleeping powers of intellect and imagination, and they lose sight of him in the luxuriance of the ideas he has conjured into existence. Figuratively he hides himself in the light of his own thought. It is for this reason that he is seldom called eloquent, and never while he is speaking. But for all this depend upon it, he is the true orator; not a man whose words cease to ring with the voice that uttered them; not one whose magnetism martials our powers of mind merely to make them gaze spell-bound at him, the man; rather is he one who, forgetting self, strives to make his thoughts breed high resolve and lofty action in all who hear him.

But conversational oratory is a most difficult acquirement, one rarely more than approached in its perfection. It can be imagined, however. On the part of the speaker, there is the rich and varied glow of colloquialism intensified, but otherwise unmodified, according to the size of the audience; on the part of the congregation, there is the sensation felt by each listener as of being singled out and specially favored.

Oratorical Delivery.—"'Tis modulation that must charm the ear," says the poet. We may add also, "inform the mind." But this is the very quality most likely to be sacrificed by the young speaker when he is compelled to rise above his usual pitch or go beyond his habitual force. Let us suppose that in order to reach an audience he must multiply his conversational delivery by ten. Then it is quite safe to assert that out of, say, one hundred graphic variations of voice which make his conversation charming, ninety will be lost when he rises into the higher plane. Of the ten remaining the chances are, that fewer than half will be used constantly.

I have listened to many speakers who rung all their changes on three or four variations of voice. The best way to test a speaker on this point is to listen just far enough outside the building to catch his voice but not his words. The sing-song and monotony of it often become painful.

This is the so-called oratorical style of delivery. We have become so accustomed to the artificiality of it as to think it quite the proper thing for the preacher. Our Elders are often so much addicted to this high-sounding but really empty style, that they cannot lay it aside even to address a family gathering.

By way of contrasting the merits of this method with the merits of the conversational method, let us suppose a speaker of each kind addressing an audience of five thousand people. In the middle of the finest passage in each, let all the listeners save the one farthest away vanish as by magic. Picture the result! Granting that both would be self-possessed enough to be otherwise undisturbed, the first speaker might go on without perceptible change in style, because he always talks to individuals; but what of the second? He must inevitably collapse. His style is wholesale; he talks only to areas of humanity. The prop would therefore be knocked out from under him.

"Audiences," says Prof. Shoemaker, "are made up of individual souls, not one of which loses its individual character because in juxta-position with another. The soul of an audience can be reached only by reaching the individual souls that compose it. An individual being addressed, each person regards himself the individual, and accordingly appropriates the thought; and each having received it, all have received it. We submit that there is no one fault among public speakers more common, or one more baneful than the habit of addressing a mass of individuals as if their souls had also massed and that, therefore, they must resort to some unnatural and monstrous means of access to it."

Dramatic Delivery.—Little need be said here of the third division, the dramatic style. When perfected it is most powerful in moving an audience; but he who would thus excel must be a consummate actor. To attempt to act the emotions one feels and fall below the fusing point in the emotions of others is to advertise one's self as a spectacle.

The basis of dramatic speaking is of course conversational. To this is added the attempt to depict by gesture and attitude the ideas and feelings that make up the speech. I have seen it done twice successfully, the more notable instance being the lectures on life in the Orient by Madam Von Finkelstein Mountford; but I have seen it fail so often, especially in political harangues, that I would caution young speakers against attempting to carry their audiences in this way. It is far more dignified to suggest the thing you are tempted to portray, and trust to the imaginations of your hearers to complete the picture, than to run the risk of acting it with ten chances to one that it will fall flat, or at best appeal only to the gallery gods.

Attributes of Voice.—Voice production is usually treated under the following heads: Form, Quality, Force, Stress, Pitch, Movement, and Grouping. What I shall have to say about these subjects will relate to the development of the first style of delivery discussed above, which I regard as the most desirable for young Elders to cultivate.

The form of the voice has reference to the manner—the abruptness or smoothness—with which the sound issues from the vocal organs. Many classifications might be made, but the simplest as well as most logical, is to consider it under three heads, the two extremes and the mean. The extreme on the side of smoothness may then be called effusive form, the extreme on the side of abruptness, explosive form, and the mean, expulsive form.

The Effusive Form.—From the very exegency of life, the last two forms of voice will receive more or less cultivation, but the first is universally neglected and yet to the preacher it is the most important of the three. "The effusive form," says Prof. Hamill, "gives a smoothness to the tone and a mildness to the utterance which, in the expression of pathos and solemnity, reverence and devotion, produce one of the most pleasing effects in delivery, calling out at once all the purer and nobler feelings, and fitting the mind for higher and holier contemplations. The absence of this element in the utterance of sublime passages in prayer and praise gives a harshness to the expression. In the milder forms of awe and horror the effusive gives intensity to the utterance."

Indeed, for the expression of the beautiful, the sublime, the pathetic, or of those emotions which call for reverence, devotion, or adoration, the voice must be smooth, gentle, and subdued. To use the same abrupt tones with which we make our ordinary communications or transact business, grates upon the finer feelings not unlike the first clods that fall upon the coffin.

Physical Basis of Tone.—As set forth in the last chapter the physical basis of tone-production is breathing; and in no other attribute is voice modified by the manner of the breathing so much as in form. It is almost entirely dependent upon the muscles that control respiration. If inhalation and exhalation result from that frictionless muscle, the diaphragm, the voice will be able to respond to the slightest touches of thought or sentiment; but if the shoulders must rise and fall, or the rib-cage expand and contract, to furnish air necessary to vocalization, loudness, abruptness, and harshness will be inevitable.

The main difficulty lies in exhalation; for it is with the outgoing air that voice is produced. I have occasion to test hundreds of young people each year in voice-production, and they are invariably weak in those muscles which control the expulsion of the breath. While most of them can inhale steadily for ten seconds, it is rarely the case that they can exhale smoothly and evenly for the same length of time; whereas to be able to produce the tones required by effusive utterance, they should be able to prolong the exhalation for a full half minute.

As will be seen, therefore, the first requisite of vocal training is a steady, uniform bellows-power; attention must be given rather to the breathing than to the voice. To overcome the short, choppy, barking tones so common and so distressing in ordinary speaking and reading, is well nigh impossible without breaking up old, and establishing new habits of lung movement. When this has been done, however, let the student practice prolonging the vowel sounds, then words alone, then phrases and short sentences, and at length connected thoughts requiring the effusive form of voice. Care should be taken to avoid monotony and to preserve in the slow, smooth utterance the modulation which characterizes the rapid speech of habit.

The expulsive form of voice is no whit less necessary or useful to the preacher than is the effusive. "It is the expulsive that gives life, energy, and spirit to all forcible speaking," says the authority above quoted. "The speaker who fails in regard to the effect of this property of utterance solicits our pity rather than commands our respect. Divested of this form of voice, the manly and powerful eloquence of Demosthenes, Webster, Catham, and Clay would become ridiculous and contemptible."

"To produce the expulsive form the breath must be forced from the lungs to the larynx by a vigorous inward and upward action of the abdominal muscles and diaphragm. The larynx is the instrument of sound, the lungs the reservoir of air, and the abdominal muscles and diaphragm the power for propelling the air. It is the inward and upward action of the abdominal muscles that compresses the lungs, and thus keeps the larynx supplied with a sufficient supply of air. Many cases of speaker's sore throat are caused by inefficient action of the diaphragm."

Although the expulsive is our habitual form of voice, it does not follow by any means that it is faultless. Deducting the weaknesses which result from failure to mould accurately the sound by the teeth, tongue, lips, and palate (See articulation and pronunciation in last chapter), we still fail in producing the firm, rounded and well-sustained tones of the ideal expulsive; and our failure is due to the same cause that prevents us from producing the effusive. We make our vowels mere dots of sound when they should be bars. Technically the fault is called want of vowel quantity. The defect will disappear only when we have mastered the effusive form, and learned to make use of it in tempering all degrees and shades of utterance.

The Explosive Form.—Of the explosive a noted authority in elocution says: "This form of the human voice is one of the most impressive in its effects. By a law of our constitution it acts with an instantaneous shock on the sympathetic nerve, and rouses the sensibility of the whole frame; it summons to instant action all the senses, and in the thrill which it sends from nerve to brain, we feel its awakening and inciting power over the mind. With the rapidity of lightning it penetrates every faculty and sets it instinctively on the alert. It seems designed by nature as the note of alarm to the citadel of the soul."

So important a form of voice as this ought surely to be at the instant command of every preacher. Habitually our utterances range very little beyond the expulsive either way, so it will generally turn out that he whose muscles are unused to the effusive on one extreme will be unprepared for the explosive on the other. It can, however, be attained by vigorous drill.

"The breath in this process is, as it were, dashed against the glottis or lips of the larynx, causing a loud and instantaneous explosion. Just before the act of the explosion, the chink of the glottis is for a moment closed, and a resistance offered to the escape of the breath, by a firm compression of the lips of the larynx, and downward pressure of the epiglottis. After this instant pressure and resistance follows the explosion caused by the appulsive

PREACHING AND PUBLIC SPEAKING. 409

act of the abdominal muscles and diaphragm propelling the breath with powerful and irresistible force on the glottis and epiglottis which at length give way, and suffer the breath to escape with a loud and sudden report of a purely explosive character."

X.

QUALITY OF VOICE—FORCE, STRESS, PITCH, MOVEMENT, AND GROUPING.

Voice may next be considered as respects its quality. The following varieties are usually treated at length in works on elocution: Normal tone, Orotund, Oval, Aspirate, Pectoral, Guttural, Nasal and Falsetto. I shall discuss only the first two.

Pure tone [a beter name is normal tone] is that quality of voice in which all the breath is converted into a clear, round, smooth, musical sound with the resonance in the back part of the roof of the mouth. It is free from all aspirate, oral, nasal, or other impure qualities. Owing to our neglect of voice-culture, this quality, so peculiar to childhood, is rarely possessed in more mature age. The restraining influences of the school-room tend directly to destroy all the natural purity and sweetness of the voice.

"The advantages of pure tone are two-fold—first, to the speaker; second, to the hearer. It is produced with less expenditure of breath than any other quality; its effect upon the vocal organs is beneficial rather than injurious; with the same effort it is heard at a greater distance than any other quality; its clear, musical properties give a distinctness to articulation and an ease to utterance grateful to the ear; it produces none of the jarring effects experienced in listening to a speaker whose voice is harsh, hard, or in any way impure in quality."

Nine-tenths of all communication is made with the pure or

normal tone. It is the natural tone of conversation, and is suitable for the expression of all ordinary ideas and emotions. When used in the effusive form it is the appropriate voice for the expression of pathetic, solemn, serious, and tranquil thought; with the expulsive form, it is appropriate for narrative, descriptive, diadactic, and argumentative thought, such as makes up the staple of lectures, sermons, and political addresses; with the explosive form it is chiefly used in the expression of ecstatic joy and mirth, which last is especially illustrated in the ringing laughter of children.

Pure tone is interfered with by any position of the organs of speech which obstructs the passage of the sound; such as, not opening the mouth widely enough, and bad habits of the tongue. Practicing on the vowel elements tends to purity of tone; but perhaps the most generally available means of culture is for the Elder to join a choir or take lessons in singing under a competent teacher of music; or in lieu of such an opportunity, take every occasion to sing as best he can alone, always striving for such an adjustment of the organs as to secure freedom and purity of tone.

"The Orotund is that quality of voice in which the breath is converted into a full, round, deep, musical tone, with resonance in the upper part of the chest. It is distinguished from the pure tone by a fulness, clearness, strength, smoothness, and sub-sonorous quality resembling the resonance of a musical instrument. In the orotund, volume and purity of tone to the greatest extent of the one and the highest perfection of the other, are blended in one vast sphere of sound.

"This quality is possessed naturally by very few. Even among public speakers it is rarely heard, save in a limited degree. Actors and orators of eminence and distinction understand and appreciate the volume of the orotund and have spared no pains to obtain control of it. It is heard in all their utterances of grand, lofty, and sublime thoughts. Though rarely possessed it is susceptible of cultivation, and may, by judicious practice, be acquired by almost every one."

So says Prof. Hamill; but it is difficult to give directions for private study; however, it may be said that whatever helps to develop the so-called chest tones in singing, directly serves to give a speaker control of the deep, rich voice of the orotund. If the Elder will constantly be on his guard against high pitch as a means of reaching his audience, and depend instead upon 'organ tones,' low but intense, he will be unconsciously cultivating this quality.

All the other qualities are impure or defective and consequently are valuable only for the purposes of imitation or the expression of exceptional emotions. Like weeds, these qualities so far at least as the preacher is concerned, will not need much cultivation. They grow up of themselves wherever the pure tone or orotund is not preserved and cultivated.

Force may be defined as the degree of intensity with which the sound is sent forth from the vocal organs. It is the carrying power of the voice, and should be increased or decreased according to the sentiment expressed and the size of the audience. Volume and loudness though not identical with force, are dependent upon it. Volume relates to the amount of space filled with the sound; loudness to the distance at which a sound can be heard. The low, deep tones of the organ fill a vast space, though they would not be heard at a long distance. The high, shrill notes of the fife can be heard at a long distance, yet they do not have great volume of sound. A full volume is produced by energetic or impassioned force with pure tone or orotund in all forms; great loudness by impassioned force joined with high pitch in connection with pure tone and orotund in all the forms.

"Perfect command of every degree is indispensable to excellence in expression. In the expression of pathos, the force must be subdued; in the utterance of bold and lofty thought, it rises to the impassioned; in the delivery of diadactic thought, it is pleasingly modulated to the moderate; speaking in a small room, the degree of force should be so modulated as not to be painful to the hearer; addressing a vast assembly in the open air, the voice should be perfectly audible to the most distant hearer; speaking under the influence of strong excitement the intensity of feeling should not hinder utterance, nor degenerate into ranting and vociferation."

The ability to move instantly from one degree of force to another marks the polished speaker and the man of self-control. Such a speaker is listened to with pleasure, simply because he relieves the strain on his hearers ere it becomes wearisome. On the other hand the ranter, that is, the man who has but one degree of force, one level of pitch, one rate of speed, and one quality and form of voice, quickly drives his audience to one of two attitudes of mind: they become nervous and restive, or they become callous and oblivious, in either of which cases the thought falls unheeded. Let the Elder practice reading much aloud, employing subdued force in pathetic, solemn, serious, and tranquil thought; moderate force in narrative, descriptive, diadactic, and unimpassioned thought, and the milder forms of sublimity, reverence, devotion and adoration; energetic force in profound sublimity, grandeur, reverence, joy, gladness, mirth, or in the delivery of strong, forcible argumentative speeches, orations, and sermons; impassioned force in calling and commanding, in the utterance of rousing and exciting applause, and in the expression of fear, anger, threatening, scorn, defiance, and revenge.

Stress may be defined as force applied to individual words or parts of words. It includes emphasis, and is consequently the principal means whereby shades of thought are discriminated. Stress is the edge which the tongue puts on words—sometimes making them keen and cutting, at other times bold and startling, then soft and enticing. The effective speaker has all methods of stress at his command and varies the enunciation of his words with every change of thought and sentiment.

Median Stress is the application of the force to the middle of the word or sound. Judiciously used it "gives a most impressive beauty, power, and grandeur to the utterance of pathos, sublimity, reverence, devotion, and adoration." But it can easily be overdone. "Stage agony," which is manifested mainly in the tortuous "windings of the lengthened O," is due almost entirely to the excessive use of median stress. A tearful voice uttering thoughts not tearful creates disgust in the listener. Do not let sentiment become maudlin in expression.

Radical Stress is by all odds the most important of stress acquirements for the Elder. It is this which gives distinctness to the enunciation even aside from the effects of force and pitch. Radical stress gives sharpness and incisiveness to the beginning of words. It can take place only after a momentary interruption of the voice. "It would seem as if there is some momentary occlusion in the larynx, by which the breath is barred and accumulated for the purpose of a full and sudden discharge."

The argumentative speaker who has not this property at hand fails to produce conviction. "It is this," says Dr. Rush, "which draws the cutting edge of words across the ear, and startles even stupor into attention; this which lessens the fatigue of listening and out-voices the stir and rustle of an assembly;" and Murdoch and Russel say: "The utter absence of radical stress bespeaks timidity and indecision, confusion of thought and feebleness of purpose * * * The right degree of this function indicates the manly, self-possessed speaker."

Every work on elocution has a long series of exercises to develop this attribute of enunciation. But perhaps the best rule that can be given here is to urge compliance with the law of articulation: "Strength of contact and quickness of release." Bring together the organs of speech with vigorous force, and release the moulded word with the suddenness of an explosion. In other words, do not suffer the organs to do their work languidly or lazily.

The other Forms of Stress are: final, which resembles radical, save that the incisiveness is applied to the end of words; compound, which combines both radical and final, and is used to express surprise, contempt, mockery, raillery, and sarcasm; thorough, which applies the force equally to all parts of the word or sound, and is used to express rapture, joy, exultation, lofty command, indignant emotion, oratorical apostrophe, and virtuous indignation; intermittent, which makes the word tremulous, and is appropriate, either to indicate feebleness and old age, or emotions which make the frame tremble and therefore give an unsteadiness to the voice. Of these, space will not permit further mention.

Pitch is the place which the voice takes on the musical scale, "Both in music and elocution perfect control of pitch is essential. Without it there can be no natural, pleasing, or impressive utterance. More speakers fail from an incorrect use of pitch than from any other cause. Often the voice rises to a high, unnatural tone, nearly an octave above the natural key or that which the sentiment demands, and upon this unpleasant tone the utterance is continued until the voice is injured and the hearers wearied. But again, pitch is important because different tones express and awaken different thoughts, emotions. The author of our being has so attuned our natures, that a low deep tone suggests reverence and devotion, high pitch joyous feelings, the middle key unimpassioned thought, and the lowest tones awe and dread. To express these emotions properly the pitch must be varied at pleasure."

Movement, which may be defined as the rate of speed with which words are uttered, "is an element of immense power and wonderful value when properly employed. But it must be skilfully used. Every mood of mind, every variety of emotion, every burst of passion has its appropriate movement. Solemnity must move slowly, joy rapidly, argument moderately, and excitement hurriedly.

This is indicated by the slow and measured step of the funeral march, the rapid movement of the merry dance, the firm but moderate step of the determined army. No defect sooner wearies the hearer or more certainly kills the effect of expression than a drawling lifeless movement; and continuous rapidity as certainly destroys all deep and impressive utterance. No element should be more carefully practiced than movement."

Grouping is modulation. It is the intuitive selection and combination of all the elements of utterance so as to convey the ever-varying colors of thought and emotion. Form, quality, force, stress, pitch, and movement may be acquired in all their divisions by assiduous practice; but the grouping of these qualities in any individual utterance must be left to each speaker's intuition. One cannot, as in a song, commit to memory the groupings of another; one must compose the tune of a speech under the inspiration of the occasion.

Prof. Hamill, from whom I have largely quoted in this chapter, gives the following rough outlines of what the grouping should be in the kinds of thought mentioned. While no absolute rule can be laid down to guide the speaker in modulation, he will do well to study analytically the cases here cited:—

1.—Pathos, solemnity, and tranquility, unmingled with grandeur and sublimity must be expressed with effusive form, pure tone, subdued force, medium stress, low pitch, and slow movement.

2.—Narrative, descriptive, didactic, and animated thought can be uttered only with expulsive form, pure tone, moderate force, radical stress, middle pitch, and moderate movement.

3.—Solemnity, sublimity, grandeur, reverence, adoration, and devotion require effusive form, orotund quality, energetic force, thorough and medium stress, low pitch, and slow movement.

4.—Argumentative, oratorical, and impassioned poetic thought require expulsive form, orotund quality, energetic and impassioned force, radical, final, or intermittent stress, middle and high pitch, and moderate and rapid movement.

5.—Shouting, calling, and commanding require expulsive form, orotund quality, impassioned force, thorough stress, high pitch, moderate and rapid movement.

6.—Sickness, feebleness, and weakness require effusive form, oral quality, subdued force, intermittent stress, low pitch, and slow movement.

7.—Stillness, secrecy and suppressed fear require effusive form, aspirate quality, subdued force, thorough stress, low pitch, and slow movement.

8.—Anger, revenge, scorn, defiance, and hate require expulsive and explosive form, pectoral and guttural quality; the other elements varying according to the intensity of the passion.

XI.

ACTION: MOVEMENTS OF HEAD AND TORSE; POSITIONS OF FEET; IMPROPER ATTITUDES.

If it is difficult to teach voice-culture by pen, it is doubly difficult to teach movement and gesture. And let me say here, I decline responsibility for the immediate results of this chapter and the next should any Elder pick up a system of action and gesticulation from them; just as I should be unwilling to answer for the life of any man who would confidently try, in deep water, rules of swimming recently committed to memory. But something can surely be done by theory toward improving gesture. At any rate, when I see the wild swinging of the arms and aimless sawing of the air indulged in by Elders who "take no thought" as to physical expression, I feel certain no great harm can come from a few pages devoted to the theory of this subject.

Consideration of Objections.—On the threshold I meet

the widely but not well founded objection that consciously to practice gesticulation leads to artificiality; that the best teacher of action is mother nature herself. There is this much truth in the objection: that nature—which here stands for spontaneous impulse —must be allowed nine-tenths of the motive power; perhaps even ten-tenths when duly instructed by art. But until so instructed, impulse cannot be trusted to give appropriate effect to any passage. The mannerisms in gesture, so prevalent among our Elders, is positive proof of this fact.

Why, indeed, should it be thought that a principle of development different from that of any other human acquirement holds in the case of gesture? We learn to talk spontaneously; yet does any one argue that we must not consciously study to improve our language by grammar, rhetoric, and elocution?

But why encourage gesture at all? Why not try to preach with the mouth alone? The question is not to be answered by me. If nature had so constituted man as to keep his arms and head and torse still while a sermon is in progress, these chapters would plainly be out of place; but the truth is, no sooner are the emotions stirred than they seek to vent themselves in action; and so much of our daily impression of the life about us comes to us from this sign language, that we immediately feel something is lacking, if the preacher stands stock still,—a sort of post with Prince Albert suit and a sounding orifice. What seems, therefore, so natural an endowment must have some significance in expression. And the fact is, that gesture, when it has meaning, is a powerful aid in the enforcement of thought But when it is spasmodic and meaningless, as it usually is when it results merely from uncontrolled nervous energy, it detracts from the thought. Before taking up gesture proper, which is ordinarily understood to mean the movements of the hands and arms, it will be well to consider a few principles relating to personal bearing in general.

Movements of the Head and Torse.—Of the various at-

titudes and movements of the head and torse in giving effect to the
language of emotion, I shall say nothing in this chapter, more than
to observe that nature is likely to be more dominant here than in
the use of the hands and arms, and in the play of expression on the
countenance; that is, if the body is kept limber and flexible in all
its joints. But too often it becomes so rigidly fixed in its lines that
it will no more respond to the feelings than a pump-handle or a
rake; causing the speaker to stand, muscle-bound and bone-bound,
through every variety of thought and emotion, in the one attitude
which he has suffered work and long habit to fix upon him.

One other remark it will be profitable to make in this connection: If father Time, or Death, should in the guise in which he is
ordinarily pictured, walk along-side any Elder through life, and
should occasionally lay his bony hand upon any vital part of the
Elder's body, would the latter not make a desperate effort to shake
off his gruesome claws, and try to escape such friendly touches in
the future? There can be no doubt of it—if Death accompanied
him in personal, or rather in skeleton form. Yet this is actually
what takes place with us all every day; and we tolerate his grim
clutches simply because he presents himself only in a general sensation of stiffness.

Stiffness in joint or muscle or skin means simply ossification
—the deposit of lime and other mineral matter in the tissues; and
ossification means the beginning of death—or figuratively speaking, the finger marks of that grim silent companion who walks beside each of us through life. Most of us, when his grip becomes
too painful, try to shake it off by doses of medicine; which is
usually so senseless a proceeding that I shall not stop to characterize it. What do you do with a carpet in order to clean it?
You shake it and roll it and beat it until it is freed from the particles of dust which have become lodged among its fibers. Well, do
the same thing with these clogged tissues of the body. Loosen the
lime particles by vigorous manipulation—the fashionable term, I

believe, is massage—and the blood and pores will get rid of them. Wrinkles—which are merely cracks in a tissue that has in it too much mineral matter to bend—may thus be rubbed out. Stiffness in back, in knee, in arm, in neck, or other part of the body may in like manner be cured, if we would give our own bodies the same care and "dressing down," which any jocky deems necessary to keep his horses in trim. All which means that we should pay attention to diet, so as to avoid too rapid ossification, and to breathing, bathing, and physical culture, so as to free ourselves—for a hundred years at least—from its relentless grip.

Now, if an Elder is careful to preserve throughout life the flexibility of movement that it is his privilege to enjoy, his body will naturally assume those attitudes which will best give expression to the varying emotions of his preaching. What these are can be learned from works especially given to this subject. My space will permit me to discuss only the movements of the feet and the hands.

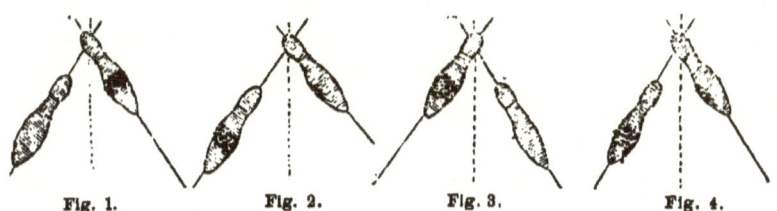

Fig. 1. Fig. 2. Fig. 3. Fig. 4.

How to Place the Feet.—The dignity of a speaker's attitude depends in no small degree upon the disposition of his feet upon the floor. In the chapter on Personal Bearing, it was insisted that the weight should be upon the balls of the feet. Another general principle to be constantly borne in mind is to keep the knees straight and energized. This in itself will tend to throw the weight forward and thus obviate the weakness of pose which comes from settling down upon the heels. But it is not the best attitude to place the weight equally on both feet. Better have, say, three-fourths on the foot behind and one-fourth on that in front.

Figure 1 represents the most natural and most graceful position of the feet for the ordinary unimpassioned discourse. The most of the weight, as indicated by the shading, is on the ball of the left foot. The right foot, as will be seen, is placed at such an angle that a line running along the middle of the sole would pass through the left heel.

When the left foot needs a rest or when the speaker is animated and leans toward his audience, the simplest change is to transfer the weight to the ball of the right foot, resulting in the position indicated in figure 2. Figures three and four are merely figures one and two reversed, and have the same general meaning and significance.

These are the only positions that the Elder need keep in mind. He should accustom himself to changing from one to the other without noise and with the least possible movement. From figure one, he can change to figure three by stepping back with the right foot, or vice versa. Should his thought become more energetic, he will naturally increase the forward distance between his feet, without much change in the relative angles of the four positions here pictured. Such an increase of distance results in the four so-called attitudes. Let the Elder practice taking them in turn and he will feel instinctively what emotion would naturally lead to each.

A Word as to Improper Attitudes.—The military position, heels together, toes outward, is too stiff and formal for any other purpose than dress parade or the subserviency of a lackey waiting for orders. To stand with the feet wide apart is to exhibit snobbishness, coarseness, and vulgarity. Such an attitude throws the abdomen forward, and generally calls for the crossing of the hands behind the back. It has its purpose in character-sketching, but no preacher of the Gospel will so forget himself as to fall into the habit. Occasionally one sees an Elder crossing one leg before the other and standing, stork-like, on one foot. He should be promptly tipped over by his missionary companion if no other lesson will cure him of it.

But these attitudes are not be compared for want of dignity with the slovenliness of leaning against the pulpit or other means of support—as if one's legs were too weak to support one's body. The whole person is thereby made to seem ungainly, every line of grace or beauty being destroyed, and the limbs presenting the aspect of something hanging in a sack. How would it be possible for vigor of thought or decisiveness to issue from such a lump of bones and flesh! And yet such attitudes are extremely common among us; and the "Rameumptums," which somehow in most of our churches do duty for pulpits, seem especially fitted to encourage this wretched habit.

Is it not about time to cut away this high lumber apron and let the Elder preach from the tip of his toes to the top of his head? Let us no longer give the audience the impression that we have some personal defects to hide. A neat pulpit with top just large enough to hold the Bible and other sacred books, and no contrivance to cover the person of the speaker, is the idea now being adopted throughout the Church.

XII.

ACTION: GENERAL MEANING AND SCOPE OF GESTURE.

We are now ready to discuss the meaning and value of gesture proper. It will not of course be expected that I enter extensively into this subject. My remarks will be very general, and I trust that on this theme, as on voice-culture and elocution, a standard manual of oratory will be consulted.

Zones of Gesture.—Gestures are made in every direction from nadir to zenith; and while it may not have occurred to the observer that each of these directions has a certain significance, this fact will become apparent by a very little reflection; and whoever gesticulates upward, downward, or horizontally, just as it happens, proclaims the fact that it is mere vagrant nervous energy, not well-defined emotion, which is guiding his arm.

A DESCENDING gesture first of all points out actual objects which are below the speaker in point of location; e. g., "This *flower-bed* is cared for by my wife;" "*Before* us lay the fragments of a beautiful jar;" "The lawn is now hidden by a *mantle* of snow." By analogy, ideas which are beneath us are also indicated by descending gestures; e. g., "I regard such conduct as vile and *contemptible;*" "Has he then sunk so *low* as that?" By a remoter analogy, whatever we feel superior to, or feel like rising above, is also so indicated; e. g., "Mr. Chairman, I *protest* against this proceeding;" "The truth of this allegation I most emphatically *deny.*"

By a little reflection it will be seen that this gesture is peculiarly a gesture of the will; that whenever the will is energized we rise superior to our environments and hence indicate our momentary exaltation by putting things below us. The gesture should slant downward at an angle of forty-five degrees, or divide into halves the quarter circle between the hands when extended horizontally, and the feet.

The HORIZONTAL zone—that indicated by stretching out the arms and moving round in a circle—is the plane of equality. The middle or horizontal gesture is appropriate, first, to point out objects located on the horizon; e. g., "A *wide* plain;" "A *distant* sail;" "The *setting* sun." Second, analogous ideas of time; e. g, "*Before* him lay the unexplored future;" "How dark is the silent ocean of the *past!*" Third, for purely intellectual ideas—ideas that are neither above us nor below us; e.g., "*Wisdom* is better than riches;" "What is man that thou art mindful of him?" Fourth, for all ideas indicative of intercourse with our equals; e. g., "I give thee in thy *teeth* the lie!" "Here, take my *hand;* let us be friends."

The ASCENDING zone is that which slants upward forty-five degrees above our extended hands. Aside from its use in pointing out geographical objects, it is the plane in which we locate all ideas superior to ourselves; all the virtues, all our hopes and aspirations of better things. Here are some examples that might be indicated by ascending gestures:—

"Hope is *above* us beckoning us onward.—*Flag* of the free heart's hope and home!—*Higher* yet rose the majestic anthem without pause.—Mighty one—all *hail*—Ye crags and *peaks*, I'm with you once again.— *High* on the political horizon stands the name of Washington."

The ZENITH gesture is used to give vent to our strongest emotions; as, in shouts of exultation, to point out our highest ideals,—those for which we would die,—and to make solemn reference to Deity or to heaven. Conversely the extreme opposite of these ideas are indicated by gestures toward the earth.

Directions of Gesture.—Besides moving upward and downward, gestures may be made to the front, to right and left oblique, to the sides, and to backward-oblique; and here also each direction has its significance. Front gestures stand, first for geographical ideas, second for future time, and third for ideas direct, pressing, distinctly marked, or strongly individualized. Oblique gestures are made half-way between the front and the side. They express ideas less pressing, direct, and individualized—that is to say, more general. Side gestures are inclusive, all-embracing, representing the acme of the general notion, when not used to point out objects in space. The backward-oblique gesture, besides its use for locating objects, is properly employed to indicate past time, departed hopes, and ideas that appeal to secrecy or that should be put behind one.

There is next the question of using one hand or two. Direct and individual ideas, or ideas merely requiring emphasis, are usually best indicated by one hand. General ideas, or ideas involving a number of objects, or wide extent in space or time or causation, will require both hands. Here are some instances of each:

Single hand gestures: "*Peace* be unto thee.—Poison and plague and yelling rage have *fled*—Justice cries—*forbear?*—I freely *grant* all you demand."

Double hand gestures: "His talents he deposited on the altar of his country.—Ye golden *lamps* of heaven, farewell.—We have no *concessions* to make, my lord.—I utterly *renounce* the project! *Spread* the glad tidings from shore to shore.—*Open* fly the infernal gates! The land was *rent* with civil strife."

Kinds of Gestures.—There remains then the discussion of the hand, the pivotal point of expression by action, the part that gives gesture its life, force, and distinctive character. The meaning of gesture changes according as the hands are supine, prone, averse, indexed, clasped, wrung, or clenched; each of which kinds we now proceed briefly to discuss.

Index.   Supine.   Prone.   Averse.

As indicated in the cut the HAND SUPINE is that in which the fingers are extended with the palm open toward the ceiling. It is the symbol of truth, candor, openness, a clear conscience, generosity—in short, of all the positive virtues that depend upon being frank, fair, and above-board. The following sets of gestures are taken from "Voice Culture and Elocution," by William T. Ross. They are arranged in series of four, of which the first is descending, the second middle or horizontal, the third ascending, and the fourth zenith. The Elder may practice them to advantage:—

Single hand, front series: 1.—See the *prize* that lies before thee. 2.—I *extend* to you the hand of friendship. 3.—The *noonday* sun looked down and saw not one. 4.—Give me *liberty* or give me death.

Oblique series: 1.—Be *firm* in the cause. 2.—Trust none but *friends*. 3.—Let your aims be *high*. 4.—And your watchword liberty.

Lateral series: 1.—I *acknowledge* the charge. 2.—Bring in *all* your evidence. 3.—Let the light of *day* shine upon my deeds. 4.—For *heaven* knows I am innocent.

Backward oblique series: 1.—Let the dead *Past* bury its dead. 2.—Free as the torrents that *leap* our rocks and plow our valleys without leave. 3.—Look on that narrow stream *high* on the mountain side. 4.—Honor the light brigade, *noble* Six Hundred.

Double hand, front series: 1.—Speak, mother, *speak!* Lift up thy head. 2.—What was Caesar, that stood upon the bank of that stream? A traitor, bringing war and pestilence into the *heart* of his country. 3.—God pity them, God *pity* them, wherever they may be. 4.—Awake, *arise!* or be forever fallen.

Oblique series: 1.—Shall *we* now contaminate our fingers with base bribes? 2.—And sell the mighty *space* of our large honors for so much trash as can be grasped *thus?* 3.—And in its hollow tones are heard the thanks of *millions* yet to be. 4.—Arm, *arm!* it is—it is the cannon's opening roar.

Lateral series: 1.—I *wash* my hands of the whole affair. 2.—And is this *all* the world has gained by thee? 3.—But one sun rules the day; by night *ten thousand* shine. 4.—Rise, fathers, *rise!* 'tis Rome demands your help.

The HAND PRONE (see cut) is in many respects the opposite in meaning of the hand supine. The general idea is that of superimposition—something placed above something else. It is generally negative and repressive, save where it blesses, or where it merely indicates place or subordination. Here are examples from the same work:

Single hand, front series: 1.—Dust thou art and unto *dust* thou shalt return. 2.—*Stay* thy impious hand. 3.—Ye gods *with-hold* your wrath!

Oblique series: 1.—It was this morning that the sun rose bright upon his hopes—it *sets* upon his grave. 2.—*Peace* dreamer! thou hast done well. 3.—The stars *went out* and down the mountain gorge the wind came roaring.

Lateral series: 1.—The wind died away to a perfect *calm*. 2.—And the death-angel flaps his broad wing *o'er the wave*. 3.—So darkly glows yon thunder cloud, that *swathes* as with a purple shroud, Ben-Ledi's distant hill.

Backward-oblique series: 1.—But she with the flash of a glance showed me the wretch I *was*, and the self I might hope to be. 2.—*Away*, slight man. 3.—His voice was heard amid the rumblings of *Mount Sinai*.

Double hand, front series: 1.—I saw the *corse*, the mangled corse. 2.—On horror's head, horrors *accumulate*. 3.—And having wound their loathsome tracks to the top of this huge mouldering monument of Rome, hang *hissing* at the nobler man below.

Oblique series: 1.—Sons of dust, in reverence *bow*. 2.—The *veil* of night came slowly down. 3.—*Hung* be the heavens with black.

Lateral series: 1.—When a great man dies the people are *overwhelmed* with grief. 2.—Sorrow mantles the *whole* earth. 3.—Let the triple rainbow rest o'er *all* the mountain tops.

The HAND AVERSE (see cut) resembles the hand prone in being repressive. It is the gesture by which we put away from us that which is distasteful or disagreeable. It is so strong a gesture and so characteristic of human nature that one has only to watch his friends during an evening's entertainment to know how truly it is the sign of being bored, or wearied, or disgusted. The hand averse also wards off attack of actual danger or of hateful ideas: Here are some examples:—

Single hand: No, *no;* no more of that. Oh, I'm *sick and tired* of all that noise. Back, *back*, I say! villain. The face of the Lord is *against* them that do evil. *Avaunt* and quit my sight. Away, *away* and follow me not.

Double hand: *Deliver* us from this cloud of mosquitoes. *Oh*, you should have *seen* that house when we came into it! With united hearts let us *drive back* the invaders. *Burst* are the prison bars! *Hide* your faces, holy angels! *Avert*, O God, the terrible calamity!

The INDEX HAND, as its name signifies, points out objects. No examples are necessary for this aspect. But it is also used to single out ideas; e. g., "Now let us look more particularly at *this* particular point. There are three aspects to this question: *First* [using the fingers of the other hand to enumerate] the cost; *second*, the profits; *third*, the people benefited."

The hands are clasped in prayer or supplication. This may be done either by interlocking the fingers, or folding the fingers over each other. In great mental agony the hands are wrung.

The clenched hand plainly enough signifies violent anger. It is generally accompanied by a striking of the table or a strong working of the muscles of the arm. There are various other gestures that it would be profitable to discuss, did space permit; such as touching the breast when referring to self, or appealing to conscience; trying to still the beating of the heart, in poignant sorrow; and grasping the head in great mental distress; but for the most part these will seldom enter into sermons.

Essential Characteristics of Gesture.—Gesture should first of all be spontaneous—almost unconscious. To divide the attention between the thought and the gesture, is to make the latter seem artificial; than which no severer criticism can be offered against expression by action. Better the rude, meaningless swinging of the arms, so far as the effect upon an audience is concerned, than the most graceful movement that indicates consciousness on the part of the speaker. But how shall the Elder pass from the crude natural to the artistic natural, save through the self-conscious or artificial? There is no way; the only advice I can give is to practice the correct forms in private and try to forget self absolutely while in public. By this means the change will in time be brought about.

In the second place, gesture should be graceful. This quality depends primarily upon well-oiled joints—especially the wrist and finger joints. Most Elders will find their wrists stiff and rigid and the fingers unflexible. The exercise of throwing the forearms up and down and allowing the hands to dangle as if lifeless, will take the habit of rigidity from the muscles. The joints should be so free that as the arm is raised preparatory to gesticulating, the hand will drop downward by its own weight, until ready to be energized. Energizing the fingers takes place on the emphatic word—that marked in italics in the foregoing exercises. The motion should move wave-like from the shoulder to the tips of the fingers, energizing each joint in turn. Where the energy gets no farther than the elbow, we have the pump-handle gesture; when it stops with the wrist, the gesture is suggestive of a paddle.

A gesture consists of two parts, preparation and termination. The gesture impulse begins to move as the thought approaches the emphatic idea. The audience should not be aware of this preparation, it should begin so smoothly and move so gradually to its climax. The arm will generally be raised with the back of the hand partly toward the ceiling, and moving slightly toward the center of the body. If the gesture be supine, the hand will be turned just before the energizing of the fingers. Care should be taken to avoid the "prevalent fault of a too wide or out-of-the-way swing of the hand in preparation; it is to gesture what flourish is to penmanship —superfluous."

The stroke or termination of the gesture is made by the spring of the hand from the wrist. "The grace of the gesture lies in the easy movement of the fingers, which should occur simultaneously with the wrist action, or so nearly so that the time between them is scarcely appreciable. The strength of the stroke should correspond with the force of the gesture, i. e., it should be gentle, moderate, or impassioned, according to the sentiment or emotion." The hand should then move so gently to the side, or make so gradual a transition to the next gesture, as not to be seen by the audience.

Grace of gesture, it may be added, depends upon moving in curved lines. But this principle can be carried too far. Strength and ruggedness are also essential qualities, and these are dependent upon straight lines.

Gesture should, in the third place, be dignified and forceful. It will be dignified if it be used sparingly and if, when used, it be free from jerkiness and other spasmodic nervous movements. "Economy of gesture," says a late writer on elocution, "is just like precision in speech. You do not want too many words, but you want enough. Not two arms when one will suffice. Not a gesture for every varying thought, and not too frequent gesture for the same thought. For example, the digital finger is very strong in gesture if used with economy. If it is used only now and then, you can send the thought right down into the hearer's heart by shaking your finger at him. But if you are shaking it all the time, what does it amount to?"

A gesture will be forceful if it is appropriate to the thought and is given without hesitation and with the same degree of emphasis that marks the tones accompanying it. The question of appropriateness is one of interpretation and good judgment on the part of the speaker, and so cannot be discussed here. As to the manner, he cannot be too strongly urged to cultivate freedom and boldness. A feeble, hesitating gesture which often results merely from bashfulness or a mistaken idea of humility, re-acts in such a way as to make the audience regard the speaker as a nobody—a man without brains or mental resources.

Let me conclude, in the language of Shakespeare, by saying: "Do not saw the air too much with your hands, but use all gently; for in the very torrent, tempest, and, as I may say, whirlwind of your passion, you must acquire and beget a temperance that will give it smoothness. * * * Be not too tame either; but let your own discretion be your tutor. Suit the action to the word, the word to the action, with this special observance, that you overstep not the modesty of nature. * * * Now this thing overdone, or come tardy off, though it may make the unskilful laugh cannot but make the judicious grieve, the censure of which one must, in your allowance, out-weigh a whole theater of others."

XIII.

STAGES OF GROWTH: FIRST, CRUDE NATURAL; SECOND, CONSCIOUS ARTIFICIAL; THIRD, ARTISTIC NATURAL.

By way of concluding this treatise, I wish to answer certain criticisms which I plainly foresee will be leveled against young men who shall try to put into practice the principles laid down in the foregoing pages. They will be judged, not by what they are trying to do, but by what they actually accomplish; for the ordinary critic has no other criterion than that expressed in the proverb: "The proof of the pudding is in the eating." And measured by this rule, they will for a long time, perhaps for years, seem at a disadvantage with those that take no thought as to how they express themselves. Lest such criticisms should counteract this reform movement in preaching, I wish to show how perfectly natural it is for the speaker who has begun a course of self-improvement, to be less capable for a time than before he began such a study.

The Crude Natural.—What we admire above all things in a speaker—or in anyone else, for that matter—is naturalness. Every man and woman soon comes to be known for certain individual traits or characteristics—certain idiosyncracies of dress or bearing, of voice, gesture, disposition, or expression. These peculiarities are so intimately associated with our idea of the person that if upon any occasion he acts without them, we note the fact at once, and feel a sort of grievance against him, as if he had been trying to impose upon us. His eccentricities may be such that we can never become intimate with him; nevertheless, he is what he is, we say, and so we learn to tolerate him. As a speaker we may never come to appreciate him, but we get accustomed to his oddities—squeaky voice, ungainly gesture, or whatever they may be —and listen with more or less charity, simply because we feel he is himself.

But while the crude-natural speaker finds toleration, he is seldom effectual in creating great impressions. The reason is to be found in the fact that his process is wasteful. Since no part of his mental energy is diverted to deploring or guarding against blunders, he has plenty of power to put upon his theme; his weakness lies in want of science. He lays about him without knowing when he hits and when he misses; in which respects he resembles the Anglo-Saxon who vainly opposed his sturdy strength against the Norman's dapper skill. Being utterly empirical in his methods, his only resource is imitation when conditions are similar to, and blind experiment when they differ from, what he has been accustomed to. While therefore there will always be, in his speaking, a certain naturalness and freedom that are gratifying, it is plain that he can never attain eminence by this method.

The Self-conscious Artificial.—Has it ever occurred to the reader to ask why gracefulness is counted natural to this person and awkwardness to that? The reason is to be found in—habit. When any characteristic has become so fixed that the mind ceases to take note of it—at that moment it becomes second nature, and therefore seems to our friends an integral part of our personality. But there is no insuperable reason why any one trait should thus become fixed. True, every one has certain inherited tendencies, which, if nothing be done to counteract them, will fashion us after our forefathers; but the fact still remains, had training been persistently carried out with certain definite ends in view, there is not one of us but that might be different from what he is—creditably different, let us say.

Now suppose this truth has not dawned upon the preacher until crudities in bearing and speech have been ingrained in him. What will happen through his reading (and believing) this book on preaching? First of all he will be made self-conscious—aware of his many defects; second, timid, as one who feels that critical eyes are upon him; third, artificial—attempting to do and say things in a way that does not fit him; fourth, weak and halting in expression, as one who is feeling his way. Thus it is easy to see why his natural force or power will be weakened. If he has begun the work of self-improvement, part of his energy goes to watching himself, part is wasted in useless fears, part is expended in learning to swing new methods, and the remainder goes toward appreciating and giving effect to the thought. The change at first is almost paralyzing. For real work he has but one-fourth the accustomed stream. The only compensation is in the fact that, where this stream once turned an overshot or some other old-time contrivance, it is now being concentrated upon a turbine.

The Artistic Natural.—In the meanwhile his usefulness as a preacher suffers. Crudities of all sorts will be condoned by an audience provided they seem natural; but only the teacher and the student of human development (who happen to realize what is taking place) will have charity for attempts at art which fail to hide the art. All the rest are bored or insulted, and say the speaker is trying to "put on" or "show off;" adding perhaps, "If that is what comes from studying preaching, I shall never study it."

But the stage of the conscious artificial does not last forever. Old habits at length give way to new, and that forgetfulness of self which is so necessary to naturalness, comes again. The time it takes to make the change from the crude to the artistic natural, as well as the completeness of the change, depends primarily upon the attention given to self in the middle stage, and secondly upon the temperament of the person. Some natures are so deep and fixed in their lines that they tack about with the same difficulty as did the Great Eastern; others are so versatile that to know is to do.

It might seem deplorable, at first thought, that the way to effective preaching should be through this breaking up, half-paralyzing process of self-consciousness; but a little reflection will show how natural it is; for what is finding out and getting rid of such crudities, but a kind of intellectual repentance? And when did true repentance ever take place without a period of penance followed by a period of corrected development? Looking at the three stages of growth in this light, we shall see at once how deep and eternal is the law underlying them, and hence how necessary it is to comply with it, no matter what the immediate consequences may be.

Result: Simplicity and Directness.—The reader will have noticed with what ease and naturalness the expert performs his work and also what labor and anxiety it costs the beginner. The pen is a small instrument, and needs but little muscular energy. Yet I have seen a lusty young giant rolling his tongue, growing red in the face, and sweating great beads of perspiration in learning how to handle it. The same principle is observable in mechanics. The first machines for any purpose are invariably complicated, clumsy, and wasteful of energy. Improvement is always along the line of simplicity of construction and directness in the transmission of force.

The essential difference between the expert and the amateur in any line of work is in the conservation and application of energy. The first uses just enough for the purpose, applying it at the proper time and place; the second in order to touch the thing at all is compelled to spread his energy out over everything in the vicinity of it. The first cuts his cocoa-nut off the tree by a neat rifle ball, scarcely touching leaf or twig beside it; the second reaches the same result—by cutting down the tree! Applied to preaching this principle means simply that what the rambling speaker takes an hour to tell, the speaker who talks to the point can make plain in three minutes.

Applications.— Often the amateur preacher, when he begins to take thought as to his sermons, expands in the direction of sound rather than sense. What he strives for is oratorical effect. The finished speaker, on the contrary, is guided by the thought and aims only at conviction. The first is given to showy figures of speech, and chooses words for their euphony and cadence; the second is content to be simple as a child and direct as a sunbeam.

But it is not alone in preaching that simplicity and directness characterize the artistic natural. Compare the examples of prayer which our Savior has left us—the Lord's prayer, the blessing on the Sacrament, the form for baptism, the words used by John in conferring the Aaronic Priesthood—with the wordy effusions of our Elders on various occasions, if you would know how many intellectual sins we have still to repent of. It was in more senses than one that Christ said: "Except ye become as little children ye can in nowise inherit the kingdom of heaven."

[THE END.]

APPENDIX.

A SERMON BY PRESIDENT WOODRUFF.

INTRODUCED TO ILLUSTRATE SOME OF THE FOREGOING
PRINCIPLES OF PREACHING.

It gives me no little pleasure to present a sermon which exemplifies so well the principles laid down in this humble treatise. Any one can see that it is not a studied effort; just as everyone must feel that it was dictated by the Spirit of God. The fact that the sermon admits of logical analysis down to the last detail, should settle the question, once for all, that the Holy Ghost is a spirit of order, and that consequently our sermons will be logical and progressive in the exact ratio that our minds yield to this Spirit.

Note how simple is the diction, how clear and direct are the sentences, how free from attempts at oratorical effect is the style. Introduction, discussion, and conclusion take their places and do their respective work, just as set forth in chapter VIII, "Analysis of the Sermon." The prevailing form of communication is narrative, which is the method so strongly urged in Sections IV, V, and VI of Chapter VI. The title and sub-headings are of course my own arrangement.

But it is not alone because the sermon exemplifies the principles of preaching that it is here inserted. It is even more valuable as showing that the work of the preacher is vain unless he be filled and guided by the Spirit of God—a truth I have tried constantly to hold before my readers. As I said in the preface so let me say here in the conclusion, my purpose has been, not to teach how we may get along without the Spirit, but how, by accustoming our minds to order and system, we shall offer the least resistance to its guidance. Here is the sermon:

OBTAIN THE SPIRIT OF GOD.*

INTRODUCTION.

I am pleased to meet with so many of our friends this morning, and I feel desirous to talk to you upon a principle that I very seldom dwell upon before the congregations of the Saints. I have had my mind somewhat exercised of late on various things, perhaps for purposes known to the Lord better than myself, though they are principles we are all more or less acquainted with.

One of the Apostles said to me years ago, "Brother Woodruff, I have prayed for a long time for the Lord to send me the administration of an angel. I have had a great desire for this, but I have never had my prayers answered." I said to him that if he were to pray a thousand years to the God of Israel for that gift, it would not be granted, unless the Lord had a motive in sending an angel to him. I told him that the Lord never did and never will send an angel to anybody, merely to gratify the desire of the individual to see an angel. If the Lord sends an angel to anyone, he sends him to perform a work that can be performed only by the administration of an angel. I said to him that those were my views. The Lord had sent angels to men from the creation of the world, at different times, but always with a message or with something to perform that could not be performed without. I rehearsed to him different times when agels had appeared to me. Of course, I referred to the angel visiting Joseph Smith. The Revelator John said that in the last days an angel should fly in the midst of heaven, having the ever-lasting Gospel to preach to them that dwell on the earth. The reason it required an angel to do this work was, that the Gospel was not on the earth. The Gospel and the Priesthood had been taken from among men. Hence God had to restore it again.

STATEMENT OF THEME.

Now, I have always said, and I want to say it to you, that the Holy Ghost is what every Saint of God needs. It is far more important that a man should have the gift than that he should have the administration of an angel, unless it is necessary for an angel to teach him something that he has not been taught.

---

*A discourse delivered at the Weber Stake Conference, Ogden, Monday, October 19th, 1896, by President Wilford Woodruff. Reported by Arthur Winter.

I am going to refer to some of my own experiences with regard to the ministrations of angels and the operations of the Holy Ghost. I have never prayed for the visitation of an angel, but I have had the administrations of angels several times in my life.

DISCUSSION.

One visitation I received in Kentucky, at the house of A. O. Smoot's mother, while on my first mission. I went through Jackson County into Arkansas Territory, and from Little Rock waded the Mississippi swamp 180 miles to get across into Tennessee. I arrived in Henry County, Tennessee, on the west, at the same time that David Patten and Warren Parish landed in that region on the north. We met and labored together for awhile and built up some churches there. I then held the office of a Priest. I traveled thousands of miles and preached the Gospel as a Priest, and, as I have said to congregations before, the Lord sustained me and made manifest his power in the defense of my life as much while I held that office as he has done while I have held the office of an Apostle. The Lord sustains any man that holds a portion of the Priesthood, whether he is a Priest, an Elder, a Seventy, or an Apostle, if he magnifies his calling and does his duty.

FIRST GENERAL DIVISION: AS TO THE VISITATION OF ANGELS.

(a). **An Incident in Arkansas.**—I will give you an instance of the Lord's protecting care over me while I was a Priest. I had this experience while in Arkansas with my companion, who was an Elder. There was a man in that country who with his wife and five sons had been in Jackson County. His wife died there. The old gentleman was apparently in the faith when he left there. He was driven out, the same as the rest of the Saints were, and some of his sons were whipped with hickory gads during the persecutions. I knew he was in this Arkansas country, and I felt anxious to go and see him, as he was the only Latterday Saint that we knew anything about in that region. The night before I got there I had a peculiar dream. I dreamed that an angel appeared to us and pointed out a certain path to us that we must follow, and that the blessings of God would attend us in following that path. As we went along this path we came to a log cabin with a wall on each side ten or fifteen feet high. This road led right through that building. When I went to the door and opened it, it was full of large serpents. My companion said that he was not going into that room for anybody or anything. "Well," said I, "I am, or I'll die trying. The Lord told us to follow that path, and I am going to walk in it, unless I am stopped by some power that I know not of." I stepped into the door. These serpents all rose up ready to jump on me, and there was a very large one in the middle of the floor that made a pass at me. It appeared to me as though I would be destroyed, but when the serpent reached near to me it dropped dead; in fact, they all dropped dead, and they turned black and burst open, after which they took fire and burned up, and both of us went through safely.

The morning after, we arrived at this man's house. His name was Akeman. It was Sunday morning, and we went into the house. Mr. Akeman and his daughter were at breakfast. His sons were settled in cabins around him. We sat down, but there seemed to be a peculiar spirit in the place. I finally stepped up to the mantle-piece, on which I saw a Book of Mormon. I picked it up, and said, "Brother Akeman, you've got a very good book here." He said, "It's a book that came from hell." I then began to understand a little of what lay before us. He had apostatized. He cursed everything and everybody—Jospeh Smith, Lyman Wight, the Apostles and a good many others whom he named. He was very angry. I inquired about his sons. He said they were settled around him there. Well, we took up our valises and left. I looked up one of his sons,—the youngest, I believe, and the only one that was in the faith— and he was like a drowning man; but by praying with him we got the Spirit of God in him, and we had a pretty good time with him. We told him of our experience at his father's, and I said we were desirous to have some meetings there if we could. He said he did not know; his father had apostatized and was at war with everything that was Mormon. He told us, however, where an old gentleman lived close by to whom he had loaned the Book of Mormon. He was an aged man and his wife was an aged woman. Their name was Hubbard. We went to see them and they were very glad to receive us.

In the morning my companion said he was going to leave the place. Of course, he was an Elder, and I was only a Priest, and we generally suppose that the lesser should obey the greater; but I said to him, calling him by name, "You are not going to leave here, nor I either; we shall both of us stay here till I see the fulfillment of my dream. It is here, and I am going to stay to see it, and you will, too." It is not natural for me to take a stand of that kind, but I felt led to do it upon that occasion. We stopped there three weeks, and cleared land for Father Hubbard, while he fed and housed us. Three times while we were there I was warned of the Lord to go and warn Mr. Akeman. The last warning I received from the Lord was on Saturday night of the third week. I went up to his house which was about three quarters of a mile distant, and when I got there his daughter stood in the doorway. I walked in and saluted him. He was walking the room, and did not say anything to me. I told him the Lord had sent me to pay him a visit. Then he made some exclamation that was rather profane. I sat down and commenced warning him. I told him that he had apostatized from the Gospel of Christ; that he had had the Priesthood and he was pursuing a course that would send him to destruction, and the judgments of God would overtake him.

Well, he raged like a demon. That is about all I said to him. I certainly did not stay long, but I delivered my message. When I left the house he followed me, and when he came to where I was he fell dead at my feet as though he had been struck with a thunderbolt from heaven. He was a very large man and he turned black as an African, and his skin seemed almost to burst open. The next day I attended his funeral. But he had raised a mob and had sent word for them to come and drive us out of the country or hang us, and they had sent warnings to us to leave. The consequence was, there were some fifteen or twenty deaths during my stay there. Men were taken with what they called pleurisy. Doctors came and opened a vein, and they died in five minutes. One of these men sent for me, and I went and saw him. Two men were holding him. He said to me, "I wish you would cut open my side; I have a pain here and it is skin deep; you can cut it out and save my life." I looked at him, but did not say anything to him. I said to myself, "If your eyes were open, you would see the angel of death standing by your side." He died while I was there. After this my partner left me, and I went alone to Memphis, Tennessee, and met with Brothers Patten and Parish.

(b) **A Vision of the Future.**—After laboring in that part for a length of time, I received a letter from Joseph Smith and Oliver Cowdery, in which they requested me to stay in that country and take charge of the churches that we had built up there. The Prophet promised me many things, and said I should lose no blessings by tarrying in that country and doing as he wished me, and letting the other brethren go and get their endowments. I was then at the house of Brother Abraham O. Smoot's mother. I received this about sun-down. I went into a lttle room where there was a sofa, to pray alone. I felt full of joy and rejoicings at the promises God had made to me through the Prophet. While I was upon my knees praying, my room was filled with light. I looked up and a messenger stood by my side. I arose, and this personage told me he had come to instruct me. He presented before me a panorama. He told me he wanted me to see with my eyes and understand with my mind what was coming to pass in the earth before the coming of the Son of Man. He commenced with what the revelations say about the sun being turned to darkness, the moon to blood, and the stars falling from heaven. Those things were all presented to me one after another, as they will be, I suppose, wnen they are manifest before the coming of the Son of Man.

Then he showed me the resurrection of the dead—what is termed the first and second resurrection. In the first resurrection I saw no graves nor anyone raised from the grave. I saw legions of celestial beings, men and women who had received the Gospel all clothed in white robes. In the form they were presented to me, they had already been raised from the grave. After this he showed me what is termed the second resurrection. Vast fields of graves were before me, and the Spirit of God rested upon the earth like a shower of gentle rain, and when that fell upon the graves they were opened, and an immense host of human beings came forth. They were just as diversified in their dress as we are here, or as they were laid down. This personage taught me with regard to these things. Among other things which he showed me, there were several lions like burnished brass placed in the heavens. I asked the messenger what they were for. He said they were representatives of the different dispensations of the Gospel of Christ to men, and they would all be seen in the heavens among the signs that would be shown. After this passed by me, he disappeared. Now, if I had been a painter I could have drawn everything I saw. It made an impression upon me that has never left me from that day to this. The next day we had a meeting in the Academy. Brother Smoot and some others went with me; but I was a lost man. I hardly knew where I was, so enveloped was I in that which I had seen.

I refer to this as one of the visitations that were given me in my boyhood, so to speak, in the Gospel. I was a Priest at the time. Of course, there was a motive in this personage visiting me and teaching me these principles. He knew a great deal better than I did what lay before me in life. It was doubtless sent to me for the purpose of strengthening me and giving me encouragement in my labors. [Note that a conclusion is here drawn.]

(c) **An Encounter with Evil Spirits.**—The other instance I want to refer to is what I spoke about at the recent General Conference. I need not dwell particularly upon this now; but I had a motive in laying it before the people on that occasion. The history of Brother Kimball's operations with those evil spirits in England is before the Church. And while on this point I want to correct a mistake that I made in referring to this matter at our General Conference. I got the names of Brother Kimball and Brother Hyde confused in my mind, and made it appear that Brother Kimball rebuked those evil spirits from Brother Hyde, when in fact it was Brother Kimball who was afflicted with those spirits and Brother Hyde administered to him. As this is a matter of history, I wish to state it correctly, and therefore make this explanation. When Brother Kimball, Brother George A. Smith, and myself went to London, we encountered these evil spirits. They sought to destroy us. The very first house that was opened to us was filled with devils. They had gathered there for our destruction, so that we should not plant the Gospel in that great city. Brother Kimball went to Manchester on some business, and left Brother George A. Smith and myself there. One night we sat up till 11 o'clock, talking Mormonism, and then we went to bed. We had only just laid down when these spirits rested upon us, and we were in a very fair way of losing our lives. It was as if a strong man had me by the throat, trying to choke me to death. In the midst of this a spirit told me to pray. I did so, and while praying, the door opened, the room was filled with light, and three messengers came in. Who they were I know not. They came and laid their hands upon us, and rebuked those powers, and thereby saved our lives. Not only so, but by the power they held they rebuked the whole army of devils that were in that great city, and bound them so that they have never troubled any Elder from that day till this.

Now, those messengers were sent to us because it was necessary. We would have lost our lives if somebody had not delivered us. We needed help, and we could not get it anywhere else.

This is all that I want to say with regard to the administration of angels to myself. This Apostle that I refer to told me he had prayed and prayed for the administration of angels. Well, if it had been necessary to save his life, as it was in my case, he would have had the administration of

PREACHING AND PUBLIC SPEAKING. 441

angels. But he had access to the gift of the Holy Ghost, as all of us have. And that, brethren and sisters, is what I want to talk to you about. [Conclusion to first General Division.]

SECOND GENERAL DIVISION: AS TO THE NEED OF THE HOLY GHOST.

(a) **Testimony of Joseph Smith.**—One morning, while we were at Winter Quarters, Brother Brigham Young said to me and the brethren that he had a visitation the night previous from Joseph Smith. I asked him what he said to him. He replied that Joseph had told him to tell the people to labor to obtain the Spirit of God; that they needed that to sustain them and to give them power to go through their work in the earth.

Now I will give you a little of my experience in this line. Joseph Smith visited me a great deal after his death, and taught me many important principles. The last time he visited me was while I was in a storm at sea. I was going on my last mission to preside in England. My companions were Brother Leonard W. Hardy, Brother Milton Holmes, Brother Dan Jones, and another brother, and my wife and two other women. We had been traveling three days and nights in a heavy gale, and were being driven backwards. Finally I asked my companions to come into the cabin with me, and I told them to pray that the Lord would change the wind. I had no fears of being lost; but I did not like the idea of being driven back to New York, as I wanted to go on my journey. We all offered the same prayer, both men and women; and when we got through we stepped up on to the deck and in less than a minute it was as though a man had taken a sword and cut the gale through, and you might have thrown a muslin handkerchief out and it would not have moved it. The night following this Joseph and Hyrum visited me, and the Prophet laid before me a great many things. Among other things, he told me to get the Spirit of God; that all of us needed it. He also told me what the Twelve Apostles would be called to go through on the earth before the coming of the Son of Man, and what the reward of their labors would be; but all that was taken from me, for some reason. Nevertheless I know it was most glorious, although much would be required at our hands.

Joseph Smith continued visiting myself and others up to a certain time, and then it stopped. The last time I saw him was in heaven. In the night vision I saw him at the door of the temple in heaven. He came and spoke to me. He said he could not stop and talk with me because he was in a hurry. The next man I met was Father Smith; he could not talk with me because he was in a hurry. I met half a dozen brethren who had held high positions on earth, and none of them could stop and talk with me because they were in a hurry. I was much astonished. By and by I saw the Prophet again, and I got the privilege to ask him a question. "Now," said I, "I want to know why you are in a hurry. I have been in a hurry all through my life; but I expected my hurry would be over when I got into the kingdom of heaven, if I ever did."

442 PREACHING AND PUBLIC SPEAKING.

Joseph said: "I will tell you, Brother Woodruff. Every dispensation that has had the Priesthood on the earth and has gone into the celestial kingdom, has had a certain amount of work to do to prepare to go to the earth with the Savior when he goes to reign on the earth. Each dispensation has had ample time to do this work. We have not. We are the last dispensation; so much work has to be done that we need to be in a hurry to accomplish it." Of course, that was satisfactory, but it was new doctrine to me.

(b) **Testimony of Brigham Young.**—Brigham Young also visited me after his death. On one occasion he and Brother Heber C. Kimball came in a splendid chariot, with fine, white horses, and accompanied me to a conference that I was going to attend. When I got there I asked Brother Brigham if he would take charge of the conference. "No," said he, "I have done my work here. I have come to see what you are doing and what you are teaching the people." And he told me what Joseph Smith had taught him in Winter Quarters, to teach the people to get the Spirit of God. He said, "I want you to teach the people to get the Spirit of God. You cannot build up the kingdom of God without that."

That is what I want to say to the brethren and sisters here today.

(c) **Value of the Spirit as compared with Visitation of Angels.**—Every man and woman in this Church should labor to get the Spirit. We are surrounded by evil spirits—spirits that are at war against God and against everything looking to the building up of the Kingdom of God; and we need the Holy Spirit to enable us to overcome these influences. I have had the Holy Ghost in my travels. Every man has that has gone out into the vineyard and labored faithfully for the cause of God. I have referred to the administration of angels to myself. What did these angels do? One of them taught me some things relating to the signs that should precede the coming of the Son of Man. Others came and saved my life. What then? They turned and left me. But how is it with the Holy Ghost? The Holy Ghost does not leave me if I do my duty. It does not leave any man who does his duty. We have known this all the way through. Joseph Smith told Brother John Taylor on one occasion to labor to get the Spirit of God, and to follow its dictation, and it would become a principle of revelation within him. God has blessed me with that, and everything I have done since I have been in this Church has been done on that principle. The Spirit of God has told me what to do, and I have had to follow that.

(d) **The Spirit as a Guide in Missionary Labors.**—In the time of the apostasy in Kirtland, Joseph hardly knew, when he met a man, unless the Spirit of God revealed it to him, whether he was friend or foe. Most of the leading men were fighting him. Right in the midst of that darkness the Spirit of God said to me, "You choose a partner and go straight to Fox Islands." Well, I knew no more what was on Fox Islands than what was on Kolob. But the Lord told me to go, and I went. I chose Jonathan H. Hale, and he went with me. We cast out some devils there, preached the Gospel and performed some miracles. I crossed lake Ontario and went into Connecticut, where my father lived. I had not seen any my relatives from the time I embraced the Gospel. I preached the Gospel there, and baptized my father, my stepmother, my sister, and my uncles and aunts, and organized a branch there. Every member of that branch was a relative of mine, excepting one, and he was a Methodist class leader who boarded at my father's house. This was all promised to me by old Father Smith when he blessed me. I got to Fox Islands, and did a good work there. Through the blessings of God I brought nearly a hundred from there up to Zion, at the same time that the Saints were driven out of Missouri into Illinois.

(e) **How the Spirit Opened the English Mission.**—So it has been all through my life. If I have undertaken to do anything, and the Lord has wanted me to do something else, he has had to tell me. When we were sent to England, we were sent by revelation. I went into the Staffordshire potteries with Brother Alfred Cordon. We were doing a splendid work, baptizing almost every night, and I thought it was the finest mission I ever was on. I went into the town of Hanley one night, and attended meeting in a large hall, which was filled to overflowing. The Spirit of the Lord came upon me and said that that was the last meeting I should hold with the people for many days. I told the people that that was the last meeting I should be with them. After the meeting, they asked me where I was going. I told them I did not know. In the morning I asked the Lord what he wanted of me. He merely said, "Go to the south." I got into the stage and rode eighty miles. The first man's house I stopped at was John Benbow's in Herefordshire. In half an hour after I entered the house I knew exactly why the Lord had sent me. There was a people there who had been praying for the ancient order of things. They were waiting for the Gospel as it was taught by Christ and his Apostles. The consequence was, the first thirty days after I got there I baptized six hundred of those people. In eight month's labor in that country I brought eighteen hundred into the Church. Why? Because there was a people prepared for the Gospel, and the Lord sent me there to do that work. I have always had to give God the glory for everything good that has happened to me; for I have realized by what power it came.

(f) **The Spirit as a Guide in Other Matters.**—When I got back to Winter Quarters from the pioneer journey, President Young said to me, "Brother Woodruff, I want you to take your wife and children and go to Boston, and stay there until you can gather every Saint of God in New England and Canada and send them up to Zion." I did as he told me. It took me two years to gather up everybody, and I brought up the rear with a company. When I got into Pittsburg with this company it was dusk, and I saw a steamer just preparing to go out. I walked right up to the captain and asked him if he was ready to go out. He said he was. "How many passengers have you?" "Two hundred and fifty." "Can you take another hundred?" "I can." "Then," said I, "I would like to go aboard with you." The words were hardly out of my mouth when the Holy Ghost said to me, "Don't you or your company go aboard that steamer." That was enough; I had learned the voice of the Spirit. I turned and told the captain that I had made up my mind not to go at present. That steamer started out. It was a dark night, and before the steamer had gone far she took fire, and all on board was lost. We should probably have shared the same fate, had it not been for that Monitor within me.

I refer to these things because I want you to get that same Spirit. All Elders of Israel, whether abroad or at home, need that Spirit. When I was on my way east at one time I drove into a man's yard in Indiana. Brother Orson Hyde had driven in and set his wagon in the door yard, and I set mine by the side of it. I turned my mules and tied them up to an oak tree. I had my wife and two children with me in my carriage. We went to lie down, and the Holy Spirit told me to get up and move my carriage. I got right up. My wife asked me what I was going to do. I said I was going to move the carriage. She wanted to know what for. I told her I did not know. I moved the carriage about fifteen rods, looked around, and then went to bed again. The Spirit told me to get up again and move my mules. I did so. In twenty minutes there came up a whirlwind that blew that oak tree down and laid it right across where my carriage had been. By listening to that Spirit our lives were saved.

GENERAL CONCLUSION.

Now, it was not an angel that pointed out these things to me; it was the Holy Ghost. This is the Spirit that we must have to carry out the purposes of God on the earth. We need that more than any other gift. I felt impressed yesterday to teach this principle to the Latterday Saints. We are in the midst of enemies, in the midst of darkness and temptation, and we need to be guided by the Spirit of God. We should pray to the Lord until we get the Comforter. This is what is promised to us when we are baptized. It is the Spirit of light, of truth, and of revelation, and can be with all of us at the same time.

Brethren and sisters, God bless you. I am glad to meet wth you. There are very few of you as old as I am. How long I shall tarry in this country I do not know; but while I do stay I want to do what good I can. These are principles that have rested a great deal upon my mind. If we labor for this Spirit, we shall have no quarreling and no difficulty, so long as that is dwelling within us. God bless you. Amen.

www.ingramcontent.com/pod-product-compliance
Lightning Source LLC
Chambersburg PA
CBHW032008300426
44117CB00008B/948